Sensory Reflections

Sense, Matter, and Medium

New Approaches to Medieval Literary and Material Culture

Edited by
Fiona Griffiths, Beatrice Kitzinger, and Kathryn Starkey

Volume 1

Sensory Reflections

Traces of Experience in Medieval Artifacts

Edited by
Fiona Griffiths and Kathryn Starkey

DE GRUYTER

ISBN 978-3-11-070902-5
e-ISBN (PDF) 978-3-11-056344-3
e-ISBN (EPUB) 978-3-11-056286-6
ISSN 2367-0290

Library of Congress Control Number: 2018951339

Bibliographic information published by the Deutsche Nationalbibliothek
The Deutsche Nationalbibliothek lists this publication in the Deutsche Nationalbibliografie;
detailed bibliographic data are available in the Internet at http://dnb.dnb.de.

© 2020 Walter de Gruyter GmbH, Berlin/Boston
This volume is text- and page-identical with the hardback published in 2018.
Typesetting: Integra Software Services Pvt. Ltd.
Printing and binding: Hubert & Co. GmbH & Co. KG, Göttingen
Cover image: Luttrell Psalter. British Library, London. MS Add 42130, fol. 170r.
Copyright The British Library

www.degruyter.com

Contents

Acknowledgments —— VII

List of Abbreviations —— IX

Contributor Biographies —— X

Fiona Griffiths and Kathryn Starkey
Sensing Through Objects —— 1

Jesse Rodin
1 **The Songbook as Sensory Artifact** —— 22

Valerie L. Garver
2 **Sensory Experiences of Low-Status Female Textile Workers in the Carolingian World** —— 50

Elizabeth Dospěl Williams
3 **Appealing to the Senses: Experiencing Adornment in the Early Medieval Eastern Mediterranean** —— 77

Melissa Herman
4 **Sensing Iconography: Ornamentation, Material, and Sensuousness in Early Anglo-Saxon Metalwork** —— 97

Patricia Blessing
5 **The Vessel as Garden: The "Alhambra Vases" and Sensory Perception in Nasrid Architecture** —— 116

Cynthia Hahn
6 **Theatricality, Materiality, Relics: Reliquary Forms and the Sensational in Mosan Art** —— 142

Sara Ritchey
7 **The Wound's Presence and Bodily Absence: Activating the Spiritual Senses in a Fourteenth-Century Manuscript** —— 163

Alexa Sand
8 **Birds in Hand: Micro-books and the Devotional Experience** —— 181

Jennifer Borland
9   **Moved by Medicine: The Multisensory Experience of Handling Folding Almanacs** —— 203

Richard Newhauser
10   **"putten to ploughe": Touching the Peasant Sensory Community** —— 225

Beth Williamson
Reflections on Sensory Reflections: An Afterword —— 249

Index —— 259

Plates —— 265

Acknowledgments

Sensory Reflections developed out of two lively sessions that we organized through Stanford University's Center for Medieval and Early Modern Studies at the International Congress on Medieval Studies in May 2016. Based on the productive conversations that began at the Congress, and the evident richness of sensory studies in medieval scholarship, we decided to continue our discussions at a "Sensory" workshop held at Stanford University in October 2016. We are grateful to the contributors to this volume for their enthusiastic engagement in that workshop and their scholarly generosity throughout the past few years. From the outset, our interest in this collaborative and interdisciplinary project has been in exploring the varied ways that sensory experiences might be traced and understood through medieval material culture. Our goal has been to work across disciplines and methods to plumb medieval material sources for traces of sensory experience.

In Autumn 2016 and Winter 2017, we convened a graduate colloquium at Stanford on "Sensory Experience in the Middle Ages," in which we discussed recent scholarship with a terrific group of engaged and creative graduate students. As part of this colloquium, we visited the "Feast for the Senses" exhibition at the Walters Art Museum (Baltimore) and were given an insightful tour by Dr. Joaneath Spicer, the James A. Murnaghan Curator of Renaissance and Baroque Art. As the colloquium continued, our graduate students, inspired by their participation in the "Sensory" workshop, developed their own projects on the medieval senses, which they then presented at the International Congress on Medieval Studies in May 2018. What started as a series of conference sessions has thus developed into an ongoing and richly rewarding collaborative research project that continues to yield exciting cross-disciplinary scholarship. We are particularly grateful to our graduate students for their engagement in this project: Björn Buschbeck, Robert Forke, Mae Lyons-Penner, Mareike Reisch, Danny Smith, Lora Webb, and Erik Yingling.

Sensory Reflections is the inaugural volume in a new series (co-edited by Fiona Griffiths, Beatrice Kitzinger, and Kathryn Starkey) on "Sense, Matter, and Medium: New Approaches to Medieval Literary and Material Culture" published by De Gruyter press. "Sense" refers both to the act of creating meaning from artifacts and to their sensory experience. One goal of this series is to foster debate about the intellectual and sensory experience of the medieval world, and to consider how, as modern scholars, we might access ephemeral aspects of medieval culture. "Matter" may be understood as both the intellectual and physical substance of medieval cultural documentation. In attending to "matter," we ask how medieval objects created meaning for their users. "Medium" provides space for reflection on practices of cultural transmission. The series thus focuses on medieval material culture and its contexts of production and reception. We are grateful to Jakob Klingner for first approaching us about creating a new series, and to Elisabeth Kempf for guiding us through the process. We are particularly grateful to Matt Gleeson for his editorial expertise and careful attention to detail.

This book could not have been completed without generous financial and institutional support from Stanford University; we especially thank the Dean of Research, the Europe Center, the Senior Associate Dean of Arts and Science, the Stanford Humanities Center, the Center for Medieval and Early Modern Studies (CMEMS), and our respective departments, German and History.

List of Abbreviations

AA SS	*Acta sanctorum*
BL	British Library
BnF	Bibliothèque nationale de France
CCSL	*Corpus christianorum: series latina*
EETS	Early English Text Society
KBR	Royal Library of Belgium
MGH	*Monumenta Germaniae Historica*
Capit.	*Capitularia regum Francorum*
Capit. episc.	*Capitula episcoporum*
Conc.	*Concilia*
Epp. sel.	*Epistolae selectae*
Poetae	*Poetae Latini medii aevi*
SS	*Scriptores*
SS rer. Germ.	*Scriptores rerum Germanicarum*
PL	*Patrologiae cursus completus: series latina*

Contributor Biographies

Patricia Blessing is Assistant Professor of Medieval and Islamic Art History at Pomona College. She received her PhD from Princeton University in 2012. Blessing's book, *Rebuilding Anatolia after the Mongol Conquest: Islamic Architecture in the Lands of Rūm, 1240–1330* (Ashgate, 2014), investigates the relationship between patronage, politics, and architectural style after the integration of the region into the Mongol empire. Together with Rachel Goshgarian, she edited *Architecture and Landscape in Medieval Anatolia, 1100–1500* (Edinburgh University Press, 2017), a collection of essays that engages with the complex political and cultural realities of the region. Blessing's current projects focus on fifteenth-century Ottoman architecture, immersive spaces, the materiality of architecture and textiles in the medieval Mediterranean, and the historiography of Islamic architecture in the former Ottoman Empire. Her work has been supported by the Samuel H. Kress Foundation, the International Center of Medieval Art, the Society of Architectural Historians, the Barakat Trust, and the Gerda Henkel Foundation.

Jennifer Borland is Associate Professor of Art History at Oklahoma State University. Her research and teaching interests range from medieval medical and scientific imagery, to medievalism and collecting, materiality, the corporeal experience of objects and spaces, audience and reception, and representations of gender. She is currently working on a book about the illustrated manuscripts of Aldobrandino of Siena's *Régime du corps*, a late medieval health guide. A related essay, "Freeze Framed: Theorizing the Historiated Initials of the *Régime du corps*," was published in *Word & Image: A Journal of Verbal/Visual Inquiry* 32 (2016). Her articles have appeared in the journals *Gesta*, *postmedieval*, *Medieval Encounters*, and *Different Visions*, and she has published on topics including the gendered experience of medieval spaces, the material legacy of handling in medieval manuscripts, and early twentieth-century medievalist architecture. She is a founding member of the Material Collective (*thematerialcollective.org*).

Valerie L. Garver is Associate Professor of History at Northern Illinois University where she teaches medieval history and medieval studies. Her research asks and seeks to answer questions concerning the history of women, gender, childhood, and family and the historical and interdisciplinary study of material culture. She is the author of *Women and Aristocratic Culture in the Carolingian World* (Cornell University Press, 2009) and co-editor (with Owen M. Phelan) of *Rome and Religion in the Medieval World* (Ashgate, 2014). Currently she is working on a book, *Dress, Textiles, and Society in the Carolingian World, c. 715–c. 915*. Her most recent publications are "Conceptions of Children and Youth in Carolingian Capitularies," in *Childhood in History: Perceptions of Children in the Ancient and Medieval Worlds*, ed. Reidar Aasgaard and Cornelia Horn (Routledge, 2017) and "'Go humbly dressed as befits servants of God': Alcuin, Clerical Identity, and Sartorial Anxieties," in *Early Medieval Europe* 26 (2018).

Fiona Griffiths is Professor of History at Stanford University. Her research focuses on intellectual and religious life from the ninth to the thirteenth century, with particular attention to the possibilities for social experimentation and cultural production inherent in medieval religious reform movements. Her work explores questions of gender, spirituality, and authority as they pertain to the experiences and interactions of religious men (priests or monks) with women (nuns and clerical wives). Griffiths is the author of *Nuns' Priests' Tales: Men and Salvation in Medieval Women's Monastic Life* (University of Pennsylvania Press, 2018), and *The Garden of Delights: Reform and Renaissance for Women in the Twelfth Century* (University of Pennsylvania Press, 2007); and co-editor (with Julie Hotchin) of *Partners in Spirit: Women, Men, and Religious Life in Germany*, 1100–1500 (Brepols, 2014).

Cynthia Hahn is Professor of Art History at Hunter College and the Graduate Center of the City University of New York. She has published extensively on many aspects of medieval art, including pilgrimage, and manuscripts with narratives of saints' lives, but of late has focused on reliquaries. Her publications include: *Portrayed on the Heart: Narrative Effect in Pictorial Lives of the Saints from the Tenth through the Thirteenth Century* (University of California Press, 2001); *Strange Beauty: Origins and Issues in the Making of Medieval Reliquaries, 400-circa 1204* (Penn State University Press, 2012); and, as editor with Holger Klein, *Saints and Sacred Matter: The Cult of Relics in Byzantium and Beyond* (Dumbarton Oaks, Harvard University Press, 2015). Her most recent book is: *The Reliquary Effect: Enshrining the Sacred Object* (Reaktion Books, 2017). *Capturing Fragments of the Divine: Passion Relics and their Reliquaries* will soon appear, published as the Franklin D. Murphy Lectures.

Melissa Herman was awarded a PhD (2013) in the History of Art from the University of York for her thesis on the development of iconography on Early Anglo-Saxon Metalwork. She remains affiliated with the History of Art Department at the University of York. Her research has focused on the impact of cultural contact on traditional art and society broadly in the early Anglo-Saxon period. She has published a co-edited volume (with Meg Boulton and Jane Hawkes) of collected essays, *The Art, Literature and Material Culture of the Medieval World* (Four Courts Press, 2015), as well as a number of chapters in assorted volumes on topics including the materiality of Anglo-Saxon metalwork, the persistence of early Anglo-Saxon iconography, and the development and transmission of the Anglo-Saxon aesthetic.

Richard Newhauser is Professor of English and Medieval Studies, Arizona State University, Tempe, and has been a visiting professor at universities in Nijmegen and Graz. His major areas of research are focused on the moral tradition in Western thought, Middle English literature, and sensology. He has directed two NEH Summer Seminars on "The Seven Deadly Sins as Cultural Constructions in the Middle Ages." He has published numerous essays on the senses in medieval culture, theology, and literature. His recent monographs include *The Early History of Greed* (Cambridge University Press, 2000; reprint 2006); *Sin: Essays on the Moral Tradition in the Western Middle Ages* (Ashgate, 2007); (co-editor) *Sin in Medieval and Early Modern Culture* (York Medieval Press, 2012); (translator) Peter of Limoges, *The Moral Treatise on the Eye* (Pontifical Institute of Mediaeval Studies, 2012); (editor) *A Cultural History of the Senses in the Middle Ages* (Bloomsbury, 2014); and (co-editor) *Optics, Ethics, and Art in the Thirteenth and Fourteenth Centuries* (Pontifical Institute of Mediaeval Studies, 2018). He is editor-in-chief of *The Chaucer Encyclopedia* (for Wiley-Blackwell in 4 volumes) and is directing a project to edit and translate William Peraldus' *Summa on the Vices* (for Oxford University Press in 3 volumes).

Sara Ritchey is Associate Professor of History and Affiliated Faculty in Religious Studies at the University of Tennessee at Knoxville. She has published widely on the intersection of gender, health, and devotion in late medieval Europe and is the author of *Holy Matter: Changing Perceptions of the Material World in Late Medieval Christianity* (Cornell University Press, 2014).

Jesse Rodin is Associate Professor of Music at Stanford University and co-editor of the *Journal of Musicology*. He is the author of *Josquin's Rome: Hearing and Composing in the Sistine Chapel* (Oxford University Press, 2012), editor of a volume for the New Josquin Edition (2014), and co-editor of the *Cambridge History of Fifteenth-Century Music* (2015). As Director of the Josquin Research Project (josquin.stanford.edu), he uses digital tools to subject fifteenth-century repertories to both close and "distant" reading. As Artistic Director of the ensemble Cut Circle (cutcircle.org), he works with world-class singers to recapture early music's intensity and grit. Rodin has been recognized with awards and fellowships from institutions such as the Guggenheim Foundation, the American Council of Learned Societies, and the Université Libre de Bruxelles. Current projects include a monograph on musical form (Cambridge University Press) and a series of recordings devoted to French songs of courtly love (Musique en Wallonie). At Stanford, Rodin directs the Facsimile Singers, which helps students develop native fluency in old musical notation. He also co-teaches a course on the art of feasting in which students cook medieval recipes in Stanford's Teaching Kitchen.

Alexa Sand is Professor of Art History, Associate Vice President for Research, and Associate Dean at Utah State University. Her research centers on the intersections of manuscript culture, gender, vernacular texts, and religiosity in late-medieval francophone Europe. She is the author of *Vision, Devotion, and Self-Representation in Late Medieval Art* (Cambridge University Press, 2014). Her work has appeared in *The Art Bulletin, Gesta, Word & Image, Yale French Studies, Different Visions,* and numerous volumes of collected essays. She is currently completing a book on the pictorial tradition of *La Somme le Roi*.

Kathryn Starkey is Professor of German at Stanford University. Her research focuses on medieval German literature of the twelfth and thirteenth centuries. She has worked extensively on visual and material culture, and manuscript illustration and transmission. Starkey is the author of *A Courtier's Mirror: Cultivating Elite Identity in Thomasin von Zerclaere's "Welscher Gast"* (University of Notre Dame Press, 2013), and *Reading the Medieval Book. Word, Image, and Performance in Wolfram von Eschenbach's "Willehalm"* (University of Notre Dame Press, 2004). She is the co-author (with Edith Wenzel) of *Neidhart: Selected Songs from the Riedegger Manuscript* (Western Michigan University: TEAMS series in bilingual medieval German texts, 2016), and co-editor (with Jutta Eming and Ann Marie Rasmussen) of *Visuality and Materiality in the Story of Tristan* (University of Notre Dame Press, 2012). With Horst Wenzel she additionally co-edited *Imagination und Deixis: Studien zur Wahrnehmung im Mittelalter* (Hirzel, 2007), and *Visual Culture and the German Middle Ages* (Palgrave Press, 2005).

Elizabeth Dospěl Williams is Assistant Curator of the Byzantine Collection at the Dumbarton Oaks Research Library and Collection in Washington, D.C. Her PhD dissertation at the Institute of Fine

Arts at New York University (2015) evaluated evidence for jewelry and its wear in the Byzantine and early Islamic eastern Mediterranean. At Dumbarton Oaks, she has researched and published on the collection of late antique and medieval textiles from Egypt. She previously worked at the George Washington University and at the Metropolitan Museum of Art. She has served as curatorial consultant for several recent exhibitions, including *Jerusalem 1000–1400: Every People Under Heaven* (The Metropolitan Museum of Art, 2016) and *Ancient Mediterranean Cultures in Contact* (The Field Museum, 2017).

Beth Williamson studied at Merton College, Oxford, where she was trained as a historian, specializing in late medieval and renaissance cultural history. She then completed an MA and a PhD in Art History at the Courtauld Institute in London. She is now a Reader in History of Art at the University of Bristol, UK. Her research concerns late medieval devotional imagery, and she has published both on iconographical topics, and on questions of religious practice. Her particular current interests range across questions of materiality and relics, as well as sensory dimensions of religious ritual and behavior, and relationships between the visual and the aural in devotional practice. Her work brings the aural, and questions of the imagining of music and sound, into dialogue with the visual in explorations of religious practice. A recent research project, Sound and Silence in the Ecology of the Cathedral, investigated contemporary attitudes to sound in Bristol Cathedral.

Fiona Griffiths and Kathryn Starkey
Sensing Through Objects

An anonymous pen-drawn image in a fifteenth-century print commentary on Aristotle by the Cologne philosopher Gerard of Harderwyck (d. 1503) depicts three competing views of the functioning and sites of the senses (Figure 1). The two heads at the top of the page represent the medical teachings of Galen and Avicenna (left), contrasted with the philosophical views of Thomas Aquinas and Albertus Magnus (right). The figure below, and the one that concerns us here, portrays the Aristotelian point of view.[1] Lines connect the figure's eye to a mirror and his ear to a bell. His right hand reaches into a fire, while a serpent bites him above the elbow. He stretches his tongue into a goblet and holds a flower to his nose. Labels identify the man's senses, and associated sensations, with their physical sources: the material objects, or stimuli, that prompt sensory perception. Thus the bell is the *obiectum auditus* (object of hearing), the flower the *obiectum olfactus* (object of smell), the contents of the goblet the *obiectum gustus* (object of taste), the mirror the *obiectum visus* (object of vision), and the fire the *obiectum tactus* (object of touch). Other lines lead from the sensory organs to the brain and then to the heart, which is the focal point of the image, the central sensory organ (*organum sensus communis*) that governs and unites all the senses.[2]

The sensory man in the Harderwyck commentary focuses our attention on the physiological experience of the senses, but also – and importantly for the subject of

---

[1] Wellcome Library, London, 2.b.5 (SR), no pagination. The commentary is Gerardus Harderwyck, *Epitomata seu Reparationes totius philosophiae naturalis Aristotelis* (Cologne: H. Quentell, 1496). For a more detailed discussion of this image, and particularly its relationship to the other images on the page, see Annemieke Rosalinde Verboon, *Lines of Thought: Diagrammatic Representation and the Scientific Texts of the Arts Faculty, 1200–1500* (PhD thesis, Leiden University, 2010), esp. 218–221 and 261. For discussion of this image in the context of visual depictions of the senses, see Carl Nordenfalk, "The Five Senses in Late Medieval and Renaissance Art," *Journal of the Warburg and Courtauld Institutes* 48 (1985): 1–22, at 5–6; and *Immagini del sentire: I cinque sensi nell'arte*, ed. Sylvia Ferino-Pagden (Milan: Leonardo Arte, 1996), 78–79.
[2] As Verboon observes, the brain is also labeled as the site where common sense resides, with no explanation of this ambiguity. Verboon, *Lines of Thought*, 221. On Aristotle's theory of the "common" senses, see Pavel Gregoric, *Aristotle on the Common Sense* (Oxford: Oxford University Press, 2007); and Daniel Heller-Roazen, "Common Sense: Greek, Arabic, Latin," in *Rethinking the Medieval Senses: Heritage, Fascinations, Frames*, ed. Stephen G. Nichols, Andreas Kablitz, and Alison Calhoun (Baltimore: Johns Hopkins University Press, 2008), 30–50. For a survey of medieval philosophical views on the senses, see Simo Knuuttila and Pekka Kärkkäinen, "Sense Perception: Medieval Theories," in *Sourcebook for the History of the Philosophy of Mind: Philosophical Psychology from Plato to Kant*, ed. Simo Knuuttila and Juha Sihvola (Dordrecht: Springer, 2014), 61–79; and Simo Knuuttila and Pekka Kärkkäinen, "Medieval Theories of Internal Senses," in *Sourcebook*, ed. Knuuttila and Sihvola, 131–145.

https://doi.org/10.1515/9783110563443-001

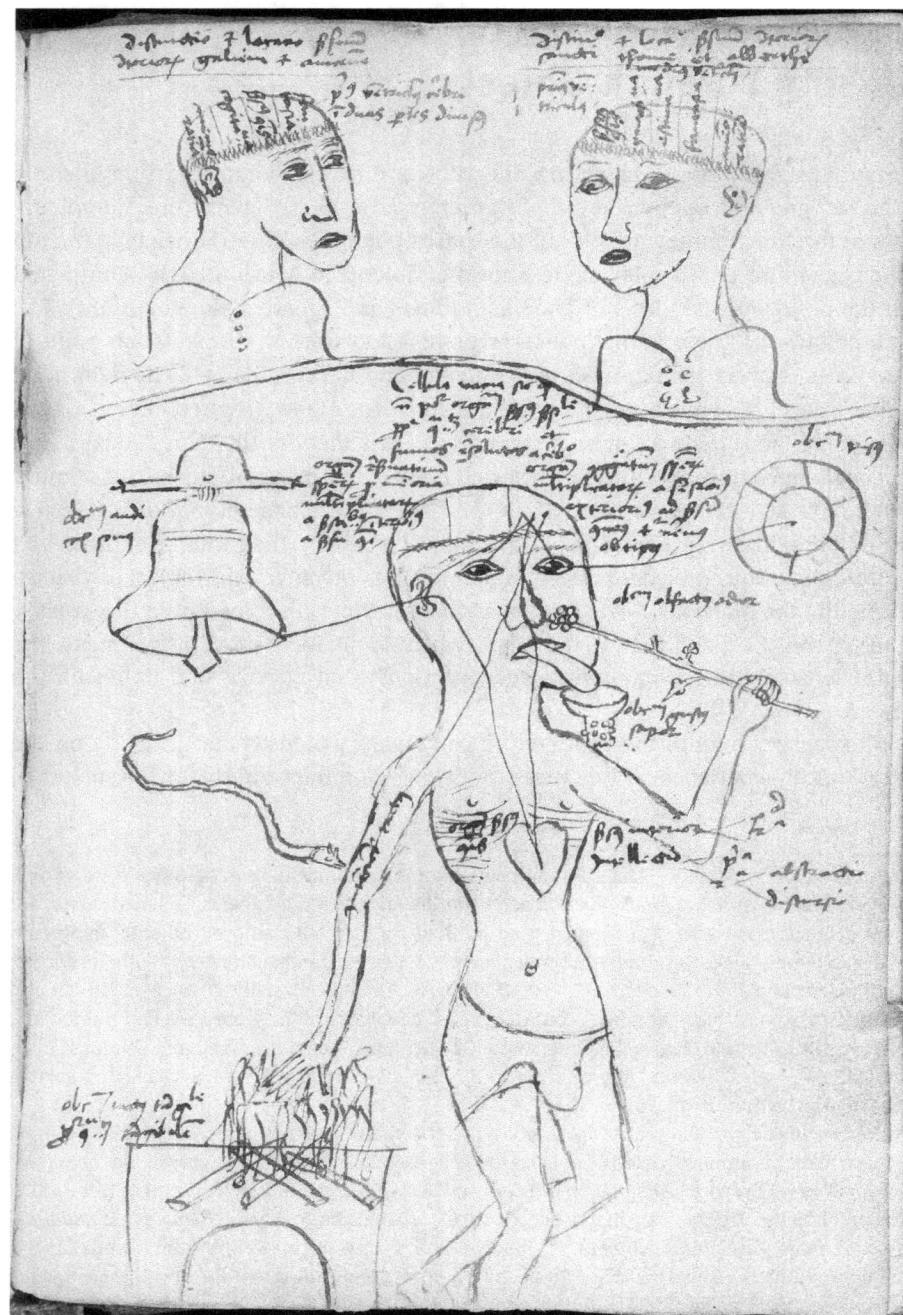

Figure 1: The Aristotelian sensory system: illustrations of senses and faculties of brain function. In Gerardus Harderwyck, *Epitomata seu Reparationes totius philosophiae naturalis Aristotelis*, Cologne, 1496. Wellcome Library, London, 2.b.5 (SR). Courtesy of the Wellcome Collection CC BY.

this book – on the everyday objects associated with them.³ The image, which appears on a blank page between Harderwyck's commentaries on Aristotle's treatises *De anima* and *De sensu et sensato*, follows Aristotle in associating the senses with their physical stimuli rather than with the symbolic representations found in other traditions.⁴ One tradition representative of the latter tendency, attested from at least the thirteenth century, associated the five senses with five animals, each of which was supposedly endowed with superior perception in its corresponding sense: the boar for hearing, the lynx for sight, the ape for taste, the vulture for smell, and the spider for touch.⁵ A fourteenth-century wall painting at Longthorpe Tower in England exemplifies this tradition, presenting the senses as animals on a sensory wheel, ruled by a crowned figure.⁶ Aristotle's *De anima* and *De sensu et sensato*, which were known in western

---

3 On the recent growth of sensory history as a field within the discipline, see the *AHR* forum "The Senses in History," *American Historical Review* 116 (2011): 307–400. Essays include Martin Jay, "In the Realm of the Senses: An Introduction"; Sophia Rosenfeld, "On Being Heard: A Case for Paying Attention to the Historical Ear"; Mark S. R. Jenner, "Follow Your Nose? Smell, Smelling, and Their Histories"; Jessica Riskin, "The Divine Optician"; Priscilla Parkhurst Ferguson, "The Senses of Taste"; and Elizabeth D. Harvey, "The Portal of Touch." Foundational to the study of the medieval senses are Richard G. Newhauser, "The Senses, the Medieval Sensorium, and Sensing (in) the Middle Ages," in *Handbook of Medieval Culture: Fundamental Aspects and Conditions of the European Middle Ages*, ed. Albrecht Classen, 3 vols. (Berlin: De Gruyter, 2015), 3:1559–1575; and Richard G. Newhauser, "Introduction: The Sensual Middle Ages," in *A Cultural History of the Senses in the Middle Ages*, ed. Richard G. Newhauser (London: Bloomsbury Academic, 2014), 1–22.

4 For visual traditions of the depiction of the senses, see Nordenfalk, "The Five Senses"; Eric Palazzo, "Art, Liturgy, and the Five Senses in the Early Middle Ages," *Viator* 41 (2010): 25–56; Elizabeth Sears, "Sensory Perception and its Metaphors in the Time of Richard of Fournival," in *Medicine and the Five Senses*, ed. William F. Bynum and Roy Porter (Cambridge: Cambridge University Press, 1993), 17–39; Michael Camille, "Sensations of the Page: Imaging Technologies and Medieval Illuminated Manuscripts," in *The Iconic Page in Manuscript, Print, and Digital Culture*, ed. George Bornstein and Theresa Tinkle (Ann Arbor: University of Michigan Press, 1998), 33–53; and Florentine Mütherich, "An Illustration of the Five Senses in Medieval Art," *Journal of the Warburg and Courtauld Institutes* 18 (1955): 140–141. The exhibition catalogue *A Feast for the Senses* is a valuable resource for medieval sensory studies: Martina Bagnoli, ed., *A Feast for the Senses: Art and Experience in Medieval Europe* (Baltimore: The Walters Art Museum, 2016).

5 As Thomas of Cantimpré wrote in the thirteenth century, solidifying the association of the senses with specific animals:

> Nos aper auditu, lynx visu, simia gustu,
> Vultur odoratu praecellit, aranea tactu.

Thomas of Cantimpré, *Liber de natura rerum*, ed. Helmut Boese (Berlin: Walter de Gruyter, 1973), 106. Cited in Nordenfalk, "The Five Senses," 1. A thirteenth-century copy of Richard de Fournival's *Bestiaire d'amour* identified five animals with the senses. Bagnoli, *A Feast for the Senses*, no. 7.

6 The crowned figure represents the overarching governance of either Reason or the "common" sense. On Longthorpe Tower, see Gino Casagrande and Christopher Kleinhenz, "Literary and Philosophical Perspectives on the Wheel of the Five Senses in Longthorpe Tower," *Traditio* 41 (1985): 311–327; and Edward Clive-Rouse and Audrey Baker, "The Wall-Paintings at Longthorpe Tower, near Peterborough, Northants," *Archaeologia* 96 (1955): 1–57.

Europe by the second half of the twelfth century, provided a different foundation for medieval understandings of the senses, reflecting on sensory *experience* rather than on acuity or (as in the moral tradition) spiritual danger.[7] As Aristotle observed in *De anima*, it is *objects* that "excite the sensory powers to activity."[8] Manuscript redactions of *De sensu* in particular introduced new ways of visualizing the senses by focusing on sensory stimuli rather than allegory or symbolism. Several extant manuscripts containing this text open with a historiated initial depicting five figures, each of whom has attributes that exemplify a distinct sensory experience. The elegant and carefully drawn historiated initial in a late thirteenth-century manuscript including *De sensu*, for example, depicts five male figures who respectively look into a mirror, pluck a harp, eat, blow a flute, and sniff a flower; this image provides an early model for the type of connection between objects and experience that the Harderwyck image invokes (Figure 2).[9]

The sensory man in Harderwyck's commentary on Aristotle provides a useful starting point for this volume on *Sensory Reflections*. The chapters that follow mark a new direction in medieval sensory studies through their focus on objects and on the particular sensory experiences that can be traced through medieval artifacts. Privileging material rather than textual evidence, these chapters seek to consider the senses as they were experienced by medieval women and men of differing social statuses, and not – as they have more typically been considered by scholarship – as they were theorized and debated by medieval exegetes and scholars.[10] Churchmen, whose concerns are most often reflected in the textual record, frequently warned against the spiritual dangers of sensory indulgence. As heirs to a long tradition within Christian thought of moralizing the senses and emphasizing the potential sinfulness of sensory experience, they were skeptical of the urge

---

[7] Nordenfalk, "The Five Senses," 2. See also Thomas J. Slakey, "Aristotle on Sense Perception," *Philosophical Review* 70 (1961): 470–484; George Lacombe, "Medieval Latin Versions of the *Parva naturalia*," *New Scholasticism* 5 (1930): 289–311; and Pekka Kärkkäinen, "The Senses in Philosophy and Science: Mechanics of the Body or Activity of the Soul?" in *A Cultural History*, ed. Newhauser, 111–132. For a discussion of the dating of the Latin translation of *De sensu*, see David Kristian Bloch, "Nicholaus Graecus and the *Translatio Vetus* of Aristotle's *De Sensu*," *Bulletin de philosophie médiévale* 50 (2008): 83–104.
[8] Aristotle, *De anima* 2.5. English translation by J. A. Smith in *The Complete Works of Aristotle: The Revised Oxford Translation*, ed. Jonathan Barnes, 2 vols. (Princeton, NJ: Princeton University Press, 1995), 1:664.
[9] Bibliothèque de Genève, Geneva, Ms. lat. 76, fol. 327r. Accessible online at http://www.e-codices.unifr.ch/en/bge/lat0076/327r. For discussion, see Sears, "Sensory Perception and its Metaphors," 35; and Camille, "Sensations of the Page," 34–36.
[10] Christopher Woolgar marks an exception, paying attention to the practical rather than the ideological in his study of the senses in late medieval England. Christopher M. Woolgar, *The Senses in Late Medieval England* (New Haven: Yale University Press, 2007).

Figure 2: The five senses depicted through objects, late thirteenth century. Bibliothèque de Genève, Ms. lat. 76, fol. 327r, detail.

to "see" or to "touch."[11] Since the senses were rooted in the body, theologians and exegetes viewed them as gateways to the soul, and potentially to sin. As Jerome had warned in his early fourth-century work *Against Jovinian*, "Through the five

---

[11] Carla Casagrande, "From Vigilance to Temperance: The Senses, the Passions, and Sin," in *A Feast for the Senses*, ed. Bagnoli, 85–93. On the positive role of sensation in medieval spirituality, see Martina Bagnoli, "Longing to Experience," in *A Feast for the Senses*, ed. Bagnoli, 33–45. As Richard Newhauser has noted, the senses had a role in medieval society that was both ideological and cultural. Newhauser, "Introduction: The Sensual Middle Ages," 1. For general discussion of the ethical understanding of the senses, see Newhauser, "The Senses, the Medieval Sensorium, and Sensing (in) the Middle Ages"; Newhauser, "Introduction: The Sensual Middle Ages"; Camille, "Sensations of the Page"; and, focusing on the later period, the essays in Lisa M. Rafanelli and Erin E. Benay, eds., *Faith, Gender and the Senses in Italian Renaissance and Baroque Art* (Burlington: Ashgate, 2015). For the late medieval debate over the role of images in Christian belief, see Jeffrey F. Hamburger, "Seeing and Believing: The Suspicion of Sight and the Authentication of Vision in Late Medieval Art and Devotion," in *Imagination und Wirklichkeit: Zum Verhältnis von mentalen und realen Bildern in der Kunst der frühen Neuzeit*, ed. Klaus Krüger and Alessandro Nova (Mainz: Philipp von Zabern, 2000), 47–69.

senses, as through open windows, vice has access to the soul."¹² In keeping with Jerome's interpretation of Jeremiah 9:21 ("Death is come up through our windows") as a reference to sensory intrusions, medieval artists sometimes depicted the sense organs as portals to a castle, as in one late thirteenth-century manuscript of Richard de Fournival's *Bestiaire d'amour*, which depicted the "tower of memory" with windows embellished by an ear and an eye.¹³ According to exegetes and theologians, the sense organs – eyes, ears, tongue, nose, skin – required vigilant oversight and safeguarding.

Despite this potential for spiritual danger, the senses were nevertheless recognized as practical cognitive tools and even (when properly defined and deployed) as spiritually instructive. Nothing is "conceived in the intellect that was not first in the senses," observed the Parisian schoolman Henry of Ghent (d. 1293) in his *Summa of Ordinary Questions*, explicitly acknowledging the centrality of the senses to learning and cognition.¹⁴ Writing somewhat earlier, the philosopher Alan of Lille (d. 1202/1203) had conceded that the senses – when guided by Reason and Prudence – could aid in comprehension, a model reflected in the so-called Wellcome Apocalypse, an early fifteenth-century German spiritual compendium (ca. 1420). Here, Prudence is depicted as a charioteer being drawn to the heavens by five horses identified as the senses (Figure 3).¹⁵ The positive potential of

---

12 "Per quinque sensus, quasi per quasdam fenestras, vitiorum ad animam introitus est." Jerome, *Adversus Jovinianum*, 2.8, in PL 23:297. English translation by W. H. Fremantle, G. Lewis, and W. G. Martley, in *Jerome: Letters and Select Works*, Nicene and Post-Nicene Fathers, ed. Philip Schaff and Henry Wallace, 2nd series, vol. 6 (Buffalo, NY: Christian Literature Publishing Co., 1893; repr., New York: Cosimo Classics, 2007), 394.
13 Bibliothèque nationale de France, Paris, Ms. français 412, fol. 237v. The depiction drew on the Augustinian model of the senses as gateways to memory and cognition. Willem P. Gerritsen, "Memory's Two Doors: Mnemotechnical Aspects of Richard de Fournival's *Bestiaire d'amours* and the Low-Rhenish Morality Book (Hannover, SLB, IV 369)," in *Medieval Memory: Image and Text*, ed. Frank Willaert, Herman Braet, Thom Mertens, and Theo Venckeleer (Turnhout: Brepols, 2004), 61–75. For an edition of the *Bestiaire d'amour*, see Richard de Fournival, *Bestiaire d'amour et la Response du Bestiaire*, ed. Gabriel Bianciotto (Paris: Champion, 2009). On textual and thematic echoes between Richard de Fournival and Peter of Limoges, see Richard Newhauser, "Educating the Senses on Love or Lust: Richard de Fournival and Peter of Limoges," in *Public Declamations: Essays on Medieval Rhetoric, Education, and Letters in Honor of Martin Camargo*, ed. Georgiana Donavin and Denise Stodola (Turnhout: Brepols, 2015), 213–228.
14 *Henry Of Ghent's* Summa of Ordinary Questions: *Article One: On The Possibility Of Knowing*, trans. Roland J. Teske (South Bend, IN: St. Augustine's Press, 2008), 22. This idea, expressed by Aquinas as well as Henry of Ghent, was originally found in Aristotle. Paul F. Cranefield, "On the Origin of the Phrase 'Nihil est in intellectu quod non prius fuerit in sensu,'" *Journal of the History of Medicine and Allied Sciences* 25 (1970): 77–80. See also Bernd Goehring, "Henry of Ghent's Use of Aristotle's *De anima* in Developing His Theory of Cognition," in *Medieval Perspectives on Aristotle's De Anima*, ed. Russell L. Friedman and Jean-Michel Counet, Philosophes Médiévaux 58 (Louvain: Peeters, 2013), 63–99.
15 Wellcome Library, London, Ms. 49, fol. 68r. Bagnoli, *A Feast for the Senses*, no. 10. See also Martina Bagnoli, "Making Sense," in *A Feast for the Senses*, ed. Bagnoli, 17–30, at 21–22; Mütherich, "An Illustration of the Five Senses"; and Sears, "Sensory Perception and its Metaphors," 29–33.

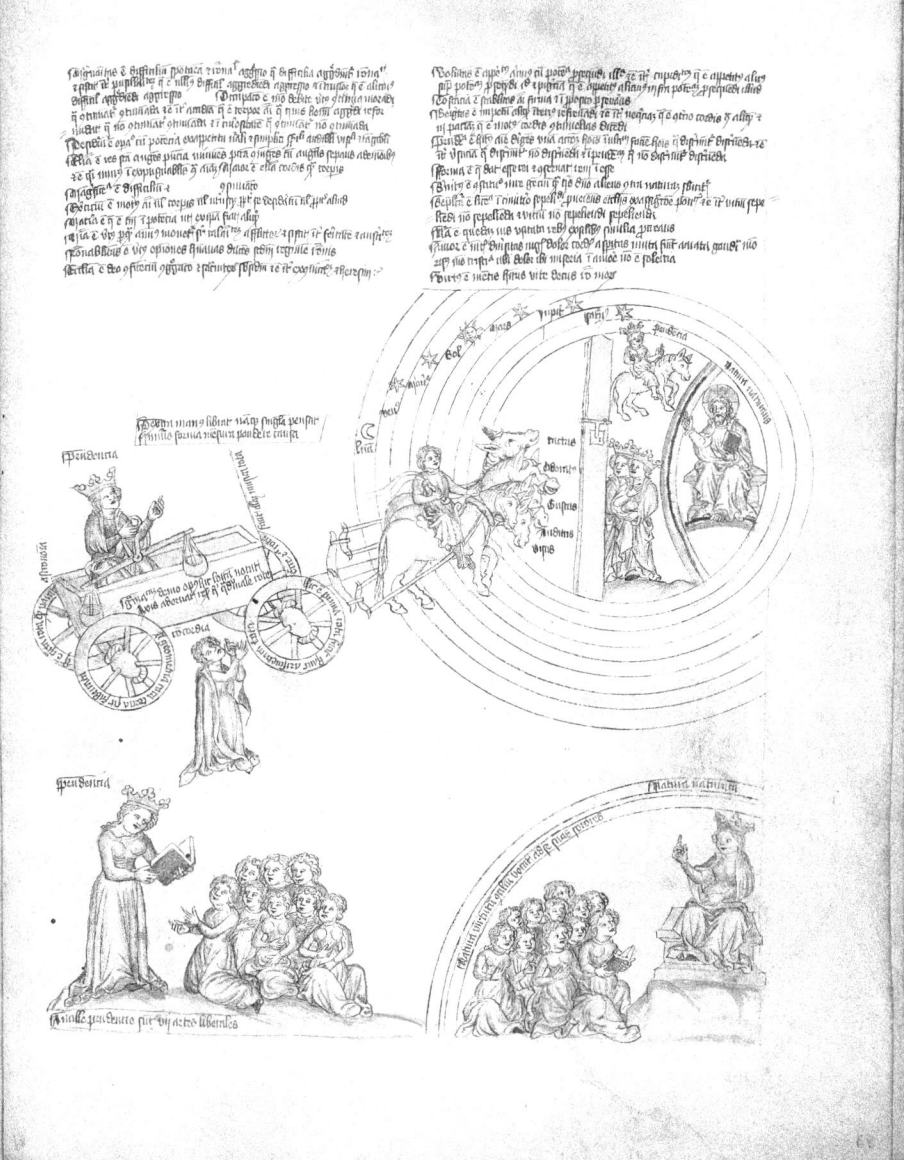

Figure 3: Prudence as a charioteer with five horses. Wellcome Apocalypse, 1420, Wellcome Library, London, MS. 49, fol. 68r. Courtesy of the Wellcome Collection CC BY.

the senses was underscored, too, by distinguishing between the inner and outer senses (which were sometimes identified as spiritual versus corporeal senses).[16] According to the philosophical tradition, which drew on early Latin and Arabic ideas, the inner senses were post-sensory faculties, among them imagination, cogitation, and memory.[17] From the spiritual perspective, the inner senses contrasted favorably with the outer senses. While the outer senses allowed only mundane understanding, the inner senses offered a means by which human beings might gain spiritual experience of the divine. As Jeffrey Hamburger and Anne-Marie Bouché have shown in their work on the "mind's eye," along with Beth Williamson in her important 2013 article "Sensory Experience in Medieval Devotion," the senses could be conceived of as spiritual pathways to God, if properly honed and guided.[18]

The image of the sensory man in the Harderwyck commentary, although modest in its execution, engages in a vibrant medieval debate concerning the site and purpose of the senses, underscoring the practical importance of the senses and sensory input to medieval people as they sought to decode and safely navigate their environment.[19] Absent from the image is the sort of moral stance that Jerome and subsequent theologians assumed; instead, the image of the sensory man depicts the senses in an everyday frame, presenting them alongside material objects and clearly indicating the mediation of these objects through sight, sound, taste, touch, and smell. Reliance on the senses was determinative in medieval daily life: women and men smelled fire, listened for thunder, felt hot or cold, tasted (or smelled) food that was good or had gone rotten, and saw (or perceived, drawing on all the senses) danger. In elite contexts too, objects served as focal points for sensory experience. The famous unicorn tapestries (ca. 1500) on display in the Musée national du Moyen Âge in Paris depict refined circumstances and experiences, yet they too link the senses to material objects: in each tapestry a noble lady invokes an individual sense through her handling of an object.[20] To represent touch, she stands stroking the unicorn's horn and holding a pennant. In the tapestry depicting taste, the lady takes sweetmeats from a dish. The

---

16 Still foundational is Harry Austryn Wolfson, "The Internal Senses in Latin, Arabic, and Hebrew Philosophic Texts," *The Harvard Theological Review* 28 (1935): 69–133.
17 For a more detailed enumeration of the internal senses, see Wolfson, "The Internal Senses," 96; for the Latin tradition (influenced by translations of Avicenna and Averroes beginning in the twelfth century), see 114–129.
18 Jeffrey F. Hamburger and Anne-Marie Bouché, eds., *The Mind's Eye: Art and Theological Argument in the Middle Ages* (Princeton, NJ: Princeton University Press, 2005); Beth Williamson, "Sensory Experience in Medieval Devotion: Sound and Vision, Invisibility and Silence," *Speculum* 88 (2013): 1–43.
19 Nordenfalk remarks that the image "bears every mark of a non-professional draughtsman." Nordenfalk, "The Five Senses," 6.
20 On the sensory experience of late medieval tapestries, see Laura Weigert, "Chambres d'amour: Tapestries of Love and the Texturing of Space," *Oxford Art Journal* 31 (2008): 317–336.

flowers that she weaves into a wreath invoke the sense of smell, and the organ she plays portrays the sense of hearing. Finally, sight is depicted by the lady's mirror, which reflects the unicorn's gaze. While the interpretation of the visual program in the tapestries is controversial, the connection drawn between objects and sensation both here and in the image of the sensory man brings to light a discourse on sensory experience that scholastic and theological texts – typically the focus of scholarship on the senses – do not fully explore.[21]

These examples – the sensory man, the unicorn tapestries, and the many manuscript depictions of the senses – convey sensory experience predominantly through the visual: by looking at these images, we *see* rather than feel, taste, hear, or smell the sensory. Privileging the visual is – at least in part – a function of modern proclivities. Sound (and silence) was central to medieval devotional practice, as Beth Williamson has reminded us. Touch, too, was spiritually significant. As Jacqueline Jung argues, medieval people recognized that while vision could be "weak and unreliable," touch was a "robust sense."[22] Making a case for the centrality of sculpture to devotion, Jung notes that three-dimensional images were "far more publicly accessible" in medieval culture than were two-dimensional ones.[23] Sculpture was, moreover, designed to be *touched*. Whereas modern interaction with the plastic arts is typically limited to looking (particularly in the modern museum, with its glassed-in cases, security guards, and alarms), medieval people stroked, held, and cradled sculptural representations. Indeed, the *vita* of Hedwig of Silesia (d. 1243) reports that the saint carried "on her person a little image of [Mary] in ivory, often holding it in her hands so that she could gaze upon it lovingly."[24] Like Williamson and Jung, the contributors to this volume look beyond vision, focusing – as Aristotle did – on the sensory implications of objects in an effort to bring us closer to medieval experience.

---

[21] Representative of many similar studies, the essays in a recent collection focus on the epistemology of the senses and literary discourses about them: Nichols, Kablitz, and Calhoun, eds., *Rethinking the Medieval Senses*. As Hans Ulrich Gumbrecht observes in his introduction to that volume, the senses are a "stubbornly centrifugal topic" in that they can "only be accessed through a thick and intrinsically complex layer of medieval erudition." Hans Ulrich Gumbrecht, "Erudite Fascinations and Cultural Energies: How Much Can We Know about the Medieval Senses?" in *Rethinking the Medieval Senses*, ed. Nichols, Kablitz, and Calhoun, 1–10, at 2.
[22] Jacqueline E. Jung, "The Tactile and the Visionary: Notes on the Place of Sculpture in the Medieval Religious Imagination," in *Looking Beyond: Visions, Dreams and Insights in Medieval Art and History*, ed. Colum Hourihane (Princeton: Index of Christian Art, 2010), 203–240, at 208.
[23] Jung, "The Tactile and the Visionary," 215.
[24] Cited in Jung, "The Tactile and the Visionary," 205. The essential tactility of medieval devotion is also apparent in studies of prayer nuts: see Evelin Wetter and Frits Scholten, eds., *Prayer Nuts, Private Devotion, and Early Modern Art Collecting* (Riggisberg: Abegg-Stiftung, 2017). See also Bagnoli, *A Feast for the Senses*, no. 58 (prayer nut pendant).

Approaching the Ephemeral: Studying Experience and the Senses through Objects

In spring 2012, the Walters Art Museum mounted an exhibition that invited visitors to engage physically with art pieces: to touch rather than simply look.[25] While modern museums have traditionally privileged the visual to the exclusion of other senses (discouraging not only touch but even overly close visual inspection), the Walters installation encouraged tactile interaction with replicas of pieces from its collection, acknowledging the significance of the nonvisual senses in the design and historic experience of the objects on display.[26] One of these objects, a Renaissance statuette of *The Shepherd Daphnis Playing a Pipe* (ca. 1520–1530), offers a particular example of the tactile appeal of the artworks; a note from the exhibition explained that this statuette was created in the context of an interest at the turn of the sixteenth century "in art that was pleasurable to hold."[27] Of modest size, the piece is 21.3 cm in height – only slightly longer than the hand of an adult man. While it is pleasing to the eye, the statuette was clearly designed to be held: it fits perfectly in the palm of one's hand, where Daphnis – a nude, seated figure – can be most easily and naturally supported (Figure 4). The satisfying weight of the piece, the smooth coolness of its bronze, and the ergonomic design of the figure – whose form is best admired when cradled in the palm – together imply that this statuette was as much intended to be enjoyed through touch as admired through sight.[28] The patina on its polished bronze surface serves as a witness to centuries of human touch.

---

[25] "Touch and the Enjoyment of Sculpture: Exploring the Appeal of Renaissance Statuettes," at The Walters Art Museum (January 21–April 15, 2012), online at https://thewalters.org/news/releases/article.aspx?e_id=333.

[26] On the privileging of the visual in museum design, see David Howes and Constance Classen, "Mixed Messages: Engaging the Senses in Art," in *Ways of Sensing: Understanding the Senses in Society*, ed. David Howes and Constance Classen (New York: Routledge, 2014), 17–36. See also Nina Levent and Alvaro Pascual-Leone, eds., *The Multisensory Museum: Cross-Disciplinary Perspectives on Touch, Sound, Smell, Memory, and Space* (Lanham, MD: Rowman & Littlefield, 2014); Catherine P. Foster, "Beyond the Display Case: Creating a Multisensory Museum Experience," in *Making Senses of the Past: Toward a Sensory Archaeology*, ed. Jo Day (Carbondale, IL: Southern Illinois University Press, 2013), 371–389; and *Museum Materialities: Objects, Engagements, Interpretations*, ed. Sandra H. Dudley (New York: Routledge, 2010).

[27] The statuette is attributed to Andrea Briosco (1470–1532). See above, n. 25, for the note from the exhibition. Concerning the role of touch in the appreciation and enjoyment of early modern art, see James Hall, "Desire and Disgust: Touching Artworks from 1500 to 1800," in *Presence: The Inherence of the Prototype within Images and other Objects*, ed. Robert Maniura and Rupert Shepherd (Aldershot: Ashgate, 2006), 145–160.

[28] This type of enjoyment of an object is what Hans Ulrich Gumbrecht advocates in his book *Production of Presence*. Challenging scholars of past societies to focus less on "meaning" and more on "presence," Gumbrecht advocates what he terms the "presentification of the past." As Gumbrecht writes,

Figure 4: *The Shepherd Daphnis Playing a Pipe*, Andrea Briosco, 1520–1530, The Walters Art Museum, Baltimore, accession number 54.234. Courtesy of The Walters Art Museum.

The Shepherd Daphnis Playing a Pipe is not a medieval object and it was, in any case, a prestige piece – unlike many of the objects considered in the following chapters. Yet considering the staging of this piece in the Walters installation raises some important methodological questions. The first, and most obvious, has to do with the historic specificity of the senses and the epistemological limits of modern experience in accessing the medieval sensory experience. When we cradle *The Shepherd Daphnis* in our hands (or grip the handle of a medieval plow, or open a folding almanac, or listen to the tinkling of tiny bells dangling from early Islamic jewelry), we must consider what sort of understanding we gain of the societies in which these objects were

---

our "desire for presence makes us imagine how we would have related, intellectually and with our bodies, to certain objects (rather than ask what those objects 'mean') if we had encountered them in their own historical everyday worlds." Hans Ulrich Gumbrecht, *Production of Presence: What Meaning Cannot Convey* (Stanford, CA: Stanford University Press, 2004), 124. For a thoughtful assessment of Gumbrecht's book and its intellectual aims, see Lloyd Kramer, "Searching for Something that is Here and There and also Gone," *History and Theory* 48 (2009): 85–97.

produced, or of the people who made or used them. As historian Martin Jay has observed, the senses are situated at "the unstable crossroads of nature and culture" – that is to say, although they have roots in biology (in the sense "organs" of tongue, nose, ear, etc.), they are interpreted through culturally and historically bounded minds and bodies.[29] Thus Mark Smith cautions that "how a lemon tastes is contingent on the tongue doing the licking, its specific history and culture."[30] Even if we *could* recapture the sounds, smells, and tastes of a bygone era, we cannot interpret them as women and men at that time might have, and did. Holding *The Shepherd Daphnis* is a pleasing experience – and it is important for our understanding of the object in many dimensions – but our experience in this case cannot replicate the historic experience of its Renaissance patrons, makers, or owners.[31]

With that caveat in mind, there is nevertheless much to learn through objects about the senses, or through both objects and senses about the cultures and people of the medieval European past. Without assuming that our experience is historically authentic, we clearly can gain new and critically important insights through the study of objects (rather than texts alone), as scholars across the disciplines have long acknowledged.[32] Not only do objects often tell a different story than texts (even, in some cases, directly disproving the claims of the written record), but they often shed light on communities and aspects of medieval life and culture that texts – produced in literate, generally elite, and often male clerical environments – do not address.

---

29 Jay, "In the Realm of the Senses," 309. David Howes, a pioneer of sensory studies, observes that "sensation is not just a matter of physiological response and personal experience. It is the most fundamental domain of cultural expression, the medium through which all the values and practices of society are enacted." David Howes, *Sensual Relations: Engaging the Senses in Culture and Social Theory* (Ann Arbor: University of Michigan Press, 2003), xi. For critical discussions of experience as a basis for historical knowledge, see Joan W. Scott, "The Evidence of Experience," *Critical Inquiry* 17 (1991): 773–797; and Martin Jay, *Songs of Experience: Modern American and European Variations on a Universal Theme* (Berkeley: University of California Press, 2005), 216–260.
30 Mark M. Smith, "Producing Sense, Consuming Sense, Making Sense: Perils and Prospects for Sensory History," *Journal of Social History* 40 (2007): 841–858, at 847.
31 In this assessment, we disagree with Peter Hoffer. Although Hoffer acknowledges that "all sensation is culturally bound" and "relative," he nevertheless allows that the senses might serve to connect us with the past. As he writes: "Can we use our senses to replicate sensation in a world we have (almost) lost? ... I think the answer is yes." Peter Charles Hoffer, *Sensory Worlds in Early America* (Baltimore: Johns Hopkins University Press, 2003), 2. For a thoughtful critical assessment of Hoffer, see Smith, "Producing Sense."
32 On the "material turn" in scholarship, see Leora Auslander, "Beyond Words," *American Historical Review* 110 (2005): 1015–1045; and Aden Kumler and Christopher R. Lakey, "*Res et significatio*: The Material Sense of Things in the Middle Ages," *Gesta* 51 (2012): 1–17. A plea for reconciliation between text and artifact appears in Martin Carver, "Marriages of True Minds: Archaeology with Texts," in *Archaeology: The Widening Debate*, ed. Barry Cunliffe, Wendy Davies, and Colin Renfrew (Oxford: Oxford University Press, 2002), 465–496.

Yet the question is not simply one of object history, but of the senses: how might studying an object in light of its presumed activation and sensory effect deepen our understanding of the past? Engaging in, or observing, activities that are thought to approximate past actions offers one route to a historical "sensorium," which we define along with Richard Newhauser (drawing on the foundational work of anthropologists David Howes and Constance Classen) as "the 'sensory model' of conscious and unconscious associations that functions in society to create meaning in individuals' complex web of continual and interconnected sensory perceptions."[33] Art historian Candace Weddle engaged in a project of autoethnography to aid in her understanding of blood sacrifice in the Roman imperial cult. Attending the Kurban Bayram sacrifices in Istanbul in December 2008 was an experience that, Weddle writes, "changed my understanding of the processes of ancient sacrifice in several fundamental ways."[34] The sights, sounds, and smells of animal sacrifice were striking, she notes, as was the waste that resulted – an element of sacrifice that she had not previously considered. While necessarily speculative, Weddle's autoethnography offers one path toward the sensory past, through modern analogues. Medievalist Jeff Rider proposes a further way of capturing the sensory experience of the past, one that promotes an experiential interaction with past objects and situations that is not passive, based on observation, but active, based on direct re-creation and enactment.[35] Rider's ideas draw in part on findings from neuroscience, in particular the argument that "mirror neurons" might allow humans to experience an action by watching another perform it, and the related idea that performing a given physical action fires the same activity in the brain that it would for another person performing the same action in another time or place. According to this model, lifting a sword (like writing with a quill, opening a folding almanac, or milking a cow) will have a neurological impact on modern "reenactors" similar to the impact it had on medieval knights, scribes, or farmers.

Medievalists have not typically embraced reenactment or re-creative experience as credible sources of knowledge about the past; indeed, reenactment is often viewed as anachronistic and distortive, and has been dismissed by some as a pastime for "the mad, the vain and the foolish."[36] However, within other fields

---

33 Newhauser, "The Senses, the Medieval Sensorium, and Sensing (in) the Middle Ages," 1559.
34 Candace Weddle, "The Sensory Experience of Blood Sacrifice in the Roman Imperial Cult," in *Making Senses of the Past*, ed. Day, 137–159, at 147.
35 Jeff Rider, "The Middle Ages Are within Your Grasp: Motor Neurons, Mirror Neurons, Simulacra, and Imagining the Past," *Medievalism on the Margins: Studies in Medievalism* 24 (2015): 155–175.
36 Jerome de Groot, "Affect and Empathy: Re-Enactment and Performance as/in History," *Rethinking History* 15 (2011): 587–599, at 587. De Groot offers a review of recent studies in reenactment and performance as they relate to history and historical knowledge making. By contrast, David Lowenthal dismisses reenactments as "patent anachronisms." David Lowenthal, *The Past Is a Foreign Country – Revisited* (Cambridge: Cambridge University Press, 2015), 490. On reenactment, see "Extreme and

(notably theater and performance studies) and other geographies and periods (notably American history), reenactment has gained a stronger foothold and developed more pronounced theoretical underpinnings.[37] The limits of experience as a form of historical evidence are clear, yet experience can nevertheless be evocative and even instructive. Following on the success of the "Touch" exhibit at the Walters Art Museum, the curators launched an exhibit in 2016 on the senses: "A Feast for the Senses." The "Feast" exhibit sought to promote a multisensory experience of medieval objects, incorporating such elements as the sounds of birdsong and church bells, the smells of roses and incense, and the feel of rosary beads. These modern re-creative elements were presented alongside treasures of medieval sensory history: the ninth-century Fuller Brooch, the late thirteenth-century *Bestiaire d'amour*, a fifteenth-century crib of the Christ Child, and several images of the wound of Christ. The layering of sight, sound, smell, and touch enriched visitors' experiences of the objects, even as the modern surround of the museum space mitigated against any illusion of an immersive or historically authentic experience.

The benefits of a reconstructive approach to the medieval sensorium are particularly apparent in Jesse Rodin's contribution to this volume, an immersive study of medieval songbooks. A performer and historian of Renaissance music, Rodin refuses conventional scholarly methods of analysis that subordinate experience and performance to a "harmonious" interpretive paradigm in which the music serves primarily to illuminate a context beyond itself. Rodin proposes an immersive approach to medieval songbooks that involves "memorizing the poems and the tunes … living inside them for weeks and months and years, and … coming to understand what it means to sing a given gesture at a given moment." By imagining a lived experience that reflects the careful and skillful execution of the songbook, Rodin offers a means of considering these late medieval works that highlights their unique qualities as documents of performed and *experienced* art. Rodin's methodology – requiring the imaginative performance of a musical piece – is intensive, yet not ahistorical. As Alexa Sand argued in her 2014 article on the Rattier Virgin

---

Sentimental History," special issue, *Criticism* 46 (2004), especially Vanessa Agnew's introductory essay, "Introduction: What is Re-Enactment?" (327–339). See also Vanessa Agnew, "History's Affective Turn: Historical Reenactment and its Work in the Present," *Rethinking History* 11 (2007): 299–312; and Iain McCalman and Paul A. Pickering, eds., *Historical Reenactment: From Realism to the Affective Turn* (Basingstoke: Palgrave Macmillan, 2010).

37 On the culture of reenactment in America, see Tony Horwitz, *Confederates in the Attic: Dispatches from the Unfinished Civil War* (New York: Pantheon Books, 1998). For an academic account of Civil War reenactment, see Rebecca Schneider, *Performing Remains: Art and War in Times of Theatrical Reenactment* (New York: Routledge, 2011). For an academic history of the sensory Civil War, see Mark M. Smith, *The Smell of Battle, the Taste of Siege: A Sensory History of the Civil War* (Oxford: Oxford University Press, 2014).

(ca. 1280–1300), imagination and intersensory association were central to medieval sensory experience as well.[38] Focusing on the small-scale Virgin and Child now in the Victoria and Albert Museum, Sand proposed that medieval devotional pieces – even when they depicted and seemingly invited touch – may not always have been touched. Highlighting the role of imagination and experience for medieval users engaging with devotional sculpture, Sand argued that "the tactile nature of these works has less to do with being handled than with being haptic."[39] The contemplation of touch, rather than actual physical contact, defined the user's experience. For medieval people (as for modern scholars), imagination and re-creative experience could function productively in tandem to convey meaning.

As contributors and editors, we grappled throughout this project with the tension between the demands of scholarly objectivity and the desire to "feel." We considered how modern experience might productively inform our understanding of the medieval past, and we tested the limits of scholarly evidence and knowledge as we explored the many ways that sensory experience might be communicated through material culture. As we found, examining objects from the perspective of the sensory pushes the boundaries of what we can know about medieval experience in a sometimes speculative but always productive way, showing us how objects shaped experience and how, in turn, experience was imprinted on objects.

Chapter Outlines

The chapters that follow are divided into two groups, based on whether the objects under consideration seem to provoke a particular sensory experience or script a particular handling. The chapters in part 1 seek to reconstruct sensory experience by paying careful attention to what objects might tell us about how they were experienced *in situ*. The songbooks, weaving implements, jewelry, and large vases discussed in these chapters are highly suggestive of the ways in which their medieval users may have experienced them. Each chapter attempts to reconstruct medieval experience, exploring different methods of approaching and capturing experience across time and cultures. In part 2, the chapters examine objects that require some form of activation in order to be used: unfolding, touching, transporting, or contemplation. These objects derive their meaning for a medieval person from sensory engagement: relics are transported and become part of a performance of piety; devotional books are

---

38 Alexa Sand, "*Materia Meditandi*: Haptic Perception and Some Parisian Ivories of the Virgin and Child, ca. 1300," *Different Visions* 4 (2014): 1–28. For an image of the Rattier Virgin, see Sand's chapter in this volume, Figure 4 (194).
39 Sand, "*Materia Meditandi*," 5.

fondled, kissed, and meditated upon; medical almanacs are noisily unfolded, moved around, consulted, and refolded; and the touch of the plow is defended as a constitutive element of male peasant experience.

The first two chapters showcase the difficulties of understanding medieval sensory experience and present different methodological approaches. Jesse Rodin identifies the limitations of current methodological practices in historical musicology, particularly when it comes to capturing the sensory experience of music. Rodin's chapter makes the case for a new and somewhat speculative approach to late medieval songbooks that might enable us to "occupy the body-and-mind of an actual late-medieval person looking or listening" and thus shed light on the compositional intent and sensory effect of specific late medieval songs. Rodin approaches the fifteenth-century Dijon Chansonnier as a sensory artifact through which he envisions individual experiences of the song and its manuscript presentation. In his methodologically unusual and provocative chapter, Rodin imagines the responses of three late-medieval singers and a music connoisseur to their performance and experience of *Je m'esbaïs de vous mon cuer*, composed by Antoine Busnoys, while they together examine the manuscript redaction. The imagined discussion draws our attention to striking qualities and compositional elements of the song that both delight and challenge the singers.

In the second chapter, Valerie Garver turns to a form of sensory experience that, like that of the singers discussed by Rodin, has left only trace evidence in the textual sources: the sensations and physical experiences of low-status Carolingian women engaged in the grueling work of textile production. Drawing on archaeological evidence from Carolingian-era sites – which yield such textile implements as spindle whorls, loom weights, pin beaters, needles, and shears – Garver explores the ways in which these objects may have been used by women, noting the physical effects and sensory experiences that they imply. For the low-status women who used these objects, textile work involved long hours in damp conditions, often in sunken huts with low light and high humidity; the work was repetitive, damaging to fingers and eyes, and noxious due to the smell of rotting fibers that the production of linen involved. Attending to the materiality of archaeological remains, Garver's chapter takes us beyond textual sources and the prestige objects that more generally capture scholarly attention, to focus on the work and conditions of low-status women whose textile production clothed an empire.

The next two chapters examine the sensory experience of adornment. Medieval jewelry is most often studied for its appearance, and not – as Elizabeth Dospěl Williams notes in her chapter – with attention to the sensory experiences of its wearers. What it *felt* like to wear jewelry is largely ignored in art historical scholarship, despite significant attention to the senses in recent years. Instead, questions of manufacture and attribution have typically dominated scholarship relating to jewelry and adornment. In her chapter, Dospěl Williams considers the effects on the senses of adornment in the early medieval eastern Mediterranean, showing the ways in which jewelry was perceived not just visually, but in tactile, aural, and olfactory terms. The feel, sound, and smell of jewelry feature centrally in this chapter, which pioneers a new approach to such adornment. As Dospěl Williams argues, "Considering evidence of sensory experience in Byzantine and Islamic jewelry requires a major shift in scholarly attention." Her chapter demonstrates the benefits to scholarship of such a shift, showing how the sound and smell of women's jewelry fueled religious concerns regarding women's public presence. Women – even when they were not seen – could be sensed in other ways, just as their jewelry – even when concealed from sight – could be announced through sound and smell.

Similar to Elizabeth Dospěl Williams, Melissa Herman considers how Anglo-Saxon adornment was perceived through the senses, both by its wearer and by other viewers. Herman argues that, despite the lack of textual witnesses to debates on the senses, the Anglo-Saxons considered sensory experience – sight, sound, and touch – when designing the intricate metalwork used to adorn accessories such as brooches, buckles, and clasps. Anglo-Saxon metalwork is minutely and deftly executed, making use of specific properties of the material and design to dictate the way in which the viewer's eye moves across the surface. Anglo-Saxon poetry underscores the idea that Anglo-Saxons were particularly attentive to adornment, which enabled them to make assumptions about its wearer's identity. Herman further suggests that "a kind of graphic synesthesia" in jewelry design may reflect the Anglo-Saxon preoccupation with sound. She describes these designs in terms of rhythm and tone, and notes that the stylized depictions of animals might have been associated with their natural sounds. With its emphasis on visual complexity, texture, luminescence, and patterning, Anglo-Saxon adornment thus bears testimony to a cultural preoccupation with sensory experience prior to the introduction of a Christian theological discourse.

Part 1 concludes with Patricia Blessing's chapter, which focuses on the so-called Alhambra Vases and the extent to which they reflect the larger aesthetic principles of the fourteenth-century Nasrid palace in Granada. The spaces of the palace were carefully crafted to entice the senses at various levels, with grand and elegant architecture, poetic epigraphy announcing the beauty of the site, fountains gurgling with the musical sounds of falling water, and gardens replete with the sweet scent of colorful flowers – all motifs that also appear in the poetry itself. The large-scale Alhambra Vases, objects connected to the palace by their close engagement with its aesthetic, appeal to perception through the poetic inscriptions written on them and through complex modes of ornament and the luster of their glaze. This chapter argues that the vases are both small pieces in the *Gesamtkunstwerk* of the Alhambra and *pars pro toto*, in that they mirror the aesthetic devices employed in the monument as a whole, and thus they can provide further inroads into a multisensory understanding of the palace.

Part 2 of the volume opens with three chapters that explore different ways in which the senses were instrumentalized in medieval Christian devotional practice.

Cynthia Hahn turns our attention to the sensory experience of relics. As she explains, ecclesiastics designed reliquaries to invoke a multisensory experience, intending in this way to "overcome spiritual complacency" and create the perception that the saint was "truly present in the relic." These relics were staged in elaborate presentations throughout the period, particularly in the region of the Meuse River valley in the duchy of Lotharingia, an area that was at the forefront of reliquary design. Focusing on Abbot Wibald's innovative reliquary ensemble for the body of Saint Remaclus at the monastery of Stavelot and drawing on descriptions of the movement and staging of relics, Hahn argues that reliquaries were "activated" to invoke communal sensory experiences, which were considered an integral part of medieval devotion. The reliquary of Saint Remaclus, with its moveable chasse, was incorporated into multisensory processions to great effect. The sight of the chasse, the smell of candles and incense, the flickering light, the noise of singing, chanting, and processing – all these sensory experiences created a heightened impression of the saint's presence. But even when the chasse was at rest, the space designed to hold it staged its power by reminding the viewer of its potential for activation. This reliquary was part of a larger effort by the abbots of Stavelot to strengthen the importance of their monastery; other projects, including the triptych reliquary also designed by Wibald, were undertaken with the same aim.

In the following chapter, Sara Ritchey challenges the presumption that later medieval devotion to the wounds of Christ was fundamentally aimed at inciting the physical senses. Rather, as Ritchey shows, the goal of devotion – even to the spectacularly corporeal side wound of Christ – could be to prompt an internal sensory experience that was founded on spiritual imagination rather than physical interaction. Focusing her analysis on a vivid fourteenth-century manuscript depiction of Christ's side wound, Ritchey advocates a reading of the wound in context as one component of a set of devotional practices carefully choreographed by the book's makers, monks at the Cistercian monastery of Villers in Brabant. Placing the wound alongside hymns, poems, depictions of the *arma Christi*, indulgences, and other texts, the book's makers intended for it to serve as an important threshold to a spiritual sensorium that was imagined and compassionate. The wound image shows no traces of abrasion, suggesting that it was not touched, kissed, or otherwise physically activated. Instead, the book's users were guided by the book's devotional program to switch registers from the bodily to the spiritual senses.

Alexa Sand's chapter examines a series of very small books, considering the sensory experiences of creating, holding, and reading them in the context of medieval religiosity. Focusing in turn on the minuscule Psalter of Saint Ruprecht (the smallest surviving book from the Carolingian period), very small books of hours from the late thirteenth to the mid-fourteenth centuries, and early modern miniature girdle books, Sand explores the connection between diminutive scale and the haptic and devotional experience of using these books. Such tiny books engage the body in a manner distinct from larger codices, requiring both user and maker to focus body and mind in a particularly concentrated fashion. Their manufacture required painstaking and minute craftsmanship, while their reading demanded a keen eye. Their small size suggests, moreover, that they may have been kept on the body and even have functioned as amulets. Engagement with small books could potentially be a form of Christomimesis, connecting the reader with Christ's voluntary adoption of the vulnerability of the human form through the Incarnation; this self-belittlement may have been especially fraught with meaning when it was prescribed to female book owners who lacked power and importance.

In chapter 9, Jennifer Borland turns our attention to medieval "folding almanacs," small manuscripts containing six to ten parchment leaves which were folded into a pocket-sized book. To read the contents, the user had to unfold the leaves and hold the almanac in a certain way, offering a particularly potent example of how an object scripted its own use. Specific sensory experiences would certainly have been generated by the manipulation of these manuscripts, and above all by the multiple and habitual unfolding and refolding of their folios. Even now, the parchment pushes to open up and stretch, while the deep folds creased into it cause it to snap back from its flattened state. This constant tension between open and closed, folded and unfolded, is made manifest in movement and in noise. The folding almanacs choreograph their handling practices: moving and resisting movement, activating their materiality, and manipulating the experiences of users.

In the final chapter of the volume, Richard Newhauser explores the sensory significance of the plow in medieval England, arguing that touching the plow ("putten to ploughe") was a physical, sensory experience that defined adult masculinity for the English peasantry. Although the plowman and the plow both figure centrally in Middle English poetry (notably Langland's *Piers Plowman* and Chaucer's *Canterbury Tales*), the peasant perspective is rarely addressed in such texts, which, like manuscript illuminations featuring the rural peasantry at work, generally reflect an elite and idealized view, offering little insight into the peasant community. As Newhauser shows, the experience of plowing – of grasping the plow handle and tilling the soil, usually in a communal or familial context – was practical and necessary, but also crucially constitutive of male peasant community, agency, and identity.

***

The chapters gathered in this volume reflect a wide range of disciplinary approaches and address a rich diversity of objects, from tools fashioned and used by unnamed and unknown peasant women and men to devotional books, almanacs, relics, jewelry, music, and decorative arts. Ranging geographically across Europe and around the Mediterranean, and temporally from the fifth to the fifteenth century, these chapters offer new perspectives on the medieval senses, urging us to focus first on objects and medieval experiences, and then on texts. A central goal of this volume is to advance conversations about medieval experience as it was imprinted in artifacts, plumbing medieval material sources for traces of ephemeral and physical experiences that were rarely fully described or articulated in texts. While objects form our starting point, the goal of each chapter is to reveal an experience, which is – by definition – fleeting and consequently often lost to history.

One insight that emerges clearly from the collected chapters is the importance of objects and sensory perception *together* as constitutive of the very identity of medieval communities. As several contributors show, objects were important to medieval individuals and groups of people, but these alone did not define community so much as the common experience of them did: a number of chapters indicate that sensory experience of shared objects could serve to identify and even maintain a medieval community. While scholars have long acknowledged the place of shared texts in the definition of "textual communities," drawing on the foundational work of Brian Stock, and more recently in the definition of "emotional communities," as Barbara Rosenwein has taught us to interpret evidence of shared affective language, the contributors to this volume encourage us to consider the existence of medieval sensory communities founded on the experience of particular (and sometimes proprietary) objects.[40] The notion that medieval communities could be founded on *both* the tangible (shared objects) and the affective (shared experience) significantly advances our understanding of identity and of the nexus between the object and its activation. Particularly promising for future research is the potential for scholars to use objects as a means of accessing communities for which we have little textual documentation. If objects and their experiences can shed light on communal identity and community formation, then – as Valerie Garver and Richard Newhauser show for low-status workers, and as Elizabeth Dospěl Williams implies for women – an object-oriented approach may yield insights into other medieval communities that have left no textual witness.

Attending to the senses enlivens our understanding of medieval societies in ways that are immensely productive for scholars, opening new research questions and prompting the development of new methodologies and fresh approaches to a broader array of materials. The theological and philosophical traditions that are represented in medieval texts and images, and which have provided the focus for much scholarship on the senses, do not typically shed light on the lived sensory experience of medieval men and women, being concerned rather with cataloguing and theorizing the senses, often from a moral perspective. Yet the medieval layperson's experience was one of sensory saturation and immersion with little concern for or awareness of the scientific, philosophical, and theoretical debates. As the chapters in this volume show, every experience, whether past or present, is a multisensory one. Although

---

40 Brian Stock, *The Implications of Literacy: Written Language and Models of Interpretation in the Eleventh and Twelfth Centuries* (Princeton, NJ: Princeton University Press, 1983); Barbara H. Rosenwein, *Emotional Communities in the Early Middle Ages* (Ithaca, NY: Cornell University Press, 2006).

medieval people may not have been familiar with the teachings of Aristotle, they too would have recognized the connection between objects and the senses. Their experiences may have been ephemeral, but the objects that stimulated sensation have often survived, offering scholars the opportunity to consider an aspect of medieval life that, lacking textual witnesses, has rarely been seen as worthy of study. Approaches such as the ones developed in this volume offer new and important insights into medieval notions of gender, faith, and identity – both communal and individual – as well as the embodied experience of medieval spaces and the activities for which they served as a stage.

Jesse Rodin
1 The Songbook as Sensory Artifact

Mirror in hand, a jester lovingly regards himself (Plate I). Encased in a pink-and-blue costume with dunce cap to match, he has wedged his way into the inner part of a large illuminated *J*. Behind the *J*'s back, a slightly less ridiculous pair of lovers in courtly dress (but the same color scheme) embraces, gazing into one another's eyes. The man leans far forward.[1]

On the facing recto things are even sillier. At the top of the page, an errant rat runs along the roof of a large *T*. Beneath it we find three figures with mouths agape: on the left, a balding man and an angry fox singing (or yelling) into each other's faces; on the right, a massive-lipped grotesque with equally massive teeth and blue glasses. Lower down on the page, a half-smiling male face hovers inside an illuminated *C*.

What might these grotesques have to tell us?[2] What sort of gloss do they provide on the text and music they adorn? To approach these questions, we first need to get our bearings: these figures decorate Antoine Busnoys's song *Je m'esbaïs de vous mon cuer*, preserved on folios 53v–54r of a book known to its friends as the Dijon Chansonnier.[3] Dijon is the longest of six surviving small-format songbooks (it measures 6.9 by 5 inches) copied in the orbit of the French royal court during the 1460s and '70s.[4] Without these chansonniers our understanding of a central musical repertory would be radically impoverished: indeed, in the context of a very poor survival rate for musical sources in fifteenth-century France, the Dijon

---

[1] My thanks to Cecilia Nocilli for confirming that the lovers are not, in fact, dancing. (Dancers would stand side by side, their hands close to their waists.)

[2] Following Peter Fingesten, it would perhaps be more appropriate to refer to these figures as "quasi-grotesques," for they feature a grotesque subject but not a grotesque concept: "they do not arouse the emotions, they produce no shudder, nor leave us cold." See Peter Fingesten, "Delimiting the Concept of the Grotesque," *The Journal of Aesthetics and Art Criticism* 42 (1984): 419–426, at 425.

[3] Throughout this essay I refer to the modern foliation. A full-color digital facsimile is available at http://patrimoine.bm-dijon.fr/pleade/img-viewer/MS00517/viewer.html?ns=FR212316101_CITEAUX_MS00517_000_01_PS.jpg. An extensive description and commentary are available on the website The Copenhagen Chansonnier and the "Loire Valley" Chansonniers, ed. Peter Woetmann Christoffersen, http://chansonniers.pwch.dk/LISTS/DijDes.html. See also Jane Alden, *Songs, Scribes, and Society: The History and Reception of the Loire Valley Chansonniers* (Oxford: Oxford University Press, 2010), appendix A, available at http://global.oup.com/us/companion.websites/9780195381528/resources. All three sites accessed 26 November 2017.

[4] Bibliothèque Municipale, Dijon, MS 517 (formerly 295). The others are Laborde, Wolfenbüttel, Nivelle, Copenhagen, and the newly identified Leuven Chansonnier, made known to me by David Fallows and David Burn; my thanks to Professor Burn for sharing with me slides from a recent presentation as well as transcriptions of the book's twelve unica. For concise descriptions of the other five songbooks, see David Fallows, *A Catalogue of Polyphonic Songs 1415–1480* (Oxford: Oxford University Press, 1999), 5ff. See also David J. Burn, ed., *Leuven Chansonnier: Facsimile and Study* (Antwerp: Davidsfonds, 2017).

Chansonnier, copied circa 1470, preserves a full 161 songs, of which 61 (including this one) are unica.

As plate I makes clear, *Je m'esbaïs de vous* is composed for three voices: a high voice (the discantus) that carries the melody, and two lower voices that interweave with the discantus to form a coherent whole.[5] Our *J* adorns the discantus, notated on the verso; the tenor (T) and contratenor (C) appear on the facing recto. This configuration of voices and voice types (high, medium, and medium-low) is absolutely standard in polyphonic songs of this period; *Je m'esbaïs de vous* is a paradigmatic example of the so-called Burgundian chanson, a repertory cultivated above all in the courts of France and Burgundy. At the top of the page we find the name of the composer, [Antoine] Busnoys, who, perhaps even more than Johannes Ockeghem, was the leading chanson composer of the mid-fifteenth century. Busnoys probably wrote this piece in France in the 1460s.[6]

Like more than half the songs in the repertory, *Je m'esbaïs* is a rondeau, a *forme fixe* poem with a textual and musical organization denoted somewhat confusingly by the pattern AB aA ab AB (Figure 1).[7] In fact the form is fairly simple. Each poetic stanza is divided into two portions.[8] The capital letters *A* and *B* indicate the two halves of the refrain ("Je m'esbaïs ... erreur"); this refrain appears in full at the beginning and the end of the poem (AB ... AB) and in partial form in the middle (A). Each lowercase letter indicates a unique non-refrain text. Thus in a complete performance one hears first a full refrain (AB); then a half stanza of new text followed by a half stanza of the refrain text (aA); then a full stanza with completely new text (ab); and, to conclude, the entire refrain (AB). The music is composed in just two sections but otherwise follows the same scheme, repeating according to the sequence AB AA AB AB. One consequence of this musical organization is that at the end of each A section one of two things happens: the performers either pause, returning to the beginning of the music, or move seamlessly forward into the B section.

---

5 My heartfelt thanks to Sean Gallagher for introducing me to this song and alerting me to its high quality.

6 See David Fallows, "Trained and Immersed in All Musical Delights: Towards a New Picture of Antoine Busnoys," in *Antoine Busnoys: Method, Meaning, and Context in Late Medieval Music*, ed. Paula Higgins (Oxford: Clarendon Press, 1999), 21–50. Cf. Sean Gallagher, "Busnoys, Burgundy, and the Song of Songs," in *Uno gentile et subtile ingenio: Studies in Renaissance Music in Honour of Bonnie J. Blackburn*, ed. Gioia Filocamo and M. Jennifer Bloxam (Turnhout: Brepols, 2009), 413–429.

7 The text survives in a slightly different version in the Rohan Chansonnier. See http://www.goldbergstiftung.org/file/dijongesamtmodern.pdf (accessed 26 November 2017).

8 Each half tends to be two or three lines long, such that a complete stanza of a rondeau is almost always four lines (divided 2+2) or five lines (divided 3+2, as here). Indeed *Je m'esbaïs* is a *rondeau cinquain* with eight-syllable lines, the most common type set to music in this period.

A	Je m'esbaïs de vous, mon cuer,	You astound me, my heart,
	Dont tant mainctenez la foleur	By persisting so much in the folly
	De plus servir nostre maistresse.	Of still serving our mistress,
B	Veu que savez qu'elle a fait cesse	Since you know she's put a stop
	De nous aimer, c'est grant [erreur].	To loving us—it's a great error.
a	Vray est que tant a de valeur	It's true that she has such worth
	Que c'estoit pour nous grant honneur.	That it was a great honor for us.
	Mais toutesfois, quis qu'elle lesse,	Nevertheless, since she's dropping us,
A	Je m'esbaïs de vous . . . maistresse.	You astound me, my heart . . . mistress.
a	Deportez vous, c'est le milleur,	Leave—it's the best thing to do—
	Sans plus acroistre ma douleur;	Without further increasing my pain;
b	Par dieu j'en ay assez, Largesse,	By God, I've had enough, Largesse;
	Votre bonté et gentillesse	Your goodness and kindness
	Me facent paie[r] pour ma faveur.	Make me pay for the favor I've enjoyed.
AB	Je m'esbaïs de vous . . . erreur.	You astound me, my heart . . . error.

Figure 1: Text of *Je m'esbaïs de vous mon cuer.*

The poem is classic unrequited love. The speaker – a man, as in more than nine out of ten rondeaux – is distressed at having lost the object of his affection.[9] He does not, and perhaps cannot, speak directly to the woman who has spurned him; instead he addresses his heart, whose feebleness in persisting in her service causes him genuine astonishment. In the manuscript these elevated sentiments are matched by a handsome and careful textual and musical script (Plate I). By convention, the refrain text (AB) is copied underneath the notes of the discantus. Also by convention, at the bottom of the verso we find the non-refrain texts written out: one half-stanza (a) and one full stanza (ab). The scribe's only slip, one that would probably not have confused anyone, was to have failed to copy the refrain incipit after each of these. Instead, the words "Je m'esbaïs de vous" float somewhat inanely below the last line of music.

Speaking of the music: it, too, is copied in a handsome hand, and features the diamond-shaped noteheads characteristic of fifteenth-century musical notation. The standard layout used here – one voice on the verso, two on the recto – dictated the graphic approach of the so-called Dijon Scribe. On the verso, notice how he has taken care to space both the words and the notes relatively evenly across the page, so as to fill exactly four staves.[10] On the recto, where by convention the tenor and contratenor are texted only with incipits ("Je m'esbaïs" or "Je"), he was able to copy the notes more closely together, such that each voice fills less than three staves.[11] This represents

---

[9] Fallows, *Catalogue of Polyphonic Songs*, helpfully identifies poems in which a woman speaks.
[10] As was common in this period, the music was copied before the text. The scribe follows standard practice in making little effort to align individual words, let alone syllables, with their associated notes.
[11] Lower voices are occasionally texted in fifteenth-century songbooks. See Louise Litterick, "Performing Franco-Netherlandish Secular Music of the Late 15th Century: Texted and Untexted Parts in the Sources," *Early Music* 8 (1980): 474–485; and Denis Slavin, "In Support of 'Heresy': Manuscript

a significant compression, since, as opposed to 113 symbols (notes and rests) in the discantus, one finds 110 in the tenor and 101 in the contratenor. In other words, the scribe has squeezed an average of 37 musical symbols onto each line of the recto, as compared to only about 28 per line on the verso. One might surmise that this solution would produce considerable visual disjunction; and yet when one examines the entire manuscript opening, the recto hardly looks cramped. On the contrary, owing to an almost complete lack of text on the recto and an empty staff separating the two lower voices, the overall impression is one of remarkable visual balance.

This quasi-symmetrical layout is so compelling, in fact, as to offer up insights into a long-standing conundrum of performance practice.[12] The absence of text in the lower voices of chansons has been taken as evidence of either instrumental or "vocalized" performance (the latter meaning that the singer would sing exclusively "ah," "ooh," or something of the sort). Both solutions are clearly possible, and were doubtless adopted for performances of polyphonic songs at various times during the fifteenth century.[13] That having been said, there is a danger, with respect to books such as this, of taking the absence of evidence as evidence of absence.[14] Consider first the discantus. It is surely owing to the practical constraints of page layout that scribes *never* crammed in all three texts sung to the A music (in this case, "Je m'esbaïs," "Vray est," and "Deportez vous") among the musical notation, with one stanza underneath the next[15]; performers were clearly expected to memorize or partially memorize the

---

Evidence for the *a cappella* Performance of Early 15th-Century Songs," *Early Music* 19 (1991): 178–190. Even in such cases the tenor and contratenor rarely carry *all* the text, as the discantus invariably does: see for example David Fallows, "Texting in the Chansonnier of Jean de Montchenu," in *Songs and Musicians in the Fifteenth Century* (Aldershot: Ashgate, 1996), chap. 10, 1–13, at 3.

12 What follows builds on arguments in David Fallows, "Secular Polyphony in the 15th Century," in *Performance Practice: Music before 1600*, ed. Howard Mayer Brown and Stanley Sadie (London: Macmillan, 1989), 201–221, at 209–212; and Fallows, "Texting."

13 See Peter Urquhart and Heather de Savage, "Evidence Contrary to the *a cappella* Hypothesis for the 15th-Century Chanson," *Early Music* 39 (2011): 359–378, and the literature cited there, above all Craig Wright, "Voices and Instruments in the Art Music of Northern France during the 15th Century: A Conspectus," in *Report of the 12th Congress of the IMS, Berkeley, 1977*, ed. Daniel Heartz and Bonnie Wade (Basel: American Musicological Society, 1981), 643–649; and David Fallows, "Specific Information on the Ensembles for Composed Polyphony, 1400–1474," in *Studies in the Performance of Late Medieval Music*, ed. Stanley Boorman (Cambridge: Cambridge University Press, 1983), repr. in David Fallows, *Songs and Musicians in the Fifteenth Century* (Aldershot: Ashgate, 1996), chap. 11, 109–159, at 128–132, esp. 128–129.

14 As Fallows notes ("Secular Polyphony," 212): "What we have are homogenized records reduced to their essence: superfluous information is difficult to find in these manuscripts. They can therefore be very misleading for the reader who goes to them expecting information they were not intended to provide."

15 In virelais it is common for scribes to underlay both B texts to the music of the discantus. But this is something of an exception that proves the rule, for B sections of virelais are often notated on separate manuscript openings, where there is ample space to make this work. Moreover, only two texts are

words.[16] The same logic applies to the lower voices: as should by now be clear, to underlay even the refrain text alone, as in the discantus, would all but preclude the horizontal compression of notes described above, which in turn would force the lower voices to be notated on four staves each, for a total of eight – or nine, if they were to be separated by a blank staff.[17] It is therefore difficult to imagine how the scribe could have texted both lower voices on the seven staves provided here – indeed, how any scribe could have done so when copying a book in which the three voices are arrayed one and two across an opening.

There is more. By convention the contratenor occupies a wide melodic range, such that the distance between its lowest and highest notes is greater than it is for either of the other voices.[18] Notice how, even in just the beginning of the contratenor's first line of music, the notes rise up, then careen downward.[19] The stems issuing

---

sung to the same music rather than three, as in the A sections of rondeaux. In rondeaux, non-refrain texts are virtually never underlaid.

16 Several factors indicate that chansonniers like this one were rarely used for performance; among the most important is the small size of these books. See Wright, "Voices and Instruments," 644–645. Nonetheless, the approach to page layout we find here (above all, the disposition and extent of text underlay) is extremely common among the surviving sources. It therefore seems reasonable to surmise that performers regularly interacted with this type of mise-en-page. On mise-en-page in a slightly later period, see The Production and Reading of Music Sources, a digital project directed by Thomas Schmidt, http://www.proms.ac.uk.

17 Alternatively (but with a similar effect), the scribe could have compressed the words horizontally, which is precisely what happens in the few chansonniers that text the lower voices. These sources, most of which date from slightly later and preserve a different repertory, generally lack the visual appeal of books like Dijon. (An exception, from the 1470s, is the ultra-deluxe Cordiforme Chansonnier, which achieves considerable visual balance even in a section where all voices carry the text. In this case the book's shape – a heart – demanded a sui generis approach to mise-en-page. See Fallows, "Texting," 1–4.)

18 In part for this reason, the contratenor may have been played rather than sung more often than the other voices; see Urquhart and de Savage, "Evidence Contrary to the *a cappella* Hypothesis." Compelling though their discussion is, the authors' claim that split-notes "prove that the contratenor was plucked on a lute or harp, vielle or vihuela, or other instrument" (370) seems overstated: these examples prove that in certain cases, the composer had in mind for the contratenor either an instrument or multiple singers – or (more prosaically) that composers sometimes included an option for such performance situations. Moreover, with regard to sustained (rather than plucked) sonorities that give rise to problems of dissonance treatment, one can also point to "offending" passages – a concept that needs to be handled with care – in upper voices, as in measure 13 of the anonymous virelai *A ceste derraine venue* (Dijon, 39v–41r, accessible at http://josquin.stanford.edu/work/?id=Ano3097). Even the tendency for contratenor voices to incorporate more leaps (including more large leaps) in songs than in three-voice mass sections is subject to interpretation: the difference could owe to issues of genre rather than performance practice.

19 In principle, the scribe could have introduced a change of clef (i.e., a change to the staff line associated with the note we would call "middle C") to mitigate this vertical disjunction – but contratenor voices are characterized by so many rapid changes of register that the widespread application of this solution would prove impractical.

northward from the highest notes penetrate the staff above to the point of precluding the notation of music there, let alone text[20]; the lowest notes, too, move well beyond the borders of the five-line staff, such that the scribe would have needed to employ some fancy footwork to fit words beneath them.[21] All of this suggests that the lack of text (save incipits) in the tenor and contratenor owes to practical and aesthetic choices concerning mise-en-page, and carries no implication that the words are optional. On the contrary, there is every reason, at least with respect to most of the repertoire in chansonniers like this one, to take the incipits at face value. In both cases they mean: "Sing the text that begins with these words."[22]

To sum up: we have here a perfectly conventional rondeau by the most famous song composer of the period, copied by a scribe who, impressively but unremarkably for books of this type, paid careful attention to page layout. The song is scored for three voices; the most likely performance scenario is three singers each singing all the words. Generous accompanying decorations appear, the work of someone who evidently possessed both imagination and humor.

Methodological Roadblocks

At this stage, a musicologist who has learned anything from the postmodern turn of (in our discipline) the 1980s and '90s might ask: What can these visual elements tell us about the music, and vice versa? Can a multidisciplinary approach make legible the cultural context in which songs like *Je m'esbaïs* circulated? And what about that rat?

The impulse to ask these questions is reasonable. But it also betrays a bias toward what I'll call "interpretive harmony" that too often beclouds our engagement with historical materials. We have been told that our arguments will be more interesting if, to stick with the example at hand, we can connect the illuminations to the text to the mise-en-page to an often ill-defined "context" beyond them – and, more damningly, we have been told that there is less "there" there if we can't. Wouldn't it be exciting if I could show that the rat is a commentary on the text of the song, which Busnoys has set to music in a way that imitates the creature's slithering? Even better, would my

---

[20] In contrast to modern practice, in which stem direction is determined by the position of the note on the staff, the Dijon Scribe's stems almost always point upward. This practice, common to all six Loire Valley chansonniers, would seem to reflect aesthetic concerns (in manuscripts of sacred music, stems do sometimes point downward, though not as often as they do today).

[21] In *Je m'esbaïs* the tenor, too, occupies a wide range (twelve notes, the same as the contratenor).

[22] This solution can be heard on a series of landmark recordings by Gothic Voices, directed by Christopher Page, most famously *The Mirror of Narcissus* (Hyperion A66087) – though Page's preference for voices that blend as perfectly as possible to produce pure, "clean" sonorities is by no means a necessary consequence of this approach.

contribution not be more "important" if I could reveal that the patron for whom this book was made was known to have been obsessed with rodents?

To make such claims I would need to demonstrate that the illuminator responded with appropriate imagery to the music and text of Busnoys's song, and that aspects of the nonmusical world affected the specifics of Busnoys's and the illuminator's creative activities. The problem is that, as is so often the case with respect to fifteenth-century polyphony, one can show neither of these things. First, both the maker and recipient of the Dijon Chansonnier are unknown – so establishing anything about how the nonmusical world might have directly impinged on the rat, the jester, the poem, or the polyphony is all but impossible. Second, Busnoys probably had no involvement in the creation of this book; unlike the words and the notes, the images belong squarely to the realm of the work's reception. This point is relevant not because reception is less important than composition, but because the overwhelming likelihood is that the creative acts of the composer and the illuminator were separate. Had the five or ten chansonniers in which this song probably once circulated all survived, we would undoubtedly find that the rat did not follow the music from book to book.[23]

To insist on a connection between music and image, then, we must limit our interpretive activities to the contributions of a single illuminator. But even this won't work – for the compositional choices that make the sneering rat and the dunce-capped jester compelling are unrelated to those that animate Busnoys's song. The two creative acts are distinct. This point extends well beyond *Je m'esbaïs de vous*: in the entire repertory, direct connections between song texts and illuminations are extremely rare.[24] Jane Alden has pointed to the example of Jean Delahaye's *Mort j'appelle de ta rigueur*, copied by the Dijon Scribe in the Laborde Chansonnier (fols. 88v–89r): illuminated initials depict a man pleading (verso) and the figure of Death mortally wounding his lover (recto).[25] Here – and evidently only here – the illuminator put actual thought into the relationship between text and image: the text, by Villon, speaks of a man who, addressing Death, mourns his departed love. And yet no laughing faces accompany *Ma bouche rit* (Dijon, fols. 9v–10bis); on the contrary, most everyone looks quite serious. And the doleful *Fors seulement l'attente que je meure* (Dijon, fols. 28v–29r)

---

23 This point can be confirmed by examining pieces that survive in multiple sources. To take a song that was copied into all six Loire Valley chansonniers (Ockeghem's *D'ung aultre amer*), we find no consistency from source to source. (The man who wears a bench as a hat turns up – alas – only once, in the Copenhagen Chansonnier.)

24 Cf. Jane Alden, "*Ung Petit cadeau*: Verbal and Visual Play in the Wolfenbüttel Chansonnier," in *Essays on Music in Honour of David Fallows: Bon jour, bon mois, et bonne estreene*, ed. Fabrice Fitch and Jacobijn Kiel (Woodbridge, UK: Boydell, 2011), 33–43, esp. at 39–43. In other contexts such connections are easier to establish. See Tim Shephard, "Seeing and Singing: Interpreting Decoration in Italian Music Manuscripts c. 1500," *Journal of the Alamire Foundation* 6 (2014): 153–166, and the literature cited there.

25 Alden, *Songs, Scribes, and Society*, 84, 86. The same song appears on an opening of the Dijon Chansonnier that lacks decorated initials (fols. 44v–45r).

is inexplicably adorned with a trio of snails.[26] Moreover, notwithstanding a healthy variety of images in these books, the visual repertoire is not endless. Silly faces are standard fare, as are animals.[27] Embracing couples, as in *Je m'esbaïs*, are not, but one does find an equally unlikely example in another song as well.[28] For these reasons it seems justifiable to conclude that when it comes to how the songbook's visual imagery connects to the music and the texts, there is less than meets the eye.

All of this, I blushingly acknowledge, is obvious. It bears saying because in the present moment we are caught in something of an epistemological feedback loop: scholars are rewarded for identifying new and expanded meanings, but almost never for narrowing possibilities or foreclosing synergies. To narrow and foreclose, some say, would impoverish our understanding rather than expand it. More, we are repeatedly told, is more. And so we leap across chasms of uncertainty in order to connect pieces of music to wider contexts, in the process confusing forests with trees, molehills with mountains.[29] Indeed with respect to these examples, I assert that the pathways that might at first seem the most promising are in fact not promising. I suggest that we should instead begin by acknowledging our bias toward interpretive harmony and moving beyond it. Once we do that, we come upon a bifurcation.

On the one hand, I hope no one would wish to claim that the musical notation, the mise-en-page, or – heaven forbid – the rat are *uninteresting*.[30] Rather, the bulk of the interest they hold, at least as it pertains to books like this one, lies squarely in the realm of generality. Taken in the context of other poems, other songs, and other grotesques, these features can help us think harder about everything from the aesthetics of bookmaking to the role of play in fifteenth-century courtly culture. *Pace* my scoffing above, we can even profit from considering why these elements are clustered within the same manuscript opening: what did it mean to juxtapose these sorts of drawings with this sort of poetry and this sort of music in a book probably destined

---

26 As Emily Zazulia kindly points out (personal communication), even random chance makes it exceedingly unlikely that not a single illumination in all six Loire Valley chansonniers would match the theme of the associated song text in an apparently meaningful way.
27 Alden's description of the illustrations is worth quoting in full: "The designs in the initials include grotesque faces (with exaggerated noses, lips, and protruding chins, generally scowling); figures with bishops' miters; jesters; people in courtly attire; obscene figures defecating; hybrid creatures; various animals, birds, snails, fish, and insects; bagpipes; bells; flowers; and acanthus-leaf patterning (red and pink or gray and white). A yellow wash was used as background." See Alden, *Songs, Scribes, and Society*, appendix A.
28 *Helas que pourra devenir* (Dijon Chansonnier, fols. 81v–82r).
29 See Jesse Rodin, "Form and Experience in Fifteenth-Century Music: Problems, Fallacies, New Directions," *Journal of the Alamire Foundation* 8 (2016): 275–292; and Emily Zazulia, "Out of Proportion: *Nuper rosarum flores*, Cathedralism, and the Danger of False Exceptionalism," *Journal of Musicology*, forthcoming 2019.
30 I mean this seriously. The rat is fantastic – it's just important to acknowledge what it is doing and what it is not doing.

for a higher-up in the orbit of the French royal court? In what situations would such a person open to this page – and what might they make of what they saw?

The answers to these questions undoubtedly varied from reader to reader. Still, because we are talking about elements that are more or less generic rather than keyed to the details of a given chanson, it is not unreasonable to posit some more or less generic explanations. In most songs in Dijon and books like it, every element other than the illuminations projects a serious, high-minded, luxurious, courtly milieu. The grotesques, surely, are playful: they indiscriminately lighten the mood, providing respite from the heavy theme of unrequited love.[31] They give the eye something silly to look at. They also tempt the mind in a "the grass is always greener" sort of way, letting a fancy person looking at a fancy book imagine herself as part of a culture bound by fewer rules and regulations.[32] Over-the-top though they are, the grotesques conjure up a world of peasants, jesters, and musicians – a world that orbited but could never be fully integrated into the activities of an aristocratic patron. These images delight the imagination, expanding the registral horizon of a book that is otherwise mostly serious.[33] They are commensurate with a widespread tendency in this period for serious and humorous, real and magical, rural and urban, sacred and secular to intermingle and intertwine. For all these reasons, we ought to spend more time with them. And then there's another reason: silly pictures are fun.

On the other hand, generality has its limits. While the rat (and the question of why the artist felt free to insert it, along with the large-lipped tooth man, here) can shed light on aspects of late-medieval culture, it can't do much for our understanding of this song in particular. Taking *Je m'esbaïs de vous*, its illuminations, and its mise-en-page chiefly as *an example of something* starts us down the road toward sentences that begin, "For late-medieval readers ..." – sentences that can't help us occupy the body-and-mind of an actual late-medieval person in the act of looking or listening. Such sentences hail from the land of Academese: a well-formulated, well-footnoted country whose very conventions distance, anonymize, and render impersonal.

To be clear, I am not trying to problematize the sorts of observations that flow from the study of a songbook or group of songbooks. To take the most prominent publication to have emerged in recent years, Alden's monograph on the so-called Loire Valley chansonniers offers up rich insights into the cultural milieu in which

---

[31] On marginalia more generally, see Michael Camille, *Image on the Edge: The Margins of Medieval Art* (London: Reaktion, 1992); and, even more, Jeffrey Hamburger's critical review in *The Art Bulletin* 75 (1993): 319–327.

[32] In part for these reasons, I find it hard to read these books as conduct manuals for the elite. Cf. Honey Meconi, "A Cultural Theory of the Chansonnier," in *Uno gentile et subtile ingenio: Studies in Renaissance Music in Honour of Bonnie J. Blackburn*, ed. Gioia Filocamo and M. Jennifer Bloxam (Turnhout: Brepols, 2009), 649–657, at 650–654.

[33] Occasionally the text and music join in on the fun. See, for instance, Emily Zazulia, "'Corps contre corps,' voix contre voix: Conflicting Codes of Discourse in the Combinative Chanson," *Early Music* 38 (2010): 347–359.

such books were produced; without contributions of this sort we would be more or less lost.[34] Rather, I am suggesting that if we *also* want to ask more specific and more personal kinds of questions, we will need to make different sorts of observations. If, that is, we want to say something that applies to *this and only this* song – if we want to glimpse something we can hear and even feel, if we want to know why someone bothered to compose *these* words and *these* notes, if we want to access an individual singer's or listener's experience of *sensing* this song in real time, of internalizing its twists and turns and imagining what meanings they might have held and might still hold – then we must begin elsewhere. We must begin by memorizing the poems and the tunes, by living inside them for weeks and months and years, and by coming to understand what it means to sing a given gesture at a given moment.

At this stage heads will start to shake, for I am advocating something like an aural version of Michael Baxandall's "period eye" – and musicologists have, after much theorizing, concluded that, on balance, this is out of reach.[35] The reasons bear repeating: in stark contrast to visual culture, we have no aural documents from the fifteenth century. It's a sobering thought that, apart from a baby's cry or (maybe) the clearing of a throat, there are few human-produced sounds we experience today that we can be sure are materially the same as the sounds that were experienced at that time. Moreover, fifteenth-century musical notation, elegant and complete though it is, was not designed to inscribe information that performers did not need or want in written form. Thus music manuscripts preserve no instructions about timbre (that is, the quality of the sound), dynamics (how loud the singers should sing), where to breathe, or the expected quality of attacks (i.e., how strongly to strike a note).[36] We also possess only relative information about tempo, of the type, "This section should be about four-thirds the speed of the previous section." There are even cases when we're not sure exactly which notes to sing (this issue is commonly known as *musica ficta*): rather than clutter up the notation with what we now call sharps and flats, composers expected singers to rely on generally understood guidelines about when to "inflect" a note upward or downward. And while the situation is not nearly as complex as it is sometimes

---

34 Alden, *Songs, Scribes, and Society*.
35 Michael Baxandall, *Painting and Experience in Fifteenth-Century Italy: A Primer in the Social History of Pictorial Style* (Oxford: Oxford University Press, 1972). The literature on "authenticity" and "authentic listening" is considerable, occupying several book-length studies and many pages of the journal *Early Music*. A useful introduction to the central issues is Shai Burstyn, "In Quest of the Period Ear," *Early Music* 25 (1997): 692–701. A refreshing take (from an Anglocentric perspective) is found in Nick Wilson, *The Art of Re-enchantment: Making Early Music in the Modern Age* (Oxford: Oxford University Press, 2014).
36 With respect to breathing, they do provide instruction in the sense that it is natural to breathe during rests. But there are many phrases that, even at a brisk tempo, cannot be sung in one breath.

made out to be, there are cases where we cannot be sure if the note B should, to use modern parlance, be sung as B-natural or B-flat.[37]

For all these reasons, the notion of the "period ear" has been largely discredited. In a widely cited study, Richard Taruskin heaps scorn on "authentic performance practice," that movement of the late twentieth century that sought to use what information could be gleaned from historical sources to reproduce as closely as possible the sounds of the music as they were experienced in the past. For Taruskin, authenticity is a modernist project whose goals are more about us than them. And of course he's right, up to a point: no matter how hard we try, we can't escape our modernity.[38]

This seemingly self-evident conclusion, I suggest, is precisely where we go astray. We genuflect before the altar of cultural distance, insisting on our feeble inability to close the epistemic gap. But we are sometimes so busy wringing our hands that we forget to delve into our historical materials.

To be sure, there is much to wring our hands about. Indeed the study of music presents unique challenges that have long stymied musicologists. To take an issue that bears heavily on the present subject, how should we engage with the musical texts? I've mentioned that *Je m'esbaïs de vous*, like virtually all fifteenth-century music, is notated in parts – that is, voices that are meant to sound simultaneously are written in different places on the page. How are we to study the piece as a whole? Looking at the notation, it is all but impossible, even for a modern scholar trained in late-medieval musical notation, to hear all three lines in one's head without aligning them vertically on the page, in score. And yet the moment we retranscribe the notation in a modern edition, we lose important aspects of the original. Above all, we lose the Dijon Scribe's elegant horizontal compression (to varying degrees) of the notes; instead we must spread the music out from left to right, such that the most active voice at any given moment, the one with the most notes per temporal unit, determines the width of the voices that sound against it. When we adopt this lowest-common-denominator approach to music spacing, which includes regular bar lines that interrupt the visual flow of the music, we make it harder to look ahead in a given voice and quickly see what's coming; melodic phrases that the Dijon Scribe manages to fit onto a single line now typically spill over onto two (see Figure 2 for a comparison of the first five measures in each of the two formats).

This problem, and many others like it, can be overcome through a combination of elegant editorial solutions and practice using modern editions. Still, the very fact of

---

[37] A useful introduction is Rob C. Wegman, "Musica Ficta," in *Companion to Medieval and Renaissance Music*, ed. Tess Knighton and David Fallows (Berkeley: University of California Press, 1992), 265–274.

[38] See Richard Taruskin, *Text and Act: Essays on Music and Performance* (Oxford: Oxford University Press, 1995), and the literature cited there. A subtle, if critical, reading of Taruskin's views appears in John Butt, *Playing with History: The Historical Approach to Musical Performance* (Cambridge: Cambridge University Press, 2002), 14–24 and passim.

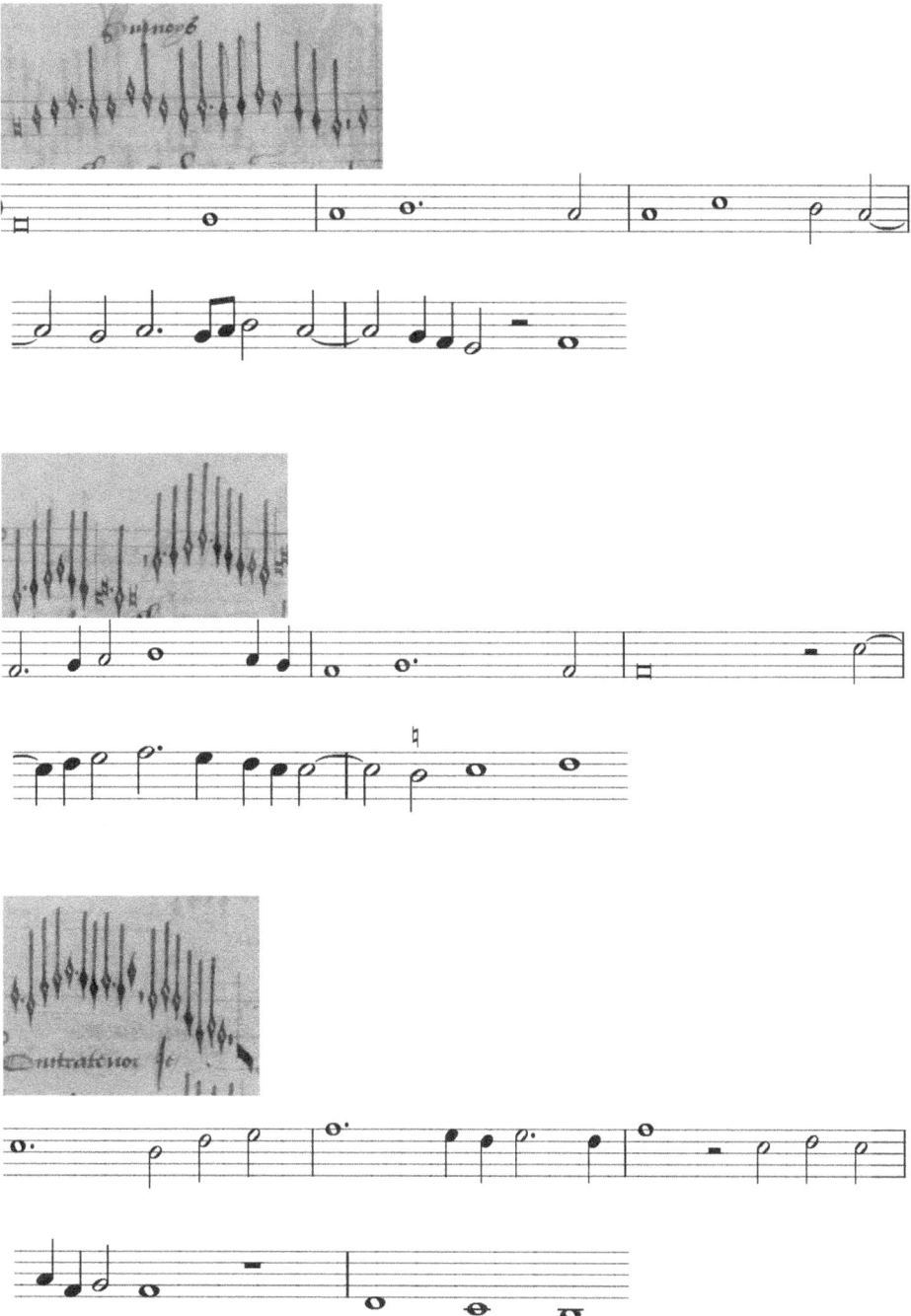

Figure 2: Voice-by-voice comparison of *Je m'esbaïs de vous*, measures 1–5, in the Dijon Chansonnier and a modern edition.

a vertically aligned score removes us from the physicality of the small songbook, the particular way the text of the poem is (and isn't) underlaid to the notes – the whole gestalt of the manuscript opening. Even more significant is that this methodological problem forces us to spend a lot of time and intellectual energy worrying about how to represent the "original" notation in modern form, which is time not spent on the notes or the words. Different editors arrive at sometimes radically different solutions; as such we lack a stable visual means of accessing our proto–sound object. We therefore find ourselves in a lose-lose situation: the original notation fails to offer the holistic overview we seek, and yet modern re-creations that facilitate score-based analysis wrench us away from the very documents that formed the basis of our forebears' musical experiences.

The hand-wringing doesn't stop with problems of edition making. All too reasonably, we worry about our capacity to discern a late-medieval composer's or poet's intentions – and about whether sussing out the intentions of an (almost invariably) white male who has been dead for more than five hundred years is worthwhile in the first place. We agonize over fifteenth-century performance practices and how they might have varied from court to court, performer to performer, decade to decade, even minute to minute. We get nervous about matters of pronunciation, trying to banish modern French from our minds and accept that, for example, the syllable "-ois" is pronounced "-oué." Setting aside issues of performance, we obsess about the impossibility of *listening* authentically, particularly in light of all the music we know now that they didn't then. And we fret over the variability of fifteenth-century listening practices and the danger of imagining an idealized, all-encompassing listener.

These problems are even more acute for performers of this repertoire. I've explained that we lack basic information about parameters such as vocal production and dynamics. While in theory every performer must therefore begin ex nihilo, with a long list of decisions to be made, in practice we face a trap: a series of well-established – if not necessarily historically informed – modern performance conventions. Alongside this trap lurks still another: an aesthetics of transgression, inherited from the nineteenth century, that leads performers always to seek out a provocative, untried approach. And so we stretch even the evidence we do have so as to make our performances more "interesting." In concerts and published recordings, one often hears instruments foreign to fifteenth-century Europe, strange transpositions and doublings, tempi that fly in the face of what we know about performance practice, frenetic changes of scoring (from purely instrumental performance to a cappella performance to solo voice with accompaniment), and the addition of drum parts, the evidence for which is thin to nonexistent.[39] None of this is "bad," exactly; assuming that modern performers own up to what they are doing, they should have the right to

---

[39] The two traps I've described intersect inasmuch as some of the practices just mentioned have been normalized.

make these and still more outlandish choices. Even so, when confronting a musical culture as foreign as that of late-medieval Europe, would it not be sensible to establish a corpus of performances and recordings that, however varied, aim to re-create the fifteenth-century sound world as best we can?[40]

But the biggest challenge of all is that these problems of mediation are ultimately a distraction, an excuse to stop thinking. Taruskin risks throwing out the baby with the bathwater, seeming almost to adopt a logic that claims, "We can't possibly recapture the past without revealing ourselves, so let's not bother." In this, the age of the selfie, we've spent so much effort reveling in the "me"-ness of everything we do that we're liable to neglect the very historical objects we're trying to study.

For we music historians – it's not pretty to admit it, but it must be admitted if progress is to be made – no longer know the repertoire.[41] To be fair, knowing *the repertoire* is impossible: even leaving aside the issue of lost works, from the fifteenth century alone we possess thousands of manuscript pages. There is too much music to get to know it all intimately, even in a lifetime – and especially in this era of work speedup and multitasking. To come to know a piece from the inside, one has to move through it in real time ten, twenty, or even a hundred times. Modern performances and recordings are, relatively speaking, scarce. It is hard even to gain the sort of rough knowledge that, in the realm of painting, can be had after several minutes of close looking. We therefore lean heavily on canonical works, and on observations that can be made from a quick glance at the score. All too often we relegate the stuff of the music to a pile of examples from which we draw when needed. And so of course our writings foreground the unknowability of it all: that's the only way to avoid admitting how steep the challenge is and how far we are from meeting it.

I count myself squarely among those who know little. Still, I was fortunate as a student to have had mentors who modeled a devotion to singing, listening, reading music manuscripts and scores, leading performances, and memorizing.[42] In my

---

40 An inverse of this problem, often encountered in performances by English ensembles, is the unfortunate idea that the best way to navigate any parameter for which we lack textual evidence is not to navigate it at all. To take dynamics, for example: even in the face of all-but-obvious musical cues (see, for instance, the discussion of "mainctenez" below), many ensembles eschew the slightest contrasts in volume, in deference to a notion of authenticity that unreflectively equates dynamic contrast with a Romantic sensibility.
41 In this respect we used to be better off. Even before the widespread availability of recordings and critical editions, scholars such as August Ambros and (several generations later) Heinrich Besseler attained sufficient mastery of the repertoire to characterize individual pieces and styles with clarity and eloquence, though their descriptions lack the analytical precision we crave today. August Wilhelm Ambros (1816–1876), *Geschichte der Musik*, vols. 1–4 (Breslau and Leipzig: F. E. C. Leuckart, 1862, 1864, 1868, 1878); and Heinrich Besseler (1900–1969), *Die Musik des Mittelalters und der Renaissance* (Potsdam: Akademische Verlagsgesellschaft Athenaion, 1931).
42 In this regard I am especially grateful to Caroll Goldberg, Lawrence F. Bernstein, Cristle Collins Judd, Peter Urquhart, David Fallows, Sean Gallagher, Alejandro Planchart, and Joshua Rifkin.

case this process has included extended periods of singular focus on a given genre or composer to the exclusion of later musics. Does this mean that I and the small but robust minority of scholars with a similar orientation can forget the Mozart and Madonna we know? Certainly not. But after enough years of immersion, certain truths unavoidably start to reveal themselves. In this context one is reminded of the words of Jack Westrup, who more than sixty years ago advocated listening "with the ears of another age and with all subsequent music banished from the mind."[43] Nowadays all anyone can do is focus on the naïveté of such a statement. What if we instead took it seriously?

Sensory Analysis

In an attempt to access the experience of performing and listening to *Je m'esbaïs de vous*, I am going to try something that to my knowledge has not been tried before. I am going to tell the story of this song from four perspectives: those of three imaginary singers reflecting on a recent performance, and a connoisseur listening to them. It is in this latter figure that modern scholars typically put our energies: we try to uncover the composer's intentions as filtered through an idealized listener. Such a listener is worth our efforts, for the elitist world of books like the Dijon Chansonnier must have included musicians and enthusiastic connoisseurs who knew hundreds of songs by heart. Indeed chansons such as *Je m'esbaïs* give the impression of having been composed with great care, in a way that invites us to attend to the subtlest details of musical construction and to the experiences of their creators, practitioners, and fans. For these reasons I am not going to channel a lay listener, the kind of person who would say, "The music was very sweet," and leave it at that; my auditor will be an insider to this practice. But I think it's also important to consider the individual experiences of the people making the music: each of them has a unique story to tell, even if (by definition) his is not the whole story.[44]

My analyses depend on immersion in *the notes*, which can be examined in a modern edition in the appendix.[45] Nonspecialist readers should be assured that

---

[43] Jack Allan Westrup, *An Introduction to Musical History* (London: Hutchinson's University Library, 1955), 152; quoted in Burstyn, "In Quest of the Period Ear," 694.
[44] In making this claim I wish to question the ideal of timbral homogeneity (i.e., having the voices blend as much as possible) that has arisen over the last several decades, and with it the conflation of timbre and forces, as in the equations: voices + instruments = timbral variety and melodic independence; voices alone = blend and sonority. Cf. Christopher Page, *Discarding Images: Reflections on Music and Culture in Medieval France* (Oxford: Oxford University Press, 1993), 41.
[45] This edition is available through the Josquin Research Project, http://josquin.stanford.edu/data?a=notationEditText&f=Bus3028. See also Clemens Goldberg's online edition, http://www.goldbergstiftung.de/forum/index_de.php?a=topic&t=113; and Leeman L. Perkins, *Antoine Busnoys: The Collected Works*,

knowledge of musical notation is emphatically not needed to understand what is coming.[46] What is needed – at least as emphatically – is engagement with the accompanying online recording; however personal, subjective, and idiosyncratic it may be, this modern realization is as good a starting point as any, particularly when one approaches it with knowledge of which parameters are encoded in the musical text (notes, rhythms, words, and some information about tempo) and which aren't (everything else).[47]

To be more specific, we know that *Je m'esbaïs* is in triple meter (1-2-3, 1-2-3) and should proceed at a moderate tempo, but we can't give "moderate" a numerical value.[48] We know that the song begins with a sonority built on the note F, but the sounding frequency of that note surely varied from performance to performance; while it may often have been close to the F on a modern piano, we can hardly lend our F any kind of authority. Even though it is fair to call the discantus "the melody," this song is polyphonic, which is to say scored for multiple, independent voices. The tenor and contratenor lines do not camp out on a single note, biding their time while the action happens above; instead they each weave an independent melodic web, complementing and at times imitating the discantus but rarely becoming fully subservient to it. This melodic independence is why it makes sense to take account of what it might feel like to be inside each vocal line as it bumps into the others.

Let us imagine, then, that we are seated in a dining hall somewhere in northern France. The year is 1475. It is late in the evening. We are reflecting on our dinnertime performance, which took place during the partridge course. And we are privileged to have in front of us a recently copied chansonnier known today as Dijon.

The goal of this exercise is to explore reactions to the music that are at once personal and communal: to use our knowledge of a much larger musical corpus to meditate on what is special in this rondeau, and on how the song's meanings emerge only

---

Part 1; Works with Texts in the Vernacular, Masters and Monuments of the Renaissance Series (New York: Broude Bros., forthcoming).

46 Such readers can take comfort that – here's another dirty secret – musical examples are rarely read carefully, in part because the details within them usually do relatively little work for the argument. Musical examples often serve as a kind of decoration, a gesture toward the musical text; in many cases the point could have been made without reproducing the given passage.

47 The recording can be heard at https://www.degruyter.com/books/9783110562347; the singers are Michela Macfarlane, Steven Soph, and Bradford Gleim. This performance will form part of a series of three albums by Cut Circle, forthcoming with the label Musique en Wallonie, that present the complete songs of Johannes Ockeghem together with selected chansons by Busnoys and newly discovered, anonymous works from the Leuven Chansonnier.

The recording intentionally uses a dry acoustic, which makes the details of the music more audible. As Anna Zayaruznaya has recently noted, a video recording would be even better, a live performance better still. See her "Intelligibility Redux: Motets and the Modern Medieval Sound," *Music Theory Online* 23 (2017), sec. 3.

48 Among other reasons, this song predates the invention of the pendulum by more than a century. The metronome was not known in the West until ca. 1812.

when activated by coordinated bodies in motion. Our conversation proceeds from the idea that the songbook is a sensory artifact – a record of experiences whose contours we can glimpse through empathetic, immersive engagement.

Dialogue on *Je m'esbaïs de vous*

To be read in conjunction with the accompanying sound file, plate I, and figure 1.[49]

Tenor: Is the opening of this song not extraordinary?

Discantus: It certainly is. The astonishment I am expressing ("You astound me") is the kind that makes you stop in your tracks. My opening melody glides gradually upward from "Je" to "-ïs," already coming to a point of relaxation [i.e., a musical arrival, or "cadence"] at "vous."[50] Indeed, this is one of the slowest starts in the repertory.[51] But at "**mon** cuer" I suddenly leap up to what will turn out to be my highest note and drive forward, expressing my angst by circling around a single note (*a'*) and using jumpy rhythms.[52] All of this makes me see how my astonishment is at once stupefying and activating. The stunned distance I am able to project in my opening phrase gives way to an anger I can't quite control.

Tenor: Fair enough, but my line makes the point more convincingly. My arrival on "vous" is more drawn out than yours and is followed by an even more dramatic shift in mood: after the cadence I leap up to a relatively high note ("mon") and ascend quickly from there (to "cuer"). So yes, this is a tale of two astonishments.

Contratenor: You've both been drinking too much gruit. The opening is hardly static: already at "-**baï**s de **vous**" I ascend to the very top of my range, to a note (*f'*) significantly higher than any I will sing again in this song. To do this I have to stretch a little, which is something you can probably hear. Affective intensity is therefore present from the start.

---

49 The sound file is available here: https://www.degruyter.com/books/9783110562347.
50 For listeners who want help with the meter, the discantus arrives on "vous" at the beginning of the third measure – that is, on the **1** following the opening **1**-2-3, **1**-2-3.
51 The only other *tempus perfectum* songs (that is, songs in a moderate triple meter) in the Dijon Chansonnier with similarly relaxed openings in the discantus are *Ma plus qu'assez et tant bruiante* (Busnoys, 31v); *Mort j'appelle de ta rigueur* (Delahaye, 44v, which begins in a remarkably similar fashion); *En tous les lieux ou j'ay esté* (Busnoys, 83v); and *Die chascun ce qu'il voudra* (anonymous, 186v).
52 Pitches are identified using Helmholtz pitch notation, where *c'* indicates what we now call middle C. (If one were to array five successively ascending Cs with middle C in the middle position, these pitches would be labeled *C, c, c', c'',* and *c'''*.)

Listener:	I can't argue with that – but I also can't help but focus on the highest, most prominent voice. While the discantus's gradual, easy ascent at the beginning is undercut a bit by the activity of the lower voices, the flurry of motion at "mon cuer" is more or less equal in all three. In any case, for me the whole first phrase seems designed to set up the second ("Dont tant mainctenez la foleur"), which is where the music really takes my breath away.
Tenor:	That's for sure. The second poetic line ("By persisting so much in the folly") starts to give the *reason* for my astonishment – and it's here, at "mainctenez" (persisting), that Busnoys really lets us have it. Notice how the energy that has been built up so far dissipates at the first important cadence ("cuer"). Motion slows. I rest. Then, trailing the discantus, I leap up to and hold the excruciatingly high note a' on the word "mainct**e**nez." It's an amazing moment. And I'm the star of the show.
Discantus:	Yes, but you've missed why it's so special. The first three notes of your line ("mainctenez") exactly imitate the music I've just sung to "Dont tant main-." By the time you reach your highest note, I've stretched even higher. The two of us actually leap upward to "nez" together, in parallel – and we pause there, on the second beat of the three-beat grouping [i.e., the second beat of the measure], metrically adrift and desperately high (especially you). After that we almost immediately stress another note: "la" of "la foleur." The effect of this passage thus depends on the sudden slowing of motion, the gathering of energy as you imitate me, our coordinated rise, and the pair of consecutive (noncadential) arrivals.
Tenor:	I was getting to that.
Contratenor:	Yeah, yeah. But you've left me out of the picture.
Listener:	For good reason, no?
Contratenor:	Harrumph. The slowdown you've described? It's the discantus and I who initiate it. The emphasis on the second beat? Same thing: the two of us land there ("mainc-") on a strangely hollow sonority. I also participate in the coordinated ascent to "-nez" (albeit with less drama) and the stress on "la" – and you neglected to explain how, from that moment until the cadence ("-leur"), we are all moving more actively, as if set aflame by the intensity of what we've just sung.
Listener:	I see what you mean – though in fact the emphasis on the second beat goes back to the arrival on "cuer," and in a way to the opening of the song

("-baïs"). It's just dramatized further by the bare sound at "mainc-" and the ascent at "-nez." Listening to this, I feel at sea: the unsettled meter captures the tug-of-war between "myself" and "my heart."

Discantus: Can we skip ahead a little? There's an interesting parallel between this passage and one later in the song. In the line "Veu que savez qu'elle a fait cesse" (Since you know she's put a stop), we again find a dramatic slowdown, followed by a sudden resumption of forward motion. The opening of my phrase is lugubrious. As I reach "cesse," I leap downward in an unusual way, as if cutting off my musical line in accordance with the text. But I only "cease" for a moment: still singing this word, I drive forward, propelling us into what has to be my favorite moment in the song (more on that in a minute). Do you agree?

Tenor: Not remotely. Well, I'll grant you that we all fleetingly slow at "cesse." But for me the earlier part of this phrase is an obstacle course. I begin by leaping once again to my highest note ("Veu que **sa**vez"), then help make a cadence ("-vez"), then continue darting around as you and the contratenor slow. Interestingly, I imitate you here (my "fait ces-" matches your "qu'elle a fait ces-"); at this point we all drive forward together. So yes, there's a pulling back at the beginning of "cesse," but it's nowhere near as dramatic as at "mainctenez."

Contratenor: On balance, I've got to side with the discantus on this one. Not only do we all slow down and move in lockstep for two notes at "cesse" (well, "fait" for me), but after that I briefly rest as you two begin to drive forward. I join you a beat later ("cesse"), intensifying things just before the cadence at the end of the word.

Listener: I also hear "cesse" as an important moment – just not as important as "mainctenez." The pause is shorter and, crucially, is not accompanied by any kind of climax: it's just a pause. Moreover, the enjambment makes me hear this as part of a much longer phrase, one that goes all the way to the end of the song.

Discantus: What do you mean? We come to a cadence at the end of "cesse."

Listener: *You* do, but it's seriously undercut. As the lower voices will doubtless agree –

Tenor and Contratenor, together: – obviously –

Listener: – as you reach the end of "cesse," their continuation of the thought ("De nous aimer, c'est grant erreur"; To loving us – it's a great error)

	has already begun. So the poetic enjambment is matched by a musical one. Indeed this is the only line in the refrain that isn't matched musically by a clear point of arrival.⁵³
Discantus:	I see what you're saying. From this vantage point, "cesse" is only a bump in the road on the way to "De nous **aimer**," where I sing a characteristically Busnoysian gesture that he seems to reserve for special occasions: a held note followed by a rapid descent with a slightly "twisty" melodic shape [down-down-up-down-down-down-down].⁵⁴ I like this gesture so much that before dinner I searched this entire chansonnier: it occurs in only five other melodic phrases, of which three are in songs by Busnoys. In almost all these examples, the gesture seems to be used at a moment of intensity. And this is one of only three cases in which the note at the beginning of the gesture is held so long.⁵⁵ There's no question Busnoys is using this music to do something special.
Contratenor:	Nice detective work! I agree this is a crucial passage. Starting on the word "nous," the tenor and I move slowly and in lockstep, gradually descending until the crucial syllable "-mer," which falls – sound familiar? – on the second beat of the measure. (The emphasis on "-mer" makes me think there's a pun intended: *aimer/amer* [love/bitter].) Crucially, the tenor and I land on notes that do not concord with one another. That uppity music theorist Johannes Tinctoris has been berating Busnoys for composing this kind of dissonant sonority.⁵⁶ But Busnoys is one of many composers who like this sound. Held this long, it creates a striking effect.

---

53 A partial exception is the first phrase, which concludes ("cuer") with a somewhat weak, "half" cadence.
54 Sean Gallagher (personal communication) kindly shared with me his observation that this gesture, though commonplace after ca. 1480, was initially associated mainly with Busnoys. An intervallic search (-2-2+2-2-2-2) using the Josquin Research Project (http://josquin.stanford.edu) provides support for this claim, particularly when one drills down to the details of the search results.
55 In the Dijon Chansonnier, this Busnoysian motif appears in the following passages (* indicates that the first note is a dotted semibreve – i.e., a held note): *Ma demoiselle ma maistresse* (15v–16r; Busnoys, rondeau; end, with both discantus and tenor moving together); *Bel Aceuil le sergent d'amour* (23r; Busnoys, rondeau; tenor [NB: three equal voices], starts on the highest note, in the penultimate phrase); *S'il vous plait que je vous tiegne* (119v; anonymous, rondeau; discantus, second phrase); *Puis qu'aultrement ne me peut estre* (168v; anonymous, combinative chanson; discantus, end of second phrase); *Mon mignault musequin* (181v; Busnoys, combinative chanson; discantus, beginning of B section).
56 This point was "later" (ca. 1477) formalized in Johannes Tinctoris, *The Art of Counterpoint* (*Liber de arte contrapuncti*), trans. Albert Seay (American Institute of Musicology, 1961), 130–131.

Listener: Yes: an effect that depends also on the discantus's Busnoysian gesture ("aimer"), all of which is "suspended" over your sustained dissonance. For anyone keeping track, the discantus's first, held note ("ai-") forms a dissonance with both of you, such that every note sounding as the lower voices reach "mer" is dissonant with every other.[57]

Tenor: Do you think it's an accident that this occurs so near the end of the refrain?

Listener: Is that a rhetorical question?

Tenor: Of course it's a rhetorical question. These dissonances are crushingly beautiful – and they lead immediately to the song's longest and most sustained passage of pervasive rhythmic activity ("c'est grant erreur"). And so I now see what you mean about the B section. The enjambment (musical and textual) makes everything drive toward the punch line of the phrase ("de nous aimer"), where we finally hear that what she has stopped doing is *loving us* – and then, reacting to that blow, we all drive forward angrily, singing, "It's a great error."

Discantus: That anger is projected in our melodies, I think. In my final phrase, mostly on the word "grant," I twice in a row sweep upward to emphasize the note *a'* before careening downward to the final cadence. The repetition has an intensifying effect – and though I can't really hear what you and the contratenor are doing, it certainly seems exciting.

Listener: Well, the lower voices are also moving rapidly, twisting and turning on "grant."

Tenor: Moreover, "grant" is the longest melisma [passage sung to a single syllable] in the song – or at least the longest passage in which all three of us hold a single syllable.

Contratenor: Why does that matter?

---

[57] Theoretically – but almost certainly not practically – the contratenor could have sung *e♭* ("-mer"); the same is true in contratenor, m. 2. Some of the best evidence against the idea that this regularly happened in the fifteenth century appears in Tinctoris, *The Art of Counterpoint*, where the music theorist complains about a compositional (and, by all indications, performative) practice that must surely have been widespread. See Peter Urquhart, "False Concords in Busnoys," in *Antoine Busnoys: Method, Meaning, and Context in Late Medieval Music*, ed. Paula Higgins (Oxford: Clarendon Press, 1999), 361–388, and the literature cited there.

Discantus:	Because it builds tension. Don't you feel as though during this concluding drive we're becoming ever more insistent, recognizing through our music how "grant" our "erreur" is?
Contratenor:	Yes, I suppose I can't argue with that.
Tenor:	Fair enough. But this whole conversation prompts an important question: how can we talk about text-music relationships when in the course of this rondeau we sing the B music to two different texts? Come to think of it, we sing the A music to no fewer than three texts!
Discantus:	You're right: any discussion that makes too much of the relationship between the music and a given line of poetry is probably overstating the case. And indeed Busnoys hasn't been so crass as to try to associate each word with a musical idea designed to express it precisely.[58] Still, I've noticed that in many of these songs the music seems to have been composed with special attention to the meaning of the refrain text.
Tenor:	Agreed. And I've noticed something else: often the poems are crafted in such a way that whatever musical effects are introduced in the refrain also work in subsequent stanzas.
Discantus:	In this context we should remember that Busnoys is a poet. Maybe he wrote these words – does anyone know for sure?
	[*silence*]
Listener:	Regardless, the point stands. Circling back to the moment we spent so much time on earlier ("mainctenez"), notice how easily that music accommodates the next two verses: "Que c'estoit pour **nous** grant honneur" and "Sans plus acrois**tre** ma douleur." In the first case we reach our high note on the word meaning "us," in the second on "increas**ing** [my pain]."
Discantus:	That's true, but you haven't yet explained what these verses are about.
Contratenor:	The first non-refrain text is sweeter and somewhat less personal than the others. The opening line, "Vray est que tant a de valeur" (It's true that she has such worth), feels like an opportunity to retreat a little from the strong emotions of the refrain and reflect in a less fraught way on the object of our love. But then, at the next line, "Que c'estoit pour nous grant honneur" (That it was a great honor for us), the mood subtly changes,

---

58 This practice was to emerge in the sixteenth century with the advent of the Italian madrigal.

	as we start to sing about ourselves – myself and my heart, that is. Notice that the music becomes charged just as we reach the word "nous."
Listener:	That's very astute.
Tenor:	In the next verse we're worked up from the start ("Leave – it's the best thing to do"); the second line, "Without further increasing my pain," is arguably the poem's most vehement and angry text.
Contratenor:	Yes, and during our performance this evening we adjusted the intensity of our singing accordingly.
Discantus:	I remember that well. It seems fair to say that the poem is written so that the text in each verse either corresponds perfectly to the musical climaxes or is at least amenable to them.
Listener:	Yes. But I'm not sure this principle applies in the B section as well ("Votre bonté"). The calmer music that accompanies the start of the B section is appropriate to "Your goodness and kindness" – but the musical pause that earlier fell on "cesse" now occurs inanely on "gentillesse" (kindness).
Tenor:	It doesn't feel inane to me.
Discantus:	Me neither. To be sure, the link between words and music is not as clear as it was before, but it nonetheless feels natural to pause a little as I meditate on a happier thought: the kindness of my heart toward my lady.
Contratenor:	Yes, and the next line is unquestionably a good fit: the climax that earlier fell on "ai**mer**" is now on "pa**ier**" ("Make me **pay** for the favor I've enjoyed").
Discantus:	I love this moment. The change in affect is so strong – and the dissonant music, which by now we've already heard once before, drives the knife in deeper.
Listener:	You bring up a fascinating point: like many of the best rondeaux being composed nowadays, the poem is not a static text, but rather tells a story, one amplified in real time by the musical setting.
Discantus:	Absolutely: I've been thinking about this a lot. If you'll permit me, I'll share with you my analysis of the musical and poetic form.[59]

---

59 This discussion draws on Fallows, "Secular Polyphony," 213; David Fallows, "Polyphonic Song," in *Companion to Medieval and Renaissance Music*, ed. Tess Knighton and David Fallows (Berkeley: University of California Press, 1992), 265–274; and Page, *Discarding Images*, 163–169.

Others:	Go ahead.
Discantus:	Part of this story will be familiar, because it's a function of genre. Starting with "Vray est," we experience a gradual buildup of tension, as we sing the A music three times in a row; the subsequent return to B is all the more arresting for having been withheld. The final statement of the refrain is in one respect a recapitulation – but in another respect we are somewhere very different from where we began.
Contratenor:	Care to tell us something *un*familiar?
Discantus:	I was getting to that. In this particular rondeau, the refrain text, as we've all observed, is already quite forceful, above all during the affectively charged moments we've identified. When, after "erreur," we return to the A music ("Vray est"), the character is more relaxed – I think someone even said impersonal. Yes, "pour nous" is heightened, but only in context. So the text and music ease up here.

When the refrain returns ("Je m'esbaïs"), I feel a renewed sense of angst, not least because of what has by now been revealed about our lady. But we sing only up to "maistresse"; there's no chance for these thoughts to develop.

Then comes the poem's most vehement utterance ("Leave"). Here I sense the speaker's unmitigated anger (at himself). And the intensity is somehow increased by the circumstance that we are now singing the A music for the third time in a row. Something, we are all aware, has to give.

As we finally move into the B music ("Votre bonté"), the mood momentarily lightens. But for all the reasons we've outlined, this easing of tension only serves as a baseline against which to measure the excruciating "Me facent paier pour ma faveur."

And then, after spewing forth this venom, we return one last time to the refrain. On some level this is simply a return: I feel what I did when we began. On another level these words now carry a different meaning: we have explained ourselves, and, in doing so, explored sad, wistful, bitter feelings. The journey we have taken intensifies the astonishment and woe expressed by the refrain text. There's a new awareness now, a heightened sadness that wasn't there before. |
| Listener: | Throughout this journey, the music amplifies the poem's affective shape, not only by deploying gestures that tug at our emotions, not |

	only by skillfully manipulating the boundary between conventions and exceptions, but also, crucially, by slowing the poem down. This text would never take even close to six minutes to recite on its own. The music gives weight to almost every word, and gives us time to process. It also complicates the poem's formal scheme by knowingly withholding the B music in the middle of the song, even as the poem returns to its opening words. We hear a mixture of repetitions, non-repetitions, and quasi-repetitions that are at once static and ever changing.
Discantus:	I can't say this about every rondeau I've performed, but I get lost in the world of this song. The words and the music have entered my body: I hear and feel them move through me as I go about my day.
Contratenor (to the Tenor):	What, pray tell, are you doing?
Tenor:	Oh, right, sorry. I got distracted while the rest of you were talking.... Did anyone else notice this *rat*?!

* * *

When we ask students to write analytical essays about pieces like *Je m'esbaïs de vous*, we typically instruct them to use "objective" description to justify their "subjective" responses to the music. My sense from conferring with colleagues is that when reading such work we easily recognize the difference between accurate and inaccurate, relevant and irrelevant, brilliant and bullshit.[60] But when it comes time for us to describe the song ourselves, all bets are off, both because the pull of "interpretive harmony" is so strong and – a related point – because we like to insist that everything we say is open to interpretation. This latter point is undeniable – but there's interpretation and there's interpretation. Without proper control, it's just "something I thought of"; with true immersion in the mid-fifteenth-century chanson repertory, by contrast, what happens at "mainctenez" (to give but one example) is undeniably special, subject to being missed but not dismissed.

I say this to forestall a probable objection to my imaginary dialogue: that this text merely re-performs our modernity. The would-be objector has a point. Among the many things my text gets wrong are the rhetorical conventions governing analytical musical discourse in this period – conventions that, alas, we have little chance of recovering because practically no such discourse survives.[61] And yet perhaps our

---

[60] I use this word advisedly. For context see Harry G. Frankfurt, *On Bullshit* (Princeton, NJ: Princeton University Press, 2005).
[61] See Rodin, "Form and Experience."

interpretations can be analogized to the (irrecoverable) insights of fifteenth-century musicians and listeners, our banter to their (surely equally comical) verbal skirmishes. Perhaps behind my forced jokes and misbegotten Americanisms lie aspects of the song that are profoundly knowable. *Knowable* here signifies both the intellect and the senses – an understanding of how the tenor approaches the note *a'* as well as embodied knowledge of what it *feels* like to approach it, having approached high notes in chanson tenors many times before. Indeed I want to assert that it is possible to honor the irrecoverableness and unknowability of so many aspects of fifteenth-century musical culture without becoming paralyzed: from what we *do* have, there is still so much more we can learn.

Are we willing to go down this touchy-feely road? Maybe not. Maybe it's easier to claim that even if we know *that* "mainctenez" is special, we'll never know exactly *how* it was special to the late medieval mind – but then, there's no such thing as "the late medieval mind." The claim becomes an essentialist performance of our superiority, in that we insist on our own complexity ("Look at me, I'm so different from them") while denying the Other a capacity for the same ("I can't know how *late-medieval people* thought"). We can do without this pretension. Instead we can try earnestly to get inside their musical heads: to marinate in a song and appreciate that they, too, had varied responses to it. Of course it's true that because we do things like listen to recordings and take the subway, we'll never quite capture the range of reactions available to fifteenth-century ears. Still.

Appendix

Score of Antoine Busnoys, *Je m'esbaïs de vous mon cuer*, ed. Jesse Rodin, Josquin Research Project (also available at josquin.stanford.edu).

Valerie L. Garver
2 Sensory Experiences of Low-Status Female Textile Workers in the Carolingian World

In the short story "The Cane" by Joaquim Maria Machado de Assis (1839–1908), set in early nineteenth-century Brazil, a young man named Damião runs away from seminary, determined to escape the restrictive life of a priest, a vocation his father compelled him to enter. He turns for refuge to his godfather's mistress Sinhá Rita, a woman who keeps poor, enslaved girls to make lace in her house. While waiting for his godfather to intercede so he can leave seminary, Damião witnesses the girls' daily experiences, obliquely noticing that they labor under threat of violence – anyone whose work is not finished by evening faces a caning. One girl, Lucretia, attracts Damião's attention when she smiles at him, but her lapse in concentration infuriates Sinhá Rita, who demands that she finish her work by sunset. Lucretia cannot catch up, even as she labors in the fading light. Despite having inwardly promised himself that he will save her from punishment, when the moment arrives, Damião hands Sinhá Rita the cane. "He felt a pang of guilt; but he needed to get out of the seminary so badly!"[1]

Machado de Assis and his commentary on Brazil's history of slavery may seem distant from the focus of this chapter upon eighth- to early tenth-century Carolingian-controlled Europe. His story is, nevertheless, broadly revelatory of the relationship between poor workers and any elite whose privileged lives they make possible. In comparison to later periods, we have little understanding of this relationship during the early Middle Ages, much less of the conditions under which the unfree and poor labored. Written sources, however, suggest a dynamic similar to that between Machado's protagonist and the enslaved lace makers: that is, an awareness among the elite of the low-status laborers all around them but little effort to understand their experiences.

In the Carolingian world, low-status fabrication of cloth and clothing stood in contrast to the textile work of the female elite, who often worked with lavish materials and made items that allowed them to emphasize their connections to powerful men and institutions as well as demonstrate their learning, skill, and piety.[2] The textile work

---

[1] Joaquim Maria Machado de Assis, "The Cane," in *A Chapter of Hats: Selected Stories*, trans. John Gledson (London: Bloomsbury Press, 2008), 221–230, at 230. I would like to thank Roberta Stewart for making me aware of this short story and suggesting its relevance to my research. This chapter also benefited from the feedback of anonymous readers, my fellow contributors who gathered at Stanford to discuss our research, Thomas Greene, Fiona Griffiths, and Kathryn Starkey. Special thanks to Danny Gerrets, Annet Nieuwhof, Wietske Prummel, and Marcia Tucker for helping me obtain research materials and photos.
[2] Jane Tibbetts Schulenburg, "Holy Women and the Needle Arts: Piety, Devotion, and Stitching the Sacred, ca. 500–1150," in *Negotiating Community and Difference in Medieval Europe: Gender, Power,*

https://doi.org/10.1515/9783110563443-003

of both groups of women shares, however, the problem that the relatively limited evidence of their labor survives in damaged, faded, or fragmentary condition. Most of the looms and cloth from this era have long rotted away; the male clerics and aristocrats who wrote the vast majority of texts from this time and place do not describe the exact conditions or material nature of this work; and most low-status women who engaged in textile labor remain lost to the historical record. Even in those rare cases when their names survive, little else remains to mark their lives besides a fixed location in time. Yet these humble women produced the bulk of cloth in the Carolingian Empire. Considering the nature and conditions of their work compels us to appreciate the many ways in which the learned and wealthy relied upon this crucial form of labor.

In texts that emanated from the male Carolingian elite, short passages concerning women's textile labor were intended to evoke or create ideal conditions within Carolingian-controlled lands. One example is a stipulation in the *Admonitio generalis* of 23 March 789 that forbade work on Sundays: "Moreover the textile work of women may not be done; they may neither cut out nor stitch clothing nor do needlework; nor is it permitted to card wool or to beat linen or to wash clothes in public or to shear sheep so that in every way the honor and quiet of the Sabbath is preserved."[3] Similarly, according to the Council of Meaux-Paris that met in 845–846, all work was to cease in *gynaecea* (textile workshops) during Holy Week.[4] Beyond the glimpse revealed by these normative texts, a reference to the everyday textile work of women also appears in the writings of one of the great intellectuals of the Carolingian era, Walafrid Strabo (d. 849). In the *Hortulus*, a political poem ostensibly about his garden, Walafrid wrote of the gourd: "Just as girls sewing with soft wool wind it all on a spindle in great spirals and measure off the succession of threads into beautiful balls, so the wandering vines of the gourd press together in twisted chains like stairs and there

---

Patronage and the Authority of Religion in Latin Christendom, ed. Katherine Allen Smith and Scott Wells (Leiden: Brill, 2009), 83–110; Valerie L. Garver, *Women and Aristocratic Culture in the Carolingian World* (Ithaca: Cornell University Press, 2009), 224–268; Valerie L. Garver, "Textiles as a Means of Female Religious Participation in the Carolingian World," in *Ancient and Medieval Religion in Practice*, ed. Sari Katajala-Peltomaa and Ville Vuolante (Helsinki: Acta Instituti Romani Finlandiae, 2013), 133–144. On the association of elite women's piety with textile work later in the Middle Ages, see Fiona Griffiths, "'Like the Sisters of Aaron': Medieval Religious Women and Liturgical Textiles," in *Female* vita religiosa *between Late Antiquity and the High Middle Ages: Structures, Developments and Spatial Contexts*, ed. Gert Melville and Anne Müller (Münster: LIT Verlag, 2011), 343–374; and Maureen C. Miller, *Clothing the Clergy: Virtue and Power in Medieval Europe, c. 800–1200* (Ithaca, NY: Cornell University Press, 2014), 145–175.

3 "Item feminae opera textilia non faciant nec capulent vestitos nec consuent vel acupictile faciant; nec lanam carpere nec linum battere nec in publico vestimenta lavare nec berbices tundere habeant licitum, ut omnimodis honor et requies diei dominicae servetur." MGH Capit. 1, ed. Alfred Boretius (Hanover: Hahnsche Buchhandlung, 1883), c. 81, 61. Unless otherwise noted, all translations into English in this chapter are mine.

4 MGH Conc. 3, ed. Wilfried Hartmann (Hanover: Hahnsche Buchhandlung, 1984), c. 80, 126.

Figure 1: Carolingian-era pin beater made of cattle or horse bone. Wijnaldum-Tjitsma find no. 5946. Photograph originally appeared in Wietske Prummel, Hülya Halici, and Annemieke Verbaas, "The Bone and Antler Tools from the Wijnaldum–Tjitsma Terp," *Journal of Archaeology in the Low Countries* 3, no. 1/2 (2011): 65–106, at 76. Reproduced with permission of the authors.

envelop the smooth branches."[5] Walafrid's image is lovely, but it begs the question: did the wool seem so soft and beautiful to the women laboring to spin it?

If we want to surmount our lack of knowledge about the lives of these textile workers, there is in fact material evidence we can turn to, employing it in combination with texts and according to a logic governed by the available sources and the generally accepted historical understanding of the era. By *material* I mean that which has the quality of physicality, the tangible, that which human senses can experience. As anthropologists in particular have shown, it is difficult to separate the material from the immaterial entirely, but here I distinguish between ephemeral experiences that leave no physical traces (the immaterial) and physical objects that remain to us together with the human experience of them both now and in the past (the material). I argue that it is possible to move from the seeming immateriality of low-status Carolingian cloth production to a firmer materiality by examining modest, unassuming objects that, unlike the cloth and looms themselves, have survived: pin beaters made of bone, spindle whorls, flax combs, loom weights, and metal shears.

A Carolingian-era pin beater found during the excavation of the terp settlement of Wijnaldum-Tjitsma in Frisia near the North Sea, in the current-day Netherlands, can serve as an example (Figure 1). Made from either horse or cow bone, the implement measures approximately twenty centimeters in length. Pin beaters were essential weaving implements during the early Middle Ages. Women used their tapered ends to push down weft threads in order to achieve a tight and even weave; placing the pin beater between pairs of warp threads, a weaver would work her way across the loom at regular intervals. Items such as this one provide information otherwise lost to us about low-status individuals. In particular, they can afford access to the sensory experiences of the many women who produced the bulk of cloth for this great empire. For example, this pin beater stands as evidence of women's repeated actions in fabricating cloth, and it testifies to the skill and experience they would have needed in

---

[5] "Et velut in fusum nentes cum pensa puellae / Mollia traiciunt spirisque ingentibus omnem / Filorum seriem pulchros metantur in orbes, / Sic vaga tortilibus stringunt ammenta catenis / Scalarum, teretes involvuntque ilico virgas." MGH Poetae 2, ed. Ernst Dümmler (Berlin: Weidmann, 1884), ll. 119–123, 339.

order to know exactly when to employ this tool and the most effective degree of pressure to exert with it.

The textile tools at the heart of this chapter were not prestige objects. Humble, made of inexpensive materials, often simple in design, they survive mainly because they were discarded or buried with a body, not because they were treated with the care and respect accorded to the many medieval manuscripts, relics, and churches preserved to this day. These tools also lack the textual context that surrounds prestige objects, particularly those from the later centuries of the Middle Ages. As such, they offer a view of sensory experience that both complements and contrasts with investigations of the senses and materiality in later medieval centuries, which have mainly focused on elite items.

Archaeological finds have tended to be the subject of object-centered studies, which typically focus on categorization, description, style, or function. Object-driven investigations, on the other hand, allow objects to guide research and explanation – that is, rather than defining objects, they attempt to answer the questions those objects raise.[6] Here I make textile-related implements the focus of an object-driven study because these items take one directly to the Frankish women who employed them to produce thread and cloth or to assemble other objects such as looms. Scholars have not yet considered what these implements reveal about the physical experience of creating textiles. Historians have paid rather little attention to these admittedly modest items except when they have considered early medieval grave goods.[7] Archaeologists have mainly categorized them, carried out technical analyses of their materials, worked to date them, or used them along with other site data in order to reconstruct the history of the settlements in which they were found.[8] Without the work of such researchers, along with that of textile conservators and experts, this study would be impossible. Nevertheless, my purpose here is to consider items already studied by these scholars in a new way, exploring these objects' potential to produce certain sensory experiences within the context of their time.

---

[6] Bernard L. Herman, *The Stolen House* (Charlottesville: University Press of Virginia, 1992), 4–11.

[7] Guy Halsall, "Female Status and Power in Early Merovingian Central Austrasia: The Burial Evidence," *Early Medieval Europe* 5 (1996): 1–24, at 7, 23; Christina Lee, "Grave Matters: Anglo-Saxon Textiles and Their Cultural Significance," *Bulletin of the John Rylands University Library of Manchester* 86 (2004): 203–221, at 206–220.

[8] Two of the richest studies of textile-related finds from early medieval excavations focus on technical issues and the products of textile labor rather than on the experiences of the individuals using them. Eva Andersson, *Tools for Textile Production from Birka and Hedeby*, Birka Studies 8 (Stockholm: Birka Project for Riksantikvarieämbetet, 2003); Penelope Walton Rogers, *Cloth and Clothing in Early Anglo-Saxon England, AD 450–700*, CBA Research Report 145 (York: Council for British Archaeology, 2007), 9–47.

The Carolingian Context

Historians of the Carolingian Empire have generally employed textual sources in their efforts to understand the work of low-status women living in Carolingian-controlled lands. Polyptychs (records of holdings, dependents, and dues of monastic estates), capitularies (normative documents emanating from royal and episcopal authorities), and the proceedings of church councils all offer historical evidence of the status and skills of the women who fabricated most cloth, often revealing male elite perceptions of these laborers. Capitularies and church council records include some stipulations regarding textile work, as in the cases described earlier. In many cases, polyptychs tie humble women to a range of tasks and duties related to the production of cloth, including the provision of a certain number and certain types of cloths. Historians such as Jean-Pierre Devroey and Benjamin Guérard have considered some of these references to female textile work, but few have explicated the experiences and conditions of this crucial form of labor or examined it extensively in relation to archaeological evidence.[9]

In this chapter, archaeological evidence takes primacy over texts; such material evidence can provide rich information, especially for the rural settlements and towns so often overlooked in written sources from this era.[10] Nevertheless, considering written sources and other contextual information will crucially link this study of archaeological remains and the servile women who labored with them to a broader consideration of the Carolingian world. One notable issue is the way in which these laborers' gender shaped their physical experiences. These objects were used by women, and they arguably provide a means of understanding women not mediated through the eyes of men. An obvious question remains: How can one be sure that these items reflect the experiences of women? Could men have used them too?

Textile work has not consistently been women's work throughout Western history; it is not necessarily the "natural" or "expected" work of women alone. Both men and women of all social statuses, for example, carried out the highly skilled needlework that produced *opus anglicanum*, the exquisite thirteenth- and fourteenth-century

---

9 *Polyptyque de l'abbé Irminon avec des prolégomènes*, ed. Benjamin E. C. Guérard (Paris: Imprimerie royale, 1844), 1:617–725; Jean-Pierre Devroey, "Femmes au miroir des polyptyques: Une approche des rapports du couple dans l'exploitation rurale dépendante entre Seine et Rhin au ixe siècle," in *Femmes et pouvoirs des femmes à Byzance et en occident (vi^e-xie siècles): Colloque international organisé les 28, 29 et 30 Mars 1996 à Bruxelles et Villeneuve d'Ascq*, ed. Alain Dierkens, Stéphane Lebecq, Régine Le Jan, and J. Sansterre (Villeneuve d'Ascq: Centre de recherche sur l'histoire de l'Europe du Nord-Ouest, Université Charles de Gaulle-Lille, 1999), 227–249, at 230–232; Valerie L. Garver, "Girlindis and Alpais: Telling the Lives of Two Textile Fabricators in the Carolingian Empire," in *Writing Medieval Women's Lives*, ed. Charlotte Newman Goldy and Amy Livingstone (New York: Palgrave Press, 2012), 155–172, at 162–165.
10 For such an examination of the early medieval rural world, see Christopher Loveluck, *Northwest Europe in the Early Middle Ages, c. AD 600–1150* (Cambridge: Cambridge University Press, 2013).

English embroideries that survive in so many Continental churches today. Men, as masters who oversaw workshops, came to dominate this craft by the mid-thirteenth century in and near London, in contrast to earlier references that mention mainly women, both aristocratic and low-status, as the artisans.[11] By the fourteenth and fifteenth centuries, men controlled cloth production on a large scale in medieval cities. Women, however, continued to engage in textile work both within workshops and in domestic spaces, and this form of labor still had strong associations with female virtue and domestic duties.[12] It is therefore unsurprising that many today assume that textile work has always been gendered female, but such a strict association has only rarely been in force across Western history.

In the Carolingian era, however, textile work was exceptional among the types of labor that low-status workers carried out: unlike most other tasks, for which men and women shared responsibility, it was almost certainly women's work alone.[13] Among lay aristocrats, only women engaged in the production of cloth and clothing. While religious women did textile work, it seems highly improbable that monks in the Carolingian world fabricated textiles, despite the fact that significant quantities of cloth moved through Frankish and other contemporary monasteries.[14] In his statutes of 822, written to govern the monastery of Corbie, the abbot Adalhard stipulated that, following the period of sheep shearing, the monks were to receive the best wool in quality and color as a tithe.[15] These demands for wool conform to the textile dues found in polyptychs; the statutes did not, however, include textile work among the handicrafts carried out at Corbie. The monks may have gathered that wool in order to provide it to dependent textile workshops where women could work it into items for the monks to use, sell, or give away. Without entering more deeply into a discussion of monastic economies, my point is that even if wool and textiles moved into monasteries, evidence of textile labor there is scant to nonexistent. Cloth fabrication was gendered female in Carolingian lands regardless of social status or locality. Textile-related tools are therefore gendered objects in terms of use, which not only provide points of comparison with textual information, but also yield new information about the experiences of the low-status women who employed them.

---

11 See, for example, M. A. Michael, ed., *The Age of* Opus Anglicanum (London: Harvey Miller Publishers, 2016).
12 Ruth Mazo Karras, "'This Skill in a Woman is by No Means to Be Despised': Weaving and the Gender Division of Labor in the Middle Ages," in *Medieval Fabrications: Dress, Textiles, Clothwork, and Other Cultural Imaginings*, ed. E. Jane Burns (New York: Palgrave, 2004), 89–104, at 90–97.
13 Monika Obermeier, *"Ancilla": Beiträge zur Geschichte der unfreien Frauen im Frühmittelalter* (Pfaffenweiler: Centaurus Verlagsgesellschaft, 1996), 185–229.
14 Gillian Clark, "Monastic Economies? Aspects of Production and Consumption in Early Medieval Central Italy," *Archeologia medievale* 24 (1997): 31–54, at 46–49.
15 L. Levillain, "Les statuts d'Adalhard," *Le Moyen Âge* 13, second series vol. 4 (1900): 233–386, at 376 (chap. 10).

Figure 2: Depiction of textile work in the Utrecht Psalter. Utrecht University Library, MS 32, fol. 84r, detail.

It is essential to recognize that, although low-status textile laborers often shared similar working conditions, tools, and worksites, local conditions produced variations in the textile work carried out across this vast empire. One key difference among sites is evidence of specialization in either linen or wool working. The Carolingian-era linen smoothers made of glass and the evidence of flax cultivation found in excavations at Montours, Belloy, Villiers-le-Sec, and Baillet-en-France, for example, reveal that women in these villages undertook the time-consuming and arduous work of fabricating linen.[16] In other cases, textile tools aided in the production of woolen cloth, which was common throughout the Carolingian world. While much of what can be said of linen applies equally to wool, wool working is not as fixed within the annual agricultural cycle as linen fabrication, and wool workers could more flexibly accomplish some of their tasks. Thus some questions, such as the effects of weather upon the workers, are not as straightforward for wool working. For these reasons, along with space constraints, this chapter focuses on linen production and objects used in crafting linen cloth.

Another key difference among sites concerns the exact locations of textile production. Much of the "indoor" labor appears to have been conducted on individual holdings, in workshops – often sunken huts – or, less usually, in large structures above ground. Written texts make clear that much cloth production took place in *gynaecea* (sometimes *piseles*) – that is, structures in which women fabricated cloth. An image in the Utrecht Psalter (ca. 820–830) depicts a sort of *gynaeceum* or textile workshop (Figure 2). The loom in this image is a vertical two-beam loom, constructed from two

---

[16] *Un village au temps de Charlemagne: Moines et paysans de l'abbaye de Saint-Denis du viie siècle à l'an mil* (Paris: Éditions de la réunion des musées nationaux, 1988), 276; Isabelle Catteddu, ed., *Les habitats carolingiens de Montours et La Chapelle-Saint-Aubert (Ille-et-Vilaine)*, Documents d'archéologie française 89, Série archéologie préventive (Guiry-en-Vexin: du Valhermeil, 2001), 217–218.

upright posts buried in the ground at a narrow distance from one another.[17] This depiction, however, is meant to provide an illustration of Isaiah 38:12: "My generation is at an end, and it is rolled away from me, as a shepherd's tent. My life is cut off, as by a weaver: while I was yet but beginning, he cut me off: from morning even to night you will make an end of me." Thus it may not be an accurate representation of ninth-century weaving. Complicating its interpretation is the scarcity of descriptions and depictions of weaving in most early medieval cultures. The *Admonitio generalis*, for example, did not list weaving among the textile labors prohibited on Sundays. Artistic depictions of weaving are also scarce in the Carolingian corpus. One rare example may be an image in a tenth-century manuscript of Hrabanus Maurus's *De universo* depicting a two-beam loom (Figure 3).[18] Because this manuscript presumably descends from a Carolingian exemplar, this illustration may reflect the appearance of a Carolingian loom. Nevertheless, the general lack of textual and pictorial evidence concerning weaving makes archaeological evidence all the more valuable: two-beam looms leave telltale postholes, and for that reason archaeologists are often able to identify locations of weaving in the early medieval West.[19]

Carolingian-era archaeological sites have also yielded rich evidence of textile work in the form of objects including spindle whorls, loom weights, pin beaters, needles, and shears. Returning to the pin beater found at Wijnaldum-Tjitsma, described earlier, not only does this object indicate the presence of weavers and cloth production there, as archaeologists have long noted, but excavations of this site have also provided rich contextual information. Though pin beaters survive at many sites, they are sometimes hard to date. At Wijnaldum-Tjitsma, however, most finds appeared in contexts with datable objects or structures. Thus it has been possible for archaeologists to locate in time the textile implements found there, and the rich quantity of finds from this site has permitted more detailed contextualization of textile-related objects than at some other sites of this era.[20]

When such contextualization is possible, it allows us to gather information about where, when, how, and in what social environment women used these implements: elements that are crucial in investigating the women's likely sensory experiences. Considering these tools as part of a social and working environment makes it possible to address the difficult conditions women were subject to and the toll this labor took upon their bodies. For example, the remains of certain linen-specific tools allow one to envision the conditions and expert skills required for linen work. The sunken huts

---

17 Utrecht University Library, MS 32, fol. 84r.
18 Archivio dell'Abbazia di Montecassino, Cod. Casin. 132, 31.
19 *Un village*, 276; Isabelle Catteddu, "Le site haut mediéval de Saleux 'Les Coutures': Habitat, nécropole, et églises du haut Moyen Âge," *Les Nouvelles de l'archéologie* 92 (2003): 20–23, at 21.
20 Wietske Prummel, Hülya Halici, and Annemieke Verbaas, "The Bone and Antler Tools from the Wijnaldum–Tjitsma Terp," *Journal of Archaeology in the Low Countries* 3 (2011): 65–106, at 66–67.

Figure 3: Image of a loom in a tenth-century copy of Hrabanus Maurus's *De universo*. Archivio dell'Abbazia di Montecassino, Cod. Casin. 132, 31.

in which parts of the process of linen production took place were damp and dimly lit; the low light may have strained the eyes of textile laborers and caused them physical discomfort. The seasonality of linen work also allows us to explore how the women may have experienced weather conditions, the quantity of daylight available, and the time frame for completing their work: all issues that speak to sensory experiences.

Other contextual evidence is provided by what we know about the considerable time and raw materials needed to furnish even one household with adequate clothing and textiles. Eva Andersson has estimated that to provide half the population of medieval Birka (300 individuals) with one full outfit of clothing would have required around 5,445,000 meters of thread made from about 900 kilograms of wool and/or linen – an amount that would require the wool of approximately 450 to 900 sheep. Of all the tasks involved in this fabrication, spinning the thread would have consumed the largest quantity of time (at roughly 20 meters per hour), although preparation of the loom added to the work. Thus a weaver would have been able to complete only about 70 to 80 cm of one-meter-wide cloth each day.[21] These estimates cannot simply be transferred to other early medieval sites, for each was unique; but they provide an approximation of the quantity of textile work and the time demanded by it across the early medieval world, including Carolingian lands, where many of the same tools and techniques were used.[22] In short, female textile workers had to toil many hours to produce cloth and clothing.

Considering female labor through the lens of its material remains offers opportunities to think afresh about methodological issues related to materiality and the senses. Reflecting on the functions of these items and the ways in which women held and manipulated them can lead to logical conclusions concerning the ways these tools and their associated labors engaged women's visual, tactile, and olfactory senses. The work of Daniel Miller on the ways in which Indian women physically experience the sari can provide a useful parallel. Miller noted that the sari never sits upon the human frame in exactly the same way in any two parallel spots, such as the shoulders, and he considered how women in saris learn to navigate their worlds. The discomfort caused by certain parts of the sari, for example, serves to assure women that their saris are not coming loose.[23] Carolingian textile implements undoubtedly wore at women's bodies, imposing certain positions, causing pain or other sensations, and perhaps changing their bodies permanently through injuries associated with overuse, strain, or environmental hazards.

In order to discuss the specific ways in which these objects convey the physical experiences of the women who employed them, relevant finds from two differing

---

21 Andersson, *Tools for Textile Production*, 46–47, 150.
22 Eva B. Andersson, "Textile Tools and Production in the Viking Age," in *Ancient Textiles: Production, Craft, and Society; Proceedings of the First International Conference on Ancient Textiles, Held at Lund, Sweden, and Copenhagen, Denmark, on March 19–23, 2003*, ed. C. Gillis and M.-L. B. Nosch (Oxford: Oxbow Books, 2007), 17–25, at 21–25.
23 Daniel Miller, *Stuff* (Cambridge: Polity, 2010), 23–30.

Carolingian archaeological sites will be considered. Written sources and evidence from other sites also offer some context for the tools employed by low-status workers. Women carried out textile work – though on different scales and for a range of reasons – with similar tools across much of the Carolingian world and beyond; exploring two contrasting locations can offer a means to consider the commonalities and variations of that labor with regard to sensory experiences.

Two Sites of Carolingian Textile Production

Of the two sites I will consider, Wijnaldum-Tjitsma served a regional elite in Frisia, on the northwestern edge of Carolingian-controlled lands where the climate and landscape made it possible for women to work in sod structures above ground. In East Francia, Büraburg bei Fritzlar offers a different context, reflecting the conditions of a fortified settlement near the powerful episcopal seat of Fritzlar. Written texts do not describe the working conditions or tools of the women at these two sites, but the objects found at Wijnaldum-Tjitsma and Büraburg bei Fritzlar reveal the presence of textile labor and are revelatory of female sensory experiences.

The finds from Wijnaldum-Tjitsma offer the opportunity to consider textile work that took place at an otherwise little-documented location: a regional elite center that is not mentioned in written texts. Further, the site provides an example from the hinterlands of the Carolingian Empire, though Frisia was a crucial region for early medieval trade and production. In the ninth and tenth centuries, in fact, Westergo, as the region around Wijnaldum-Tjitsma was known for much of the Middle Ages, was one of the most densely populated territories of northwestern Europe. Cattle breeding contributed greatly to the economy of Frisia – providing exports such as hides, leather, parchment, and crafted bone items – as did the raising of sheep, which allowed for the production of high-quality woolen cloth. These forms of production for export also meant that Frisians had the means to import desirable products that were unavailable locally. Wijnaldum-Tjitsma reflects that context. The site is located near the modern village of Wijnaldum on the Tjitsma terp, an artificially raised area built for human habitation and use. The extraordinarily high number of bone and antler tools that survive here from the Merovingian and Carolingian eras, along with some highly unusual finds such as musical instruments and a gold-and-garnet fibula, set Wijnaldum-Tjitsma apart from other Frisian terp settlements of the time.[24] Wijnaldum-Tjitsma appears to have served a regional elite and had quite a few artisans, parti-

---

[24] H. A. Heidinga, "The Wijnaldum Excavation: Searching for a Central Place in Dark Age Frisia," in *The Excavations at Wijnaldum: Reports on Frisia in Roman and Medieval Times*, ed. J. C. Besteman, J. M. Bos, D. A. Gerrets, H. A. Heidinga, and J. de Koning (Rotterdam: A. A. Balkema, 1999), 1–16, at 10.

cularly metalworkers. The site was rich in finds partly because of the archaeological methods used there. When excavating at Wijnaldum-Tjitsma in the early 1990s, archaeologists employed the technique of wet sieving – that is, as earth from the excavation was sifted through a fine screen mesh measuring four by four millimeters, a spray of water was applied to dissolve away the earth until the water ran clear. This careful attention allowed excavators to discover extremely small artifacts such as bone needles and environmental evidence like fish bones, which archaeologists presume are often missed in excavations of other early medieval sites (Figure 4).[25]

Twelve bone implements used for textile work were found dating from the Carolingian era (defined for this site as 750–850): nine needles, a spindle whorl, a smoother, and the aforementioned pin beater. Unlike those found at some other sites, Wijnaldum-Tjitsma's fiber tools are not associated with specific sunken huts; rather, most items came from refuse pits.[26] Among the metal finds were early medieval copper-alloy needles and four lead or lead/tin spindle whorls. It is not possible to definitively determine the precise use of the needles. Inhabitants could have used some or all for sewing skins or making and repairing fishnets rather than textile work.[27] Men may therefore have used them. The spindle whorls and pin beater, however, are unmistakable signs of textile work – of spinning and weaving, respectively (Figure 5).[28] Moreover, evidence of flax cultivation from the period 800–850 was found in a well.[29] These textile tools could therefore have served to spin flax and weave it into linen cloth.

Despite the evidence for spinning and weaving at Wijnaldum-Tjitsma, these activities likely never exceeded the bounds of small-scale production.[30] Here it seems probable that the textile workers supported only local needs. They labored under unusual conditions for the Carolingian era: instead of the sunken huts in which low-status women often worked cloth in other parts of the Carolingian world, it appears that craft production at Wijnaldum-Tjitsma, including textile work, took

---

25 Caroline Tulp, "Tjitsma, Wijnaldum: An Early Medieval Production Site in the Netherlands," in *Markets in Early Medieval Europe: Trading and 'Productive' Sites, 650–850*, ed. Tim Pestell and Katharina Ulmschneider (Macclesfield: Windgather Press, 2003), 221–233, at 221; Prummel et al., "The Bone and Antler Tools," 67, 76.
26 Prummel et al., "The Bone and Antler Tools," 75.
27 Tulp, "Tjitsma, Wijnaldum," 231–232.
28 Prummel et al., "The Bone and Antler Tools," 68.
29 J. P. Pals, "Preliminary Notes on Crop Plants and the Natural and Anthropogeneous Vegetation," in *The Excavations at Wijnaldum: Reports on Frisia in Roman and Medieval Times*, ed. J. C. Besteman, J. M. Bos, D. A. Gerrets, H. A. Heidinga, and J. de Koning (Rotterdam: A. A. Balkema, 1999), 139–149, at 145.
30 Wietske Prummel, Kinie Esser, and Jørn T. Zeiler, "The Animals on the Terp at Wijnaldum-Tjitsma (the Netherlands) – Reflections on the Landscape, Economy, and Social Status," *Siedlungs- und Küstenforschung im südlichen Nordseegebiet* 36 (2013): 87–98, at 90.

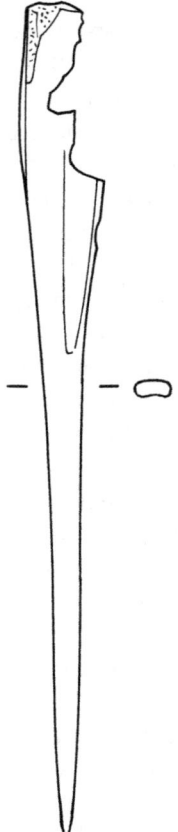

Figure 4: Merovingian-era needle or awl with a broken hole, made from the fibula of a young pig, similar to Carolingian-era bone needles from the same site. Wijnaldum-Tjitsma find no. 1525. Drawing originally appeared in Prummel et al., "The Bone and Antler Tools," 76. Reproduced with permission of the authors.

place in sod structures.[31] It is hardly surprising to encounter this type of structure in a terp settlement in Frisia, a landscape where peat and sod were found, but its use for textile production underlines the fact that variety in working conditions marked this form of female labor. Wijnaldum-Tjitsma had sunken huts, but these were not the locations of textile work. Flax cultivation and linen production fare best in cool, damp conditions; it seems probable that the climate in Frisia was humid enough to make

---

31 D. A. Gerrets, "Conclusions," in *The Excavations at Wijnaldum: Reports on Frisia in Roman and Medieval Times*, ed. J. C. Besteman, J. M. Bos, D. A. Gerrets, H. A. Heidinga, and J. de Koning (Rotterdam: A. A. Balkema, 1999), 331–342, at 335. On sunken huts, see Catteddu, "Le site haut medié-val," 21; and E. Zadora-Rio, "Early Medieval Villages and Estate Centres in France (c. 300–1100)," in *The Archaeology of Early Medieval Villages in Europe*, ed. J. A. Quirós Castillo (Bilbao: Universidad del País Vasco, 2010), 77–98, at 88.

Figure 5: Merovingian-era spindle whorl made of red deer antler. Carolingian-era bone, lead, lead/tin, and ceramic spindle whorls were found at the same site. Wijnaldum-Tjitsma find no. 1001. Photograph originally appeared in Prummel et al., "The Bone and Antler Tools," 78. Reproduced with permission of the authors.

working flax in sunken huts unnecessary there. Just as at many other Carolingian-era sites, however, the evidence from Wijnaldum-Tjitsma provides only a partial picture. Structural remains from this site have been difficult to interpret because they did not include wood, only sod.[32] Moreover, archaeologists excavated only a portion of the Tjitsma terp, and this terp is just one of many in the area. In fact, relatively few excavations among the Frisian terps have taken place, making comparisons to similar locations difficult.[33] Although this fact limits scholars' ability to draw firm conclusions regarding this site, it does not prevent them from considering the nature of the location based on the available evidence, nor does it preclude examination of the experience of textile work there.

On the other side of the Carolingian Empire, in East Frankish lands, archaeological excavations have also turned up relatively widespread evidence of weaving.[34] My case study from East Francia will be Büraburg bei Fritzlar, a fortified hilltop site that lies about three kilometers southwest of the modern town of Fritzlar in North Hessen.

---

[32] Heidinga, "The Wijnaldum Excavation," 4.
[33] Gerrets, "Conclusions," 335.
[34] Examples include Halle-Künsebeck (Westphalia), where sixth- to eighth-century clay loom weights were found; Tilleda (Saxony-Anhalt), where weaving took place in sunken huts from around the ninth to the eleventh centuries; and Runden Berg bei Bad Urach (Badem-Württemburg), a fortified site with many finds related to textile work. See, respectively, Christoph Stiegemann and Matthias Wemhoff, ed., *Kunst und Kultur der Karolingerzeit: Karl der Große und Papst Leo III. in Paderborn* (Mainz: Verlag Philipp von Zabern, 1999), 1:244; Jean Chapelot and Robert Fossier, *The Village and House in the Middle Ages*, trans. Henry Cleere (Berkeley: University of California Press, 1985), 121–122; Rainer Christlein, *Der Runde Berg bei Urach III: Kleinfunde der frühgeschichtlichen Perioden aus den Plangrabungen 1967–1972* (Sigmaringen: Jan Thorbecke Verlag, 1979), 7, 34.

This relatively large settlement also served as an episcopal and trading center.[35] Construction of fortifications began there by the late seventh century.[36] Boniface of Mainz founded a diocese there in 741/742 and had a church built. In a letter of 742 to the pope, he called the settlement an *oppidum*, and Pope Zachary recognized it as such in his reply to Boniface.[37] In 773, the *Royal Frankish Annals* referred to it as a *castrum*.[38] From the mid-eighth through the tenth centuries, it served as a place of refuge, particularly during the Saxon attacks on Fritzlar, with its cathedral and monastery, in the 770s. Hundreds of houses lay along an 1100-meter wall, which enclosed an area of approximately eight hectares with some larger houses inside it. A *suburbium* or outlying area was also fortified and contained many pit houses that functioned as workshops. This settled area appears to have prospered until around 850, when Fritzlar, down in the valley, overtook it in religious and secular importance.[39] Büraburg bei Fritzlar is among the most thoroughly excavated of such fortified sites. The Carolingian finds in this settlement relate to men, women, and children alike, including many objects of daily use. Quite a few textile implements have been found there, some in an area containing sunken hut workshops, some in the numerous graves, and some in the many structures built for defense, housing, or other changing purposes over time.[40]

---

35 Recently scholars have become skeptical of the conclusion of Norbert Wand, the principal excavator there from 1967 to 1973, who argued that it was a fortified city (*Burgstadt*). Norbert Wand, "'Oppidum Buraburg' – der Beitrag der Büraburg bei Fritlar zur frühen Stadt östlich des Rheins," in *Vor- und frühformen der europäischen Stadt im Mittelalter: Bericht über ein Symposium in Reinhausen bei Göttingen in der Zeit vom 18. bis 24. April 1972*, ed. Herbert Jankuhn, Walter Schlesinger, and Heiko Steuer (Göttingen: Vandenhoeck und Ruprecht, 1973), 163–201, at 167–168; Dieter Geuenich and Thomas Zotz, "Castra und Höhensiedlungen in der schriftlichen Überlieferung," in *Höhensiedlungen zwischen Antike und Mittelalter von den Ardennen bis Adria*, ed. Heiko Steuer and Volker Bierbrauer (Berlin: de Gruyter, 2008), 795–820, at 813–815.
36 Wand, "Oppidum Buraburg," 167–168; Joachim Henning and Richard I. Macphail, "Das karolingische Oppidum Büraburg: Archäologische und mikromorphologische Studien zur Funktion einer frühmittelalterlichen Befestigung in Nordhessen," *Universitätsforschungen zur prähistorischen Archäologie* 100 (2004): 221–251, at 221–222, 248–249.
37 MGH Epp. sel. 1, ed. Michael Tangl (Berlin: Weidmann, 1916), no. 50, 80–86, at 81; no. 51, 86–92, at 87.
38 MGH SS rer. Germ. 6, ed. Georg Heinrich Pertz and Friedrich Kurze (Hanover: Hahnsche Buchhandlung, 1895), 36.
39 Norbert Wand, "Die Büraburg – eine fränkische Großburg zum Schutz des Edergebietes," in *Fritzlar im Mittelalter: Festschrift zur 1250-Jahrfeier* (Fritzlar: Magistrat der Stadt Fritzlar, 1974), 41–58, at 45; Heiko Steuer, "The Beginnings of Urban Economies among the Saxons," in *The Continental Saxons from the Migration Period to the Tenth Century: An Ethnographic Perspective*, ed. Dennis H. Green and Frank Siegmund (Rochester: Boydell, 2003), 159–192, at 170.
40 Wand, "Oppidum Buraburg," 165, 169, 199–201; Werner Best, Rolf Gensen, and Philipp R. Hömberg, "Burgenbau in einer Grenzregion," in *Kunst und Kultur der Karolingerzeit: Karl der Große und Papst Leo III. in Paderborn; Beiträge zum Katalog der Ausstellung Paderborn 1999*, ed. Christoph Stiegemann and Matthias Wemhoff (Mainz: Verlag Philipp von Zabern, 1999), 1:328–345, at 328; Thorsten

2 Sensory Experiences of Low-Status Female Textile Workers —— 65

Figure 6: Clay spindle whorls and broken animal bone spinning rods from Büraburg bei Fritzlar. Photograph copyright Museumslandschaft Hessen Kassel.

The many Carolingian-era textile implements found at Büraburg bei Fritzlar came mainly from graves. It is therefore difficult to pinpoint their locations of use, although sunken huts and family homes appear most likely. Among the objects unearthed at the site were spindle whorls made of clay, about two centimeters each, all dating to the eighth or ninth centuries, and bone spindle rods (Figure 6).[41] The original length of the rods in figure 6 is impossible to determine because both are broken at one end. Many such rods were found in the cemetery at Büraburg bei Fritzlar. Excavations also turned up numerous clay loom weights: one large weight, dating from the eighth or ninth century and now broken, was decorated with a cross, while others were plainer

---

Sonnemann, "Neue Forschungen zur Büraburg und dem Fritzlar-Waberner Becken im frühen Mittelalter," *Hessen-Archäologie und Paläontologie in Hessen* 8 (2009): 103–107, at 103.
41 Ten-to-fourteen-centimeter spindle rods were found at Rottenburg am Neckar, Calw-Stammheim, and Merdingen. Ralph Röber, "Zur Verarbeitung von Knochen und Geweih im mittelalterlichen Südwestendeutschland," *Fundberichte aus Baden-Württemberg* 20 (1995): 885–944, at 887–889, 935.

Figure 7: Collection of Carolingian-era textile implements from the settlement of Fritzlar-Geismar, Schwalm-Eder Kreis, including two loom weights typical of the era, a tablet for tablet weaving, two spindle rods, and two spindle whorls. Photograph copyright Museumslandschaft Hessen Kassel.

(Figure 7).[42] The site also yielded metal implements, including bronze and iron needles and Carolingian-era iron shears. As with those found at Wijnaldum-Tjitsma, determining the exact use(s) of a given needle is difficult: they may have been employed in leather work and net making as well as for textiles. The shears were likely implements for textile work and/or cutting hair (Figure 8).[43] Shears rarely appear in textual or pictorial depictions of textile work, but they were necessary to such labor. Remains of shears survive in the archaeological record in association with other textile-related artifacts, particularly in earlier medieval graves that contained grave goods, confirming their use among ordinary women.

---

[42] Wand, "Oppidum Buraburg," 193; Stiegemann and Wemhoff, *Kunst und Kultur der Karolingerzeit*, 277. A clay loom weight with an incised cross was also found at Igersheim. Röber, "Zur Verarbeitung," 891–892.

[43] Carolingian shears were also unearthed at Emsdetten-Isendorf. Wand, "Die Büraburg," 54–55; Stiegemann and Wemhoff, *Kunst und Kultur der Karolingerzeit*, 76–77, 240–41, 276–277.

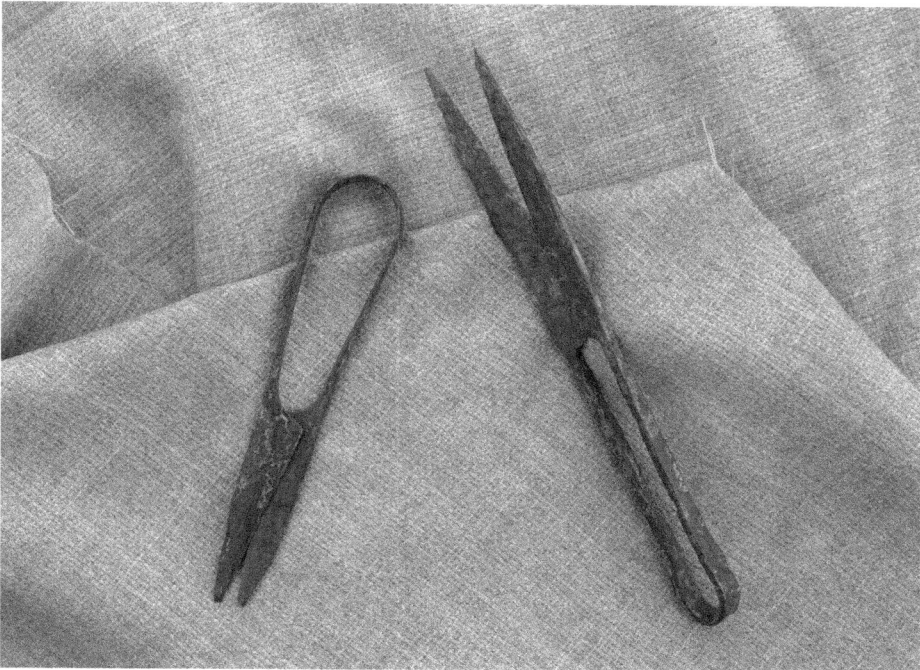

Figure 8: Two pairs of Carolingian-era iron shears from Büraburg bei Fritzlar. Photograph copyright Museumslandschaft Hessen Kassel.

Sensory Experiences

The sensory experiences of low-status women challenge cultural historians because they dislodge them from their usual considerations of elite texts and artistic production. To enter into the sensory experience of a common woman in Carolingian lands is to embrace the dull, the repetitive, and sometimes the expected. Yet conjuring their experiences can provide insight into the kinds of communities that constituted the majority of the empire. As has been mentioned, at both Wijnaldum-Tjitsma and Büraburg bei Fritzlar archaeologists have found evidence of linen production, a form of skilled labor that underscores women's contributions to Carolingian society and speaks to communities' seasonal experiences. This, together with the tools discovered, sets the stage for exploring the sensory experiences of the female workers at these sites. Linen work doubtless would have consumed much of their time, especially during the late summer and early fall, when flax, an annual crop, was ready to harvest and process. The women could then spin and weave linen thread over subsequent months. These tasks would have engaged nearly every sense.

Flax production was grueling, beginning with the labor-intensive task of separating flax fibers from the stalk in which they grew. To remove most of the stalk often

Figure 9: Early medieval glass linen smoother from the excavations of the huts for glass making at Klein Süntel. Photograph copyright Axel Hindemith.

required retting, or submersion in water in order to cause the stalk to begin to rot and make it easier to separate from the flax fibers. The smell of this rot can be powerful, and therefore the olfactory senses of the women processing flax may have been overwhelmed to the point of distracting them from other sensations. They may have grown accustomed to the smell as time passed, but certainly the odor would have alerted their communities to this labor.

Pieces of stalk usually remained in the flax following retting, so workers needed to beat the linen, then scrape it to remove the last bits of the stalk, and finally smooth the remaining fibers.[44] Many early medieval linen smoothers are made of glass or stone, such as one from Klein Süntel, Germany (Figure 9). At Wijnaldum-Tjitsma, archaeologists found a smoother made from a cow humerus (Figure 10). Both fit within the palm of an adult's hand. Given the tactile sensations that scraping and smoothing would have produced, it is worth wondering if the women would have protected their hands. Modern textile workers in industrialized countries often wear gloves in order to avoid occupational contact dermatitis – a condition often caused by chemicals and dyes, but which can also result from contact with raw materials.[45] A piecemeal survey of websites of hobbyists, re-creators, and institutional projects that document reconstructions of past methods of flax processing and linen fabrication turns up few people employing gloves; but of course these individuals engage in linen production part-time and under modern circumstances, even if the tools they use are close to historical ones. It is impossible to know if servile women in the

---

44 *Un village*, 277.
45 B. P. Soni and E. F. Sheretz, "Contact Dermatitis in the Textile Industry: A Review of 72 Patients," *American Journal of Contact Dermatology* 7 (1996): 226–230.

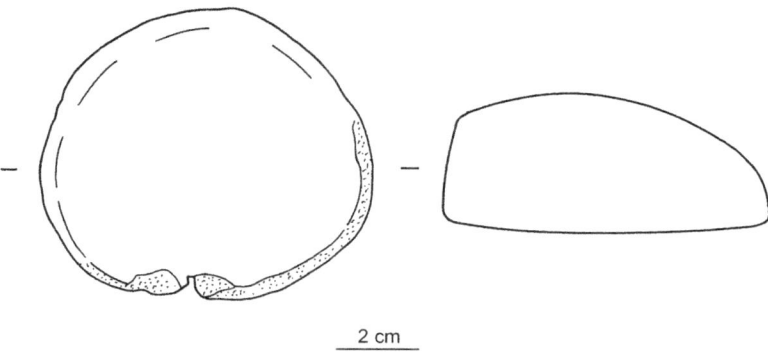

Figure 10: Carolingian- or Ottonian-era smoother made from a cow humerus. Wijnaldum-Tjitsma find no. 7025. Drawing originally appeared in Prummel et al., "The Bone and Antler Tools," 79. Reproduced with permission of the authors.

Carolingian era wore gloves to protect their hands, but one suspects they may have employed them when scraping or first breaking down flax stalk. Other processes such as combing, spinning, and weaving required a keen sense of touch, and gloves would have impeded these stages of production. Retting could have scratched, cut, and abraded skin and otherwise caused discomfort unless the women developed sufficient calluses to dull their sense of touch. Such calluses, while making retting more bearable, may have hindered their spinning and weaving; but it is also possible that their hands may have "recovered" before moving to the next stages of production. This possibility speaks to the difference between temporary and permanent alteration of the body.

After retting and smoothing, the workers then had to comb or heckle the flax to separate the useful long fibers from the short ones. An undatable flax comb from the region around Münster suggests much about the sensory experience involved in this step of linen making (Figure 11). The comb's iron spikes are mounted in two rows in a block of wood measuring 8.9 centimeters. The longest of these teeth is 9.2 centimeters.[46] It is therefore an item that can be held in the palm of one's hand. The repeated action of combing with this tool could have made muscles ache and, over time, may have caused repetitive use injuries, particularly in the hand, the wrist, and the shoulder joints. Gripping the comb may have abraded the skin, caused blisters, and/or produced calluses. Women needed to work through the fibers with their fingers as well, helping to sort the long and short fibers as the comb separated them. This work required dexterity, and the sense of touch aided in its completion.

Only after combing was the flax ready to be spun into thread and woven. Spinning was a repetitive and time-consuming activity for which skill increased through

---

46 Stiegeman and Wemhoff, *Kunst und Kultur der Karolingerzeit*, 236–237.

Figure 11: Early medieval flax comb or heckle. Photograph copyright LWL-Archäologie für Westfalen/ Stefan Brentführer.

experience. In the Carolingian world, women often employed spinning rods with whorls attached to them to make thread. Whorls of ceramic and metal were found at both Wijnaldum-Tjitsma and Büraburg bei Fritzlar, and they appear in the archaeological record at many eighth-, ninth-, and tenth-century sites. Spindle whorls sped the process of spinning; they were not necessary to that process. Their weight causes the spinning rod, inserted into them, to turn more quickly and thus more rapidly produce thread. Spindle whorls could be placed upon the rods either as bottom or top weights. Because the spindle rods and whorls rarely survive together, it is impossible to know if the women who employed them in the Carolingian world exhibited a preference between the two placements. If bottom-weighted, the whorl could spin more easily, especially in a clockwise motion, producing what is known as Z-spun thread. Right-handed spinners often prefer this method, but skilled spinners could have just as likely spun in a counterclockwise motion with the spindle whorl at the top of the rod, producing S-spun thread. When the spindle rod was top-weighted, the fabricator would have needed to support the spindle, likely on her thigh, in order to give herself more control over the spin diameter and consistency of the thread, a process that would have worked best when a woman wanted to spin two or three threads together.⁴⁷ Thus, if a low-status woman engaged in bottom-weighted spinning, she would require a sharp eye to focus on her quickly turning spindle, while carefully manipulating the flax and thread with her fingers. Top-weighted spinning would have created a specific sort of tactile engagement, for a woman had to notice the pressure on her thigh and adjust her spinning accordingly. In both cases, she would have needed to combine touch and sight to spin thread. Her sensitivity to the weight of her spindle whorl, its placement on the spindle rod, and the speed of her spinning would affect characteristics of the final product such as how tightly spun the thread would be: even five grams of difference in weight could affect the spin diameter and quality of thread.⁴⁸ The spindle rods from Büraburg bei Fritzlar have incisions on them, which probably aided women in grasping the rods, guiding them, and stopping their rotation (Figure 12). When spinning flax fibers, workers also engaged their sense of taste, because flax thread requires continual moisture. Most spinners likely used their own saliva for this purpose.⁴⁹ The taste of the flax fibers and the thirst caused by wetting the thread are other aspects of the multisensory experience of spinning.

Turning from spinning to weaving involves considering the ways in which items such as loom weights aided in the construction of other objects. Loom weights have been found at other Carolingian-era sites in addition to Büraburg bei Fritzlar and Wijnaldum-Tjitsma, particularly at the important trading center Dorestad (in the current-day Netherlands), where excavations between 1969 and 1976 turned up around two thousand whole or fragmentary weights. When one considers that a loom would have required thirty to sixty of these objects, their frequency in the archaeological record makes sense.⁵⁰ A loom would have consisted of two posts buried in the ground with a crossbeam between them, a type of object that left its telltale postholes at Wijnaldum-Tjitsma, Villiers-le-Sec, and Baillet-en-France.⁵¹ The warp threads hung vertically from the crossbeam with the loom weights pulling them downward to provide the requisite tension. Flax required heavier loom weights than wool because it lacked wool's degree of flexibility.⁵² Setting up such a loom required at least two women, who would need

---

47 Gertrud Grenander Nyberg, "Spinning Implements of the Viking Age from Elisenhof in Light of Ethnological Studies," *NESAT* 3 (1990): 73–84, at 75–79; Chrystel Brandenburgh, "Textile Production and Trade in Dorestad," in *Dorestad in an International Framework: New Research on Centres of Trade and Coinage in Carolingian Times*, ed. Annemarieke Willemsen and Hanneke Kik (Turnhout: Brepols, 2010), 82–88, at 83.
48 Evidence from Scandinavia suggests that some spindle whorls and techniques would have been better suited to linen. Andersson, *Tools for Textile Production*, 25–26.
49 Elizabeth Coatsworth and Gale R. Owen-Crocker, "Textiles," in *A Cultural History of Dress and Fashion in the Medieval Age*, ed. Sarah-Grace Heller (London: Bloomsbury, 2017), 11–28, at 17.
50 Brandenburgh, "Textile Production and Trade in Dorestad," 85.
51 *Un village*, 276.
52 Andersson, *Tools for Textile Production*, 28.

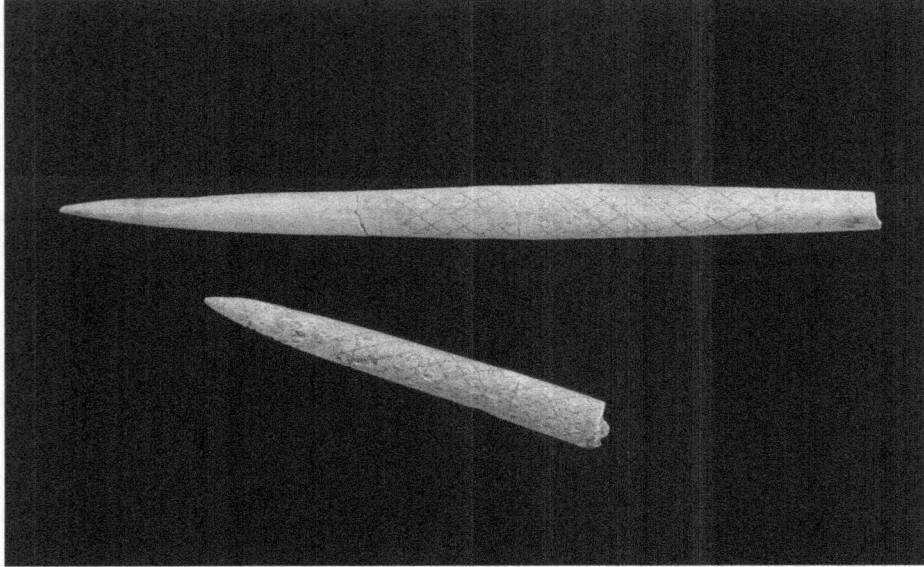

Figure 12: Carolingian-era animal bone spindle rods from Büraburg bei Fritzlar. Photograph copyright Museumslandschaft Hessen Kassel.

shears, like the ones found at Büraburg bei Fritzlar or those portrayed in the Utrecht Psalter, to cut the warp threads to the appropriate length. In fall and winter the metal shears would have felt cold to the touch, perhaps warming if used long enough. Squeezing the shears, among other tasks necessary for preparing the loom, speaks to the strength that low-status female workers likely developed in their hands.

When a woman worked at the loom, the manner in which she interlaced the weft threads with the warp created the particular weave of a given textile; weavers had to keep careful track of both pattern and thread tension. Pin beaters aided them in making well-woven cloth, but exerting the proper amount of pressure required a deft sense of touch. Viewed more closely, the pin beaters from both Wijnaldum-Tjitsma and Villiers-le-Sec have incised markings or designs on them.[53] The marks on the Wijnaldum pin beater are lines spaced at regular intervals. These decorations may have helped individuals identify their own pin beaters and may have been expressions of individuality on the part of either the users or makers of these objects; they may also or instead have served practical purposes, providing texture to help the weavers grip the tool and making it less likely to slip as they worked. Such incisions may have made the sensation of holding the pin beater more pleasurable;

---

[53] Stiegemann and Wemhoff, *Kunst und Kultur der Karolingerzeit*, 258.

perhaps the women may at times have rubbed or felt these designs, enjoying the tactile sensation.

Women's working conditions were doubtless shaped as well by constraints to their eyesight. Although the remains of lamps do not survive in close relation to evidence for looms in the sunken huts at Büraburg bei Fritzlar or in the sod structures at Wijnaldum-Tjitsma, excavators found oil lamps in proximity to looms at Baillet-en-France and Villiers-le-Sec.[54] It is therefore likely that weavers sometimes employed artificial light. The relatively low light in their worksites, combined with the need to keep track of each thread, likely strained textile workers' eyes in both the short and long term. Flickering light, awkward viewing angles, and poor visual contrast are all known causes of asthenopia, a common condition that manifests in the form of "eye fatigue, discomfort, burning, irritation, pain, ache, sore eyes, and headache."[55] Viewing conditions that created poor contrast would have been a major problem because weaving and sewing required workers to differentiate among threads, pay attention to thread tension, and assess the weave of their cloth. Weavers would also have needed to examine their work from awkward angles at times. In addition, if women had uncorrected vision problems such as hyperopia (farsightedness), these could have caused headaches when they worked in low light. As humans age, usually beginning in their forties, presbyopia, "the gradual and progressive age-related loss of accommodative amplitude," causes the lenses of their eyes to lose their capacity to focus on nearby objects.[56] Thus the declining vision of older women likely exacerbated their susceptibility to eye strain. Of course, it is impossible to measure the degree to which these medical conditions affected early medieval textile workers, but they do suggest a number of sensory experiences and possible reactions to them. On average, young women would have had less trouble working in low light than older women did, but even then, long hours of labor in those conditions may have caused pain or discomfort. Such work could also have contributed to the development of myopia (nearsightedness) in some young workers. The degree to which factors either genetic or environmental (including light levels and the act of viewing objects closely for long periods) affect the development of myopia remains a subject of debate and research among scientists and physicians. Age may play a role, given that children and young adults appear more prone to developing myopia due to environmental factors regardless of genetic inheritance.[57] Perhaps the effects of eye strain would have caused women to limit the time they spent sewing and weaving each day. They

---

54 *Un village*, 271.
55 James E. Sheedy, John Hayes, and Jon Engle, "Is All Asthenopia the Same?," *Optometry and Vision Science* 80 (2003): 732–739, at 732.
56 A. Glasser, "Presbyopia," in *Encyclopedia of the Eye*, ed. Darlene Dartt, Joseph C. Besharse, and Reza Dana (Amsterdam: Elsevier, 2010), 488–495, at 488–491.
57 Thomas T. Norton and John T. Siegwart, Jr., "Light Levels, Refractive Development, and Myopia – A Speculative Review," *Experimental Eye Research* 114 (2013): 48–57.

may have tried to set their looms up in better light when possible, as suggested by the image in the Utrecht Psalter in which a loom has been set up outdoors. Nevertheless, the effects of presbyopia meant that younger women would have been more likely than older women to perform textile labor that required looking closely at threads and cloth in lighting conditions that reduced contrast. Workers may have compensated for low light to some degree by using their sense of touch, but it was no panacea.

Linen working shaped a woman's year and thereby her family's and community's expectations and experiences. Flax is an annual crop with a hundred-day growing cycle. It therefore had a single harvest each year. The female laborers would have needed to devote concentrated blocks of time to the processing of flax, usually in late summer or early fall. Other linen work such as spinning and weaving could presumably have taken place at other times of the year, although conditions may have been too cold in the sunken huts or other structures at certain times. Scholars recognize that the climate of early medieval northwestern Europe was colder and wetter than in the preceding and following eras.[58] In the fall, or if spinning and weaving into the winter months, female textile workers may have felt chilled at times and had to dress in order to deal with the weather. Perhaps their hands became cold and felt stiff as they worked, hindering them in tasks that required their sense of touch. One wonders if they had to warm their hands occasionally to continue their work when temperatures were low.

Evidence strongly suggests the social nature of much female textile work. In addition to these low-status workers' experience of the senses of sight (low light), smell (retting), and touch (flax combing and spinning), this sociality would have engaged their aural sense. As in other eras, clerics believed women to be gossips, and Carolingian texts contain passages cautioning men to avoid gossiping women and urging women not to gossip.[59] Admittedly, churchmen directed these appeals at a limited audience, but if one sets aside the question of their effect upon actual behavior, these statements reveal the expectation of a female propensity for idle chatter. Because textile work, especially weaving, sometimes took place in groups, clerics may have perceived such moments as opportunities for gossip. Indeed, concern about women's behavior in these settings is apparent in a range of sources. Carolingian authorities often expressed suspicion of women who worked in *gynaecea*.[60] Since men had little to do with textile work, this created female spaces that lacked direct male oversight. Harder to know is whether children were present. It would be perfectly logical if children were around as women carried out this labor, but in the absence

---

58 Frederic L. Cheyette, "The Climatic Anomaly of the Early Middle Ages," *Early Medieval Europe* 16 (2008): 127–165, at 155–165.
59 *Capitulary of Riculf of Soissons*, chap. 16, in MGH Capit. episc. 2, ed. Rudolf Pokorny and Martina Stratmann (Hanover: Hahnsche Buchhandlung, 1995), 107; *Institutio sanctimonialium Aquisgranensis*, canon 10, in MGH Conc. 2.1, ed. Albert Werminghoff (Hanover: Hahnsche Buchhandlung, 1908), 445.
60 *Capitulare Olonennse*, c. 5, in MGH Capit. 1, 317; Notker the Stammerer, *Gesta Karoli*, in MGH SS rer. Germ., n.s. 12, ed. Hans F. Haefele (Berlin: Weidmann, 1959), bk. 2, chap. 4, 52.

of direct evidence it is impossible to know with certainty. Surely, though, the processing of flax, as well as labor carried out in *gynaecea*, would have involved groups of women working together. Also, many tasks related to fabric production were repetitive and time-consuming: one study has indicated that intricate embroidery of a ten-by-seven-centimeter expanse of linen could take around thirty hours of work that demanded the embroiderer's constant attention.[61] Chatting could have been a way to make the time and work pass more quickly and pleasurably. It therefore seems likely that these places were locations of chatter, laughter, and discussion, even if accounts of such aural and social sensation do not remain.

The textile work carried out at Büraburg bei Fritzlar had much in common, then, with that carried out at Wijnaldum-Tjitsma, despite the locations' differences in size, purpose, building structures, extent of modern excavation, and degree of documentation in the written record. Indeed, a range of Carolingian-era sites appear to have been the locations of similar textile work, which suggests that low-status women across much of the Carolingian world shared similar sensory experiences. Despite the rather high number of women who fabricated textiles in this world, however, contemporaries did little to document the nature and conditions of that labor. Although the elite took an interest in this world, they left no record indicating that they knew it at the intimate level explored here. Walafrid Strabo mentions "soft wool" in the *Hortulus*, but for those who spun and wove it day after day, week after week, it may not have seemed so pleasing to the senses.

Few medievalists, aside from archaeologists and textile experts with a strong interest in reconstructing the technical aspects of textile work, have taken much notice of the tools that inspired this study. In no small part, the modest appearance of these implements and their gendered and low-status nature have left them understudied in their "afterlife." Yet these humble objects allow us to see much that has vanished. Rotted looms and distaffs "appear" to us thanks to the spindle whorls, loom weights, and pin beaters discussed here. These tools reveal grueling work and remind us of the difficult labor that supported the elite culture that so often draws the attention of medievalists. This study should caution against any romanticizing of rural labor, for the reality was that much work in the medieval countryside was repetitive, wearying, and harmful to human health over the long term. In the case of linen work, it affected the body through the terrible smell of retting, the sharp gouges of the flax stalk, the strain upon eyes caused by weaving, the calluses left on the fingers by repeated spinning and flax combing, and the sound of gossip and chatter as women labored together. Perhaps this work provided a sense of satisfaction or accomplishment for some workers. Others may have found it unceasing drudgery. One could never argue that the sensory and cultural experiences essential to textile work were the same for

---

[61] Helen M. Stevens, "Maaseik Reconstructed: A Practical Investigation and Interpretation of 8th-Century Embroidery Techniques," *NESAT* 3 (1990): 57–60, at 57–58.

all individuals who undertook it. Processing flax, spinning, and weaving were ephemeral experiences that left few traces in the written record by which to judge laborers' opinions and feelings about them. The materiality of archaeological remains, however, makes these experiences discernible.

Just as Damião was aware of the clicking bobbins and the presence of the lacemaking girls in the background of his own concerns, so too were these people and objects constantly in the background of the Carolingian world. Appreciating a much wider range of lived experience and more fully comprehending the size and scope of Carolingian society poses a challenge to the typical historical frame of this empire, often presented as unified through the political and religious projects of its elite. To what extent would these female textile workers and their communities have been aware of such projects? It is impossible to say for sure, but this exploration of their sensory experience suggests not only the repetitive and sometimes grueling labor that occupied many women but also the fact that such work contributed to the construction and maintenance of the Carolingian Empire.

Elizabeth Dospěl Williams

3 Appealing to the Senses: Experiencing Adornment in the Early Medieval Eastern Mediterranean

Few artifacts of material culture evoke the human form with the immediacy of jewelry. To hold medieval jewelry and feel its heft – a privilege normally extended only to those working in museums or frequenting dealers and galleries that sell such pieces – powerfully brings its original owners to mind (Figure 1). Indeed, it is impossible to handle medieval jewelry today without imagining the spectral bodies of the pieces' original wearers: a minute ring evokes the slim fingers of a small child, an earring conjures up the countless times its wearer threaded its loop through her earlobe. These objects' intimate connections to the long-lost bodies of past owners are brought into relief as the modern-day viewer relates them to his or her own physical experience of wearing jewelry. The way in which jewelry embeds time and memory through the physical experience of wearing adds particular poignancy to working with medieval adornments. We wonder who the ring in our hands today was made for, whether it was a cherished heirloom handed down within a family, or what special significance it held for its owner.

Investigation into medieval experiences of wearing jewelry is speculative to be sure, and yet it offers profound and universal human insight beyond what is discussed in modern scholarship. In this chapter, I draw from a spectrum of evidence – including written texts, visual sources, and most of all surviving objects, all from the Byzantine and early Islamic eastern Mediterranean in roughly the sixth through twelfth centuries – to explore what this material can tell us about medieval wearers' visual, tactile, aural, and olfactory experiences of jewelry.[1] These observations in

---

[1] There has been extensive interest in Byzantine and early Islamic sensory experience in recent years, though none of this work has taken jewelry or dress into consideration, instead focusing mostly on what could be called the religious sensorium. For the Byzantine world, see, for example, Béatrice Caseau, "The Senses in Religion: Liturgy, Devotion, and Deprivation," in *A Cultural History of the Senses in the Middle Ages*, ed. Richard Newhauser (London: Bloomsbury, 2014), 89–110; Susan Ashbrook Harvey, "The Senses in Religion: Piety, Critique, Competition," in *A Cultural History of the Senses in Antiquity*, ed. Jerry Toner (London: Bloomsbury, 2014), 91–114; Susan Ashbrook Harvey and Margaret Mullett, *Knowing Bodies, Passionate Souls: Sense Perceptions in Byzantium* (Washington, D.C.: Dumbarton Oaks Research Library and Collection, 2017). A 2016 symposium held at the Freer/Sackler, "The Word Illuminated: Form and Function of Qur'anic Manuscripts," featured several papers dedicated to sensory perception in Islamic contexts, including papers dealing with incensing, chanting, and reading in mosque services in the Umayyad and Ottoman periods. Of particular note were papers by Alain George, "Sight and Sound in Early Qur'ans," and Nina Ergin, "The Qur'anic Soundscape of Mimar Sinan's Mosques." In his closing remarks, Julian Raby specifically noted that the symposium

Figure 1: Handling a Fatimid-era silver hoop. L.A. Mayer Museum of Islamic Art, Jerusalem, J130-68. Photograph: Elizabeth Dospěl Williams.

turn lead to larger questions about women's public and private presence, since an expanded view of sensory experience makes it possible to consider that outward appearance encompassed other sensory cues beyond the strictly visual, such as smell and sound.

The Sensory in Texts

The prevalence of jewelry as part of dress, its role in life-cycle events like marriage, its honorific function as part of court apparel, and its sheer value in precious metal and gemstones all help explain why it is so frequently mentioned in textual sources from the early medieval eastern Mediterranean. However, dowry lists, wills, literary texts, trade manuals, religious treatises, and legal documents – the written sources in which jewelry most often appears – only rarely provide any information about

---

broke new ground in discussing sensory perception in connection with Islamic art and ritual. The papers are now available for viewing on the Freer/Sackler's YouTube channel, https://www.youtube.com/user/FreerSackler. For program and abstracts, see http://www.asia.si.edu/research/symposia/art-of-the-quran/default.php (accessed 30 November 2017).

sensory experience. Perhaps the best-mined sources concerning jewelry from the eastern Mediterranean are marriage documents (*nedunyot*) from the Cairo Geniza, which relay extensive information about the clothing, jewelry, and household furnishings belonging to Jewish women of eleventh-century Cairo and later.[2] Because these accounts were essential in quantifying the property a woman brought into a marriage in case of later divorce, they are filled with careful descriptions of individual pieces of jewelry (including their material, form, and common name) along with their monetary value. Although a rich resource for understanding jewelry as part of broader assemblages of household items brought into medieval women's marriages, these lists reveal little about how the pieces were worn, and nothing about the women's sensory experiences. This is certainly true for many genres of textual sources from the medieval eastern Mediterranean: they are useful in what they tell about the legal details of owning jewelry, its production and trade, and its regulation as part of dress, but they tell precious little about visual, tactile, aural, or olfactory experiences related to its wear.

    A few exceptional texts, nonetheless, offer insight into the sensory qualities of adornments, providing rare glimpses into the medieval experience of wearing jewelry. The *vita* of Pelagia, a seventh-century hagiographic text, for example, deploys the sensory experience of jewelry to rhetorical ends.[3] A certain James recounts the tale of Nonnos, a monk who had become bishop of Antioch. The story opens as Nonnos delivers a pious speech before an assembly of bishops who have gathered in the city. As the monk speaks, his sermon is disrupted by the appearance of

> the chief actress ... the first in the chorus of the theater, sitting on a donkey ... adorned in the height of fantasy, wearing nothing but gold, pearls, and precious stones, [and] even her bare feet were covered in gold and pearls. With her went a great throng of boys and girls all dressed in cloth of gold with collars of gold on their necks, going before and following her. So great was her beauty that all the ages of mankind could never come to the end of it. So they passed through our company, filling all the air with traces of musk and the most sweet smell of perfume. When the bishops saw her bare-headed and with all her limbs shamelessly exposed with such lavish display, there was not one who did not hide his face in his veil or his scapular, averting their eyes as if from a very great sin.[4]

---

[2] S. D. Goitein, *A Mediterranean Society: The Jewish Communities of the Arab World as Portrayed in the Documents of the Cairo Geniza*, vol. 4, *Daily Life* (Los Angeles: University of California Press, 1983); S. D. Goitein, "Three Trousseaux of Jewish Brides from the Fatimid Period," *American Jewish Studies Review* 2 (1977): 77–110.

[3] "Pelagia, Beauty Riding By," trans. Benedicta Ward, in *Harlots of the Desert: A Study of Repentance in Early Monastic Sources* (Kalamazoo: Cistercian Publications, 1986), 57–75. Latin text in PL 73:663–672. Commentary on Pelagia's life and its moralizing messages is discussed in Lynda Coon, *Sacred Fictions: Holy Women and Hagiography in Late Antiquity* (Philadelphia: University of Pennsylvania Press, 1997), 71–94.

[4] "... ecce subito transiit per nos prima mimarum Antiochiae; ipsaque est prima choreutriarum pantomimarum, sedens super asellum; et processit cum summa phantasia, adornata ita, ut nihil videretur

The description of Pelagia and her entourage is filled with cues about the sight, sound, and odors of jewelry and dress, deployed here to evoke luxury and immoderation. It is especially notable that the narrator dwells on the appearance of Pelagia's jewelry and the smells of her entourage, likely because these were exceptional sensory experiences in the daily public life of Antioch. Equally important is the visual impact of her procession on the gathered crowd, particularly the impression made by the gemstones she wears on her nearly nude body, perhaps because these would have glittered and attracted the eye.

Few sources from the early medieval eastern Mediterranean, however, match the tenth-century *adab*, or Arabic literary work, *Kitāb al-Muwashshā* (The Brocaded Book) in including extensive detail about the sensory experience of wearing jewelry.[5] Written by 'Abbasid Baghdad's most stylish man-about-town, al-Washshā' (d. 936), the text offers a lively description of the elegant denizens of the cosmopolitan capital, their behaviors, and their fashionable dress. The first part of al-Washshā's manual is devoted to manners, including sections about proper ways to express greetings, formulate jokes, and convey feelings to friends and lovers. In the second part, al-Washshā' turns to appearance, devoting numerous chapters to both men's and women's dress. He particularly relishes the appearance, tactility, and smells of clothing and jewelry.[6] A chapter dedicated to men's clothing, for example, stipulates that their tunics should be lightweight, and describes the sources of silk and other materials for these garments.[7] When they are recovering from bloodletting, having a drink, or alone at home, al-Washshā' advises, men should wear tunics perfumed with musk, undershirts scented with ambergris, and headscarves tinted with safflower oil, which he notes are all equally acceptable scents to apply to textiles used to furnish the interiors of elegant men's homes.[8] Men are allowed to wear rings, so long as they are not made of gold, for gold rings are only worn by women and slaves.[9] A chapter

---

super ea nisi aurum et margaritae et lapides pretiosi; nuditas vero pedum ejus ex auro et margaritis erat cooperta: cum qua maxima erat pompa puerorum et puellarum in vestibus pretiosis amicta, et torques aurea super collum ejus. Quidam praecedebant, alii vero sequebantur eam: pulchritudinis autem decoris ejus non erat satietas omnibus saecularibus hominibus. Quae tamen transiens per nos, totum implevit aerem ex odore musci, vel caeterorum suavissimorum odoramentorum fragrantia. Quam ut viderunt episcopi ita nudo capite et omni membrorum compage sic inverecunde transire cum tantis obsequiis ut nec velamen super caput positum, nec super scapulas, tacentes ingemuerunt, et quasi a peccato gravissimo averterunt facies suas." PL 73:664–665. Translation in "Pelagia, Beauty Riding By," 67.

5 Al-Washshā', *Le Livre du Brocart, ou la Société raffiné de Bagdad au Xe siècle*, trans. Siham Bouhlal (Paris: Gallimard, 2004); al-Washshā', *Kitāb al-Muwashshā*, ed. Rudolf-Ernest Brünnow (Leiden: Brill, 1886).
6 Men's clothing described in al-Washshā', chaps. 23–26.
7 Al-Washshā', chap. 23.
8 Al-Washshā', chap. 23.
9 Al-Washshā', chap. 25.

on perfuming details the benefits of using musk, aloe powder, ambergris, and saffron perfume, but denounces men's use of camphor and saffron water.[10]

Kitāb al-Muwashshā considers the proprieties of women's dress and jewelry in similarly sensual terms.[11] A chapter dedicated to fashionable women's clothing, for example, stipulates that they should wear clothing that is not too brightly colored, but which may be perfumed with musk, sandalwood, ambergris, or nard.[12] Elsewhere, al-Washshā' expands the list to include perfumed ointments of sandalwood, clove, camphor, aloe, myrrh, and rhubarb, as well as oils derived from violets, jasmine, and willow, which he notes are all scents that would never be worn by men.[13] Women's jewelry, too, is described in some detail in *Kitāb al-Muwashshā*. Al-Washshā' delights in recounting the gemstones in vogue among 'Abbasid Baghdad's elite, such as pearls, amber, rubies, emeralds, and the like; he also advises women to wear pleasant-smelling jewelry, such as choker necklaces with fermented cloves or long collars filled with camphor and ambergris.[14]

The Sensory in Artifacts and Representations

The *vita* of Pelagia and *Kitāb al-Muwashshā* stand out as exceptions among Byzantine and Islamic textual sources, which are otherwise generally silent on the sensory effects of jewelry. For this reason, the close study of objects and visual representations offers potentially more fruitful avenues for gaining information about the experiences of medieval wearers. Yet mining artifacts for such traces is complicated by historiographical and methodological limitations. Studies of jewelry from the eastern Mediterranean during the Byzantine and Islamic periods are still in their infancy, as specialists grapple with the sheer quantities of jewelry, the difficulties of attributing pieces without secure provenance, and the relatively few practitioners in the field.[15] As a result, scholarship has been dominated by catalogues written by scholars attempting to identify, attribute, and organize jewelry from museum collections and archaeological excavations.[16] Catalogue entries generally quantify only the length

---

10 Al-Washshā', chap. 26.
11 Al-Washshā', chaps. 27–28.
12 Al-Washshā', chap. 27.
13 Al-Washshā', chap. 28.
14 Al-Washshā', chap. 28.
15 For a discussion of the historiography of Byzantine and Islamic jewelry studies, see Elizabeth Dospěl Williams, "Style in Ornament: 'Islamic' Jewelry at the Intersection of Art History and Material Culture," *Islamic Material Cultures* 1 (forthcoming).
16 On Byzantine jewelry, the major catalogues are Marvin Ross, *Catalogue of the Byzantine and Early Mediaeval Antiquities in the Dumbarton Oaks Collection*, vol. 2, *Jewelry, Enamels, and Art of the Migration Period* (Washington, D.C.: Dumbarton Oaks Research Library and Collection, 1962), republished

and width of pieces, without documenting details that would help reconstruct the physical experiences of wearing jewelry, including weight, diameter, thickness, and the like. Descriptions of stylistic features and technical details of the objects emphasize visual impact and privilege the singular moment of production over practices of wearing them.[17] For these reasons, considering evidence of sensory experience in Byzantine and Islamic jewelry requires a major shift in scholarly attention, and a careful reexamination of old evidence, to foreground the physicality and materiality of the pieces and to look in visual representations for information about how they were worn.

A group of large bracelets from Fatimid-era sites in Palestine and comparable examples in museum collections around the globe offer instructive examples in terms of the queries that might be brought to the fore when recasting discussions of jewelry in terms of its sensory effect. Several hoards containing large silver and gold hoops were discovered in Ramla, Jerusalem, and Caesarea, in contexts pointing to their burial in the late eleventh or early twelfth century on the eve of the Crusades (Figures 2, 3, 4).[18]

---

in 2006 with additions and corrections by Susan Boyd and Stephen Zwirn; Isabella Baldini Lippolis, *L'Oreficeria nell'Impero di Costantinopoli: Tra IV e VII Secolo* (Bari: Edipuglia, 1999); and most recently Antje Bosselmann-Ruickbie, *Byzantinischer Schmuck des 9. bis frühen 13. Jahrhunderts: Untersuchungen zum metallenen dekorativen Körperschmuck der mittelbyzantinischen Zeit anhand datierter Funde* (Wiesbaden: Reichert Verlag, 2011).

For Islamic jewelry, see Marilyn Jenkins and Manuel Keene, *Islamic Jewelry in the Metropolitan Museum of Art* (New York: Metropolitan Museum of Art, 1983); Rachel Hasson, *Early Islamic Jewellery* (Jerusalem: L. A. Mayer Memorial Institute for Islamic Art, 1987); Rachel Hasson, *Later Islamic Jewellery* (Jerusalem: L. A. Mayer Memorial Institute for Islamic Art, 1987); Na'ama Brosh, ed., *Islamic Jewelry* (Jerusalem: The Israel Museum, 1987); Marian Wenzel, *Ornament and Amulet: Rings of the Islamic Lands*, The Nasser D. Khalili Collection of Islamic Art, vol. 16 (London: Oxford University Press, 1993); Jack Ogden et al., *The Art of Adornment: Jewellery of the Islamic Lands*, The Nasser D. Khalili Collection of Islamic Art, vol. 17 (London: Oxford University Press, 2013).

17 Work by scholars like Antje Bosselmann-Ruickbie and Jenny Albani is notable in addressing questions about the function and social context of jewelry stemming from these basic formal analyses, yet this work is rare in the case of Byzantine and Islamic jewelry. See Antje Bosselmann-Ruickbie, "Byzantinisch, Islamisch oder 'Internazionaler Stil'? Email- und Körbchenohrringe aus dem östlichen Mittelmeerraum," in *Grenzgänge im östlichen Mittelmeerraum: Byzanz und die islamische Welt vom 9. bis 13. Jahrhundert*, ed. Ulrike Koenen and Martina Müller-Wiener (Wiesbaden: Reichert Verlag, 2008), 83–114; Jenny Albani, "Elegance over the Borders: The Evidence of Middle Byzantine Earrings," in *'Intelligible Beauty': Recent Research on Byzantine Jewellery*, ed. Chris Entwistle and Noël Adams (London: British Museum Press, 2010), 193–202.

18 The Ramla hoard was discovered in 2006. See Ayala Lester, "Fatimid Period Jewelry Hoard from the Excavations at Mazliah," *Qadmoniot* 41(2008): 35–39 (in Hebrew); Israel Antiquities Authority, "A unique find of gold and silver bracelets dating to the 11th century CE was uncovered in IAA excavations at Ramla," 11 April 2006, http://www.antiquities.org.il/article_Item_eng.asp?sec_id=25&subj_id=240&id=1076&module_id=#as (accessed 30 November 2017). The hoard in Jerusalem was discovered in the late 1970s to early 1980s on the Haram al-Sharif (Temple Mount). See Meir Ben-Dov, "Fatimid Silver Jewelry from the Temple Mount Excavations," *Qadmoniot* 16 (1983): 88–91

3 Appealing to the Senses — 83

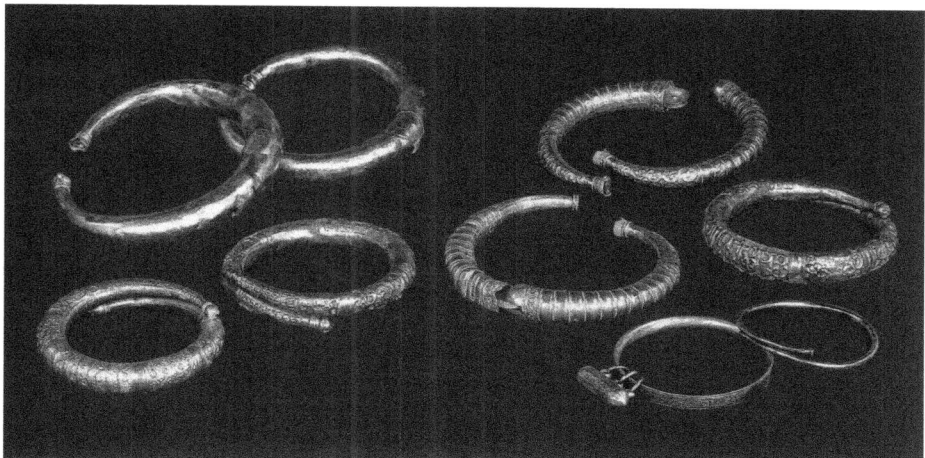

Figure 2: Jewelry hoard from Ramla, gold and silver, eleventh century. Collection: The Israel Museum, Jerusalem, IAA 2008-640-648. Photograph copyright The Israel Museum, Jerusalem.

Figure 3: Jewelry hoard from Jerusalem, silver, eleventh century. Collection: The Israel Museum, Jerusalem, IAA 1986-626-631. Photograph copyright The Israel Museum, Jerusalem.

84 —— Elizabeth Dospěl Williams

Figure 4: Jewelry hoard from Caesarea, silver, eleventh century. Collection: The Israel Museum, Jerusalem, IAA 1961-1286-631. Photograph copyright The Israel Museum, Jerusalem.

The pieces are made from sheets of silver or gold that have been worked into tubular shapes, some with hinges and clasps. The hoops vary significantly in their decoration. Some are smooth (as in the hoard from Jerusalem), while others feature ribbed designs that create a scalloped surface (as in the Ramla hoard). Still others depict lattice patterns formed out of geometric and floral designs and filled with animals, most frequently birds (as in the hoard from Caesarea). The hoops are large and heavy: the two largest pieces have an outer diameter measuring 12.5 cm, and the recorded weight of the largest hoop in the Ramla hoard is 170 g. The remaining hoops vary in diameter from approximately 7 to 10.2 cm, with weight ranging from 35 to 117 g.[19] The sheer material investment in the pieces becomes apparent when one considers that a Fatimid gold coin (*dinar*) minted in Filastin (Palestine) in the year 364 AH (974–975) weighs 4.246 g.[20]

(in Hebrew). The Caesarea hoard was excavated in 1960 in an area dating to the period of the Crusades. See Avraham Negev, *Caesarea, 66–70* (Tel Aviv: E. Lewin-Epstein Publishers, 1967); Avraham Negev, "Caesarea," *Israel Exploration Journal* 10 (1960): 264–265; and Avner Raban and Kenneth G. Holum, eds., *Caesarea Maritima: A Retrospective After Two Millennia* (Leiden: Brill, 1996), xxvii–xliv. I have discussed these hoards and included full bibliographic information in my PhD dissertation, "Worldly Adornments: Women's Precious Metal Jewelry in the Early Medieval Eastern Mediterranean (500–1100 CE)" (Institute of Fine Arts, New York University, 2015).

19 The measurements are those provided and published by the Israel Antiquities Authority. The accession numbers are, for the Ramla hoard, IAA 2008-640-648; for the Jerusalem hoard, IAA 1986-626-630; and for the Caesarea Hoard, IAA 1961-1286-1293.

20 The example used is a coin minted under the authority of al-Mu'izz, now held at the American Numismatic Society in New York, 1959.86.7, http://numismatics.org/collection/1959.86.7 (accessed 30 November 2017).

Many marriage contracts from the Cairo Geniza trove list items like these, naming bracelets, armlets, and anklets according to a variety of terms and providing precise monetary values for each item.[21] This treatment suggests that these items were commonly owned among the upper classes of medieval Cairo. Sitt al-Riyāsa, a well-off bride from Fustat whose dowry was written in August 1156, owned "a pair of granulated golden bracelets with niello work" (*mujrā sawād*) valued at eighteen dinars and "a pair of golden bracelets with niello work" appraised at twenty-eight dinars. A slave named "Beechtree" was assessed at twenty dinars, a stark reminder of the relative value of large hoops like these.[22] The sheer material investment in the precious metal used to make the jewelry – and, by extension, the pieces' weight – undoubtedly explains why large hoops counted among the most valuable items in a bridal trousseau.

Foregrounding the size of these pieces and their weightiness – rather than qualities of their manufacture or their visual attributes – leads to questions about the ephemeral experiences of wearing such jewelry. To imagine wearing large and heavy hoops around one's arms, wrists, and ankles is to invite questions about the physicality of jewelry and to evoke the concrete realities of their bodily use. For example, the varied diameters of the objects might point to a specificity of function according to the part of the body adorned, with armlets and anklets certainly requiring a wider diameter than bangle bracelets. The differing diameters might also be seen as corresponding to individual bodies, with jewelry custom-designed to the dimensions of the wearer. The large size of such hoops might furthermore indicate that they were meant to be worn *over* clothing; such a pattern of use would certainly make sense as a way to hold large pieces of jewelry in place on a moving body. That the pieces appear in multiples, and often even pairs, is also compelling, for it suggests that symmetry was important both visually and physically. Lastly, making the hoops weighty seems to have been a major concern: while many of the pieces are indeed made of hollow sheets of metal, at least one has been given additional heft thanks to a still-untested filling, which today survives as a crumbling white paste.[23] Such a filling would not only have helped the hoops keep their shape by preventing warping, it would also have weighed the pieces down so that they clustered around the wearer's wrists or ankles.

---

21 The terms derive from a variety of languages as well, suggesting their pervasiveness as part of regional costume. These include *siwar* (related to a classical Arabic term, *asuwara min fidda*, or "bracelets of silver," in the Qur'an, 76:21); *dastaynaq* (suggested by Goitein to be related to the Persian word for "hand," *dast*); *dumluj* (possibly an Ethiopian term); *hadid/hadida* (Arabic meaning "iron," though possibly specifically indicating silver or nielloed bracelets); *mi'dada* (an arm ornament that seems to be made exclusively of silver, likely also meant to hold sleeves); and *khalakhil* (anklet). See S. D. Goitein, *A Mediterranean Society*, 219–222, and appendix D with primary sources in translation.
22 Goitein, *A Mediterranean Society*, appendix D, document V, 328–332.
23 The silver hoop was found in Ramla; it measures 9.8 cm in diameter and weighs 117 g. The exact accession number is not recorded. See Lester, "Fatimid Period Jewelry Hoard."

Observations about how these objects were worn and how they affected the senses are arguably best corroborated by contemporaneous depictions of human bodies wearing jewelry, yet such images are remarkably rare in the early medieval eastern Mediterranean. The few representations of women wearing jewelry almost always portray exceptional individuals, oftentimes at the margins of society, like dancers, prostitutes, or entertainers.[24] A rare surviving drawing of a female musician, dated to the eleventh century and completed in ink and watercolor on paper, offers a case in point (Plate II).[25] Found in Fustat in Egypt, the depiction is atypical, and could even be called unique. The woman is depicted in full-figure format and is entirely nude. It is perhaps because of this nudity that the artist has chosen to devote such detailed attention to the woman's elaborate hair, her flowing headgear, her prominent tattoos, her hairless pubic area, and also to her jewelry, which consists of a heavy collared necklace, armlets, bracelets, and anklets.

Close examination of the scene provides information about the setting and clues to the figure's identity. The woman (or perhaps a second, now-lost figure to her right?) holds a wineglass in one hand and a lute in the other, while two clear vessels containing a red liquid are placed on a shelf over her shoulder. The scene appears to be set in a party atmosphere, not dissimilar to the kind described in the ninth-century *Risālat al-qiyān* (Epistle on Singing-Girls) by the 'Abbasid littérateur al-Jāḥiẓ, which praises such entertainers while also warning men against their wiles.[26] The inclusion of such dancers in court parties certainly dated to the earliest Islamic period: sculptures of dancers from the eighth-century Umayyad palace Khirbat al-Mafjar, today housed in the Rockefeller Museum in Jerusalem, even record their presence in nearly life-size dimensions.[27] In these sculptures, semi-nude women holding rattles wear substantial pieces of jewelry, notably armlets, bracelets, and anklets; traces of red paint on the women's bodies raise the possibility that they were once gilded with sheets of gold (Figures 5, 6, Plate III). That dancers are always depicted with large

---

24 Eva Baer, "Female Images in Early Islam," *Damaszener Mitteilungen* 11 (1999): 13–24; Hana Taragan, "A Matter of Looking: The Female Images in the Umayyad Palace at Khirbat Al-Mafjar," in *The Metamorphosis of Marginal Images: From Antiquity to Present Time*, ed. Nurith Kenaan-Kedar and Asher Ovadiah (Tel Aviv: Tel Aviv University, 2001), 69–78.
25 Israel Museum, Jerusalem, B65.04.0165. The drawing was recently published in Jonathan Bloom, *Arts of the City Victorious: Islamic Art and Architecture in Fatimid North Africa and Egypt* (New Haven: Yale University Press, 2007), 112–113; D. S. Rice, "A Drawing of the Fatimid Period," *Bulletin of the School of Oriental and African Studies* 21 (1958): 31–39; and Dalu Jones, "Notes on a Tattooed Musician: A Drawing of the Fatimid Period," *Art and Archaeology Research Papers* 7 (1975): 1–14.
26 A. F. L. Beeston, *The Epistle on Singing-Girls of Jāḥiẓ* (Warminster: Aris & Phillips, 1980); Lisa Emily Nielson, "*Diversions of Pleasure*: Singing Slave Girls and the Politics of Music in the Early Islamic Courts (661–1000 CE)" (PhD dissertation, University of Maine, 2010).
27 There are extensive descriptions in Robert Hamilton, *Walid and His Friends: An Umayyad Tragedy* (London: Oxford University Press, 1988).

Figure 5: Sculpture of a woman, Khirbat al-Mafjar, Jordan, eighth century. Collection: Rockefeller Museum, Jerusalem. Photograph: Elizabeth Dospěl Williams.

Figure 6: Detail of a sculpture from Khirbat al-Mafjar, Jordan, eighth century. Collection: Rockefeller Museum, Jerusalem. Photograph: Elizabeth Dospěl Williams.

hooped jewelry suggests that it was an expected part of their accoutrements and a cosmetic ideal among this exceptional class of women.

While most studies of the abovementioned drawing and the sculptures from Khirbat al-Mafjar have deployed these images to argue for early Islamic standards of beauty, these works of art are also useful in what they reveal about the sensory effects of large hoops. Tactility and movement are emphasized, particularly in the Fatimid drawing. There, the artist has provided exceptional detail in rendering the hoops in a scalloped design, perhaps an effort at indicating a textured surface similar to that of the ribbed pieces from the Ramla and Caesarea hoards. The anklets bunch up above the woman's ankles, as if to suggest dancing; the bracelet on the woman's left wrist slips halfway up her forearm, similarly implying movement. Her armlets, in contrast, are closely bound around her arms, pinching her voluptuous flesh. The overall effect is one of sensory overload, and this is certainly representative of the pleasurable atmosphere evoked in period texts about the enjoyments of the court, which included wine parties hosted by elite men.[28]

However, sound is undoubtedly the most vivid sensory effect evoked by this drawing and the dancers of Khirbat al-Mafjar: we can imagine these women's jewelry clinking as they moved and played the instruments in their hands. This leads one to wonder whether large hoops were specifically manufactured for their acoustic effects. Numerous pieces in museum collections attest to the prominence of aural experience. For example, a pair of hoops in the collections of the L. A. Mayer Museum, dated to the Fatimid era, have hollow interiors filled with pellets or small pieces of metal, which create a whooshing sound when shaken (Figure 7).[29] Other works feature charms that make sound, such as a gold bracelet or armband at Dumbarton Oaks, dating to the late sixth or early seventh century, with two small bells attached to it, which ring when shaken (Figure 8).[30] Some pieces of jewelry even "speak" in the first person, with inscriptions wishing protection to the wearer or naming the craftsman responsible for manufacture.[31]

Lastly, while the hoops from Ramla, Jerusalem, and Caesarea do not themselves show any signs of fragrance, examples of other jewelry suggest that olfactory effects were also an important component of women's adornments at the time. Two contemporaneous hoards excavated in nearby Tiberias offer a sense of the range of adornments that may have once accompanied the hoops as part of wearers' ensembles. These hoards include multiple earrings in the form of crescents and baskets, notable

---

28 Hamilton, *Walid and His Friends*.
29 L. A. Mayer Museum, Jerusalem, J242-68 and J243. The two pieces seem to be a pair. Published in Hasson, *Early Islamic Jewellery*, 71, cat. no. 86.
30 Dumbarton Oaks Research Library and Collection, Washington, D.C., BZ.1953.10. Published in Ross, *Catalogue*, 44, cat. no. 45.
31 For example, in Ramla, two pairs of bracelets include the inscription "I wish you complete blessing." A gold bracelet in the Mayer Museum (J47) similarly offers blessings (Hasson, *Early Islamic Jewellery*, 65, cat. no. 71), and three silver bracelets at the same museum (J285, J286, and J287) simply read "Perfect Blessing" and "Blessing" (Hasson, *Early Islamic Jewellery*, 69, cat. no. 82). At least one bracelet, also in the Mayer Museum (J130), names its craftsman, Isma'il (Hasson, *Early Islamic Jewellery*, 68, cat. no. 80).

Figure 7: Gold hoops, ca. eleventh/twelfth century, L. A. Mayer Museum of Islamic Art, Jerusalem, J242-68 and J243. Photograph: Elizabeth Dospěl Williams.

for their hollowed-out interiors.[32] Earrings in these shapes were very popular in the medieval Mediterranean from approximately the tenth century onward, as attested to by the innumerable examples currently in museum collections; these include luxury pieces in gold and others manufactured in baser materials like bronze, all pointing

---

32 Na'ama Brosh, "Two Jewelry Hoards from Tiberias," *'Atiqot* 36 (1998): 1–9. Examples from the 1974 hoard (IAA 1974-2128-2142) are illustrated on the website of the Israel Museum, http://www.imj.org.il/imagine/galleries/viewItemE.asp?case=7&itemNum=374328 (accessed 30 November 2017), and were published in Ayala Lester, "A Fatimid Hoard from Tiberias," in *Jewellery and Goldsmithing in the Islamic World* (Jerusalem: The Israel Museum, 1987), 21–29. The 1990 hoard (IAA 1990-1269-1275) is also on the Israel Museum's website, http://www.imj.org.il/imagine/galleries/viewItemE.asp?case=7&itemNum=374324 (accessed 30 November 2017).

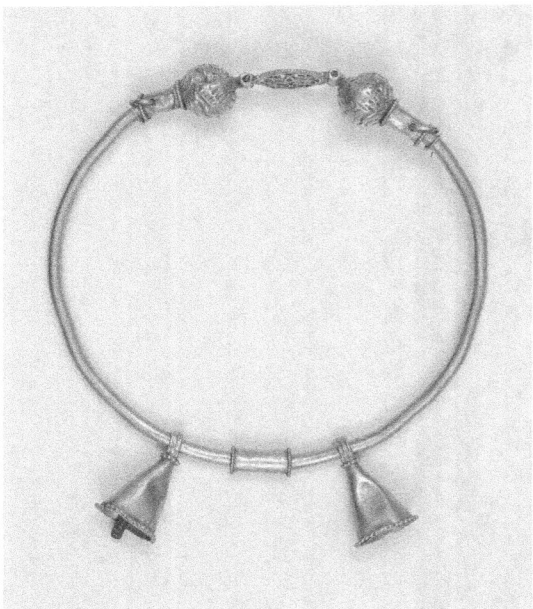

Figure 8: Gold bracelet or armband with bells, sixth/seventh century, Dumbarton Oaks Research Library and Collection, Washington, D.C., BZ.1953.10. Photograph copyright Dumbarton Oaks, Byzantine Collection, Washington, D.C.

to the wide social spectrum of people who wore such earrings (Figure 9).[33] Excavated examples are documented at a range of sites, showing that hollowed-out earrings were popular into Byzantine territory and beyond.[34] Intriguingly, at least one example of a bronze crescent-shaped earring was found with small bits of wool fiber stuck inside its hollowed core (Figure 10).[35] This small detail suggests that the vast numbers of hollowed crescent- and basket-shaped earrings that survive were in fact intended to bear fibers soaked in scent, following the fashions described in al-Washshā's guide to etiquette. Although this important detail speaks volumes about the sensory experiences of medieval wearers, it is not the kind frequently given prominence in the technical evaluations and stylistic discussions current in the fields of Byzantine

---

[33] Dumbarton Oaks Research Library and Collection, Byzantine Collection, Washington, D.C., BZ.1953.12.99. Published in Ross, *Catalogue*, 93, cat. no. 134.

[34] Basket and enamel earrings are discussed in Bosselmann-Ruickbie, "Byzantinisch, Islamisch oder 'Internazionaler Stil'?" The extensive popularity of crescent earrings is evaluated in Albani, "Elegance over the Borders." Both emphasize the appeal of the types in Byzantine and Islamic contexts.

[35] Bosselmann-Ruickbie, *Byzantinischer Schmuck*, cat. no. 74. The earring is made of bronze; it measures 2.6 cm wide and 2.8 cm tall, and it weighs 4.6 g. It is held in the Archaeological Museum, Corinth, Inv. Nr. MR 6258.

3 Appealing to the Senses — 91

Figure 9: Gold earring, ca. eleventh century, Dumbarton Oaks Research Library and Collection, Washington, D.C., BZ.1953.12.99. Photograph copyright Dumbarton Oaks, Byzantine Collection, Washington, D.C.

Figure 10: Bronze earring with remnants of wool, ca. twelfth century, Archaeological Museum, Corinth, accession number MR 6258. Photograph courtesy of Antje Bosselmann-Ruickbie.

or Islamic jewelry. As such, it serves as a reminder of the exciting reevaluations that may arise in scholarship as specialists turn to the functions of medieval jewelry rather than focusing strictly on its manufacture and attribution.

Sensory Borders between Public and Private

Thinking about jewelry in terms of sensory experience also makes it possible to expand our definitions of what constituted women's outward appearance in public and private contexts: close study of texts, objects, and visual depictions points to multisensory effects of adornments that extend beyond mere visibility. Returning to the *vita* of Pelagia, for example, we note that its author goes to great lengths to describe the sight, smell, and sound of Pelagia's costume as she processes in public before the bishops. Interestingly, the only other extensive account of Pelagia's dress occurs toward the end of the *vita*, when she prepares to donate her rich storeroom of textiles and adornments after converting to Christianity. There the narrator emphasizes her private actions: Pelagia calls on a servant to make an inventory of her wardrobe (*vestarium*) of gold and silver, jewelry, and precious clothing, and donates gold collars to each of her young servants before setting them free.

The distinction between the public spectacle of the sinful woman, in which the narrator emphasizes the scintillating, sensual delights of Pelagia's appearance, and the private setting of her personal wardrobe at home is striking. By describing Pelagia's alluring dress, luxurious jewelry, and vast personal wealth, the narrator draws on a tradition in period literature that addresses the dangers of adornments displayed in public.[36] When we consider the story of Pelagia in relation to moralists' concerns about women's appearances, we can see that the sensory associations of Pelagia's dress are linked to her public persona and, as a result, to her moral ambiguity; her actions in the home, in contrast, are understood to reflect her true nature as a pious, morally upright Christian woman.

The conceptual linking of external luxury and questionable morality has deep roots in ancient culture; the topic has been well explored by scholars focused on women's visual appearances.[37] Late Roman and early Christian moralistic sources,

---

36 Patricia Cox Miller, "Is There a Harlot in This Text? Hagiography and the Grotesque," in *The Cultural Turn in Late Antique Studies: Gender, Asceticism, and Historiography*, ed. Dale B. Martin, Patricia Cox Miller, and David Brakke (Philadelphia: University of Pennsylvania Press, 2005), 87–102.
37 Ria Berg, "Wearing Wealth: *Mundus Muliebris* and *Ornatus* as Status Markers for Women in Imperial Rome," in *Women, Wealth and Power in the Roman Empire*, ed. Päivi Setälä (Rome: Institutum Romanum Finlandiae, 2002), 15–74; Christiane Kunst, "Ornamenta Uxoria: Badges of Rank or Jewellery of Roman Wives?" *The Medieval History Journal* 8 (2005): 127–142; Maria Wyke, "Women in the Mirror: The Rhetoric of Adornment in the Roman World," in *Women in Antiquity*, ed. L. Archer et al. (London:

for example, view external fineries with suspicion, linking them to concepts of luxury and foreignness, while idealizing individuals who dress modestly with minimal ornamentation. In Tertullian's (ca. 160–ca. 220) *De cultu feminarum* (*On the Apparel of Women*), for example, Christian women are urged restraint and modesty in appearance, in order to maintain order and avoid the public attention associated with the sensory excesses of luxurious dress.[38] In Tertullian's view, inappropriately ornamented or over-ornamented individuals – like Pelagia – should be decried for showing off their wealth in the public sphere, and their moral character is called into question.

Clement of Alexandria (ca. 150–ca. 215), writing in Egypt in the late second century CE, also includes passages addressing the moral appropriateness of women's public appearance. His *Paedagogus* (*The Instructor*), a work aimed at Alexandria's upper-class Christian converts, includes many sections addressing the appropriateness of men's and women's clothes, jewelry, ointments, and perfumes.[39] Like Tertullian, Clement denounces ostentatious finery; yet Clement goes further in extending his prohibitions to sensory presence as well. He explains that women should avoid alluring smells because they incite sensual desires and lust, and that perfumes are to be condemned for their associations with luxury.[40] Clement also criticizes men for wearing perfumed ointments, arguing that by wearing fancy perfumes they may be confused with women or foreigners.

Tertullian's and Clement of Alexandria's precautions against lavish adornments or perfumes should be contextualized alongside ancient attitudes toward sensory perception more generally. As Jerry Toner explores in his introduction to *A Cultural History of the Senses in Antiquity*, managing one's sensory impression on others was linked to social status, particularly when it came to dress: looking and

---

Macmillan, 1994), 134–151; Alicia J. Batten, "Neither Gold nor Braided Hair (1 Timothy 2.9; 1 Peter 3.3): Adornment, Gender and Honour in Antiquity," *New Testament Studies* 55 (2009): 484–501.

38 Tertullian, *On the Apparel of Women*, trans. S. Thelwall, in *The Fathers of the Third Century*, Ante-Nicene Fathers, vol. 4., ed. Alexander Roberts, James Donaldson, and A. Cleveland Coxe (Buffalo, NY: Christian Literature Publishing, 1885), revised and edited for New Advent by Kevin Knight, http://www.newadvent.org/fathers/0402.htm (accessed 30 November 2017). Latin edition in *La Toilette Des Femmes (De Cultu Feminarum)*, trans. Marie Turcan (Paris: Éditions du Cerf, 1971). Extensive resources on Tertullian, including original Latin, translations, bibliography, and information about the text's transmission, are available at www.tertullian.org/works/de_cultu_feminarum.htm (accessed 30 November 2017).

39 Clement of Alexandria, *The Instructor*, trans. William Wilson, in *The Fathers of the Second Century*, Ante-Nicene Fathers, vol. 2, ed. Alexander Roberts, James Donaldson, and A. Cleveland Coxe (Buffalo: Christian Literature Publishing, 1885), revised and edited for New Advent by Kevin Knight, accessed 30 November 2017, http://www.newadvent.org/fathers/0209.htm. Greek edition: Clement of Alexandria, *Paedagogus*, ed. M. Marcovich and J. C. M van Winden (Leiden: Brill, 2002).

40 *Paedagogus*, bk. 2, chap. 8.

smelling good, for example, was essential in conveying one's social status.[41] Toner specifically argues that wanton luxury, as "a total onslaught against the senses since it reflected a coalescence of various sensory experiences," was in fact a problem because it challenged accepted notions of social status, ethnicity, and even gender performance.[42]

Tertullian's and Clement's prohibitions reflect not only efforts to define the behaviors and dress of the early Christian community, but also the deep-rooted endurance of ancient anxieties centered around public appearance, the display of wealth, gender identity, and the question of natural as opposed to artificial beauty. That Clement's regulations extend to smell underlines the importance of including other sensory effects in scholarly discussions of early Christian women's public personae, which until now have focused almost exclusively on their visual appearance.

Similar attitudes toward the public display of ornaments echo into the Islamic period, showing the long afterlives of these conceptual groupings into the Middle Ages. Compellingly, these texts, too, emphasize the sensory impact of women's dress and jewelry, suggesting that public appearance encompassed not only what was visible to the eyes, but also other effects like sound. The Qu'ran, for example, denounces women's excessive or overly visible adornment through the linked concepts of *zīnah* and *tabarrūj*. The term *tabarrūj* specifically denotes the inappropriate display of wealth, beauty, and adornment; its associations are with finery, charm, and drawing attention to oneself. In the Sūrat al-Aḥzāb (The Parties), for example, *tabarrūj* is specifically aligned with immoral public behavior. Here, jewelry's visibility outside the home is particularly decried, with issues of display coming through clearly:

> O wives of the Prophet! You are not like other women. If you are reverent, then be not overly soft in speech, lest one in whose heart is a disease be moved to desire; and speak in an honorable way. Abide in your homes and flaunt not your charms [*tabarraja*] as they did flaunt them in the prior Age of Ignorance [*jāhiliyyah*]. Perform the prayer, give the alms, and obey God and His Messenger. God only desires to remove defilement from you, O People of the House, and to purify you completely. (33:32–33)[43]

---

[41] Jerry Toner, "Introduction: Sensing the Ancient Past," in *A Cultural History of the Senses in Antiquity*, ed. Jerry Toner (London: Bloomsbury, 2014).

[42] Toner, "Introduction," 10.

[43] Sūrat al-Aḥzāb, verses 32–33: "yā-nisā'a n-nabiyyi lastunna ka-'aḥadin mina n-nisā'i 'ini ttaqaytunna fa-lā takhḍa'na bi-l-qawli fa-yaṭma'a lladhī fī qalbihī maraḍun wa-qulna qawlan ma'rūfa / wa-qarna fī buyūtikunna wa-lā tabarrajna tabarruja l-jāhiliyyati l-'ūlā wa-'aqimna ṣ-ṣalāta wa-'ātīna z-zakāta wa-'aṭi'na llāha wa-rasūlahū 'innamā yurīdu llāhu li-yudhhiba 'ankumu r-rijsa 'ahla l-bayti wa-yuṭahhirakum taṭhīra." Al-Qur'ān, accessed 30 November 2017, http://al-quran.info/#33. English translation in *The Study Qur'an: A New Translation and Commentary*, ed. Seyyed Hossein Nasr et al. (New York: Harper Collins, 2015), 1028–1029.

The term *zīnah* presents an even more interesting example, showing that appearance could encompass not only visually discernible elements like jewelry, but other sensory effects as well. *Zīnah* refers to external fineries, with a variety of meanings that encompass cosmetics, appearance, and grooming, while more generally evoking ornamentation or embellishment. It also carries negative connotations related to excessive concern with worldly wealth. Doris Behrens-Abouseif has provided the most thoughtful translation of this term, describing *zīnah* as vanity or idle pastime, "the worthlessness of ephemerality," but it could also connote excessive adornment.[44] This point comes through strongly in a particularly well-known passage from the Qur'an, in Sūrat al-Nūr (Light), which contrasts modesty and excess:

> And tell the believing women to lower their eyes and to guard their private parts, and to not display their adornment [*zīnah*], except that which is visible thereof [*mā dhahara minhā*]. And let them draw their kerchiefs over their breasts, and not display their adornment [*zīnah*] except to their husbands, or their fathers, or their husbands' fathers, or their sons, or their husbands' sons, or their brothers, or their brothers' sons, or their sisters' sons, or their women, or those whom their right hands possess, or male attendants free of desire, or children who are innocent of the private areas of women. Nor let them stamp their feet such that the ornaments they conceal become known. (24:31)[45]

Here, the act of stamping jewelry-clad feet, producing noise, is specifically decried, suggesting that the aural qualities of wearing jewelry were as morally perilous as the visual effects of showing off luxurious adornments in public. As such, it suggests that legalistic and religious concerns about women's public appearance were not limited to what was visually evident to the eyes, but also encompassed effects such as the sound of their jewelry and smell of their clothes as they moved in the public realm.

Conclusion

In this chapter, I have attempted to reframe discussions of jewelry from the medieval eastern Mediterranean by shifting attention away from the visual experience of

---

44 Doris Behrens-Abouseif, *Beauty in Islamic Culture* (Princeton, NJ: Markus Wiener, 1998), 21.
45 Sūrat al-Nūr, verse 31: "Wa-qul li-l-mu'mināti yaghḍuḍna min 'abṣārihinna wa-yaḥfaẓna furūja-hunna wa-lā yubdīna zīnatahunna 'illā mā ẓahara minhā wa-l-yaḍribna bi-khumurihinna 'alā juyūbi-hinna wa-lā yubdīna zīnatahunna 'illā li-bu'ūlatihinna 'aw 'ābā'ihinna 'aw 'ābā'i bu'ūlatihinna 'aw 'abnā'ihinna 'aw 'abnā'i bu'ūlatihinna 'aw 'ikhwānihinna 'aw banī 'ikhwānihinna 'aw banī 'akhawā-tihinna 'aw nisā'ihinna 'aw mā malakat 'aymānuhunna 'awi t-tābi'īna ghayri 'ulī l-'irbati mina r-ri-jāli 'awi ṭ-ṭifli lladhīna lam yaẓharū 'alā 'awrāti n-nisā'i wa-lā yaḍribna bi-'arjulihinna li-yu'lama mā yukhfīna min zīnatihinna wa-tūbū 'ilā llāhi jamī'an 'ayyuha l-mu'minūna la'allakum tufliḥūn." Al-Qur'ān, accessed 30 November 2017, http://al-quran.info/#24. English translation in *The Study Qur'an*, 876–877.

adornment to questions pertaining to other senses, such as touch, hearing, and smell. While texts are largely silent on the ephemeral experiences of wearing jewelry, a close study of objects in fact reveals much about medieval wearers' experiences. A shift in focus, from jewelry's formal appearance and visual effect to its physicality and multisensory qualities, adds significant nuance to our understanding of period dress practice and offers new avenues of inquiry for evaluating medieval sensory experience. In the larger picture, however, by drawing attention to the multisensory aspects of adornment, we make a strong case for reevaluating definitions of medieval women's public presence, which should encompass the smell and sound of their apparel in addition to their visual appearance.

Melissa Herman
4 Sensing Iconography: Ornamentation, Material, and Sensuousness in Early Anglo-Saxon Metalwork

It is commonly understood that there are five basic senses through which humans experience life and the world around them – sight, hearing, smell, touch, and taste – although modern neurobiological research might argue for a myriad of additional, if less observable, senses.[1] While these are human physiological traits constant throughout history, conceptions of and engagement with the senses vary between cultures and time periods. Early Anglo-Saxon England during the sixth and seventh centuries, following the withdrawal of Roman influence and before full conversion to Christianity, was a culture that embraced an oral rather than literate tradition.[2] The introduction of Christianity brought literacy and a tradition of written record; it also drew Anglo-Saxon England into closer connection with Latinate thought and exegetical writings, including those pertaining to the senses. Before this transition, however, how might the senses and sensory experiences have been understood in early Anglo-Saxon England?

Generally speaking, the task of analyzing a historical period is based on using the details that can be discovered in records from the time to create a credible and coherent account.[3] In this respect, the study of the history of sixth- and seventh-century Anglo-Saxon England is fraught with problems. The oral culture of early Anglo-Saxon society – a tradition that continued even after the introduction of literate modes of communication and documentation – means that the number of documentary sources is limited.[4] Those that do pertain to the period – whether biased and temporally distant historical narrative, or nonhistorical literature written with great

---

[1] Douglas B. Light, *The Senses*, Your Body, How It Works (Philadelphia, PA: Chelsea House, 2005), 10–11. See also the essays in Friedrich G. Barth, Patrizia Giampieri-Deutsch, and Hans-Dieter Klein, eds., *Sensory Perception: Mind and Matter* (Vienna: Springer, 2012).
[2] J. Hines, "Religion: The Limits of Knowledge," in *The Anglo-Saxons from the Migration Period to the Eighth Century: An Ethnographic Perspective*, ed. John Hines (Woodbridge: Boydell Press, 1997), 375–410, at 393–394.
[3] Marc Bloch, *The Historian's Craft* (Manchester: Manchester University Press, 1992), 40–57.
[4] For further discussion of the oral tradition of Anglo-Saxon England, see Andy Orchard, *A Critical Companion to Beowulf* (Rochester, NY: D. S. Brewer, 2003), 225–227; Mark Amodio, *Writing the Oral Tradition: Oral Poetics and Literate Culture in Medieval England*, Poetics of Orality and Literacy (Notre Dame, IN: University of Notre Dame Press, 2004), 4–7; John D. Niles, *Old English Heroic Poems and the Social Life of Texts* (Turnhout: Brepols, 2007), 53–58.

poetic license – are problematic in the accuracy of their accounts.⁵ Given the dearth and unreliability of textual sources, it is material evidence contemporaneous to the period that best illustrates the influences and considerations of early Anglo-Saxons. As products of human workmanship, artifacts represent a reaction to the events and experiences of their time and encapsulate the social, historical, and cultural context within which they were made.⁶

Many of the Anglo-Saxon objects that have survived from the sixth and seventh centuries are made of metal: jewelry, armament, and household goods which have been recovered archaeologically. These pieces of metalwork are often works of art: with a few exceptions, they tend to be extensively ornamented with intricate, meticulously executed decoration, including geometric patterns, complex interlacing linear designs, and abstracted iconography such as zoomorphic imagery. These artifacts are often recovered piecemeal, and only certain materials survive the vagaries of burial underground without significant damage and decay. Similar decorations and iconography may also have ornamented organic media such as textiles, wood, bone, or ivory, but few examples remain of these more ephemeral objects.

The imperfect nature of the information generated even by those objects found and recovered within well-established archaeological contexts means that analysis is limited without other sources of information. Much of the existing scholarship regarding the early Anglo-Saxon material record is focused on the object itself, its material construction and composition, its situation based on style and iconography within a historical context, and its archaeological impact. By nature, such examination of past societies through the material record is overwhelmingly ocular.⁷ Recent scholarship has started to become more interpretive, examining iconographic symbolism and considering objects' patronage, purpose, and use.⁸ Still, it tends to shy away from experience – that is, one's physical, emotional, and sensory engagement with an object at the moment of encounter. Attempting to reconstruct the original experience of interacting with an artifact is, by nature, speculative; the limited nature

---

5 See Walter A. Goffart, *The Narrators of Barbarian History (A.D. 550–800): Jordanes, Gregory of Tours, Bede, and Paul the Deacon* (Princeton, NJ: Princeton University Press, 2005), 296–307; Paul Meyvaert, "Bede, Cassiodorus, and the Codex Amiatinus," *Speculum* 71 (1996): 827–883, at 831–843; M. B. Parkes, "Rædan, Areccan Smeagan: How the Anglo-Saxons Read," *Anglo-Saxon England* 26 (1997): 1–22; Elizabeth M. Tyler, *Old English Poetics: The Aesthetics of the Familiar in Anglo-Saxon England* (York: York Medieval Press, 2006), 9–37.

6 For discussion of this aspect of material artifacts, see Whitney Davis, "Beginning the History of Art," *Journal of Aesthetics and Art Criticism* 51 (1993): 327–350; Evelyn P. Hatcher, *Art as Culture: An Introduction to the Anthropology of Art*, 2nd ed. (Westport, CT: Praeger, 1999), 1–2.

7 Martin K. Foys, "A Sensual Philology for Anglo-Saxon England," *postmedieval* 5 (2014): 456–472, at 461.

8 Jane Hawkes, "Symbolic Lives: The Visual Evidence," in *The Anglo-Saxons from the Migration Period to the Eighth Century: An Ethnographic Perspective*, ed. John Hines (Woodbridge: Boydell Press, 1997), 311–338.

of the material record and lack of direct experiential accounts from the time ensure that whatever conclusions are drawn must to some degree be suppositional. Nonetheless, such efforts offer insight into these objects' purposes and a means to interpret the way in which Anglo-Saxons experienced the senses and manipulated them in their deliberate decorative choices. Among the varied corpus of surviving material, selected pieces of male and female jewelry dating from the sixth and seventh century, at once decorative and practical, offer an excellent opportunity to approach these issues.

The close attention paid to the construction and decoration of personal jewelry and armament in Anglo-Saxon society indicates a culture in which displays of wealth played an important role in constructing understanding of an individual's identity. The giving of valuable gifts – money, ornaments, or property – was a way to solidify bonds in Anglo-Saxon society, particularly between a lord and his warriors.[9] Old English poetry – recorded in the later Anglo-Saxon period but understood to preserve aspects of earlier oral poetry – offers some insight into this custom.[10] The poem *Fortunes of Men*, preserved in the Exeter Book, a tenth-century compendium of Old English poetry, clearly lays out the exchange of gifts:

> Sumum wundorgiefe
> þurh goldsmiþe   gearwad weorþað;
> ful oft he gehyrdeð   ond gehyrsteð wel,
> brytencyninges beorn,   ond he him brad syleð
> lond to leane.   He hit on lust þigeð.

[For another, marvelous gifts are prepared by goldsmiths. Very often he obeyed, and he decorated the man of the powerful king well, and he gave broad lands to him as a reward. He accepts them joyfully.][11]

The transaction of finely ornamented jewelry in exchange for loyalty is less mercenary than it might initially appear, not being payment for services rendered but rather reward for friendship and fidelity – past, current, and future. This interpretation is

---

9 Paul Veyne, *Le pain et le cirque: Sociologie historique d'un pluralisme politique* (Paris Éditions du Seuil, 1976); Valerie A. Maxfield, *The Military Decorations of the Roman Army* (Berkeley, CA: University of California Press, 1981); Dominic Janes, *God and Gold in Late Antiquity* (Cambridge: Cambridge University Press, 1998), 38–39.

10 For example, the poem *The Dream of the Rood* is preserved in the tenth-century Vercelli Book; however, an earlier version can be found on the eighth-century Ruthwell Cross, suggesting a much earlier date of composition. Elisabeth Okasha, *Hand-List of Anglo-Saxon Non-Runic Inscriptions* (Cambridge Cambridge University Press, 1971), 108–112; Éamonn Ó Carragáin, *Ritual and the Rood: Liturgical Images and the Old English Poems of the Dream of the Rood Tradition* (Toronto: University of Toronto Press, 2005), 49–50.

11 *Fortunes of Men*, lines 72–76. In Bernard James Muir, ed., *The Exeter Anthology of Old English Poetry: An Edition of Exeter Dean and Chapter, MS 3501*, Exeter Medieval Texts and Studies (Exeter: University of Exeter Press, 2000), 1:246. Translations of Old English, except where noted, are by Simon C. Thomson, Ruhr-Universität Bochum, in discussion with the author.

reinforced by the use of the word *wundorgiefe*. *Wundor*, translated here as "marvelous," carries a deeper sense of astonishment, awe, and even otherworldliness than can be translated into modern English, while *giefe*, translated as "gifts," seems to refer to the freeness of giving rather than a specific gift itself.[12] The phrase *on lust þigeð* points to the deep allure of the gift and the joy of receiving it. Such rewards (aside from land) were to be worn and circulated rather than stored or hoarded. The display of riches thereby indicated both status and kinship, one's belonging to the elite group that served a generous lord. In *Beowulf*, the Geats, journeying to Danish shores, are stopped by a watchman:

> þa of wealle geseah   weard Scildinga,
> se þe holmclifu   healdan scolde,
> beran ofer bolcan   beorhte randas,
> fyrdsearu fuslicu;   hine fyrwyt bræc
> modgehygdum,   hwæt þa men wæron.
> ... meþelwordum frægn:
> "Hwæt syndon ge   searohæbbendra,
> byrnum werede,   þe þus brontne ceol
> ofer lagustræte   lædan cwomon,
> hider ofer holmas? ...
> ... Næfre ic maran geseah
> eorla ofer eorþan   ðonne is eower sum,
> secg on searwum;   nis þæt seldguma,
> wæpnum geweorðad,   næfne him his wlite leoge,
> ænlic ansyn."

[Then the guard of the Scyldings saw from the walls, he who had to guard the sea-cliffs, bright shields, prepared war-equipment, carried down the gangplank. Curiosity arose in his inner thoughts, as to what these men were. He ... interrogated them formally: "What are you, armored men, wearing mailcoats, who have come bringing this tall ship across the sea-road, across the water to this place? ... I have never seen a greater man in the world than is one of you, a man in armor. Ennobled by weapons, that is no serving man, unless his looks, his unique appearance, belie him."][13]

As evidenced by his own words in the poem and by the description of him catching sight of "bright shields," the coast guard is fixated on the new arrivals' armor. His words upon seeing the Geats up close convey interest and excitement more than fear, and he takes the fineness of their battle gear as evidence of their nobility, particularly in the case of Beowulf, who is *maran* and therefore perhaps better armed

---

[12] Thanks to Simon C. Thomson for discussion of Old English word choice and interpretation throughout.

[13] *Beowulf*, lines 229–251a. In Robert Dennis Fulk et al., eds., *Klaeber's Beowulf and The Fight at Finnsburg*, 4th ed., Toronto Old English Series 21 (Toronto: University of Toronto Press, 2009), 9–10.

or most decorated.¹⁴ The next line reinforces the point, evocatively designating Beowulf, whose physical appearance is never described in the poem, as "ennobled by weapons," thereby emphasizing the cultural value of displaying metalwork. Material evidence accords with such literary suggestions in signaling that the quality and type of objects displayed served as initial indicators of who and what an individual might be.¹⁵ The impact of these objects was intended to be visual, appealing first to the sense of sight. The more powerful and wealthy people were, the more luxurious and impressive would be their visible display of wealth, and the more respect they would garner.

Surviving pieces of Anglo-Saxon metalwork are impressive and even overwhelming to the eye, demonstrating a deliberate effort to create a dense visual field and to control and manipulate the movement of a viewer's eye across the pattern of ornamentation.¹⁶ One example of the highly ornate patterning that Anglo-Saxon craftsmen were capable of producing is a pair of triangular shoulder clasps recovered from the sixth- or early seventh-century burial mound at Taplow in Buckinghamshire (Figure 1). The buckles have a copper alloy core, wrapped in gold foil and overlain with filigree.¹⁷ These components, reducing the amount of gold needed to craft the clasps, might be seen as an indication of lower status and lesser wealth; but the precision of the ornamentation and the vitality of the design preclude the possibility that they were produced by a workshop of lesser technical accomplishment. The triangular plates and the loop of each clasp are filled with sinuous interlacing forms; the hooks are ornamented with filigree S-spirals and a ropelike plait border; the three round settings at the corners of each triangular plate would have been inlaid with contrasting material, likely shell.¹⁸ The initial impression given by these clasps is one of exuberant lines and variegated shine. With further examination, the chaos resolves itself into schematic, serpentine zoomorphs, recognizable as such only with knowledge of the conventions for depicting animals in Anglo-Saxon art.¹⁹ The forms evoke a sense of intricate complexity and restless motion barely restrained. The play

---

14 Ruth Johnston Staver, *A Companion to Beowulf* (Westport, CT: Greenwood Publishing Group, 2005), 36–38; Scott Gwara, *Heroic Identity in the World of Beowulf* (Leiden: Brill, 2008), 100–102.
15 Penelope Walton Rogers, *Cloth and Clothing in Early Anglo-Saxon England, AD 450–700* (York: Council for British Archaeology, 2007), 111; Gale R. Owen-Crocker, *Dress in Anglo-Saxon England* (Woodbridge: Boydell & Brewer, 2010), 317.
16 A more complete version of this argument can be found in Melissa Herman, "All That Glitters: The Role of Pattern, Reflection, and Visual Perception in Early Anglo-Saxon Art," in *Sensory Perception in the Medieval West*, ed. Michael D. J. Bintley and Simon C. Thomson, Utrecht Studies in Medieval Literacy 34 (Turnhout: Brepols, 2016), 159–180.
17 Leslie Webster et al., *The Making of England: Anglo-Saxon Art and Culture AD 600–900* (London: British Museum Press, 1991), 55–56, cat. no. 43.
18 Webster et al., *The Making of England*, 55–56, cat. no. 43.
19 The highly abstracted nature of Anglo-Saxon animal art means that depictions are rarely naturalistic but extremely formulaic, allowing for easy recognition once one is familiar with the modes of representation. For a comprehensive guide to deciphering this style of art, see George Speake, *Anglo-Saxon Animal Art and Its Germanic Background* (Oxford: Clarendon Press, 1980).

Figure 1: Shoulder clasps, copper core wrapped in gold with filigree, sixth or seventh century, Taplow, Buckinghamshire. Collection: The British Museum, London, 1883,1214.3 and 1883,1214.2. Photograph copyright the Trustees of the British Museum.

of light across the surface of this object is an integral part of the visual experience: the polished gold would have glinted and shone, even in low light, while the texture of the raised, beaded curves of the zoomorphs would dazzlingly reflect the light from different angles.

Another example of the creation and manipulation of a complex visual field not limited to zoomorphic or even linear designs is an early seventh-century disc brooch from Sarre (Plate IV).[20] Constructed from a gilt copper-alloy composite with a silver back plate and decorated with garnet cloisonné, white shell, and gold filigree, the brooch creates an almost dizzying effect through its multiple textures and layers of ornament. Its large central boss of shell, set with a flat, round garnet, is the center of two cruciform shapes that do not fall on the same axis: one formed by the silver bands that divide the boss, the other by four smaller shell and garnet cloisonné bosses on the outer edges of the brooch. Four concentric bands of ornament surround the central boss, alternating between garnet cloisonné and filigree, each one distinct and bordered by beaded gold wire. The complex arrangement of the textures, designs, and material variations dictates the movement of the eye over the surface of the brooch and through complex patterns within patterns that it must unravel in order to perceive.

---

20 Webster et al., *The Making of England*, 48, cat. no. 31a.

There is a sensuality in the viewing of this brooch and these shoulder clasps that is indelibly linked to both their iconographic design and their material construction. Anglo-Saxon metalwork demonstrates an understanding of the sensuousness of the materials used in its construction, particularly the way in which they appeal first to the sense of sight in terms of light and color. Gold has an enduring brilliance; it does not tarnish, reflects light, and has a color that can be manipulated from rich buttery yellow to a much paler shade through adulteration of the metal.[21] Silver is even brighter than gold when polished, but tarnishes if not handled and maintained properly, becoming dull and discolored. Garnet is a stone with distinctive light-refractive properties and a variable color ranging from bright red to a deep, dark burgundy that can appear almost purple, depending on the individual stone and how it is manipulated.[22] Other materials, like blue and millefiori glass or imported shell, offer a more subtle sheen and a counterpoint to the dominant color scheme of red and gold found in most Anglo-Saxon jewelry. Utilizing the unique and distinctive aspects of the different materials, the execution of Anglo-Saxon metalwork decoration shows a deliberate effort to influence and manipulate the viewer's sensory experience: the eye is encouraged to glide along the surface of the ornament, exploring the texture, form, color, light, and shadow of the piece. Adding materially to the sensual impact of the metalwork is the likelihood that the effect would be multiplied when pieces were worn: an early Anglo-Saxon (male or female) would rarely wear a single brooch or buckle in isolation. The wearer of a full array of pieces would glitter like Beowulf and his Geats. The deft handling of both material and iconography in the metalwork strongly suggests that early Anglo-Saxons had a deep understanding of visual perception and a delight in manipulating it to create an aesthetic and sensory experience.

The focus on manipulation of the visual in early Anglo-Saxon England is not surprising given that sight has long been thought to be dominant among our senses.[23] Modern-day studies in physiology and neurology demonstrate that visual perception has been known to supersede the information received from other senses, even when the information conflicts and the visual data is incorrect.[24] Vision also plays a

---

21 Janes, *God and Gold in Late Antiquity*, 19.
22 Noël Adams, "The Garnet Millennium: The Role of Seal Stones in Garnet Studies," in *"Gems of Heaven": Recent Research on Engraved Gemstones in Late Antiquity, AD 200–600*, ed. Noël Adams and Chris Entwistle, British Museum Research Publication 177 (London: British Museum Press, 2011), 10–24, at 10.
23 Kristine Krug, "Principles of Function in the Visual System," in *Sensory Perception: Mind and Matter*, ed. Friedrich G. Barth, Patrizia Giampieri-Deutsch, and Hans-Dieter Klein (New York: Springer, 2012), 41–56.
24 Harry McGurk and John Macdonald, "Hearing Lips and Seeing Voices," *Nature* 264 (1976): 746–748; Lawrence D. Rosenblum, Mark A. Schmuckler, and Jennifer A. Johnson, "The McGurk Effect in Infants," *Perception & Psychophysics* 59 (1997): 347–357; Dustin Stokes and Stephen Biggs, "The Dominance of the Visual," in *Perception and Its Modalities*, ed. D. Stokes, M. Matthen, and S. Biggs (Oxford: Oxford University Press, 2014), 350–378.

significant role in assisting other senses to process and interpret physical stimuli – for example, we clarify words by watching the movement of mouths, or visually judge the shape and size of objects being touched, resulting in a more complete, complex, and accurate sensory experience.[25] Within the Anglo-Saxon context, there is not much writing on the five senses, but it is possible to discern evidence of an understanding of and engagement with sensory perception on a philosophical level. Perhaps unsurprisingly, this evidence has been found in the form of iconography on metalwork. The Fuller Brooch, a large, late ninth-century Anglo-Saxon hammered-silver brooch, has a complex design inlaid with niello and ornamented with what was once thought to be the earliest depiction of the five senses in Western art.[26] The central and largest figure represents sight, arguably the most important in the scheme; it is surrounded by the other four senses in the form of four figures who each perform an action that alludes to a particular sense.[27] Preceding the Fuller Brooch by more than a century are a group of early Anglo-Saxon silver coins dated to the early to mid-eighth century, the Series K sceattas. Upon closely examining the iconography of five types of coins within this series, Anna Gannon has suggested that they are each intended to represent one of the five senses.[28] Both brooch and coins engage with the medieval understanding of the senses by means of iconographic representation but are firmly part of the post-conversion Anglo-Saxon world steeped in Christian thought and understanding. Nonetheless, the complexity and multilayered patterning of the earlier Anglo-Saxon metalwork seems to suggest that, prior to England's reconnection with the exegetical Latinate world and the creation of objects demonstrating obvious engagement with medieval philosophies of the five senses, there existed an understanding of the centrality of visual perception and a desire to manipulate visual experience.

Vision may have dominated the medieval (and early Anglo-Saxon) hierarchy of sensation, but the other senses had their roles. The sense of hearing was considered to be second in importance, with subordinate senses of smell, taste, and touch ranking lower in the order.[29] Sound had an important place in Anglo-Saxon life, central to

---

[25] Stokes and Biggs, "The Dominance of the Visual," 360–367.
[26] Carl Nordenfalk, "The Five Senses in Late Medieval and Renaissance Art," *Journal of the Warburg and Courtauld Institutes* 48 (1985): 1–22.
[27] Rupert Leo Scott Bruce-Mitford, "The Fuller Brooch," *British Museum Quarterly* 45 (1952): 75–76; Rupert Leo Scott Bruce-Mitford, "The Christian Saxon and the Viking Age: Late Saxon Disc-Brooches," in *Dark-Age Britain: Studies Presented to E. T. Leeds with a Bibliography of His Works*, ed. Donald Harden (London: Methuen, 1956), 169–258.
[28] Anna Gannon, *The Iconography of Early Anglo-Saxon Coinage: Sixth to Eighth Centuries*, Medieval History and Archaeology (Oxford: Oxford University Press, 2003).
[29] Robert Jütte, *A History of the Senses: From Antiquity to Cyberspace* (Cambridge: Polity, 2005); Annette Kern-Stähler and Kathrin Scheuchzer, "Introduction," in *The Five Senses in Medieval and Early Modern England*, ed. Annette Kern-Stähler, Beatrix Busse, and Wietse de Boer (Leiden: Brill, 2016), 1–17, at 3.

people's daily experiences, if somewhat fleeting.[30] The impact of aurality in Anglo-Saxon life becomes evident in the surviving literature, which often provides rich descriptions of both organic and man-made sounds, and even in the very language, which offers a plethora of words that take their meaning from sounds.[31] For example, it is the sound of their call that distinguishes the array of native black-colored corvids (ravens, crows, and rooks) and informs their Old English names (*hrefn*, *crawe*, and *hroc*).[32] Returning to the poem *Fortunes of Men*, the description of two men's fate in the great hall resounds with the sounds found within:

> Sum sceal on heape   hæleþum cweman,
> blisian æt beore   bencsittendum;
> þær biþ drincenda   dream se micla;
> sum sceal mid hearpan   aet his hlafordes
> fotum sittan,   feoh þicgan,
> ond a snellice   snere wræstan,
> lætan scralletan   sceacol, se þe hleapeð
> nægl neomengende.

> [One will delight the assembly of heroes, please those sitting on benches with beer; there will be great joy among the drinkers there. One will sit with a harp at his lord's feet, receiving payment, and swiftly work the strings, letting the plectrum – that which leaps – produce a loud sound, the peg produce sweet sounds.][33]

Within the oral tradition of Anglo-Saxon England, poetry would have been performed aloud, likely with musical accompaniment, for example by the harp.[34] The sounds of the words in this passage replicate those of plucked strings and leaping melody, while their meaning reinforces the role of music as a communal experience, shared

---

30 Steve Mills, "Sensing the Place: Sounds and Landscape Perception," in *(Un)settling the Neolithic*, ed. Douglass W. Bailey, A. W. R. Whittle, and Vicki Cummings (Oxford: Oxbow, 2005), 79–89; C. M. Woolgar, *The Senses in Late Medieval England* (New Haven, CT: Yale University Press, 2006); Kristopher Poole and Eric Lacey, "Avian Aurality in Anglo-Saxon England," *World Archaeology* 46 (2014): 400–415, at 400–401.
31 Foys, "A Sensual Philology for Anglo-Saxon England," 466–470; Poole and Lacey, "Avian Aurality in Anglo-Saxon England," 400–405.
32 Poole and Lacey, "Avian Aurality in Anglo-Saxon England," 403; Eric Lacey, "When Is a Hroc Not a Hroc? When It Is a Crawe or a Hrefn: A Case-Study in Recovering Old English Folk-Taxonomies," in *The Art, Literature and Material Culture of the Medieval World*, ed. Meg Boulton, Jane Hawkes, and Melissa Herman (Dublin: Four Courts Press, 2015), 138–152.
33 *Fortunes of Men*, lines 77–84. Muir, *The Exeter Anthology of Old English Poetry*, 1:246–247.
34 For discussion of the performance of oral poetry in Anglo-Saxon England, see Roberta Frank, "The Search for the Anglo-Saxon Oral Poet," *Bulletin of the John Rylands Library* 75 (1993): 11–36; John D. Niles, "The Myth of the Anglo-Saxon Oral Poet," *Western Folklore* 62 (2003): 7–61; Chris Jones, "Where Now the Harp? Listening for the Sounds of Old English Verse, from Beowulf to the Twentieth Century," *Oral Tradition* 24 (2009): 485–502; Lisa M. Horton, "Singing the Story: Narrative Voice and the Old English Scop," *The Hilltop Review* 4 (2010): 48–57.

between the men in the social context of the hall. And back in *Beowulf*, while the hero fights the monster Grendel under cover of darkness, the gathered Danes listen blindly to the cacophony, relating the sounds of battle to the familiar sounds of feasting in the same hall:

>Dryhtsele dynede;   Denum eallum wearð,
>Ceasterbuendum,   cenra gehwylcum,
>eorlum ealuscerwen. Yrre wæron begen,
>reþe renweardas.   Reced hlynsode.

>[Noise filled the noble hall – to all of the Danes, townsmen, to each of the bold men, it was a sharing of ale. They were both enraged, the savage hall-guardians. The hall resounded.][35]

Thus it is in the literature and the language that the sounds of Anglo-Saxon England most obviously echo. But perhaps they can also be found resonating in the material record, evoked through visual iconography.

Scholarship in neuroscience and psychological studies over the last two decades has formed a subfield addressing multisensory perception, which acknowledges that the sensory information that allows humans to perceive the world does not come from individual senses in isolation, but rather amalgamates the multiple senses together.[36] Studies show that there are connections between the auditory and visual portions of the brain at the cognitive level and that when the information from one sense is ambiguous, another sense can step in to clarify or confirm the perception.[37] More colloquially, words associated with auditory stimuli and descriptions are often used in visual descriptions of art or architecture, such as *harmony*, *rhythm*, *discordant*, or even *noisy*. Such word choices enhance a visual description with a sense of meaning drawn from the experience of sound.

There is undeniable rhythm and variable tones in the ornament of early Anglo-Saxon metalwork; with that in mind, it is possible to use those attributes here to perform a purposefully synesthetic reading that mingles sight and hearing. A seventh-century gilt-bronze disc brooch (Figure 2) bears relatively simple geometric decoration but can be read with a certain sense of musicality. The brooch has five concentric bands of ornamentation starting with the central round boss of enamel set in a metal collar. The next layer is a double band of repoussé rings with a series of

---

[35] *Beowulf*, lines 767–770. Fulk et al., *Klaeber's Beowulf*, 28. This passage has been a controversial one for translators and scholars, interpreted in widely differing ways, specifically with regard to the word *ealuscerwen*. A discussion of these differing arguments can be found in Fulk et al., *Klaeber's Beowulf*, 126–127. The translation used here follows Foys, "A Sensual Philology for Anglo-Saxon England," 462.
[36] Fiona Newell and Ladan Shams, "New Insights into Multisensory Perception," *Perception* 36 (2007): 1415–1417.
[37] Robyn Kim, Megan A. K. Peters, and Ladan Shams, "0 + 1 > 1: How Adding Noninformative Sound Improves Performance on a Visual Task," *Psychological Science* 23 (2012): 6–12.

Figure 2: Disc brooch, gilt copper alloy with enamel inlay, seventh century, Oxfordshire. Collection: Ashmolean Museum, Oxford, AN1992.162. Reproduced courtesy of the Ashmolean Museum, University of Oxford.

hatch marks cut into it, alternating between the inner and outer rings: these marks, cut into the metal with such deliberate alternation, evoke a sense of percussion in the design. Next comes a narrow band, raised and flattened, inset with contrasting material, likely niello. We might say that it offers a dark counterpoint to the brightness and pattern of the bands on either side. The penultimate band is the widest; it bears a ring of repoussé ribbons each striped with two grooves. These ribbons twist together, with no visible starting or ending point, to form an infinite serpentine pattern endlessly circling the brooch in harmony. Finally, the outermost band is a smooth edge revealing the coppery color of bronze in contrast to the bright yellow of the gilt that covers the rest of the brooch. As the eye moves from band to band around the brooch, the tones and syncopation change, offering rhythm, cadence, and harmony.

The late sixth to early seventh-century gold shoulder clasps (Plate Va) found in Mound 1 at Sutton Hoo – each one formed from two nearly identical halves and joined with a pin – display a very different decorative program. The rectangular portion of each clasp has a central panel with a regular pattern of alternating stepped lozenges made of garnet and millefiori set against a garnet cloisonné ground. The different, alternating colors of these panels act like staccato notes. The tonal quality of the coloration may be likened to auditory tones, bright gold contrasting with rich reds and a checkerboard pattern of deep blues. Surrounding the panel is a frame of gold with a frieze of interlaced garnet serpents with blue glass eyes. This serpentine border has an undeniable rhythm to it, twisting and looping at longer or shorter intervals. Each of the multiple patterns in this ornamentation follows its own rhythm but remains in harmony with the other iconographic fields on the object. Another auditory aspect may perhaps be found in the recognizable zoomorphs: the borders with their snakes, and the curved ends of the clasps, which depict two bisected boars with gold filigree zoomorphs between their legs. Above and beyond their role in the overall graphic noise of the scheme, these animals might evoke the sounds they make in nature.

Given the absence of textual sources from the period, it is impossible to state unequivocally that an Anglo-Saxon viewer would have found an aural quality and sense of musicality in the decoration of these objects. However, recent art historical work on the Bayeux Tapestry – an Anglo-Saxon artwork, albeit one made several centuries after the metal artifacts under consideration – has argued that a kind of graphic synesthesia can be read in the iconography. Richard Brilliant explores how the auditory violence of battle, as depicted on the tapestry, is visually evoked not only through images of figures and actions that might have made noise, but also through compositional choices that create a jagged sensation of cacophony.[38] As different as the tapestries are from the metal artifacts considered here, it is possible that a similar interpretation of compositional choices can be applied to the earlier Anglo-Saxon iconography found on the metalwork. In both cases the question remains: would this synesthetic experience have been intentional, and, if so, would it have been recognized and appreciated by Anglo-Saxons? The adept weaving of sound into Anglo-Saxon literature suggests an understanding of the complexity of aural sensation, and the sensory manipulation evident in both the literature and the art makes it plausible, though not provable, that there was a deliberate intent to create a multisensory experience.

Another sense inextricably engaged in the original experience of Anglo-Saxon metalwork is that of touch. In the medieval hierarchy of the senses, touch was considered the lowest and basest sense, disdained for its bestial carnality.[39] Yet, as Mark Paterson

---

[38] Richard Brilliant, "Making Sounds Visible in the Bayeux Tapestry," in *The Bayeux Tapestry: New Interpretations*, ed. Martin K. Foys, Karen Eileen Overbey, and Dan Terkla (Woodbridge, UK: Boydell Press, 2009), 71–84, at 76–78.

[39] Mark Paterson, *The Senses of Touch: Haptics, Affects and Technologies* (Oxford: Berg, 2007), 1.

so clearly points out, the sense of touch is inseparable from embodied existence.[40] The pieces of Anglo-Saxon jewelry examined here were for the most part functional items, used to secure garments and accessories; as such, they would have been handled regularly when they were fastened and unfastened. The repeated cutaneous contact would lead an Anglo-Saxon to become very familiar with the tactile qualities of his or her jewelry: the physical weight and texture of the material, its temperature before and after extended wear, and the surface variations created by the patterns of ornamentation. By extension, an Anglo-Saxon would recognize the tactile qualities of similar objects owned by others. This is not to suggest that Anglo-Saxons would have had the freedom to access or closely examine another individual's personal ornament, but rather that knowledge of their own jewelry would have given them a sense of familiarity with the physical presence of other contemporaneous pieces.

This suggests that even in the absence of touch, vision can still offer an impression of the tactile nature of an object; put another way, there is a tactile aspect to the visual perception of an object's materiality and iconography. A mid- to late seventh-century disc pendant (Plate Vb) can stand as an exemplar of the tactile experience of early Anglo-Saxon metalwork. This object is part of a well-established group of filigree-ornamented disc pendants, usually bearing a cross shape, that proliferated in the second half of the seventh century.[41] Its design is relatively spare compared to the aesthetic complexity of much early Anglo-Saxon iconography, but notable amongst its type for its use of polychrome and its poorly executed cloisonné.[42]

Despite the paucity of decoration, there are myriad tactile experiences to be found within it. The round sheet of polished gold from which the pendant is made carries an even shine and would be smooth to the touch. The rough but regular texture of the filigree borders at the edge of the disc and the central cross is clearly evident, and would have been recognizable to most Anglo-Saxons, as filigree was a very common decorative convention. Anyone familiar with metal would know that the pendant would be cold to the touch until warmed by a body or other external heat source. The glossy, flat garnets on the arms of the cross and the slick, rounded glass of the central boss differ from the metal components in texture, as well as having different reactions to temperature: being less conductive of heat, the garnet and glass retain coolness even as the surrounding metal warms up. All of these tactile qualities would be sensed if physical contact could be made with the pendant. But even absent actual touch, they could still be noted and perceived visually.

---

40 Paterson, *The Senses of Touch*, 1–2.
41 Helen Geake, *The Use of Grave-Goods in Conversion-Period England, c.600–c.850* (Oxford: British Archaeological Reports, 1997), 38.
42 Christopher Scull, *Early Medieval (Late 5th–Early 8th Centuries AD) Cemeteries at Boss Hall and Buttermarket, Ipswich, Suffolk*, Society for Medieval Archaeology Monograph 27 (Leeds: Society for Medieval Archaeology, 2009), 100.

Given the dominant role that vision plays in gathering sensory information and the assistance that sight can provide to other senses, might it be plausible that sight can allude to or mimic the perception of other senses that are not being directly stimulated? When early Anglo-Saxon metalwork is considered in this light, it is conceivable that the complex visual elements were intended, above and beyond their dominant ocular effect, to allude to other senses. Perhaps modern thought is too eager to draw firm divisions between the different senses; perhaps they were not considered to be singular and disparate in earlier historical periods, but in the medieval mind were instead combined at times.[43] Smell can affect taste, and sound can be physically felt; thus, within the medieval sensorium, sight might perhaps inform all the other senses.[44] Recent scholarship has begun to approach visual representations of music – such as musical notations or images of music making – not as mere artifacts of performance but rather as deliberate visual evocations of auditory experience.[45] Vision, through imagery strongly associated with sense memories, can recall past sensory experiences and map them onto the perception of an object that is seen but not experienced through the other senses.[46] While these echoes of disparate sensory perceptions are in no way equivalent to actual sensory experience, the role that vision plays in supplementing and even evoking the other senses is significant.[47] Returning to the metalwork, the contemporary experience would without question have been predominantly visual; however, it could also be a synesthetic encounter, in which sight embeds suggestions of sound and touch.

These physical objects, imbued with their materiality and multisensory experience, offer a link between modern scholarship and the historical period that produced them. Materially, the objects remain much the same as they were in their own time – rarely pristine but often recoverable or reconstructible. Nevertheless, as modern viewers of historical artifacts, we encounter the objects in a dramatically different way than audiences of the original time did. Technological advances and curatorial practice serve to distance a modern viewer from the artifact, yet at the same time make it more accessible in many ways than it would have been in its own day.

One of the most dramatically effective modern-day aids to viewing Anglo-Saxon metalwork has been the use of high-resolution digital photography, which allows the image of an object to be enlarged many times in order to examine its diminutive

---

43 Foys, "A Sensual Philology for Anglo-Saxon England," 463.
44 Leigh Eric Schmidt, "Hearing Loss," in *The Auditory Culture Reader*, ed. Michael Bull and Les Back, Sensory Formations Series (Oxford: Berg, 2006), 42–59, at 52.
45 This is a tremendous oversimplification of nuanced and complex scholarship relating to the experience of sound and music. For further reading, see Emma Dillon, *Medieval Music-Making and the Roman de Fauvel* (Cambridge Cambridge University Press, 2002), 45–46; Beth Williamson, "Sensory Experience in Medieval Devotion: Sound and Vision, Invisibility and Silence," *Speculum* 88 (2013): 1–43; and Jesse Rodin's contribution to this volume.
46 Stokes and Biggs, "The Dominance of the Visual," 360.
47 Stokes and Biggs, "The Dominance of the Visual," 373–374.

details with perfect clarity. These images are often made accessible to the public so that a much wider modern audience can engage with, if not experience, the artifact. We possess a greater ability to manipulate light, both when photographing and, to a lesser degree, in the actual display of an object. The use of diffuse or well-directed light can minimize the glare from reflective objects such as Anglo-Saxon metalwork, allowing the decorative program to be more clearly and completely seen. Another advance in modern technology is the use of other forms of imaging, such as X-rays and computer or artist's renderings, to clarify aspects of construction or ornamentation that time or damage have made less legible. In addition to these advances in clarity of viewing, modern access to these artifacts, whether in person or through photography, offers the opportunity to take time with the object: we have extensive or even limitless time to closely observe all the small details and nuances of construction, material, and iconographic decoration.

With so much gained through modern technological advances, what has been lost? Does a modern viewer "see" what an Anglo-Saxon viewer "saw"? Modern curatorial practice in galleries and museums gives primacy to sight and isolates artifacts from all human contact, encasing them in glass-fronted displays and demanding that gloves be worn on the rare occasions when they are allowed to be handled.[48] This is by no means a castigation of such practices, which are intended to preserve and maintain the integrity of these delicate and valuable objects; nonetheless, they severely limit one's experience of the physical item. Even this shred of physicality is lost when the artifact is accessed through photography alone. Thus modern viewers are denied sensory engagement with the object's physical presence. Jonathan Wilcox wrestles with this issue for medieval manuscripts, which, like early medieval artwork, are currently being digitized and disseminated to a wide audience.[49] His remedy for reclaiming the sensory experience of the book's material is to reengage with the physical craft that went into making it.[50] Such a process could be possible, to some degree, with early Anglo-Saxon metalwork. But, absent a detailed knowledge of the practice of goldsmithing, an understanding of the sensory experience of the objects might be better achieved through the admittedly speculative process of reconstruction.[51]

In her chapter in this volume, Valerie Garver illustrates how archaeological evidence, tangential textual sources, and modern experimentation can be

---

[48] Jonathan Crary, *Techniques of the Observer: On Vision and Modernity in the Nineteenth Century* (Cambridge, MA: MIT Press, 1992), esp. 16.
[49] Jonathan Wilcox, "The Sensory Cost of Remediation; Or, Sniffing in the Gutter of Anglo-Saxon Manuscripts," in *Sensory Perception in the Medieval West*, ed. Michael D. J. Bintley and Simon C. Thomson, Utrecht Studies in Medieval Literacy 34 (Turnhout: Brepols, 2016), 27–52.
[50] Wilcox, "The Sensory Cost of Remediation," 40–51.
[51] Toward the aim of reengagement, a comprehensive discussion of the craft of the Anglo-Saxon goldsmith can be found in Elizabeth Coatsworth and Michael Pinder, *The Art of the Anglo-Saxon Goldsmith: Fine Metalwork in Anglo-Saxon England: Its Practice and Practitioners*, Anglo-Saxon Studies (Woodbridge, England: Boydell Press, 2002).

used to approximate an unrecorded medieval activity (and its associated sensory experience).[52] Similar methodology, although with significantly fewer evidentiary resources, can be used to reconstruct an idea of early Anglo-Saxon life and the experience of engaging with metalwork in its original context. Such imaginative forays can prove to be surprisingly valuable to scholarly research into past societies. Re-creating possible historical scenes based on material and/or fragmentary textual evidence is similar to the practice of experimental archaeology, which makes use of accepted archaeological and historical evidence to replicate past cultural practices in order to test theories and hypotheses about that culture.[53] In the process of proving or disproving the original thesis, these experiments provide a wealth of information about the materials, means, and customs used by the historical society under consideration.[54] Re-creations, even imaginary ones, that are grounded in valid evidence can provide some modern access to the experiences of historical cultures, like the early Anglo-Saxons, and their interactions with the surviving objects of their workmanship, like ornamented jewelry.

First a location must be pictured – for example, an Anglo-Saxon feasting hall, the gathering place in which a community was entertained. Archaeological excavation has uncovered the remains of several buildings that are likely great halls, such as the one identified at Yeavering, thought to be an early Anglo-Saxon royal site, and the smaller feasting hall discovered recently at Lyminge in Kent.[55] Descriptions of feasting halls and the behaviors engaged in within them can be found with some frequency in Old English poetry, particularly those poems thought to preserve variations of earlier compositions. In addition to the passage from *Fortunes of Men* discussed earlier, the great hall in *Beowulf* is described in rhapsodizing terms, using epithets like "the timbered hall, stately and decorated with gold."[56] All of this evidence intimates that the Anglo-Saxon great hall was a large timbered building filled with benches and tables for the gathered people, likely lit by firelight and torches and a little hazy from the smoke, and filled with sounds of festivity: drinking, merrymaking, conversation, and singing by the resident scop. Into this context a metal artifact, like the Sarre brooch discussed earlier (Plate IV), can be inserted, worn by one of the people in the hall.

---

52 See Valerie Garver's chapter in this volume.
53 James R. Mathieu, ed., *Experimental Archaeology: Replicating Past Objects, Behaviors, and Processes*, BAR International Series 1035 (Oxford: Archaeopress, 2002), 12.
54 Alan K. Outram, "Introduction to Experimental Archaeology," *World Archaeology* 40 (2008): 1–6, at 1–3.
55 Brian Hope-Taylor, *Yeavering: An Anglo-British Centre of Early Northumbria*, Department of the Environment Archaeological Reports 7 (London: Crown, 1977); Gabor Thomas and Alexandra Knox, "Lyminge Excavations 2013: Interim Report on the University of Reading Excavations at Lyminge, Kent," Lyminge Archaeological Project (Reading: University of Reading, 2013); Alexandra Knox, "Discovering an Anglo-Saxon Royal Hall: Harnessing Community Archaeology at Lyminge," *Current Archaeology* 284 (2013): 20–25.
56 *Beowulf*, lines 307b–311. Fulk et al., *Klaeber's Beowulf*, 12–13.

The Sarre brooch was excavated from a woman's grave, where it had been interred as part of her burial attire.[57] The large circular brooch would have been one of a number worn to keep her clothes fastened; but, given its size and ornamentation, it would have been displayed prominently.[58] Drawing upon the assorted evidence, we can imagine the brooch, now undamaged and gleaming with fresh gilding and bright cloisonné, on a woman in the feasting hall. It sits among layers of cloth, fastening her dress shut at chest level. Other flashing jewelry glitters at the wearer's wrists and neck. The surface of the brooch catches the flickering firelight, and the smoke and dimness make it difficult to see the piece from a distance. At the same time, the woman is moving to pour more drinks and chatting to her companions while the scop sings a saga in the corner. There is no opportunity to fully observe the brooch, as the line of sight is continually being interrupted by moving fabric, reflected light, and bodily position, due to the crowds enjoying the festivities in the hall, leaving the viewer with only fleeting impressions of the decoration. Obviously this imagined encounter is not a replacement for contemporaneous accounts; however, it offers a means, grounded in personal sensory experience and what little knowledge of the original context survives, by which to reclaim the sensory experience of a viewer of the period engaging with the object.[59]

While modern examination allows for undistracted, unobstructed views and time to scrutinize an artifact, this imagined encounter offered anything but. There is no evidence in either the archaeological or literary record indicating that early Anglo-Saxons had cultural conventions that encouraged or even allowed close viewing of personal ornament – for example, admiring a brooch or pendant. However, there is no evidence to the contrary either, and it is certainly possible that these intricately decorated objects were much admired. Nonetheless, an early Anglo-Saxon encounter would always be impacted by factors such as time, sensory distractions (including competing jewelry), and visual obstructions. It seems unlikely that a viewer of the time would have been able to properly process and appreciate the iconography. But did the objects need clear and close viewing in order to be visually perceived and interpreted? Returning to the coast guard, who was so sure of Beowulf's prowess and nobility due to the quantity and quality of his armament, it must be asked what he could really see and know of the Geats apart from their shining metal.

Many of the early Anglo-Saxon objects embellished by intricate, minute ornamentation are small in scale and personal in function, such as brooches, buckles, clasps, pendants, and sword or dagger pommels. For example, a set of late sixth- or seventh-century gold miniature buckles found at King's Field in Kent (Figure 3) each measure just 3.15 cm tall and 2.2 cm wide. Small, though by no means the smallest, even in the corpus of early Anglo-Saxon England, these tiny buckles were likely used

---

57 Webster et al., *The Making of England*, 48, cat. no. 31a.
58 Owen-Crocker, *Dress in Anglo-Saxon England*, 138–139.
59 Stokes and Biggs, "The Dominance of the Visual," 360.

Figure 3: Miniature buckles, gold with filigree, sixth or seventh century, Faversham, Kent. Collection: The British Museum, London, .1094.'70 and .1094.a.'70. Photograph copyright the Trustees of the British Museum.

to fasten garters.[60] Despite the buckles' reduced size, the decorative program is no less intricate and deftly executed than it is on larger pieces. Each buckle shows two pairs of linked and confronting predatory bird heads with curved beaks, surrounding a rectangular central panel filled with interlacing snakes. The base of each buckle is a gold foil openwork plate, utilizing repoussé for the iconographic pattern, while an extensive filigree decoration variegates the texture from plain to beaded.

Given the intricacy of the design and the small scale of the buckles, it must be asked: who would or could have seen them? The display of such items, while an integral part of personal identity and identification, was indelibly tied to their placement on the body (in the case of jewelry) or their close possession (in the case of armament). This suggests that the only people given access to closely observe the exquisite iconographic programs of the metalwork would have been the object's craftsman and its owner. However, it seems excessive and impractical for such precise and elaborate decoration – whether it appears on expensive high-status items or on less costly, arguably lower-status objects – to be only intended for an audience of one.

While unfettered visual access to the artifact is a luxury that modern viewers enjoy, it is by no means a necessity in order to unravel the iconographic program ornamenting the object. As discussed earlier, there is a formulaic component to most of the iconography of early Anglo-Saxon metalwork, with which viewers of the time would likely have been familiar and capable of deciphering. Human visual acuity is predicated on our brains' ability to recognize visual objects quickly and accurately

---

[60] Susan Youngs et al., *"The Work of Angels": Masterpieces of Celtic Metalwork, 6th–9th Centuries AD* (London: British Museum Publications, 1989), 57, cat. no. 43.

despite the vagaries of altered appearance and context.[61] This means that recognition is not based solely on a clear and complete view of what is being seen but rather informed by a series of rapid guesses about the object's "identity" and its relationship to the context in which it appears.[62] Furthermore, human perception is able to ascertain meaning from what it sees even when the view is fragmented, transitory, or fleeting.[63] This suggests that for the Anglo-Saxon viewer, the sustained and unobstructed viewing of a piece of ornamented metalwork was not necessary in order to perceive and understand the iconography. Instead, it seems plausible that an Anglo-Saxon viewer well versed in the iconographic and aesthetic conventions of the time could observe a multitude of informational cues from viewing a piece of ornamented metalwork, noting geometric or zoomorphic patterns, colors and reflectivity, and perhaps the complex synesthetic experiences created by the iconography of the ornament.

It has become evident in both the surviving material culture and poetry that the Anglo-Saxon understanding of the senses is both complex and nuanced, often creating an intertwining of sensory perception, a kind of deliberate synesthesia. Further, there seems to have been a willingness and ability to manipulate the sensory experience of an audience for effect. Whether demonstrated in the performance of a poem like *Fortunes of Men*, which offers multiple iterations of auditory experience through content and delivery, or in the multisensory materiality of the ornamented metalwork, the early Anglo-Saxons seem to show insight into the interrelationship between different senses and how such interplay can enhance an experience. Although such interpretations of Anglo-Saxon culture are, to some degree, speculative, they can offer an opportunity to rethink accepted information about the period and open new opportunities for evaluation and dialogue.

---

61 Mark J. Fenske et al., "Top-down Facilitation of Visual Object Recognition: Object-Based and Context-Based Contributions," in *Visual Perception Part 2: Fundamentals of Awareness, Multi-Sensory Integration and High-Order Perception*, ed. Susana Martinez-Conde et al. (Amsterdam: Elsevier, 2006), 3–21, at 3.
62 Fenske et al., "Top-down Facilitation," 16.
63 Aude Oliva and Antonio Torralba, "Building the Gist of a Scene: The Role of Global Image Features in Recognition," in *Visual Perception Part 2*, ed. Martinez-Conde et al., 22–36, at 22–23.

Patricia Blessing

5 The Vessel as Garden: The "Alhambra Vases" and Sensory Perception in Nasrid Architecture

A poem from the Hall of the Abencerrajes, a major structure within the Alhambra, offers the opportunity to observe the poetic devices that are at play within the palace complex of the Nasrid rulers of Granada. Like other poems found in the epigraphy of the Alhambra, this text is attributed to court poet Ibn Zamrak (d. 1393), a major literary figure at the Nasrid court in the second half of the fourteenth century. The poem serves the purpose of giving voice to the monument. Its author created a first-person speaker – the building – to establish comparisons between the specific part of the monument in question, certain objects held within it, and the architecture of the palace as a whole. The poem exalts the monument's beauty and, toward the end, in a seeming afterthought that is in fact central to both text and building, glorifies the patron:

1. The Imam Muhammad inherited the same grandeur
   inna l-imāma Muḥammadin waritha l-'ūlā
   as his father, our lord Abu-l-Hajjaj
   k-abīhu mawlānā Abī-l-Ḥajjāj
2. Behold the vase standing at its door
   fa-unẓur ilā l-ibrīqi qāma bi-bābihi
   surrounded by me with adornments like brocade
   fa-ḥafaftu bil-washī kal-dībāj
3. There, sitting on a throne, it will seem
   wa-qad i'talā l-kursī taḥsibu annahu
   as a valiant sultan, sitting on his throne
   sulṭanun fārisun qā'idan bil-tāj.[1]

Note: For suggestions on this chapter, I thank the editors Fiona Griffiths and Kathryn Starkey, Beatrice E. Kitzinger, all participants of the Sensory Reflections workshop at Stanford University in October 2016, Anja Heidenreich, Rikard Nordström, and Bissera V. Pentcheva. I am grateful to Cristina Partearroyo Lacaba at the Instituto Valencia de Don Juan in Madrid and Moya Carey at the Victoria and Albert Museum in London for granting me access to objects relevant to this study. For research support, I thank the Society of Architectural Historians and the Gerda Henkel Stiftung.

---

1 José Miguel Puerta Vílchez, *Reading the Alhambra: A Visual Guide to the Alhambra through Its Inscriptions* (Granada: Patronato de la Alhambra y Generalife, 2011), 174. Unless otherwise noted, all transliterations are mine, following the Arabic printed text published by Puerta Vílchez. Translations follow Puerta Vílchez, with some modifications.

Taking this poem as a starting point, I will propose a discussion of the so-called Alhambra Vases: large-scale luster-ceramic vessels, some of which carry poetic inscriptions akin to those on the building. Through these inscriptions, a close connection is formed between the monument, the vases, and the visitor who has been invited into the multisensory space of the Alhambra. Thus the vases offer a concrete starting point from which to discuss the sensory experience of this monument and – short of a reenactment of poetry readings within the space – provide inroads into understanding the building's immersive nature.[2] Overall, the Alhambra Vases and the architectural decoration of the palace are closely intertwined. This is true not only of the objects that bear inscriptions and the sections of poetic text in the Alhambra, but also of the vegetal and geometric motifs that appear in textiles, in the monumental decoration, and on at least some of the vases.[3] Thus, imagining a reconstruction of the palaces with the objects in place – vases in niches, curtains and wall hangings over openings and along walls – we can begin to understand the level of intense sensory effects at work in the Alhambra.[4]

In the rich haptic and aural space created, objects such as the so-called Alhambra Vases and various types of textiles were integral. Aurally, the sound of water running through the monument's myriad fountains and the rustle of curtains suspended in doorways, niches, and windows would have become part of this multisensory landscape.[5] The haptic aspects of architecture – according to Juhanni Pallasmaa, the ways in which touch can influence human perception of space – are central in the Alhambra, with its multiple surfaces of different textures: sleek tiles, deep reliefs in stucco, polished marble.[6] While some of these surfaces lie within reach of human hands, along with ephemeral, movable objects such as vases and curtains, others are too far away to touch and remain in the realm of desire. This tension is part and parcel of the artifice established in the Alhambra, a combination of accessible haptic space and evoked desire for the surfaces far above, such as the *muqarnas* dome of the Hall of the Abencerrajes. The notion of artifice – that is, the purposeful creation of highly sophisticated and carefully orchestrated spaces in which nothing has been left to accident – is crucial in order to understand the Alhambra as a multisensory space, and the poetic epigraphy of the monument is an integral part of this design

---

2 See the discussion of reenactments in the introduction to this volume, 10–15.
3 On textiles and architectural decoration, see Purificación Marinetto Sánchez, "El uso del tejido y su decoración en los palacios de la Alhambra," in *A la luz de la seda: Catálogo de la colección de tejidos nazaríes del Museo Lázaro Galdiano y el Museo de la Alhambra; Orígenes y pervivencia* (Alcobendas: TF, 2012), 19–31.
4 With its focus on the vases, this chapter is a first step in what I hope will become a more in-depth exploration of the materiality and sensory world of the Alhambra, and of medieval Islamic architecture in the Mediterranean.
5 José Miguel Puerta Vílchez, *La poética del agua en el Islam / The Poetics of Water in Islam* (Sabarís, Baiona Pontevedra: Trea, 2011).
6 Juhanni Pallasmaa, *The Eyes of the Skin: Architecture and the Senses* (Chichester: Wiley-Academy, 2005).

process. Throughout the palace complex, poetic inscriptions present the monument as a first-person narrator. These poems add layers of perception to the monument: in addition to seeing the decoration, the beholder can also potentially engage with the building through the poetry. Indeed, these and similar texts were not only inscribed on the walls of the Alhambra but might potentially have been recited during court ceremonials (as certain other poems were).[7] In many instances, the poems are written in such a way as to steer the visitor's perception of the structure, highlighting certain elements or suggesting comparisons and metaphors. In this sense, the poetic inscriptions are essential for the activation of the multisensory space.

Scholarship on the Alhambra is extensive, but so far has only marginally addressed modes of sensory experience beyond vision. Thus, Olga Bush has considered how the visual overload created in the architectural decoration of the Alhambra was combined with poetic descriptions – some inscribed onto walls, others recited at royal ceremonies – in order to impress the beholder.[8] Yet even though poetry and textiles are central to Bush's insightful study, she does not examine aural and tactile properties. Similarly, focusing on the Mirador de Lindaraja, a small belvedere within the complex of the Alhambra, D. Fairchild Ruggles has emphasized the presence of poetic inscriptions, representations of Nasrid power, and their relationship to the visually overwhelming architectural decoration.[9] Still, the experience of the Alhambra described in these studies remains a visual one, focusing on the eye of the beholder.[10] Cynthia Robinson has suggested that interpretations need to be revisited in light of deeper understandings of aesthetics and philosophy based on studies of Nasrid poetry.[11] José Miguel Puerta Vílchez has opened new avenues by discussing the Alhambra's poetic epigraphy in relation to notions of aesthetics in Arabic thought and language.[12]

The presence of the haptic and the aural in the Alhambra's inscriptions and objects needs to be considered in order to reach an understanding of the space as a

---

[7] Emilio García Gómez, *Foco de antigua luz sobre la Alhambra: Desde un texto de Ibn al-Jaṭīb en 1362* (Madrid: Instituto Egipcio de Estudios Islámicos en Madrid, 1988); Olga Bush, "Architecture, Poetic Texts and Textile in the Alhambra" (PhD dissertation, New York University, 2006), 331–342. I was not able to consult the recent book by Olga Bush, *Reframing the Alhambra: Architecture, Poetry, Textiles and Court Ceremonial* (Edinburgh: Edinburgh University Press, 2018), published after this chapter was completed.
[8] Bush, "Architecture, Poetic Texts and Textile in the Alhambra."
[9] D. Fairchild Ruggles, "The Eye of Sovereignty: Poetry and Vision in the Alhambra's Lindaraja Mirador," *Gesta* 36 (1997): 180–189.
[10] Bush, "Architecture, Poetic Texts and Textile in the Alhambra"; Olga Bush, "'When My Beholder Ponders': Poetic Epigraphy in the Alhambra," *Artibus Asiae* 66 (2006): 55–67.
[11] Cynthia Robinson, "Marginal Ornament: Poetics, Mimesis, and Devotion in the Palace of the Lions," *Muqarnas* 25 (2008): 185–214.
[12] José Miguel Puerta Vílchez, "Speaking Architecture: Poetry and Aesthetics in the Alhambra Palace," in *Calligraphy and Architecture in the Muslim World*, ed. Mohammad Gharipour and Irvin Cemil Schick (Edinburgh: Edinburgh University Press, 2013), 29–45.

product of artifice, rife with different media that are geared toward the creation of an immersive experience. The space engages the senses not only through fixed structures, but also carefully designed portable elements. The poetry so insistently refers to such elements, including water, garden, and textile metaphors, that it amounts to a set of instructions in how to read the space and become absorbed in its artifice. These poetic texts comment on the monument's beauty in metaphorical terms – for instance, in repeated comparisons between the building and a bride in her finery. Such metaphors appear in several instances, including in the second verse of a poem inscribed on the frame of a niche on the left-hand side of the entrance to the Comares Hall:

1. I resemble a nuptial throne, or even exceed it,
   wa-ḥakaytu kursīya l-'arūsi wa-zidtuhu
2. and I assure the happiness of bride and groom
   annī ḍamintu sa'ādata l-azwāji.[13]

Despite the rich record of multisensory engagement that appears in these poems, we do not have texts that comment on these features of the Alhambra and their effects from the point of view of a medieval visitor. Only the mid-fourteenth-century account of Ibn al-Khatib, describing royal celebrations, provides an occasional glimpse of the palace's and court's splendor, although in rather general terms.[14] Thus, Valérie Gonzalez's attempt to understand the immersive experience of the Comares Tower within the Alhambra in comparison to a work by current-day artist James Turrell, as problematic as it may be from the point of view of historical context, offers reflections about aesthetic experiences in the absence of relevant statements in primary sources.[15]

In this chapter, I investigate how the Alhambra Vases fit into the framework of the fourteenth-century Nasrid palace, a space carefully crafted to entice the senses at various levels.[16] While it is not verifiable that most of these large-scale vases (most complete examples are about 120 to 135 cm tall; see Table 1) were used in the Alhambra itself, they clearly engage with the aesthetic proposed by the palace. Those vases with poems inscribed on them most closely correspond to these aesthetic principles. Here I insert the surviving pieces into the premises of multisensory space established at the Alhambra, a space that includes vision, hearing, and touch. The inscriptions provoke a visual engagement with the complex ornament and the luster of the glaze on the vases, but also invoke the haptic potential of textile motifs and metal sheen, calling attention

---

13 Puerta Vílchez, *Reading the Alhambra*, 120.
14 Commentary in García Gómez, *Foco de antigua luz sobre la Alhambra*. For the Arabic text and Spanish translation, see García Gómez, 123–169.
15 Valérie Gonzalez, "The Comares Hall in the Alhambra and James Turrell's Space That Sees: A Comparison of Aesthetic Phenomenology," *Muqarnas* 20 (2003): 253–278.
16 Other furnishings would also need to be considered, although furniture belonging to the Alhambra has yet to be identified, if indeed it has been preserved.

Table 1: Overview of extant vases and large fragments

Name	Museum; inventory number	Provenance	Height	Color	Date
Simonetti Vase	Museo Nacional de Arte Hispanomusulman, Granada	Attilio Simonetti, Rome; Fortuny; bought by the Spanish government in 1934.	121cm	glaze damaged	eary 14th c
Gazelle Vase	Museo Nacional de Arte Hispanomusulman, Granada, inv. no. 290	Presumed to have been produced for the site.	136cm	blue	14th or 15th c. [Al-Andalus, cat. 112]
Osma Vase	Instituto Valencia de Don Juan, Madrid	From mid-nineteenth-century excavation at Mazara del Vallo, Sicily; Count Burgio di Villafiorita; called Burgio Vase by Van de Put, and there noted as recorded by Michele Amari in 1872	120cm	gold	c. 1333–54
Jerez Vase	Museo Arquelogico Nacional, Madrid, inv. no. 1930/67	Excavation in monastery of Santa Maria de la Defension near Jerez de la Frontera; found in 1927; in the museum since 1930	126cm	gold	c. 1354–91
Hornos Vase	Museo Arquelogico Nacional, Madrid, inv. no. 50419	Found in Jaen	135cm	blue	c. 1333–54
	Galleria Regionale della Sicilia, Palermo, inv. no. 5229	From excavation at Mazara del Vallo, Sicily; then sacristy of the church of Our Lady of Paradise in Mazara, in museum since 1880s	128cm	gold	late 13th c, [Al-Andalus, cat. 110]
Fortuny Vase or Salar Vase	State Hermitage Museum, St. Petersburg, inv. no. F-317	From El Salar, Andalusia; Collection Fortuny since 1871; Fortuny sale 1875, n. 42; Collection Prince Basilevsky; Hermitage since 1885	117cm	gold	early 14th c. [Al-Andalus, cat. 111]
	Nationalmuseum Stockholm, inv. no. NMK 47	part of the so-called Prague booty of 1648 when the Swedes occupied Prague at the end of the Thirty Years War.	125cm	gold	c. 1333–54

Table 1 (Continued)

Name	Museum; inventory number	Provenance	Height	Color	Date
Freer Vase	Freer Gallery of Art, Washington, DC, inv. no. F1903.206a-b	Mariano Fortuny bought the Freer Vase from a tavern in Granada; sold with Fortuny collection in 1875; C. Stein sale, Paris, May 1886; bought by Charles Davis of London for Freer collection in 1903; gift of Charles Lang Freer	H: 77.2cm W: 68.2cm	blue	c. 1354–91
	Museum of Islamic Art, Cairo, inv. no. 25777	Gift Bank Nasr, 1983, see: Bernard O'Kane, ed. *The Treasures of Islamic Art in the Museums of Cairo*. Cairo and New York: American University in Cairo Press, 2006, cat. 254.	82cm	blue	Late 14th c.
Berlin fragment	Museum für islamische Kunst, Berlin, inv. no. 1900.113		58cm	blue	c. 1354–91
Heilbronner Vase	No longer extant	J. Seligmann sale 1925, sold to Spaniard, destroyed in fire in customs storage at Irun in 1936	123cm	gold	c. 1333–54
Neck	Hispanic Society of America, New York, inv. no. E576		43cm	blue	c. 1375–1400

to the vases' semblance of precious materials. Thus the vases are both small pieces in the *Gesamtkunstwerk* of the Alhambra and *pars pro toto*, in that they mirror the sensory devices employed in the monument. Within the Alhambra, sight, sound – that which is implied in poetic inscriptions (with the option of recitation) as well as that of the water in the fountains – and the haptic potential of architectural decoration all together form a sensory space that is at once closely tied to the architecture itself and beyond physical presence. Thus, a discussion of the vases can provide insights into the ways in which the space operated at the level of artifice, beyond the architecture itself.

As Elizabeth Dospěl Williams points out in her study of jewelry from the late antique eastern Mediterranean in this volume, reactions to the visual, aural, and olfactory properties of objects often need to be retrieved from references that appear few and far between in late antique and medieval sources.[17] In the case of the Alhambra,

---

17 See the chapter by Dospěl Williams in this volume.

the poetry inscribed on the monument should perhaps be viewed as such a source; this is the approach that I propose in analyzing the poem on one of the vases as it relates to the texts on the building. First, I will introduce the Alhambra Vases and the discussion of their provenance and dates. Then, I will turn to the so-called Freer Vase as a case study, in order to propose an analysis of the ways in which poetic epigraphy, used in a range of materials, becomes a means to construct and understand a multisensory space.

Introducing the Alhambra Vases

The set of known Alhambra Vases comprises a substantial number of pieces. As shown in Table 1, nine nearly complete vases and three large fragments have survived. While detailed studies of their material and formal qualities exist, the vases have yet to be fully understood within the dialogue of multisensory perception that is established in the Alhambra. Following an overview of the extant vases and their background, this chapter will seek insights into the ways in which these pieces were an essential part of the monument's proclivity for artifice.

The connection of these large ceramic vessels to the Alhambra is not necessarily straightforward. Several vases are mentioned as being located on-site in sources from the seventeenth and eighteenth centuries, but these pieces have, for the most part, not been preserved.[18] Two of these vases were depicted in *Antigüedades árabes de España* in 1804.[19] One of the two is the so-called Gazelle Vase preserved in the Museo Nacional de Arte Hispanomusulman at the Alhambra (Plate VI).[20] The second has been lost.[21] Hence the Gazelle Vase, combined with seventeenth- to nineteenth-century sources indicating the presence of other such vases on-site, provides the strongest connection between the objects and the Alhambra.

---

18 José Ferrandis Torres, "Los vasos de la Alhambra," *Boletín de la Sociedad Española de Excursiones: Arte, Arqueología, Historia* 33 (1925): 73–75, with relevant sources.
19 Digital images of the publication are available online, courtesy of the Biblioteca del Patronato de la Alhambra y Generalife, http://www.alhambra-patronato.es/ria/handle/10514/6006 (accessed 8 January 2017)
20 Jerrilyn D. Dodds, ed., *Al-Andalus: The Art of Islamic Spain* (New York: Metropolitan Museum of Art, 1992), 358–359, cat. no. 112; Ferrandis Torres, "Los vasos de la Alhambra," 74; A. Van de Put, "On a Missing Alhambra Vase, and the Ornament of the Vase Series," *Archaeologica* 92 (1947): 44. Van de Put indicates 1777–1792 as the date of publication for *Antigüedades árabes de España*. The library record of the Biblioteca de la Alhambra y Generalife indicates 1780–1804: see http://www.alhambra-patronato.es/ria/handle/10514/6006 (accessed 8 January 2017).
21 Ferrandis Torres, "Los vasos de la Alhambra," 74 and plate 9, reproducing the image from the 1804 publication. Van de Put, "On a Missing Alhambra Vase," 44n2.

Figure 1: Osma Vase, second quarter of fourteenth century, Instituto Valencia de Don Juan, Madrid. Image: Album/Art Resource, NY.

Other vases have varied provenances, as shown in Table 1, and only a few of them come from documented archaeological contexts, including the Jerez Vase, found in a monastery near Jerez de la Frontera.[22] The Osma Vase at the Instituto Valencia de Don Juan, Madrid (Figure 1), and the vase now in Palermo (Figure 2) were both discovered

---

22 Museo Arqueológico Nacional, Madrid, inv. no. 1930/67; Gaspar Aranda, *Jarrón nazarí llamado de la Cartuja de Jerez*, Pieza del mes (Madrid: Museo Arqueológico Nacional, May 2007), 1–12; *Los jarrones de la Alhambra: simbología y poder* (Granada: P.C. Monumental de la Alhambra y Generalife, Consejería de Cultura, Junta de Andalucía, 2006), 162–165.

Figure 2: Unnamed Alhambra Vase, late thirteenth to early fourteenth century, Galleria Regionale della Sicilia, Palermo, inv. no. 5229. Image: Album/Art Resource, NY.

in Mazara del Vallo in Sicily in the nineteenth century, although the exact circumstances of the find are not documented.[23]

Two vases are securely connected to the collection, sold in 1875, of Spanish painter Mariano Fortuny Marsal (1838–1874).[24] These are the so-called Fortuny or

---

23 The vases are: Galleria Regionale della Sicilia, Palermo, inv. no. 5229; Instituto Valencia de Don Juan, Madrid, acquired in 1924. They are published in Van de Put, "On a Missing Alhambra Vase," 75; *Los jarrones de la Alhambra*, 158–161; Dodds, *Al-Andalus*, 354–355, cat. no. 110. For the provenance of both vases, see Ferrandis Torres, "Los vasos de la Alhambra," 67–68.

24 Not to be confused with his son, Mariano Fortuny Madrazo (1871–1949), a fashion and textile designer active in Venice. On the son's life, see *Encyclopedia Britannica Online*, s.v. "Mariano Fortuny, Spanish-Italian multimedia artist [1871–1949]," accessed 8 January 2017, https://www.britannica.com/biography/Mariano-Fortuny-Spanish-Italian-multimedia-artist-1871-1949. The online object record for the Freer Vase confuses father and son: http://www.asia.si.edu/collections/edan/object.php?q=fsg_F1903.206a-b&bcrumb=true (accessed 8 January 2017).

Figure 3: Fortuny or Salar Vase, early fourteenth century, State Hermitage Museum, St. Petersburg, inv. no. F-317. Image: Album/Art Resource, NY.

Salar Vase (Figure 3), today preserved in the Hermitage in St. Petersburg, and the Freer Vase, a large fragment missing neck and wings, preserved in the Freer Gallery in Washington, D.C.[25] Fortuny designed the bronze lion stands that these two vases still have.[26]

The so-called Simonetti Vase is reported to have been in Fortuny's collection, although it is named after an earlier owner, Attilio Simonetti; the Spanish government

---

[25] The Fortuny Vase: inv. no. F-317; Dodds, *Al-Andalus*, 356–357, cat. no. 111; Ferrandis Torres, "Los vasos de la Alhambra," 66. The Freer Vase: inv. no. F1903.206a-b.
[26] Ferrandis Torres, "Los vasos de la Alhambra," 67, 75. For more on the collection and the design of the stands, see Carlos González López and Montserrat Martí Ayxelà, *Mariano Fortuny Marsal, 1838–1874*, 2 vols. (Barcelona: Diccionari Ràfols, 1989), 1:146–157.

acquired it in 1934 for the Museo Nacional de Arte Hispanomusulman in Granada.[27] The Hornos Vase was found in Jaén.[28] The vase in the Nationalmuseum in Stockholm was part of the so-called Prague booty of 1648, taken when the Swedes occupied Prague at the end of the Thirty Years' War; it entered the royal collections at that point and was transferred to the museum in the late nineteenth century. The vase had reached Prague in the late sixteenth century, where it became part of the collection of Emperor Rudolph II after being bought by Ambassador Joachim von Sinzendorff in Istanbul. Before that, the vase is reported to have been located in Cyprus until the Ottoman conquest of the island in 1571.[29]

Numerous catalogues and lists of the vases and fragments exist, pointing to the interest that these pieces have elicited among scholars since the 1920s.[30] Since little is known about the circumstances of their production, scholarship on the Alhambra Vases has been largely concerned with proposing sequences for dating the extant pieces based on types of decoration and colors of glaze (silver/blue versus white/gold).[31] As places of production, Málaga and Granada have been suggested.[32] In the first systematic publication of the Alhambra Vases in 1925, José Ferrandis Torres collected the ensemble of extant vases and large fragments; his catalogue for the most part remains valid today.[33] The exception is the addition of the Jerez Vase, which was found in 1927 (two years after Ferrandis Torres published his article) and acquired by the Museo Arqueológico Nacional in Madrid in 1930.[34] Another vase, depicted in Ferrandis Torres's article in plate 4 and labeled as being held in Berlin, may be

---

27 Summer A. Kenesson, "Nasrid Luster Pottery: The Alhambra Vases," *Muqarnas* 9 (1992): 103.
28 Kenesson, "Nasrid Luster Pottery," 107; *Los jarrones de la Alhambra*, 146–149.
29 "Alhambra Vase," Collections Database, Nationalmuseum, Stockholm, accessed 26 July 2018, http://collection.nationalmuseum.se/eMP/eMuseumPlus?service=ExternalInterface&module=collection&objectId=37866&viewType=detailView; *Los jarrones de la Alhambra*, 156–157. High-resolution images of the vase can be viewed on Google Arts & Culture, https://www.google.com/culturalinstitute/beta/asset/jarra-or-alhambra-vase-granada-spain/dwGWNN9mm-kzuA (accessed 12 January 2017). For an introduction to Rudolph II's collection, see Jacob Wisse, "Prague during the Rule of Rudolph II (1583–1612)," *Heilbrunn Timeline of Art History*, Metropolitan Museum of Art, accessed 27 October 2017, http://www.metmuseum.org/toah/hd/rupr/hd_rupr.htm.
30 Ferrandis Torres, "Los vasos de la Alhambra"; Van de Put, "On a Missing Alhambra Vase"; Alice Wilson Frothingham, *Lustreware of Spain*, Hispanic Notes & Monographs, Peninsular Series (New York: Hispanic Society of America, 1951); Richard Ettinghausen, "Notes on the Lustreware of Spain," *Ars Orientalis* 1 (1954): 133–156; Carmen Serrano García, "Los jarrones de la Alhambra," in *Estudios Dedicados a Don Jesús Bermúdez Pareja (1908–1986)* (Granada: Asociación cultural de amigos del Museo Hispanomusulman, Granada, 1988), 127–162; Kenesson, "Nasrid Luster Pottery"; *Los jarrones de la Alhambra*.
31 Ferrandis Torres, "Los vasos de la Alhambra"; Van de Put, "On a Missing Alhambra Vase"; Ettinghausen, "Notes on the Lustreware of Spain"; Serrano García, "Los jarrones de la Alhambra."
32 Ferrandis Torres, "Los vasos de la Alhambra," 60–65; Arthur Lane, "Early Hispano-Moresque Pottery: A Reconsideration," *The Burlington Magazine for Connoisseurs* 88 (1946): 246–253.
33 Ferrandis Torres, "Los vasos de la Alhambra," 65–77 and plates 2–8.
34 Aranda, "Jarrón nazarí llamado de la cartuja de Jerez."

the Heilbronner Vase, destroyed in a fire in a Spanish customs storehouse in 1936.[35] Writing in 1947, Van de Put describes the same set of objects, adding the Jerez Vase, which had been found in the meantime, and including a detailed appendix of complete vases and large fragments.[36]

Later publications have contributed to the detailed analysis of decoration that has led to a clearer chronology of the vases, although not, in the absence of excavated kilns, to a better sense of their production. Ferrandis Torres, basing his conclusions especially on the large number of tiles preserved in the Alhambra (although hardly any in luster technique remain on-site), argues for their local production in Granada, although difficulties ensue in distinguishing this from Málaga's production.[37] He attributes the gold-glazed vases to Málaga, the blue-and-gold ones to Granada, and dates the former group to the second half of the fourteenth century, the latter to the early fifteenth century.[38] The only dated piece of luster ceramic connected to Nasrid Granada is a large tile preserved in the Instituto Valencia de Don Juan in Madrid; its inscription mentions the name of Nasrid ruler Yusuf III (r. 1408–1417).[39]

The chronologies and attributions established in the 1920s have largely been maintained in later publications. Richard Ettinghausen focuses on the question of dates, seeking to establish the oldest piece in the group.[40] Although he concedes that analysis of the epigraphy remains inconclusive, Ettinghausen posits the Osma Vase as the oldest, followed by the pieces in Palermo and St. Petersburg.[41] More recently, Carmen Serrano García has proposed further detailed analysis of decoration and measurements, suggesting that production continued for longer than previously thought; this change in chronology leads her to date the Osma Vase to the last quarter of the thirteenth century. The date range for the other pieces remains the same as Ferrandis Torres suggested.[42]

The function of the vases is unclear. Although their basic shape recalls that of storage vessels, the luster glaze – both expensive and difficult to produce – would have precluded such use for the Alhambra Vases. As Ferrandis Torres points out, the glaze would have prevented the clay bodies of the Alhambra Vases from breathing, thus subverting a main function of storage vessels: namely, to keep liquids cool.[43] The large size of the vases poses the problem of portability – or rather, their lack thereof. It is clear that the vases were not designed to be handled frequently and with ease,

---

35 Kenesson, "Nasrid Luster Pottery," 102–103 and fig. 11.
36 Van de Put, "On a Missing Alhambra Vase," 73–77.
37 Ferrandis Torres, "Los vasos de la Alhambra," 63–64, 69.
38 Ferrandis Torres, "Los vasos de la Alhambra," 65.
39 Ferrandis Torres, "Los vasos de la Alhambra," 72 and plate 10; Dodds, *Al-Andalus*, 360–361, cat. no. 113.
40 Ettinghausen, "Notes on the Lustreware of Spain," 145–148.
41 Ettinghausen, "Notes on the Lustreware of Spain," 148.
42 Serrano García, "Los jarrones de la Alhambra," 160–161.
43 Ferrandis Torres, "Los vasos de la Alhambra," 65.

considering their large size and considerable weight.⁴⁴ The flat, smooth, wing-shaped handles do not, in fact, seem to be easy to grasp. Even with the vases stabilized on stands, maneuvering one would probably require at least two adults.⁴⁵ At the same time, a court like that of the Nasrids would have had a sufficient number of slaves to ensure that such work could be completed, and so perhaps we should not insist on modern notions of portability that tend to imply small and lightweight objects.⁴⁶

Thus, to experience the vases likely required movement on the viewer's part rather than the object's. The circular nature of the decoration on many of the vases further supports this idea, particularly in the case of those vases that have poetry inscribed on them. In order to fully appreciate a piece like the Freer Vase, one needs to be able to walk around the object to read the inscription that runs in a band around its body without being repeated on each side. Thus, placement in a niche would not be the best option to ensure a viewer's interaction with a piece: Figure 4 shows a modern copy of the Gazelle Vase placed in a niche in the northeastern corner of the Courtyard of Myrtles, a few meters from the entrance to the Comares Hall.

While these issues have been pointed out, they have not yet been pursued in detail. In methodological terms, a central problem is posed by the nature of the sources. Although all of the extant vases have various kinds of text written *on* them, known medieval sources do not contain any passages *about* them. Not all the vases have legible poetic text: some have pseudo-writing, others have phrases invoking blessings and luck for the owner. While both features are common within medieval Islamic art, and also occur frequently within the Islamic art of Spain, it is nevertheless relevant to note that the presence of text is highly valued, even if it isn't legible. The illusion of text, in fact, enhances the value of those passages – such as the poems – that *are* legible. In what follows, I will focus on the Freer Vase, one of the extant pieces inscribed with a poem. While this text has been read and translated, an analysis within the larger context of poetic epigraphy and sensory perception in the Alhambra remains to be done. Notably, the poem on the Freer Vase works to engage the viewer using many of the same devices that are employed in the poetic inscriptions of the Alhambra, evoking the beauty of the object and a range of materials.

---

44 Unfortunately, no data is available on the weight of these vases.
45 It is unclear what kinds of stands these vases originally had. For examples of twelfth- and thirteenth-century cylindrical clay stands used to support large storage amphorae, see Bulle Tuil Leonetti, Yannick Lintz, and Claire Déléry, eds., *Le Maroc médiéval: Un empire de l'Afrique à l'Espagne* (Paris: Hazan and Musée du Louvre, 2014), 344, cat. no. 197, and 345, cat. no. 199.
46 For a discussion of notions of portability, see Avinoam Shalem, "The Poetics of Portability," in *Histories of Ornament: From Global to Local*, ed. Gülru Necipoğlu and Alina Payne (Princeton, NJ: Princeton University Press, 2016), 250–261.

5 The Vessel as Garden — 129

Figure 4: A modern copy of the Gazelle Vase on view in the Courtyard of Myrtles at the Alhambra in 2014. Photograph: Patricia Blessing.

The Freer Vase

The Freer Vase is not preserved in full: the neck and wings are missing, and only the body remains (Plate VII). The first recorded owner of the vase, Mariano Fortuny Marsal, bought it from a tavern in Granada. The bronze stand, inspired by the Fountain of the Lions at the Alhambra, was designed by Fortuny, as was the stand for the Hermitage Vase, also in his collection prior to being sold.[47] The Freer Vase was in the sale of the Fortuny collection in 1875, a year after the owner's death. It next appeared in the C. Stein sale in Paris in May 1886.[48] Charles Davis of London bought the vase for the Freer Collection in 1903.[49]

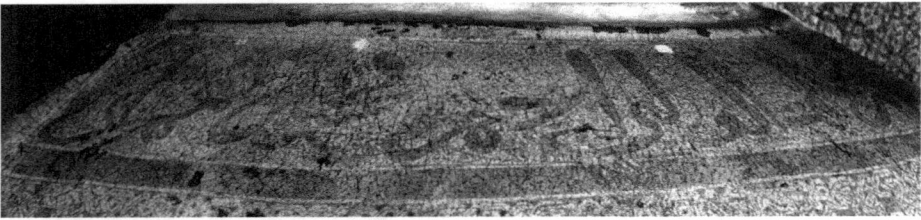

Figure 5: Detail of poetic inscription, Stockholm Vase, second quarter of fourteenth century. Photograph courtesy of Nationalmuseum Sweden, Stockholm, inv. no. NMK 47.

The body of the vase is painted with blue motifs on a white background, a type of design that appears generally in those vases dated to the late fourteenth or early fifteenth centuries. From top to bottom, the decoration of the fragmentary piece shows a pair of gazelles (closely connected to those on the Gazelle Vase preserved at the Alhambra; see Plate VI) with a medallion of palmettes in between them, an inscription in cursive Arabic letters that runs around the thickest part of the body (this will be discussed below), and a lower zone where large stars alternate with palmette motifs. While the occurrence of poetic inscriptions is rare on the vases, this case is not unique: the vase in the Nationalmuseum in Stockholm has a similar band around the top part of the body between the two handles (Figure 5). To my knowledge, the inscription on the vase in Stockholm is unpublished, and I am currently working on reading it based

---

47 Dodds, *Al-Andalus*, 356–357, cat. no. 111; Freer Vase object record, inv. no. F1903.206a-b, Collections Database, Freer Gallery of Art, accessed 7 March 2018, http://archive.asia.si.edu/collections/edan/object.php?q=fsg_F1903.206a-b.
48 Van de Put, "On a Missing Alhambra Vase."
49 Freer Vase object record, inv. no. F1903.206a-b, Collections Database, Freer Gallery of Art, accessed 7 March 2018, http://archive.asia.si.edu/collections/edan/object.php?q=fsg_F1903.206a-b.

on photographs provided by the museum.⁵⁰ The difficulty of this task is due to the fact that, because of the luster glaze, the vases are difficult to photograph without glare.

A further poem can be found on the Hornos Vase in the Museo Arqueológico Nacional in Madrid, at the base of the neck in between the wings. It reads: "All fountains spring and seem the most perfect flow/and increase abundant kindness and great good fortune./And confirm the memory of happiness and the poverty/that the fortune of time banished morning and evening."⁵¹ Unlike some of the other poems, in particular the one on the Freer Vase, this text does not establish comparisons to other materials, nor does it evoke the glaze of the vase. Nevertheless, the mention of fountains and the flow of water is significant in order to connect the piece to the presence of such features within the architecture of the Alhambra. Thus, indirectly, the multisensory nature of the monument is part of the Hornos Vase as well.

On the Freer Vase, the poem endeavors to provoke the multisensory engagement of the viewer by establishing the vase as a first-person narrator who addresses the beholder. The poem is rendered below in the reading and translation offered by Alois Richard Nykl (with slight modifications):

1. O you onlooker who are adorned with the splendor of the dwelling
    Ayyuhā l-nāẓiru lladhī zānahu rā'iqu l-dāri
2. Look at my shape today and contemplate: you will see my excellence
    Unẓur al-yawma ṣūratī wa-ta'ammal tara khayrī
3. For I appear to be made of silver and my clothing from blossoms
    Fa-ka-annī min fiḍḍatin wa-libāsī mina-l-zahrī
4. My happiness lies in the hands of he who is my owner, underneath the canopy
    *Sa'dī bi-yadāya lladhī nāla mulkī bi-miẓalla.*⁵²

The poem places the vase front and center in a first-person discourse: the object introduces itself and invites the gaze of the onlooker (or beholder; the Arabic term *nāẓir* can mean one or the other), pointing out its own beauty. The vase is presented not simply as an object of ceramic, but also of metal, alluding to the luster glaze that both creates a silver sheen and actually contains metal – a necessary technical feature to attain the metallic aesthetic. The ambivalence of its nature is stated in the poem: First, the vase compares itself to a vessel made of silver (*ka-annī min fiḍḍatin*).

---

50 Only older black-and-white photographs of the inscription are available: email communication from Rikard Nordström, Picture Officer, Nationalmuseum, Stockholm, 12 January 2017. The object is currently in storage since the museum is closed until the end of 2018 for renovations.
51 English translation in Puerta Vílchez, *La poética del agua en el Islam*, 66, after the Spanish text in a translation by Eduardo Saavedra in *Los jarrones de la Alhambra*, 148. The Arabic text has not been published.
52 A. R. Nykl, "The Inscriptions on the 'Freer Vase'," *Ars Orientalis* 2 (1957): 496. In the final line of the poem, *miẓalla* can be translated as "canopy" but literally means "an object providing shade".

In the same line of the poem, the vase refers to its apparent clothing (*libāsī*) made of flowers. This last phrase evokes a garden motif but also establishes one of the textile metaphors frequent in the poetic epigraphy of the Alhambra. Thus, precious metal and textiles are evoked in the self-description of the vase. Both are sources of wonder or amazement (*'ajab*, in Arabic) – notions that can be closely tied to literature, but also to objects.[53] The emphasis on the object's own happiness points to the larger issue of personification, in that the vase receives the power to speak and feel. Thus, the object is not simply a lifeless piece of furniture but rather an actor in the larger scheme of things, moving under the auspices of the owner who, in most of these poems, appears as the culmination. Viewed by itself, the poem may not be all that remarkable, but in the context of the larger multisensory space that is the Alhambra, it becomes significant.

Olga Bush briefly discusses this vase in her study of the Alhambra, connecting the Freer Vase to prosopopoeia in poetic inscriptions on a range of objects from the medieval Islamic world.[54] With regard to the poem on the vase, Bush states that the text contains a repertoire of features that are of interest to her study of prosopopoeia, including "staging ... the encounter between object and beholder".[55] This relationship between object and beholder, as Bush defines it, stands at the center of sensory perception within the Alhambra. The object might be a vase, or a curtain. Yet within the framework of a multisensory space that encompasses everything within it, the "object" might also be the building. Since the object takes on the role of guide through the building, the visitor is actively placed within the immersive space. The distinction between the different senses is dissolved, in that several of them – vision, hearing, touch – are directly addressed and included in this space of artifice. The sense of smell can also be evoked by the images that refer to flowers, with their pleasant fragrance (or even overpowering fragrance, thinking of a hedge of jasmine on a summer night). Such imagery is used on the Freer Vase, and in the following verse from a poem at the entrance of the Hall of the Two Sisters:

---

53 Roy P. Mottahedeh, "'Ajā'ib in The Thousand and One Nights," in *The Thousand and One Nights in Arabic Literature and Society*, ed. Richard G. Hovannisian and Georges Sabagh (Cambridge: Cambridge University Press, 1997), 29–39; Nasser Rabbat, "'Ajīb and *Gharīb*: Artistic Perception in Medieval Arabic Sources," *The Medieval History Journal* 9 (2006): 99–113; Matthew D. Saba, "Abbasid Lusterware and the Aesthetics of 'Ajab," *Muqarnas* 29 (2012): 187–212. On the challenges of studying literary expressions of 'ajab and related emotions: Lara Harb, "Poetic Marvels: Wonder and Aesthetic Experience in Medieval Arabic Literary Theory" (PhD dissertation, New York University, 2013), 1–11.
54 Bush, "Architecture, Poetic Texts and Textile in the Alhambra," 109–111. Bush also discusses prosopopoeia in medieval Islamic objects in a recent study that focuses on a tenth-century ivory pyxis from Umayyad Spain: Olga Bush, "Poetic Inscriptions and Gift Exchange in the Medieval Islamicate World," *Gesta* 56 (2017): 179–197.
55 Bush, "Architecture, Poetic Texts and Textile in the Alhambra," 110.

1. and who [referring to Muhammad V, the patron] has endowed you [the palace] with this fair garden, in which the flowers
   wa-ḥabāka bil-rauḍi l-anīqi fa-zahruhu
2. smile when they boast of your regalia
   mutabassim lammā azdahathu ḥulākan.⁵⁶

Thus, the task in the remainder of this chapter will be to understand, firstly, how the vase as an object is designed to address the viewer through shape, text, and references to other materials; secondly, how the object relates to the space surrounding it; and thirdly, how it mimics the larger space to the extent that a multisensory experience is incited in the object as much as in the Alhambra as a whole.⁵⁷

Poetic Epigraphy and Multisensory Space

Indeed, because of its mimetic capacity, the Freer Vase can serve as a hinge between the group of vases and the Alhambra as a whole: the text on this vase is closely connected to the poetry inscribed on the monument.⁵⁸ The poetic inscriptions on the monument were for the most part written by court poet Ibn Zamrak.⁵⁹ Born in Granada in 1333, Abu Abdallah Muhammad b. Yusuf al-Surayhi, known as Ibn Zamrak, entered the service of the Nasrid administration in his native city. He remained in the service of Sultan Muhammad V during the ruler's exile in Fez (Morocco) from 1359 to 1362, and was private scribe and court poet both during this time and after the court's return to Granada. In 1371, Ibn Zamrak became chief minister in place of his teacher Ibn al-Khatib (d. 1374), who had fled to the rival court of the Marinids in Fez and was captured and executed a few years later. Ibn Zamrak remained in office until 1391; after this, he was deposed and reappointed several times until his assassination in

---

56 Puerta Vílchez, *Reading the Alhambra*, 207.
57 I thank Richard Newhauser for suggesting the term "mimics."
58 The text on the Freer Vase directly connects to the poetic epigraphy from the Alhambra that appears in José Miguel Puerta Vílchez's detailed study together with drawings of its locations on the walls of the palaces: Puerta Vílchez, *Reading the Alhambra*. For more on issues of aesthetics by the same author, see José Miguel Puerta Vílchez, *Historia del pensamiento estético árabe: Al-Andalus y la estética árabe clásica* (Madrid: Akal, 1997). I was unable to access the English translation, published after this chapter was completed: José Miguel Puerta Vílchez, *Aesthetics in Arabic Thought: From Pre-Islamic Arabia through al-Andalus*, trans. Consuelo López Morillas (Leiden: Brill, 2017). Olga Bush and Cynthia Robinson have explored the monument's poetic inscriptions and proposed interpretations: Bush, "'When My Beholder Ponders': Poetic Epigraphy in the Alhambra"; Olga Bush, "The Writing on the Wall: Reading the Decoration of the Alhambra," *Muqarnas* 26 (2009): 119–147; Cynthia Robinson, "Marginal Ornament: Poetics, Mimesis, and Devotion in the Palace of the Lions," *Muqarnas* 25 (2008): 185–214.
59 Akiko Motoyoshi Sumi, *Description in Classical Arabic Poetry: Waṣf, Ekphrasis, and Interarts Theory* (Leiden: Brill, 2004), 185–186.

1393.⁶⁰ A major figure in the literature of Islamic Spain, Ibn Zamrak left poems that have been documented on the walls of the Alhambra as well as in collections by Ibn al-Khatib (before the master's death in the 1370s) and the seventeenth-century historian al-Maqqari, who compiled a wide range of sources on al-Andalus.[61]

The poetry of the Alhambra does not simply describe objects and architecture but rather, as Akiko Motoyoshi Sumi suggests in her discussion of Ibn Zamrak's ode to Muhammad V, offers a carefully curated experience: "The poet imitates and improves on both nature and architecture, the palace, in his ode. That is to say, both of them are materials for his poetry, because he even idealizes the palace that is already a complete architectural work of art. What we experience is not the palace itself, but the mediated, i.e. verbalized, form ennobled by him".[62] Thus Sumi argues that the poem is both an engagement with nature (in its curated form in the gardens, and in general) and with the monument. Of course, due to its place in the epigraphy of the palace, the poetry also becomes an element of the architecture, a building stone of text within the larger project of artifice. Text, palace, and nature are closely connected, to the point of becoming one.

A second poem from the Hall of the Abencerrajes, attributed to Ibn Zamrak, enhances the issues raised in the first poetic epigraph discussed in the opening section of this chapter:

1. In this palace, Ibn Nasr has achieved his ambitions
   nāla Ibn Naṣrin bi-hādha l-qaṣri mā-(i)qtarahā
   For its door has opened to sublime victory
   fa-bābuhu li-ʿazīzi l-naṣri qad futiḥā
2. Observe the vase in my *miḥrāb* and you will see it
   fa-unẓur li-(i)brīqi miḥrābī tarāhu bihi
   as the imam beginning prayers
   mithla l-imāmi idhā ṣalātahu (i)ftataḥā
3. My Lord, allow my owner to last forever as with him
   adāma rabbi li-mawlāya l-baqāʾ kamā
   his gifts will last for the world and for religion
   adāma lil-dīn wa-l-dunyā bihi l-minḥā.[63]

---

60 F. de la Granja, "Ibn Zamrak," in *Encyclopaedia of Islam, Second Edition*, ed. Peri Bearman et al., accessed 16 January 2017, http://referenceworks.brillonline.com/entries/encyclopaedia-of-islam-2/ibn-zamrak-SIM_3419; Emilio García Gómez, *Ibn Zumruk, el poeta de la Alhambra* (Madrid: E. Maestre, 1943); H. Hadjadji, *Le poète vizir Ibn Zamrak: Du faubourg d'Albaycine au palais de l'Alhambra* (Beirut: Albouraq, 2005).

61 Evariste Lévi-Provençal and Charles Pellat, "Al-Maḳḳarī," in *Encyclopaedia of Islam, Second Edition*, ed. Peri Bearman et al., accessed 18 January 2017, http://referenceworks.brillonline.com/entries/encyclopaedia-of-islam-2/al-makkari-SIM_4832.

62 Sumi, *Description in Classical Arabic Poetry*, 185–186.

63 Puerta Vílchez, *Reading the Alhambra*, 174.

Both poems – the one above and the one that opens this chapter – are relevant in the present context because both of them describe a vase (*ibrīq*, better translated as "ewer") that is placed in a niche within the monument-narrator. While one can only speculate on the placement of vases within the Alhambra, the prevalence of deep niches of various sizes throughout the complex suggests that they did indeed hold objects, rather than standing empty as they do in the current museum space. Artifice is used to improve on nature: the latter is harnessed in order to establish the palace as a major source of artifice and amazement.

While the vases are important parts of this setup, they are not the only objects that contribute to the multisensory space. Textiles such as curtains, hangings, and cushions were other elements in this setting, appealing to the senses with the sounds that they made when moved and the sheen of their threads. This idea connects to the larger discussion of textile motifs in stucco and woodcarving at the Alhambra, and their connection to extant pieces of fabric.[64] Although none are preserved on-site today, a substantial number of textiles associated with the Alhambra through their patterns, aesthetics, dates, and possibly place of production exist.[65] These include large-format pieces such as the so-called Alhambra curtains.[66] These textiles tie into the same discourse of *'ajab* that is evoked in the poem on the Freer Vase.[67] In this line of thinking, Lisa Golombek has ascribed to medieval and early modern Muslim culture a sensibility particularly attuned to textiles and their patterns.[68] Golombek emphasizes the rich textile production of the Islamic world and the use of architectural decoration that refers to woven models. Following Golombek, Oleg Grabar has suggested that a prevalent textile aesthetic exists in Islamic architecture, closely connected to the geometric ornament that covers large sections of monuments.[69] Both arguments are certainly convincing, considering the fluidity with which textile patterns appear in other materials and contexts while architectural decoration is evoked in textiles. These patterns, in turn, cannot be divorced from the actual textiles that would have been used within spaces.

---

[64] Bush, "Architecture, Poetic Texts and Textile in the Alhambra"; Marinetto Sánchez, "El uso del tejido y su decoración en los palacios de la Alhambra"; Cynthia Robinson, "Towers, Birds and Divine Light: The Contested Territory of Nasrid and 'Mudéjar' Ornament," *Medieval Encounters* 17 (2011): 27–79.

[65] Louise W. Mackie, *Symbols of Power: Luxury Textiles from Islamic Lands, 7th–21st Century* (Cleveland, OH, and New Haven, CT: Cleveland Museum of Art and Yale University Press, 2015), 192–203.

[66] The Hispanic Society of America, New York, H 931; Mackie, *Symbols of Power*, fig. 5.26. The Cleveland Museum of Art, Leonard C. Hanna Jr. Fund, 1982.16; Mackie, *Symbols of Power*, fig. 5.29. For more on these textiles, see Mackie, *Symbols of Power*, 192–203.

[67] See note 53 above and Sumi, *Description in Classical Arabic Poetry*.

[68] Lisa Golombek, "The Draped Universe of Islam," in *Content and Context of Visual Art in the Islamic World: Papers from a Colloquium in Memory of Richard Ettinghausen*, ed. Priscilla Soucek and Carol Bier (University Park, PA: Pennsylvania State University Press, 1988), 25–50.

[69] Oleg Grabar, *The Mediation of Ornament* (Princeton, NJ: Princeton University Press, 1992), 141–142, 145.

Figure 6: Silk lampas with horizontal bands of calligraphy, Granada, fourteenth century. Collection: The Victoria and Albert Museum, London, inv. no. 821–1894. Image courtesy of the Victoria and Albert Museum, London.

Poems similar to those in the Alhambra and on the Freer Vase also appear on textiles that were produced in the context of Nasrid Granada and perhaps used within the palace. A fragment (Figure 6) in the collection of the Victoria and Albert Museum in London speaks in the first person, evoking the pleasure conferred on its viewer:

1. *Anā lil-faraḥ lil-faraḥ anā ahlan wa man ra'ānī ra'[ā] surūr ra'[ā] hanā'*
   I am for pleasure. Welcome. For pleasure am I. He who beholds me sees joy and delight.[70]

Larger pieces of the same textile, sewn together to form a chasuble, are preserved in the Textile Museum in Washington, D.C.[71] Despite the fact that two of these pieces were joined upside down, their size manages to suggest the effect of the original textile as a whole, in which the circular nature of the poem and the potentially infinite continuation of the woven pattern come together. Thus, the initial phrase "I am for pleasure" is repeated in inverted form: "For pleasure am I." In this lies a

---

[70] Mariam Rosser-Owen, "Andalusi and Mudéjar Silk Textile in the Victoria and Albert Museum: 'A School of Design in This Beautiful Class of Sumptuary Art,'" in *La investigación textil y los nuevos métodos de estudio*, ed. Laura Rodríguez Peinado and Ana Cabrera Lafuente (Madrid: Fundación Lázaro Galdiano, 2014), 177, accessed 23 October 2017, http://www.flg.es/images/publicaciones/investigacion-textil-nuevos-metodos.pdf.

[71] Textile Museum, Washington, D.C., inv. no. 84.29. Briefly mentioned in Bush, "Architecture, Poetic Texts and Textile in the Alhambra," 107; Mackie, *Symbols of Power*, 207; *Unraveling Identity: Our Textiles, Our Stories*, object labels for exhibition at the Textile Museum, Washington, D.C., 21 March–9 August 2015, 43–44, accessed 23 October 2017, https://museum.gwu.edu/sites/museum.gwu.edu/files/Unraveling-Identity-Expanded-Labels.pdf.

chiasm, following Bissera Pentcheva's concise definition of the term: "Chiasm in literature operates through repetition of a word or phrase in a mirroring structure that establishes a frame arranged centripetally, about a center. As a result, the structure focuses attention on the center, which, in a chiasm occupying several lines, embodies the main idea, understood as a premeditated action, a counsel, or a promise".[72] The mirroring that hinges on a central concept here highlights pleasure (*faraḥ*). Hence, the pleasure taken by the viewer (or wearer) in the textile as well as the overall focus on just such pleasure within Nasrid poetry and aesthetics stand at the center of the poem. At the same time, the entire poem appears over and over again, forming the repeat of the weave pattern.[73] The repetition of these phrases draws the viewer into the beauty of the language, and even more so into the beauty of the object, which is emphasized by the poem. Thus, even though the poems – on the Freer Vase, in various parts of the Alhambra, and on the textile fragment just mentioned – do not directly address the senses, they allude to multiple levels of perception.

Imagery related to various materials addresses the properties inherent in these materials and the ways of perceiving them. While vision takes a central place, the comparisons to textile and metal invite the poem's reader or hearer to imagine these precious materials, also creating imagined experiences of touch. In the case of textiles, the sound of rustling fabric may be added to this multisensory illusion. The presence of sound is extended to the fact that poetic inscriptions might potentially have been read and recited, along with other poems that were known to the court's poets but not part of the building's epigraphy.

Moreover, the sound of water flowing in the many fountains of the Alhambra and running through channels in the Courtyard of Lions and adjacent rooms would have added to the immersive experience of the palace (Figure 7).[74] In this sense, another poem is crucial in that it establishes a connection between water, perception, and artifice. The poem is inscribed on the rim of a marble fountain basin that was installed in the sixteenth century in the garden at the foot of the Mirador de Lindaraja,

---

[72] Bissera V. Pentcheva, *Hagia Sophia: Sound, Space, and Spirit in Byzantium* (University Park, PA: Pennsylvania State University Press, 2017), 85.
[73] On technical problems when weaving textiles with inscriptions, see Regula Schorta, "Technische Aspekte gewebter Inschriften," in *Islamische Textilkunst des Mittelalters: Aktuelle Probleme*, Riggisberger Berichte 5 (Riggisberg, Switzerland: Abegg-Stiftung, 1997), 139–143.
[74] As evocative as photographs of water flowing through the fountains and marble channels of the Alhambra are, it is also important to note that the water features have been restored and the fountains largely replaced by copies to protect the originals. On the multiple layers of restoration and change at the Alhambra since the sixteenth century, see D. Fairchild Ruggles, "Inventing the Alhambra," in *Envisioning Islamic Art and Architecture: Essays in Honor of Renata Holod*, ed. David J. Roxburgh (Leiden: Brill, 2014), 1–21.

Figure 7: Fountain of Lions (modern copy), Courtyard of Lions, the Alhambra, Granada. Photograph: Patricia Blessing.

although its original location is unknown.[75] Two lines of the poem are particularly pertinent in establishing the image of water:

1. a piece of ice, some of which has melted, and some of which hasn't melted
   qiṭʿatun min baradin fa-baʿḍuhā dhāʾibun wa-baʿḍuhā lam yudhab
2. and when the bubbles float, you imagine that I am a heaven in which all kinds of stars arise
   wa-idhā ṭafā l-ḥabābu khiltanī falakan aṭlaʿa shattā-l-shahab.[76]

In this poem the water metaphors are taken to a higher level, connecting them to the firmament, and hence to other structures within the Alhambra such as the wooden ceiling of the Comares Hall (Figure 8), which has been interpreted as representing

---

75 The original basin is now in the archaeological museum of the Alhambra, and a copy is installed in the garden: Puerta Vílchez, *Reading the Alhambra*, 355.
76 Lines 9 and 10 of the poem. Line 9: my translation after García Gómez, *Poemas árabes en los muros y fuentes de la Alhambra*, 129; line 10: after Puerta Vílchez, *La poética del agua en el Islam*, 46. Two slightly conflicting readings of the entire poem with Arabic text and Spanish translation are published in García Gómez, *Poemas árabes en los muros y fuentes de la Alhambra*, 128–132; and Antonio Almagro Cárdenas, *Estudio sobre las inscripciones árabes de Granada* (Granada: Imp. de Ventura Sabatel, 1879), 117–120.

5 The Vessel as Garden — 139

Figure 8: Ceiling of the Comares Hall, the Alhambra, Granada. Photograph: Patricia Blessing.

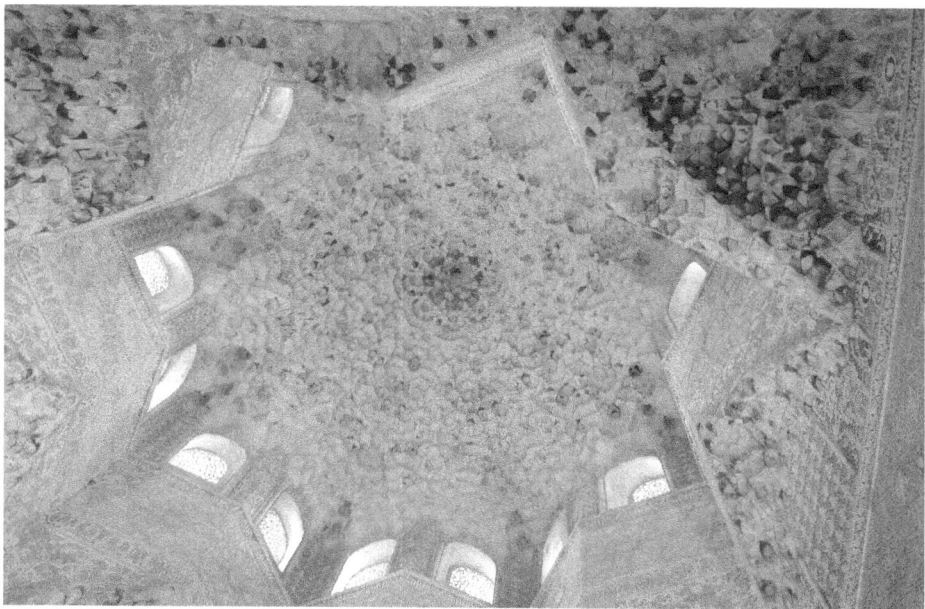

Figure 9: Ceiling of the Hall of Abencerrajes, the Alhambra, Granada. Photograph: Patricia Blessing.

the firmament based on inscriptions, including Qur'anic texts, within the hall.[77] The same metaphors are evoked in the *muqarnas* domes of the Hall of the Abencerrajes (Figure 9) and the Hall of the Two Sisters, two spaces located across from each other on either side of the Courtyard of Lions.[78] Within this larger play of metaphors, objects such as the fountain basins – both the so-called Fountain of Lindaraja and the fountain basin in the Courtyard of Lions – are joined with curtains and vases in a discourse of beauty and amazement that is directly inscribed within poems in the structure and on these objects. This observation raises the question of the larger discourse on beauty and perception in medieval Islamic thought, and the aesthetics of wonder.

Conclusion: The Alhambra and Beauty in Medieval Islamic Thought

Perceptions of beauty and aesthetics were often connected to the notion of God and the Qur'an as paragons of beauty. Discussing the work of philosopher al-Ghazālī (d. 1111), Doris Behrens-Abouseif notes:

> But beauty is not only visual; it can be perceived by smell and touch as well as cognition, which lead to corresponding pleasures. The more exalted the subject of our knowledge, the higher the pleasure. Al-Ghazālī distinguishes between aesthetic beauty and beauty perceived by the intellect. Only external beauty is sensed through sight, hearing, touch, and taste, but there is also the beauty of abstract things such as knowledge and virtue, which are perceived by the "inner sight" *(baṣīra bāṭina)*, not by the senses. Knowledge of God is the perfect perception of beauty and the utmost form of pleasure, surpassing all satisfactions of the senses and the intellect.[79]

The scientific discussion on optics in the works of scholars such as Ibn al-Haytham (d. 1039) also had a significant impact on the ways in which visual perception was understood and connected to the intellect.[80] A difficulty in applying these ideas to the visual arts is that the medieval authors themselves did not do so. Rather, the concepts noted above were first and foremost relevant for the assessment of aesthetics in

---

77 Puerta Vílchez, *Reading the Alhambra*, 124–126.
78 Puerta Vílchez, *Reading the Alhambra*, 172–185, 206–219.
79 Doris Behrens-Abouseif, "Aesthetics," in *Encyclopaedia of Islam, THREE*, ed. Kate Fleet, Gudrun Krämer, Denis Matringe, John Nawas, and Everett Rowson, accessed 23 October 2017, http://dx.doi.org/10.1163/1573-3912_ei3_COM_23736.
80 Alhazen, *The Optics of Ibn Al-Haytham, Books I–III: On Direct Vision*, trans. A. I. Sabra (London: Warburg Institute, University of London, 1989); Puerta Vílchez, *Historia del pensamiento estético árabe*, 696–720.

literature or poetry, but not architecture or objects.⁸¹ Due to this discrepancy between a rich tradition of thought on aesthetics and an apparent disregard for the visual arts, certain limits remain to the ways in which we can approach sensory perception in medieval Islamic art. Nevertheless, these philosophical works also open up the possibility of a larger understanding of aesthetics that, as Puerta Vílchez argues, can be connected to the visual.⁸² In this sense, the Alhambra can be an important connecting point between the two modes of aesthetics, in that the space of the palace serves to demonstrate that the building, the poetic texts of the period (whether recited within or inscribed on the monument), and the portable objects that are part of the same aesthetic discourse all form a *Gesamtkunstwerk*.

With this unified aesthetic of architecture, object, and poetry in mind, the Alhambra as a space is the ultimate source of *'ajab*. Indeed, the thirteenth-century Iranian polymath Qazvini (d. 1283/1284) defines this notion as "the sense of bewilderment a person feels because of his inability to understand the cause of a thing".⁸³ Applied to the multisensory space of the Alhambra, the sense of wonder is palpable in that a range of materials (stone, tile, wood, stucco) are used in the architecture, but often in ways that belie their physical characteristics. Thus, stucco takes on textile patterns, seemingly dissolving walls. At the same time, objects are added to this space and enhance the wonder it creates: vases made of ceramic are said to be of metal or wrapped in fabric; textiles embrace their own woven nature, but also show motifs that connect them closely to the walls. Often, in fact, one cannot tell whether the wall is a textile or the textile a wall. Similarly, in the case of the Alhambra Vases, the ceramic medium of their bodies is hidden behind layer upon layer of metal and textile metaphors as well as water motifs connecting them to the larger garden space that is also part of the Alhambra. In this sense, a deeper understanding of the Alhambra Vases offers insights into the ways in which this multisensory space is constructed, taking into account both the architecture and the objects placed within it.

---

81 Doris Behrens-Abouseif, *Schönheit in der arabischen Kultur* (Munich: C. H. Beck, 1998), translated into English as Doris Behrens-Abouseif, *Beauty in Arabic Culture* (Princeton, NJ: Markus Wiener, 1998); Behrens-Abouseif, "Aesthetics."
82 Puerta Vílchez, *Historia del pensamiento estético árabe*. Further investigation requires close reading of this extensive study together with the existing art historical narrative.
83 Persis Berlekamp, *Wonder, Image, and Cosmos in Medieval Islam* (New Haven, CT: Yale University Press, 2011), 23.

Cynthia Hahn
6 Theatricality, Materiality, Relics: Reliquary Forms and the Sensational in Mosan Art

Considerable thought and significant resources have always gone into the presentation of holy relics. In the eleventh century, Abbot Gauzlin of Fleury Monastery used the novel form of a reliquary shaped like an arm to enclose a cloth relic associated with the Passion, and, during a procession on Ascension Day, he gestured with that arm so that he "strengthened [the crowd] by a benediction made by the relics."[1] In the early thirteenth century, Abbot Berthold of Weingarten Abbey saved relics of Saint Martin from being deposited in an altar and put them instead in a spectacular reliquary in the shape of the saint's head "in order to encourage the faith and piety [of the people]."[2] In the late tenth century, Archbishop Egbert of Trier founded workshops to produce stunningly beautiful reliquaries in enamel and gold, and the artisans in his employ created innovative reliquary shapes for use in his cathedral.[3] Throughout the Middle Ages, liturgies were written that used music to provoke an emotional response and involved the display and procession of reliquaries to gorgeous effect.[4] Subsequent "spontaneous" miracles, assiduously recorded in miracle books, magnified the renown and power of both relics and reliquaries.[5] Medieval examples of such multimedia provocations involving the display of relics are, in fact, legion.

The patrons of reliquaries – generally bishops, abbots, and other ecclesiastics – repeatedly went on record to assert that they created new reliquaries for the express purpose of stimulating the faith of their congregations. If we take their claims seriously and look to see how they accomplished their goals, we discover certain persistent strategies. Above all, an appeal to the senses reveals itself as their primary tactic.[6]

---

1 Cynthia Hahn, "The Voices of the Saints: Speaking Reliquaries," *Gesta* 36 (1997): 20–31, at 22n17, citing Andrew of Fleury, *Vita Gauzlini abbatis Floriacensis monasterii*, in *Vie de Gauzlin, abbot de Fleury*, ed. and trans. R.-H. Bautier and G. Labory (Paris: CNRS, 1969), 60–63.
2 Hans Swarzenski, *The Berthold Missal and the Scriptorium of Weingarten Abbey* (New York: Pierpont Morgan Library, 1943), 117–118.
3 He made both a staff reliquary today preserved at Limburg an der Lahn, and the Andreas reliquary with a foot on top of a box shape, still located at Trier. Hiltrud Westermann-Angerhausen, "Überlegungen zum Trierer Egbertschrein," *Trierer Zeitschrift für Geschichte und Kunst des Trierer Landes und seiner Nachbargebiete Trier* 40–41 (1977): 201–220.
4 See essays in Susan Boynton and Diane J. Reilly, eds., *Resounding Images: Medieval Intersections of Art, Music, and Sound* (Turnhout: Brepols, 2016); see also Chiara Mercuri, *Corona di Christo, Corona di Re: La Monarchia Francese e la corona di spine nel medioevo* (Rome: Edizioni di storia e di letteratura, 2004).
5 Ronald C. Finucane, *Miracles and Pilgrims: Popular Beliefs in Medieval England* (Totowa, NJ: Rowman and Littlefield, 1977).
6 See Anne-Marie Yasin, "Sacred Space and Visual Art," in *Oxford Handbook of Late Antiquity*, ed. Scott Fitzgerald Johnson (Oxford: Oxford University Press, 2012), 935–969; Martina Bagnoli, ed.,

Means included innovative designs, sumptuous materials, and magnificent presentation and ceremony. It would seem that, first and foremost, patrons hoped to overcome spiritual complacency with striking displays and multisensory extravaganzas. They sought to create a perception that the saint was truly present in the relic.

In this chapter, I want to focus on an aspect of this topic that is not often enough considered when discussing medieval art – that is, the inherent changeability and movement in relic display and reliquary objects, and the performative, sense-stimulating presentation of the relic to its audience. Instead of iconography, I will consider installation; instead of design, I will consider presence; instead of craft, I will consider spectacular materiality.[7]

An initial example, although it concerns textual rather than material evidence, is telling. In 1030, the Cathedral of the Virgin Mary in Cambrai was dedicated by Bishop Gerard. As G. J. C. Snoek reports, to bolster the impact of the ceremony, the bishop

> caused relics to be brought from the entire diocese and grouped them hierarchically around the altar. The relics of his predecessor St. Gaugerik, who had died five centuries before, were placed on the bishop's throne. Thus the saint took possession of his episcopal throne for one more day and was considered to be presiding at the consecration.[8]

Such an "installation" of relics is exemplary, reminding us of two important features of reliquary use and display. The first feature to remark is the essential portability of most reliquaries – they were made to be moved. Second, the willingness of a bishop to employ the available relics and reliquaries like actors in a play is striking. Saint Gaugerik was pressed into resuming his role of bishop "for a day," asserting the viability and

---

A Feast for the Senses: Art and Experience in Medieval Europe (Baltimore, MD: The Walters Art Museum, 2016); Éric Palazzo, "Les cinq sens au Moyen Âge: L'état de la question et perspectives de recherche," *Cahiers de Civilisation Médiévale, Xe–XIIe Siècles* 55 (2012): 340–366. Of interest for its discussion of material religion is Webb Keane, "The Evidence of the Senses and the Materiality of Religion," *Journal of the Royal Anthropological Institute* 14 (2008): 110–127: "Religions may not always demand beliefs, but they will always involve material forms. It is in that materiality that they are part of experience and provoke responses, that they have public lives and enter into ongoing chains of causes and consequences. A few things follow from the relative autonomy of semiotic forms. First, material forms do not only permit new inferences, but, as objects that endure across time, they can, in principle, acquire features unrelated to the intentions of previous users or the inferences to which they have given rise in the past. This is in part because as material things they are prone to enter into new contexts" (124).

7 I would call attention to the following works: Jill Stevenson, *Performance, Cognitive Theory, and Devotional Culture* (Basingstoke, UK: Palgrave Macmillan, 2010); Jacqueline Jung, *The Gothic Screen: Space, Sculpture, and Community in the Cathedrals of France and Germany, ca. 1200–1400* (Cambridge, England: Cambridge University Press, 2012); and Elina Gertsman, *Worlds Within: Opening the Medieval Shrine Madonna* (University Park, PA: Pennsylvania State University Press, 2015). Also noteworthy is *Gesta* 51 (2012), edited by Aden Kumler and Christopher R. Lakey.

8 G. J. C. Snoek, *Medieval Piety from Relics to the Eucharist: A Process of Mutual Interaction* (Leiden: Brill, 1995), 22.

importance of his continuing presence. The reliquary, in this case, literally represents the saint. At Cambrai, these two features of reliquaries allowed the saintly bishop and his retinue to perform the role of heavenly witnesses to the consecration of the altar.

Surviving reliquaries and reliquary groups similarly attest to the robust exploitation of Christian materiality elsewhere in the duchy of Lotharingia, especially the Meuse River valley area, and they present us with a fascinating "intervisual" as well as "intertextual" case study. The Meuse River valley, whose art is called Mosan by art historians and associated with precocious stylistic achievements and high-quality design in metalwork, can indeed be considered a hotbed of reliquary innovation.[9]

Elsewhere I have praised Abbot Wibald of Stavelot for advances in reliquary design, but he is not the only impresario of the region to use the effective presentation of sacred artworks to win strategic advantage and prestige for his foundation.[10] Although it has often been suggested that stylistic "advances" are prompted by competition, in the Mosan area the competition may have been most acute between patrons rather than artists, with each churchman seeking to present his relics more dramatically than the last. A closer examination of the relics and reliquaries – in particular the *chasses* (the large church-shaped "coffins" that held the bodies of important patron saints) and the triptychs, which often housed the most revered relics of all, those of the True Cross – will repay our attention.

Among his many striking relic presentations, one of Abbot Wibald's efforts stands out as especially remarkable in many aspects. Although unfortunately no longer extant – only a drawing made in 1661 and a few fragments of the enameling attest to its form and beauty – Wibald's reliquary ensemble for the body of his patron saint Remaclus at the monastery of Stavelot was perhaps the largest project to ever be executed in the newly prestigious technique of champlevé enamel (the piece, dated ca. 1150, is more than 3 yards in height, about 275 centimeters square; see Figure 1).[11]

---

9 For a brief discussion, see Peter Lasko, *Ars Sacra 800–1200*, 2nd ed. (New Haven: Yale University Press, 1995), chap. 18; at greater length, see F. Rousseau, *La Meuse et le pays mosan en Belgique: Leur importance historique avant le XIIIe siècle* (Brussels: Éditions Culture et Civilisation, 1977); and Jacques Stiennon, *Art mosan des XIe et XIIe siècles* (Brussels: Cultura, 1964).

10 My praise of Abbot Wibald: Cynthia Hahn, *Strange Beauty: Issues in the Making and Meaning of Reliquaries, 400–circa 1204* (University Park, PA: Pennsylvania State University Press, 2012), chap. 12. Beyond Wibald's reliquaries, it has been suggested that the famous baptismal font by Renier de Huy was produced as a special attraction for its church. For discussion and bibliography: Jean-Louis Kupper, "Les fonts baptismaux de l'église Notre-Dame à Liège," *Feuillets de la Cathédrale de Liège* 16–17 (1994): 1–11.

11 Susanne Wittekind, *Altar – Reliquiar – Retabel: Kunst und Liturgie bei Wibald von Stablo* (Cologne: Böhlau Verlag, 2003); Susanne Wittekind, "Liturgiereflexion in den Kunststiftungen Abt Wibalds von Stablo," in *Art, Cérémonial et Liturgie au Moyen Âge: Actes du Colloque de 3e Cycle Romand de Lettres*, ed. Peter Kurmann and Nicolas Bock (Rome: Viella, 2000), 503–524; Wolfgang Kemp, "Substanz wird Form. Form ist Beziehung. Zum Remaklus-Altar der Abtei Stavelot," in *Kunst und Sozialgeschichte*, ed. M. Papenbrock and G. Schirmer (Pfaffenweiler: Centaurus-Verlagsgesellschaft, 1995), 219–234; Ulla Krempel, "Das Remaclusretabel in Stavelot und seine künstlerische Nachfolge," *Münchner Jahrbuch*

Figure 1: Drawing from 1661 of the shrine of Remaclus from Stavelot Abbey (original shrine ca. 1150), Archives de l'État, Liège. Copyright IRPA-KIK, Brussels.

Additionally, it is multipart and specifically oriented toward viewers in the space of the church. It was made not of bronze but of equally impressive materials: gilded and silvered copper alloy and jewel-like enamel, a glittering surface that would have caught the light of the candles surrounding it. In its day, it must have shone seductively at the eastern end of the monastery church. Like many reliquary presentations, it was constructed of various parts; but in this case, rather than a temporary

---

der bildenden Kunst 22 (1971): 23–45. In a lengthy inscription on the arch, the dependencies of the monastery are listed – indeed, this was why the drawing was made, as a source of evidence for a legal proceeding (although the surviving drawing is a copy of another drawing and was not done from the original), as discussed by Krempel. Krempel (29) claims a precedent for the shrine at Waulsort where Wibald studied (now lost); she also discusses a Byzantine influence on the style of the shrine.

assemblage of multiple reliquaries, the result is more like a stage set with changeable props. The rest of our discussion of the piece will concern its potential for activation. Although the materials and iconography of this reliquary ensemble are impressive, its effect is primarily created by its powerful structuring of a point of view – like a stage set, it presumes a particular vantage point for its audience. Equally important, its nature is that of an ensemble only momentarily stilled, always poised and ready for action.

The center of the shrine, the reliquary chasse that held the body of Remaclus, was one of its smallest parts but surely the epicenter of potential "action."[12] It is the heart of the ensemble, the element from which the rest of the ensemble "emanates" and to which it returns. It is the powerful center that, although small, is amplified by its location in a larger whole that scales up its effect.[13]

A good portion of the shrine is concerned with Remaclus's deeds, including his founding of monasteries and relationships with the king, which are narrated on either side of the chasse in eight scenes; pictured above are images linking him to cosmic and Old Testament themes. The chasse, thus framed by "action" and glorified in its position, lies beneath and in alignment with the image of Christ as Lord in Heaven. It is further enclosed within the great arch of the shrine, with its inscription enumerating sixty-three possessions of the abbey, and centered beneath a "ciborium."[14] The ciborium, an essential feature of the shrine, at once projects commandingly forward into the space of the viewer and retreats to provide a dramatic void into which the chasse is inserted. Finally, the pediment of the ciborium features the recognition of the saint by the Holy Spirit, depicted in the form of a dove descending from the cosmic power of the *Majestas* above. But let us remember: all of this "staging" holds the potential for disruption – or, perhaps better, enlivenment – with the removal of the central element, the chasse.

It is highly likely that on a regular basis, for feasts and celebrations, the chasse component of Remaclus's shrine was moved and carried in procession by the monks. The predecessor of this chasse, an earlier reliquary that held the body of the patron saint (and which likely supplied reused materials, or spolia, for the manufacture of Wibald's version, which was in turn replaced around 1265), was carried forth from the

---

12 I will refer to the whole as the *shrine* and the reliquary as the *chasse*. This terminology is not consistent in the literature and, especially in German, such a chasse is often referred to as a *Schrein*. By *chasse*, I mean a generally church-shaped reliquary with peaked roof and gable ends. These vary in size. I use the word *shrine* for the ensemble because it is suggestive of a location where the cult of the saint is fixed.

13 For "nesting" effects in reliquary presentation, see Cynthia Hahn, *The Reliquary Effect: Enshrining the Sacred Object* (London: Reaktion, 2017). Here we will not discuss architectural settings even though they are equally important in terms of effect.

14 Although Lasko calls it a "porch," I think it was inspired by the structures over altars that center attention on them. Some were even fitted with curtains, which could have also existed at Stavelot. See Lasko, *Ars Sacra*, 193–195.

monastery on multiple occasions to great effect.¹⁵ In its twelfth-century iteration in Wibald's shrine, the chasse was treated as the saint himself, testifying to the power of its contents and exhibiting the joining of "container and contained" so typical of reliquary ensembles.¹⁶ An exploration of previous travels of the first reliquary of Remaclus will clarify the "potential" of action that was incorporated into Wibald's chasse.¹⁷

At an early moment, after a Viking attack of 881, Remaclus's body was removed from his tomb and taken by the monks "on tour." As Ellen Arnold argues, the body, in some sort of reliquary, was used "to remind residents of the broader region of the presence and miraculous powers of St. Remacle."¹⁸ These lessons were reinforced by the writing of a second book of *Miracula Remacli*, which included almost forty miracles. Such manifestations and subsequent hagiographic documentation and reinforcement were common strategies used by monasteries to raise funds for building and other purposes.¹⁹

---

15 Wibald's chasse must have survived until the period when the first drawing was done (of which the copy was made in 1661), but it was no longer the principal shrine and the relics had been removed to the new shrine: Benoît Van den Bossche, "La châsse de saint Remacle, les orfèvres, l'atelier: État de la question," in *A la recherche d'un temps oublié: Histoire, Art et Archéologie de l'Abbaye de Stavelot-Malmedy au XIIIe siècle; Actes du colloque*, ed. Alain Dierkens and Nicolas Schroeder (Stavelot: L'Abbaye de Stavelot, 2014), 79–85, at n. 16. Such replacements and renewals are common: see the story of the shrine of Gertrude of Nivelles in Ulrich Rehm, "Schatz aus den Trümmern: Kolloquium zum Gertrudenschrein im Schnütgen-Museum am 5.2.1996 aus Anlaß der Ausstellung 'Schatz aus den Trümmern: Der Silberschrein von Nivelles und die europäische Hochgotik' [...]," *Kunstchronik* 49 (1996): 181–189. Monks regularly upgraded the shrines of their saintly patrons, often reusing parts as spolia. Wibald remade much of the interior of Stavelot, so the fact that he reworked this chasse indicates the power it was thought to hold, as if it were almost a relic in itself.
16 Hahn, "The Voices of the Saints"; Hahn, *Strange Beauty*, 23 (discussion of Thiofrid of Echternach).
17 There are no documents concerning the first reliquary, although we might assume it existed from the moment the body was removed from its grave after the Viking raids. Zimmerman discusses the miracles and notes an "arva": Matthew Zimmerman, "Hagiography and the Cult of Saints in the Diocese of Liège, c. 700–980" (PhD dissertation, St. Andrews University, 2007), 197. Alternatively, multiple iterations of reliquaries may have existed in addition to the three of which there is documentation, so "first" may be a misnomer here. Christina Normore, "Navigating the World of Meaning," *Gesta* 51 (2012): 19–34, has similarly traced the history of a reliquary through various iterations, but in that instance a ship form was finally remade into a secular object.
18 Ellen F. Arnold, *Negotiating the Landscape: Environment and Monastic Identity in the Medieval Ardennes* (Philadelphia: University of Pennsylvania Press, 2012), 16.
19 P.-A. Sigal, "Les voyages de reliques aux onzième et douzième siècles," *Voyage, quête, pèlerinage dans la littérature et la civilisation médiévale: Senefiance* 2 (1976): 75–104; Renate Kroos, "Vom Umgang mit Reliquien," in *Ornamenta Ecclesiae: Kunst und Künstler der Romanik*, ed. A. Legner (Cologne: Schnütgen-Museum der Stadt Köln, 1985), 3:25–49; T. Snijders, "'Obtulisti libellum de vita domni Remacli': The Evolution of Patron Saint Libelli as Propagandist Instruments in the Monastery of Stavelot-Malmedy, 938–1247," *BMGN: Low Countries Historical Review* 128, no. 2 (2013): 3–30.

The eleventh-century *Triumphus sancti Remacli* tells the story of yet another momentous occasion when the body left the monastery.[20] As reported in the remarkable account of a dispute, Remaclus decisively won back privileges that had been illicitly appropriated from one of his abbeys, vanquishing both imperial and episcopal forces in favor of his home institution. In the lengthy narrative, we have direct evidence about the use of the reliquary by the monks and can witness something of its power for its community as a material, mobile, and "sensible" object.

The dispute arose over the allotment of income. Stavelot had long been paired administratively with another monastery, Malmédy, as both had been founded by Remaclus (both were also ruled by Abbot Wibald in the mid-twelfth century). However, despite their geographic proximity, Stavelot was in the bishopric of Tongeren-Maastricht and Malmédy in the bishopric of Cologne. In a period when abbots were often nonresident and/or appointed by the emperor, Malmédy and its wealth were usurped by Anno II, the archbishop of Cologne.[21] In the early days of the dispute, the monks of Stavelot attempted to elicit help in their efforts to recover their sister monastery through the stratagem of placing the reliquary on the floor of the church. Perhaps this was a variant of the ceremony called the humiliation of saints; at any rate, it seems they thought Remaclus would hear them better from the floor.[22] The abbot, who had been away during this episode, did not approve, and he placed the reliquary back in its normal elevated position. On another occasion, the abbot and monks took the chasse to legal proceedings in Aachen but did not win satisfaction.

In 1071, with the dispute still unresolved, the monks and Abbot Theodoric took more drastic action. According to the *Triumphus sancti Remacli*, they processed their patron saint in his reliquary to the imperial Easter Court in Liège, passing through

---

[20] Discussed and translated in part by Robert Bartlett, *Why Can the Dead Do Such Great Things?: Saints and Worshippers from the Martyrs to the Reformation* (Princeton, NJ: Princeton University Press, 2013), 318–320. The Latin text is in *Triumphus sancti Remacli*, ed. D. W. Wattenbach, in MGH SS 11, ed. G. H. Pertz (Hanover: Hahn, 1879), 433–461. Discussed in G. Jenal, *Erzbischof Anno II. von Köln (1065–75) und sein politisches Wirken: Ein Beitrag zur Geschichte der Reichs- und Territorialpolitik im 11. Jahrhundert* (Stuttgart: Hiersemann, 1975), 2:56–109; T. Vogtherr, *Der König und der Heilige: Heinrich IV., der heilige Remaklus und die Mönche des Doppelklosters Stablo-Malmedy* (München: Oldenbourg, 1990); Anton Legner, *Reliquien in Kunst und Kult zwischen Antike und Aufklärung* (Darmstadt: Wissenschaftliche Buchgesellschaft Darmstadt, 1995), 37–40; Ellen F. Arnold, *Negotiating the Landscape*. Also, Alison Elliott argues that the *Triumphus* provides unique evidence of oral composition: Alison Elliott, "The *Triumphus sancti Remacli*: Latin Evidence for Oral Composition," *Romance Philology* 32 (1978–1979): 292–298.

[21] Later known in Cologne as Saint Anno: see Kroos, "Vom Umgang mit Reliquien." In this case Anno did not attempt to take any relics, but see J. Rotondo-McCord, "Body Snatching and Episcopal Power: Archbishop Anno II of Cologne (1056–1075), Burials in St Mary's ad gradus, and the Minority of King Henry IV," *Journal of Medieval History* 22 (1996): 297–312.

[22] Patrick J. Geary, "Humiliation of Saints," in *Saints and their Cults*, ed. S. Wilson (Cambridge: Cambridge University Press, 1983), 123–140.

towns and accumulating supportive monks and the bodies and reliquaries of *their* patron saints along the way. After the first night's stop in Louvegne, the monks were granted a vision of a shining path hanging in the air leading to their destination.[23] Clearly their trip was divinely guided.

The saintly cohort ultimately included Saint Semetrius (a saint who had been translated from Rome to Stavelot as a show of support from the Pope), Saints Servatius, Monulphus, and Gondulphus (all bishops of Tongeren-Maastricht), Saint Quirin (of Malmédy), Saint Marcel, and even relics of John the Baptist.[24] Each of these was surely in a reliquary, but, given that the reliquaries were considered not only to hold but to *be* the saint, these reliquaries go unmentioned in the *Triumphus*.

Entering the cathedral of St. Lambert, the chanting crowd of monks, accompanied by their patron saints, placed the Remaclus chasse on the altar, singing the *Veni Creator Spiritus* and the Seven Penitential Psalms; that is, they humbly and specifically prayed for intercession and called upon the Spirit to do the work of strengthening souls.[25] Summoning the Holy Spirit with the hymn used at Pentecost, the dedication of churches, the consecration of bishops, the election of popes, and the coronation of kings, they intoned the following provocative verses:

> Come, Holy Ghost, Creator, come
> from thy bright heav'nly throne;
> come, *take possession of our souls*,
> and *make them all thine own*.
> ....
> Thou who art sevenfold in thy grace,
> *finger of God's right hand*;
> his promise, teaching little ones
> *to speak and understand*.
> O guide our minds with *thy blest light*,
> with love our hearts inflame.[26]

The hymn (per my emphasis above) invokes sound, touch, light, and sight in its project of the arousal and edification of the soul by the Holy Spirit, identified as the "finger of God." (I would also note that surely incense and candles would have been involved, as

---

23 Arnold, *Negotiating the Landscape*, 201.
24 Ellen F. Arnold, "Environment and the Shaping of Monastic Identity: Stavelot-Malmédy and the Medieval Ardennes" (PhD dissertation, University of Minnesota, 2006), 82; Arnold, *Negotiating the Landscape*, 200–203.
25 Bartlett, *Why Can the Dead Do Such Great Things?*, 319.
26 H. Henry, "Veni Creator Spiritus," *The Catholic Encyclopedia* (New York: Robert Appleton Company, 1912), online at New Advent, accessed 21 January 2017, http://www.newadvent.org/cathen/15341a.htm. All emphasis above is mine. Full translation, audio text, and Latin text at https://en.wikipedia.org/wiki/Veni_Creator_Spiritus#cite_note-3:

they represented another sensory form of prayer.)²⁷ Thus, by singing these hymns in this performance at Liège, the monks asked that witnesses be converted anew in their fervor for God through the full authority of the Roman Church and the power of the relics of the bishop saint. It seemed they expected this conversion to occur through the actions of sensory stimulation upon the soul. They were not disappointed.

After the dramatic opening salvo, the monks processed the chasse around the church and placed it a second time on the altar of the Trinity. Suddenly the reliquary made a sound and rose into the air. Mightily encouraged, the monks set out to find King Henry IV and discovered him dining alfresco with Anno, the archbishop of Cologne, the defendant in their suit. Despite their animated protest, Anno continued to resist the Stavelot faction and urged the king to ignore their entreaties as well.

Indignant at this rebuff, the monks heaved the shrine onto the middle of the dinner table. Orders were issued for its removal but it proved immensely heavy – in

Veni, Creator Spiritus,	Come, Holy Ghost, Creator, come
mentes tuorum visita,	from thy bright heav'nly throne;
imple superna gratia,	come, take possession of our souls,
quae tu creasti, pectora.	and make them all thine own.
Qui diceris Paraclitus,	Thou who art called the Paraclete,
donum Dei altissimi,	best gift of God above,
fons vivus, ignis, caritas,	the living spring, the living fire,
et spiritalis unctio.	sweet unction and true love.
Tu septiformis munere,	Thou who art sevenfold in thy grace,
dextrae Dei tu digitus	finger of God's right hand;
tu rite promissum Patris,	his promise, teaching little ones
sermone ditans guttura.	to speak and understand.
Accende lumen sensibus,	O guide our minds with thy blest light,
infunde amorem cordibus,	with love our hearts inflame;
infirma nostri corporis	and with thy strength, which ne'er decays,
virtute firmans perpeti.	confirm our mortal frame.
Hostem repellas longius	Far from us drive our deadly foe;
pacemque dones protinus;	true peace unto us bring;
ductore sic te praevio	and through all perils lead us safe
vitemus omne noxium.	beneath thy sacred wing.
Per te sciamus da Patrem	Through thee may we the Father know,
noscamus atque Filium,	through thee th'eternal Son,
te utriusque Spiritum	and thee the Spirit of them both,
credamus omni tempore.	thrice-blessed three in One.
Amen.	Amen.

27 Catherine Saucier, "The Sweet Sound of Sanctity: Sensing St Lambert," *The Senses and Society* 5 (2010): 10–27.

effect, immovable.[28] After the departure of the king's party and a long night standing vigil by the chasse, the monks finally agreed to return to the cathedral with the again-portable reliquary. In the church, it once more performed dramatically. Again it rose into the air, now making a noise the chronicler describes as "like that of a spirit arriving."[29] This sound was answered by a noise from the crypt where the body of Saint Lambert resided. Then a witness saw a cloud of smoke and a blazing light issuing from the crypt, containing apparitions of the figures of the two saints conversing. The bells of the cathedral rang of their own accord and miracles ensued. The emperor, upon hearing of these events, finally relented and came to the cathedral; he placed Remaclus's staff (conveniently supplied by the monks) on the reliquary as sign of his capitulation and the restoration of Malmédy to Stavelot.

This miracle story records material witness of various sorts: the reliquary with its relic, the bells, the staff, the table, the altar. It invokes sounds: chants, prayers, the ringing bells, the spooky noises of the shrine. It has spectacular visuals: the smoke and blazing light, the gleaming shrine itself. Finally, it does not neglect either the sense of smell – surely incense – or an audience: the townspeople and fellow saints collected along the way, the canons of the other church in Liège, the court, and the spirit of the saint rising from the crypt. Above all, the presence of the saints was *palpable*. Some of this was spontaneous; a good deal was undoubtedly stage-managed to be quite literally spectacular. And the monks themselves prayed that the Spirit make it all entirely effective: "Accende lumen sensibus," or, "Kindle the light of our senses."

---

28 Bartlett, *Why Can the Dead Do Such Great Things?*, 320. This was not unusual for a saint's body and a sign that the saint was acting: Patrick J. Geary, *Furta Sacra: Thefts of Relics in the Central Middle Ages* (Princeton: Princeton University Press, 1978), 97, 105.

29 See Bartlett, *Why Can the Dead Do Such Great Things?*, 320. The passage at length reads:

> Morantibus nobis Leodii in domo sancti Lamberti, factus est denuo sonus tanquam advenientis spiritus, qui humanos replens auditus templum pariter replevit, quo multi convenerant ex diversis partibus. Facta igitur concussione non modica ubi sancti ossa quiescebant sacratis sima, visum est palam moveri scrinium, ac sublevari quasi uno cubito in aera. Non minor quam superius factus est subtus in cripta eodem momento sonitus, ubi pretiosi martyris Lamberti quiescit sacratissimum corpus. Illic ea hora intentus erat psalmodiae cum suis clericis Lietbertus episcopus Cameracensis, qui ex eo quod acciderat aliquantulum pavore perterritus, fugientibus aliis, ut vir Deo plenus et altioris ingenii divinum quiddam intelligens, restitit, nosse desiderans quis esset rei exitus, quae tam prodigialiter insonuit. Nam ut ipse testatus est, densa nebula primitus locum illum offuscatum reddidit, qua statim dis parente subsecuta lux sole clarior resplenduit. In medio illius splendoris velut in excessu mentis effectus antistes conspicatur duos apparuisse mira claritate fulgentes, Remaclum delicet ac Lambertum sanctissimos aeque pontifices, quos audivit archano quodam murmure de his quae acciderant inter se colloquentes. (*Triumphus sancti Remacli*, 2.22; MGH SS 11, 457)

Here the spirit could be that of Saint Lambert, or the Holy Spirit, as above, when it is joined to Remaclus. It could be, in Gregory the Great's words, a more general "spirit of the just": see Cynthia Hahn, *Portrayed on the Heart: Narrative Effect in Pictorial Lives of Saints from the Tenth through the Thirteenth Century* (Berkeley: University of California Press, 2001), 39. For music and smell in the hagiography of Lambert, see Saucier, "The Sweet Sound of Sanctity."

If we return to the Stavelot shrine in its later incarnation, we see that Wibald, in the ensemble he commissioned, demonstrates how such a powerful reliquary could be reinserted into an environment that activated the relic while it remained motionless and "at home." At Stavelot, the reliquary would be returned from procession and nested back into a setting that magnified its importance, reminding the viewer of its power. Using uniform materials to build what can only be called a kind of stage set, Wibald constructed a space where the reliquary slotted into place end-on in the ciborium-like setting of the shrine, while facing and almost challenging the viewer with its presence.

Wibald conveyed the scope of Remaclus's power as Stavelot's patron saint by, as noted above, listing in an inscription on the shrine the monastery's many dependencies. Furthermore, he disseminated relic fragments and founded prayer brotherhoods with regional monasteries.[30] Just before this period, abbots of Stavelot had created libelli that asserted the importance of Remaclus by gathering the textual evidence of his sanctity (including the *Triumphus*); but Wibald, as abbot, rather than disseminating texts, chose sumptuous visual materiality to make his case.[31]

Chasses comparable to the now-lost Remaclus chasse often have figures of a patron saint depicted on their gable ends. One can look to examples from the same region: one depicting Saint Oda, abbess of Amay, between Religion and Charity (ca. 1170, British Museum), or a later image of the enthroned Saint Amandus of Saint-Amand (early thirteenth century, Walters Art Museum, Plate VIIIa), or that of Servatius of Maastricht with deacon and priest (Figure 2).[32] In each of these examples, the end of the chasse becomes the face, the "leading" surface in a procession, even the site for interaction and intercession. In effect, as the comparable examples demonstrate – especially that of Amandus – this face becomes a kind of icon of the saint, and the reliquary/relic *is* the presence of the saint.

In the case of the Remaclus chasse, however, on the gable end we see not a simple portrait, but a more complex statement about the saint's identity – an image that shows him joined in spirit with Peter and Christ, with Peter depicted as the first pope and Remaclus in his role of apostolic missionary to the Ardennes and founder of churches. The two earthly servants stand on either side of their Lord, representing the unified power of the Church.

---

[30] Philippe George, "Les confraternités de l'abbaye de Stavelot-Malmedy," *Bulletin de la Commission royale d'histoire: Académie royale de Belgique* 161 (1995): 105–169.

[31] Snijders, "Obtulisti libellum de vita domni Remacli." The evidence of other earlier texts implies the rewriting of the Remaclus *vita* to bring it up to date to increase the saint's prestige: J. R. Webb, "The Decrees of the Fathers and the Wisdom of the Ancients in Heriger of Lobbes' Vita Remacli," *Revue Bénédictine* 120 (2010): 31–58.

[32] The chasse with Oda can be seen on the British Museum research website: http://www.britishmuseum.org/research/collection_online/collection_object_details.aspx?objectId=51129&partId=1 (accessed 8 December 2017); that of Amandus is discussed at http://art.thewalters.org/detail/22284/shrine-of-saint-amandus/ (accessed 8 December 2017). For Servatius, see Renate Kroos, *Der Schrein des heiligen Servatius in Maastricht und die vier zugehörigen Reliquare in Brüssel* (Munich: Deutscher Kunstverlag, 1985).

Figure 2: Servatius with deacon and priest, chasse of Saint Servatius (the "Noodkist"), Sint-Servaaskerk, Maastricht. CC BY-SA 4.0.

Furthermore, we must recognize that the architectural "slot" that holds the chasse is not a neutral construction. Ciboria were often part of altars and relic ensembles. The example at Stavelot recalls the ciboria of Italy, especially one in St. Peter's in Rome, where the Veronica was displayed (displayed by clerics on a second level of the ciborium, similar to the way in which reliquaries were displayed on choir screens, according to Jackie Jung).[33] At San Ambrogio in Milan, a ciborium similarly encloses the golden altar/reliquary of Saint Ambrose (and looks very much like the structure in the Remaclus drawing).[34] In a photograph of a liturgy celebrated at San Giorgio al

---

33 Jung, *The Gothic Screen*.
34 Cynthia Hahn, "Narrative on the Golden Altar of Sant' Ambrogio: Presentation and Reception," *Dumbarton Oaks Papers* 53 (1999): 167–187.

Velabro in Rome (Plate VIIIb), one can see that with proper lighting, a ciborium can highlight the actions and centrality of the priest at the altar to great effect.

As an important component of the Remaclus shrine, the ciborium was singled out for lavish decoration. It is here that we see the Holy Spirit descending to link Remaclus to Christ (Figure 1), becoming a sort of "familiar" to Remaclus and recalling both the monks' invocation of the *Veni Creator Spiritus* at Liège and the report that a white dove issued from the shrine, one of the miracles described in the *Triumphus*.[35] The primary arch of the ciborium was encrusted with gems, angels were depicted in the spandrels of the inner arch, and in the spandrels of the primary arch were located the *Operatio* and *Fides* roundels that are the only surviving portions of the shrine today (see Figure 3 for the *Operatio* roundel). These roundels reference faith and works in the Church and its liturgies. Surely this ciborium was also lavishly lit with candles, which would have been placed in any available interstices and on the altar in front. Thus it is clear that the purposeful employment of a ciborium shape in the Stavelot shrine makes powerful claims about the holiness, power, liveliness, and past service of the relic.

Above I intimated that shrines in the Mosan area participated in something of a competition for prestige. Such competition functioned in terms of both the perceived power of the relics and the spectacular quality of the reliquaries that held them. Both aspects are readily apparent in elements of the Remaclus shrine as well as in other surviving texts and objects related to this interconnected "family" of saints of Lotharingia.[36] As in the case of Remaclus, it was usually a reliquary chasse that was used to assert the power of the saint for the benefit of his or her devotees. Such chasses, in taking a church-like shape, reinforce the concept of location of power: even if the chasse, as a diminutive representation of the church, is carried outside the building in procession, it carries the full force of the sacred space of the saint's home to the exterior world.

Unfortunately, the chasses cited in the most significant historical texts rarely survive (as Remaclus's does not), but the texts are nevertheless instructive concerning the possibilities of the potential use of such objects, ranging from "testimony"

---

35 Arnold, *Negotiating the Landscape*, 202.

36 There is a growing bibliography on this community of saints: Zimmerman, "Hagiography and the Cult of Saints"; Philippe George, "Le pays mosan, laboratoire hagiographique impérial?," in *Hagiographie, idéologie et politique au Moyen Âge en Occident: Actes du colloque international du Centre d'Études supérieures de Civilisation médiévale de Poitiers, 11–14 septembre 2008*, ed. E. Bozóky (Turnhout: Brepols, 2014); Edina Bozóky, "Reliquaires et idéologie dans l'Empire, XIIe siècle," in Bozóky, *Hagiographie, idéologie et politique*; Catherine Saucier, *A Paradise of Priests: Singing the Civic and Episcopal Hagiography of Medieval Liège*, Eastman Studies in Music (Rochester, NY: University of Rochester Press, 2014). Also see Catherine Saucier, "Reading Hagiographic Motets: Christi nutu sublimato, Lamberte vir inclite, and the Legend of St. Lambert," *Journal of the Alamire Foundation* 6 (2014): 84–111. The latter, though it discusses fifteenth-century material, is instructive and cites J. R. Webb, "Cathedral of Words: Bishops and the Deeds of their Predecessors in Lotharingia, 950–1100" (PhD dissertation, Harvard, 2008).

Figure 3: Operatio, surviving champlevé medallion from the shrine of Remaclus from Stavelot, ca. 1150, Kunstgewerbemuseum, Berlin. Copyright Wikimedia: in public domain.

in legal proceedings to martial support. One account concerns the body of Saint Servatius. An early chasse (the surviving object is a later one dating to ca. 1160; see below) was brought by the canons of Maastricht to Otto I's court at Duisberg to win justice for the "many wrongs that Count Immo had inflicted on them."[37] Similarly, the reliquary of Saint Lambert of Liège (Remaclus's compatriot in the *Triumphus sancti Remacli*) was carried in procession by chanting churchmen in order to break a siege at Bouillon in 1141.[38]

---

37 Bartlett, *Why Can the Dead Do Such Great Things?*, 318.
38 Discussed in Saucier, *A Paradise of Priests*, chap. 5; Bartlett, *Why Can the Dead Do Such Great Things?*, 324. Saint Anno, the archbishop and villain of the *Triumphus*, was one of a number of saintly bodies that were regularly carried in procession in thirteenth-century Cologne – his chasse survives. See Anton Legner, *Monumenta Annonis: Köln und Siegburg, Weltbild und Kunst im hohen Mittelalter* (Cologne: Schnütgen-Museum, 1975).

In Maastricht – the original location of the cathedral of the Prince-Bishopric of Tongeren-Maastricht and a site of continuing prestige throughout the Middle Ages – a collection of relics housed in an impressive set of twelfth-century reliquaries speaks not only to the power of individual chasses but also to their presentations in reliquary ensembles. In the altar area of the Sint-Servaaskerk, surrounding the potent chasse of Servatius (the so-called Noodkist), the twelfth-century reliquaries of the sixth- and seventh-century bishops of the diocese, Monulphus and Gondulphus (featured players in the *Triumphus*), were also displayed, reinforcing the patron saint's power. A seventeenth-century drawing records what was likely the customary display (Figure 4). In this display, the viewer is confronted by five "faces": the Servatius chasse, and what appear to be two end panels or gable ends of other chasses flanking it on either side.

Figure 4: Seventeenth-century drawing of treasury and disposition of the Noodkist, first published in Renate Kroos, *Der Schrein des heiligen Servatius in Maastricht und die vier zugehörigen Reliquare in Brüssel* (Munich: Deutscher Kunstverlag, 1985), plate 11. Image in public domain.

The Servatius reliquary itself preserves the customary form: a church-like shape with steep roof and gable ends, ornamented on the roof and sides with subsidiary figures and with a portrait of the saint on the end panel (Figure 2). However, the four reliquaries of other saints displayed on either side of the chasse take quite an unusual form. They are, if I may coin a term, façade-reliquaries: false fronts that, in effect, imply the presence of a chasse that is not there (Plate IXa). It is clear from the undisturbed oak reverse sides of these panels that they were never more substantial than they are today (although there are numerous nail holes and rings intended perhaps for hanging the panels).[39] Nevertheless, as discussed above, such gable end reliquaries are sufficient to present a "face" and create a sense of the presence of the bodies and relics of the saints. Ultimately, Maastricht had a very powerful cohort of saints housed in these flexible, movable units. Such a reliquary ensemble was truly

---

39 Kroos, *Der Schrein des heiligen Servatius*.

Figure 5: Reliquary bust of Saint Servatius, 1580, Sint-Servaaskerk, Maastricht. Image courtesy of Kleon3 CC BY-SA 4.0.

ready to be put to service in creating a picture of the divine force of its heavenly community.

The continuing use and impact of these sorts of reliquary chasses is well attested to, even in visual evidence. Narrative reliefs surviving from the fifteenth-century head reliquary of Servatius, copied and used on the base that supports the sixteenth-century bust (see Figures 5–6), depict Servatius himself transporting the relics of his sainted episcopal forebears in just such a chasse.[40] (Given that his chasse in Maastricht is said to contain relics of other saints, the reliquary depicted may in

---

40 E. G. Grimme, "Die Reliquienbüste des heiligen Servatius in Maastricht: Unter besonderer Berücksichtigung der Reliefs im Hamburger Museum für Kunst und Gewerbe," in *In medias res: Festschrift zum siebzigsten Geburtstag von Peter Ludwig*, ed. R. Jacobs (Cologne: DuMont, 1995), 341–362. Discussed on the Columbia University website, Treasures of Heaven: http://www.learn.columbia.edu/treasuresofheaven/relics/Eight-Plaques-from-the-Saint-Servatius-Bust.php (accessed 8 December 2017).

Figure 6: Servatius transporting relics of previous bishops from Tongeren to Maastricht. Copy of one of eight panels for the pedestal of the bust of Servatius, original reliefs for the first bust of 1403, copies by Aachen silversmith August Witte, 1908, now in Museum für Kunst und Gewerbe Hamburg. Image courtesy of Kleon3 CC BY-SA 4.0.

some sense be a version of his own.) Once more, the traditional church shape of such reliquaries implicates, in a scalable architectural miniature, the power and prestige of the church where the relics were located. (The reliefs also depict other Servatian relics such as the key the saint supposedly received during his lifetime from Peter himself, further reinforcing the ecclesiastical brotherhood). Thus, it is abundantly clear that the case of Remaclus is not at all unusual: sacred objects such as reliquaries were used as mobile props, reiterating and carrying the power of the holy throughout the region.

It should not, however, be imagined that the aesthetic ideas for the presentation of relics that we have seen employed at Maastricht and Stavelot were exclusively local or only took the form of the chasse. Rome is one source we have cited, but we should also acknowledge the influence of another holy city: Constantinople was likely the source for the triptych, a form that came to prominence in Mosan reliquaries.

Abbot Wibald traveled to the Eastern capital as a diplomat and must have seen Byzantine reliquary presentations. Those holding relics of the True Cross, as discussed by Jannic Durand and Holger Klein, were surely the most spectacular.⁴¹ Evidently, Wibald was able to acquire relics of the Cross, perhaps on his trip of 1155–1156. The abbot dedicated another altar and reliquary ensemble at his monastery of Stavelot to the True Cross, but unfortunately that altar is also lost. However, the abbot additionally placed some tiny fragments of the relics of the Cross in the smaller Stavelot altarpiece now in the Morgan Library and Museum in New York (1156–1158, Plate IXb).⁴²

In this reliquary, the relics' potential for movement and their power to produce holy space are once again displayed. However, in this case, the space in question is not outside the church, but rather is space activated by the possibility of opening and closing the triptychs' wings – there are three triptychs in all on the Morgan reliquary! Embedded in the central surface of this Mosan champlevé masterpiece are what appear to be two tiny Byzantine triptychs. Assembled from Byzantine cloisonné enamel fragments and spolia, these seemingly intact and authentic "reliquaries" attest to the prestigious Eastern origin of the relics they contain.⁴³

And once more, as in the case of his Remaclus shrine, in this triptych reliquary Wibald has his artist supply a narrative frame for a sacred and powerful center. In six scenes, the narrative tells the story of Constantine's vision of the sign of the cross and Helena's finding of the True Cross relics. In striking contrast to the movement and action of these events, the scalloped form at the middle of the triptych is a still and focused center. In that it evokes the distinctive forms of an early Christian altar surface, this space transforms the embedded reliquaries located there into a simulacrum of the sacrifice of the Mass.⁴⁴ Finally, one additional "frame" – the columns supporting niello "domes" on the wings of the triptych – additionally conjures sacred Christian space by suggesting the shape of a ciborium, a structure that is often used, as we have seen, to shelter and enhance the altar space in medieval churches. The complexity of this relic presentation with its multiple framing devices is truly breathtaking.

Second in prestige in the Mosan area only to the chasse form, and more easily manipulated on an altar space, the triptych form was a powerful choice for the presentation of the tiny relic fragments of the True Cross. As Kelly Holbert rightly

---

41 Holger Klein, *Byzanz, der Westen, und das Wahre Kreuz: Der Geschichte einer Reliquie und ihrer künstlerischen Fassung im Byzanz und im Abendland* (Wiesbaden: Reichert Verlag, 2004); Holger Klein, "Eastern Objects and Western Desires: Relics and Reliquaries between Byzantium and the West," *Dumbarton Oaks Papers* 58 (2004): 283–314; Jannic Durand, "La relique impériale de la Vraie Croix d'après de 'Typicon' de Sainte-Sophie et la relique de la Vraie Croix du trésor de Notre-Dame de Paris," in *Byzance et les reliques du Christ: XXe Congrès International des Études Byzantines, 19–25 août 2001; Table ronde Les reliques de la Passion / Centre de Recherche d'Histoire et Civilisation de Byzance*, ed. J. Durand and B. Flusin (Paris: Association des Amis du Centre d'Histoire et Civilisation de Byzance, 2004), 91–105.
42 William Voelkle, *The Stavelot Triptych: Mosan Art and the Legend of the True Cross* (New York: Pierpont Morgan Library, 1980).
43 Hahn, *Strange Beauty*, 209, 212–215.
44 Voelkle, *The Stavelot Triptych*.

notes, triptychs were not familiar in the West before this era but were common in Byzantium in both reliquaries and beautiful ivory objects. In the Mosan region, especially in Liège with its church dedicated to the True Cross, a large number of reliquaries in the eleventh and twelfth centuries took up the triptych form after what seems to have been an initial example commissioned by Wibald.[45]

This series of reliquaries includes many variations on the stratagem of movable wings that allow for the dramatic display of relics and an amplification of the power of their presence. The Adoration of the Cross liturgy calls for the cross to be veiled and then unveiled at a dramatic juncture in its performance. A movement of triptych wings could surely supplement such a revelatory moment in the liturgy. Alternatively, when closed, the triptych form protects its contents and is perfect for use in portable or semiportable reliquaries. Although much smaller than the giant Remaclus shrine (the Guennol triptych, for example, is only 26.9 by 29.2 cm when open, and moreover is supplied with a ring for suspension), these Mosan triptychs stage their relics in a similar fashion, only now the entire "stage set" moves along with the relic.[46]

The Liège triptych of the True Cross from the now-disused church of Sainte-Croix (1160–1170, Figure 7) is an especially striking example of the type and, I would argue, develops its innovative presentation by exploiting elements of point of view and space.[47] It does this perhaps in even more sophisticated ways than did the shrine at Stavelot, but for a more privileged audience (who could linger and look closely).[48] The remarkable evocation of different spaces and viewpoints on this little piece would have forced the viewer to move around, while the reliquary itself perhaps remained fixed in place on the altar.

The composition of the lower center of the triptych encourages the viewer to assume the viewpoint of a group of saints (with the inscription RESURRECTIO

---

45 Kelly M. Holbert, "Mosan Reliquary Triptychs and the Cult of the True Cross in the Twelfth Century" (PhD dissertation, Yale, 1995); Joyce Brodsky, "The Stavelot Triptych: Notes on a Mosan Work," *Gesta* 11 (1972): 19–33; Joyce Brodsky, "Le groupe du triptyque de Stavelot: Notes sur un atelier mosan et sur les rapports avec Saint-Denis," *Cahiers de Civilisation Médiévale, Xe-XIIe Siècles* 21 (1978): 103–120.
46 For the Guennol triptych, see W. Monroe, "The Guennol Triptych and the Twelfth-Century Revival of Jurisprudence," in *The Cloisters: Studies in Honor of the Fiftieth Anniversary*, ed. E. C. Parker and M. B. Shepard (New York: Metropolitan Museum, 1992), 166–177; J. Fried, "Time and Eternity in the Eschatology of the Guennol Triptych," *Viator* 29 (1998): 363–376; Philippe George, "'Sur la terre comme au ciel': L'évêque de Liège, l'abbé de Stavelot-Malmédy, le droit, la justice et l'art mosan vers 1170," *Cahiers de civilisation médiévale* 56 (2013): 225–253.
47 The church is currently under restoration: https://www.wmf.org/project/coll%C3%A9giale-sainte-croix-de-li%C3%A8ge (accessed 8 December 2017). The triptych is now in the Grand Curtius museum in the collection of Mosan and religious objects: Philippe George, *Reliques et arts précieux en pays mosan: Du haut Moyen Âge à l'époque contemporaine* (Liège: Éditions du CÉFAL, 2002), 150.
48 Hiltrud Westermann-Angerhausen, "Das ottonischen Kreuzreliquiar im Reliquientriptychon von Ste. Croix in Lüttich," *Wallraf-Richartz-Jahrbuch* 16 (1974): 7–22. One should be aware that this object has suffered; it is missing the outer surface of the triptych, the angels are flattened, and the spears have been reconstructed so that both hold sponges.

Figure 7: Liège triptych of Sainte-Croix, 1160–1170, Grand Curtius Museum, Liège. Image courtesy of Kleon3 CC BY-SA 4.0.

SANCTORUM) who, although confined to a more earthly sphere under an arch, are anticipating the Resurrection. From this lower viewpoint, indeed, one could look up into the face of the angel *Misericordia*, positioned on a downward-angled surface, and catch sight of the wonderful cabochon behind which are relics of Vicentius and John the Baptist, labeled with an authentic. If privileged to peer directly into this gem, the viewer could apprehend yet another space, physically and metaphysically separate, a heavenly and boundless realm suggested by the effects of the somewhat cloudy crystal.[49] Finally,

---

49 Hahn, *Strange Beauty*, 241.

at the top center of the triptych, vision achieves a higher level of certainty. A tiny jeweled cross holding relics of the True Cross, once an imperial gift from Emperor Henry II, is re-presented here in its original form (inscribed *Lignum vite*). It is as if this gift – surely both imperial *and* divine – is presented by angelic courtiers along with other relics of the Passion (the nails, vinegar pot, crown of thorns, lance, and sponge are included in the relief below the relic); and, furthermore, the cross is revealed to the devotee through a small and very clear rectangular window "into heaven."[50] Finally, in the upper arched construction of the triptych, Christ opens his arms wide to display the marks of the nails, and looks down over all. Once the wings of this triptych were opened, this complex intersection of gazes and *invitations to gaze* presented the viewers with a remarkable spiritual opportunity; the whole was surely intended to stimulate faith and also to provide an opportunity for prayerful contemplation.

In sum, in this essay we have examined two magnificent reliquary displays and two powerful reliquary types along with their uses in Lotharingia. The creativity of Mosan artists of the twelfth century has proven to be remarkable, especially in its attention to the provocation of the senses. Of course, chasses and triptychs were not the only forms that patrons used to "stimulate" the faithful in the period. Head reliquaries, although for the most part of later date, were another favorite shape that had a long life in the Meuse River valley – including renowned examples housing relics of Saint Servatius in Maastricht and Saint Lambert in Liège.[51] The exploration by artists and patrons of a wide range of possibilities of relic presentation and display – which provoked sensory stimulation, included "lively" reliquaries, and made use of many other material and performative variations – continues in the Meuse and elsewhere well into the early modern period, but that is a story yet to be told.

---

50 The angels originally held the lance and sponge, as above, n. 48. The "window" is a feature of celestial vision in revelation: See Cynthia Hahn, "Vision," in *A Companion to Medieval Art*, ed. C. Rudolph (Oxford: Oxford University Press, 2006), 44–64.

51 Although the documented golden bust of Servatius made for Goslar by Henry III in 1050 was an early example, Servatius was represented by two other heads – a now-lost example from 1402 and a seventeenth-century replacement. The narrative panels that accompanied the head are discussed above. A. M. Koldeweij, "Das Servatius-Büstenreliquiar in der Maastrichter Servatiuskirche und seine liturgische Nutzung," in *Kunst und Liturgie im Mittelalter: Akten des internationalen Kongresses der Bibliotheca Hertziana und des Nederlands Instituut te Rome, Rom, 28.–30. September 1997*, ed. N. Bock (Munich: Hirmer, 2000), 217–233.

Sara Ritchey
7 The Wound's Presence and Bodily Absence: Activating the Spiritual Senses in a Fourteenth-Century Manuscript

In Royal Library of Belgium MS 4459–70, a much-discussed fourteenth-century manuscript, an illustration of the wound in Christ's side appears (Plate X).[1] A red lozenge centered in the page, the wound is framed by words verifying that the illustration's measurements are equal to those of the laceration produced in Christ's side by the lance of Longinus. Above and below, instruments of the Passion are depicted in horizontal rows. On either side are written two parallel passages of hymn texts dedicated to the side wound. Below the wound appear words addressed by Christ to the manuscript's user, describing his suffering as a remedy for the effects of wretched human sin.[2] Introduced at the top center of the page, above the uppermost renderings of the *arma Christi*, is an indulgence of forty days for those who contemplate the image. Just to the left, the scribe has wedged in a line from a text that begins on the recto, a prayerful song on Christ's Passion that embeds the wound image. As this description indicates, the wound in MS 4459–70 did not stand alone. Given its multimedia interdependence, I refer to it not simply as a wound, but as the *song-wound-indulgence complex*. A multisensory engagement with various interactive texts and images was required for the viewer to apprehend, unravel, or "activate" the complex.[3] This engagement, I will show, was not limited to physical sensation. To the contrary, I argue that the wound in MS 4459–70 was designed to steer its users from a corporeal to a spiritual sensory experience.

---

[1] The first extended modern description of the wound in MS 4459–70 can be found in Rudolph Berliner, "Arma Christi," *Münchner Jahrbuch der bildenden Kunst* 6 (1955): 35–152, esp. at 48–51. For a more recent exploration, see Flora Lewis, "The Wound in Christ's Side and the Instruments of the Passion: Gendered Experience and Response," in *Women and the Book: Assessing the Visual Evidence*, ed. Lesley Smith and Jane Taylor (London: British Library, 1997), 204–228.
[2] "Lancea crux clavi spine mors quam toleravi ostendunt qua vi miserorum crimina lavi." In a different hand: "Cetera penalia quaere post duo folia."
[3] On "activating" the image, see Beatrice Kitzinger, "The Instrumental Cross and the Use of the Gospel Book Troyes, Bibliothèque Municipale MS 960," *Different Visions: A Journal of New Perspectives in Art* 4 (2014): 1–33. By "activate," Kitzinger refers to the full constellation of an artwork's medium and materials – its contents and the physical manipulations performed by the user/observer (in this case, turning pages, gazing, reading, singing, hefting a large book onto a reading stand): "If we load the particularities of construction, content, activation, conceived purpose and possibilities of use that make up a specific work of art into the words 'object' or 'work,' we begin to approach the multivalent means by which meaning and argument are woven into medieval artistic enterprise, and the multivalent ways in which medieval artworks are construed as 'active objects'" (8).

The interactive media, which include multiple songs, illustrations, indulgences, and enumerations, are bound in MS 4459–70, a 261-folio manuscript that was produced at the Cistercian monastery of Villers. In a colophon dated 1320, a certain Brother John of St. Trond, who acted as confessor to the nuns at the nearby Cistercian monastery of Vrouwenpark, claimed to have initiated the production of the manuscript, which contains a variety of texts on religious life: visions, letters of instruction, documents on the feast of Corpus Christi, liturgical texts, and eight *Lives* of "living" saints, five of whom were local *mulieres religiosae* with Cistercian affiliation.[4] The manuscript is written in seventeen different fourteenth-century hands and composed of eleven codicological units.[5] The codicological units were all created at roughly the same time and in the same scriptorium, evident in the fact that certain hands and distinct black-and-red decorative elements are scattered throughout.[6] A table of contents on the recto of a half sheet at the front of the codex was written circa 1330, and the texts within the book reflect the order described there, indicating that it has maintained its current composition since that time.[7] This general codicological uniformity suggests that the manuscript, although composed of miscellaneous texts, contains a certain unity of purpose. John of St. Trond provides a sense of that purpose in the colophon, indicating his wish that the manuscript take effect on his very soul and act upon his person through the prayers of its users.[8] In this formulation, the prayers of

---

[4] The five female saints were Elizabeth of Hungary, Alice of Schaerbeeck, Beatrice of Nazareth, Christina of St. Trond, and Margaret of Ypres. "Living saints," or "Sante Vive," as Gabriella Zarri first called them, were those religious figures who were recognized as holy by their own contemporaries owing to their purported demonstration of prophecy, revelation, thaumaturgy, or political influence while still living. Gabriella Zarri, *Le Sante Vive: Cultura e Religiosità Femminile nella Prima Età Moderna* (Turin: Rosenberg & Sellier, 1990).

[5] Suzan Folkerts has provided a thorough codicological analysis in her *Voorbeeld op schrift: De Overlevering en toe-eigening van de vita van Christina Mirabilis in de late middeleeuwen* (Hilversum: Verloren, 2010), 126.

[6] Folkerts, *Voorbeeld*, 126.

[7] Folkerts, *Voorbeeld*, 126. Some fragmentary texts and insertions are not included in the contents. The table of contents is also not foliated, so that it functions more like an inventory than a searchable index.

[8] "Quamobrem precatur lecturos in eo quod dicere velint anima eius cum animabus omnium fidelium defunctorum per dei misericordiam et per ihesu christi sanguinis aspertionem. Et per intercessionem beate marie ac omnium sanctorum sanctarum que requiescant in pace amen amen." The contents of the book, along with John of St. Trond's position as confessor at Vrouwenpark, suggest that he may have intended the book to be used by the nuns there. The book includes letters of instruction to the nuns of Vrouwenpark, sacramental blessings that women could perform, and a mass formulary for female saints. See Suzan Folkerts, "Het handgeschreven boek als platform voor identiteitsvorming in de religieuze gemeenschap," in *Herinnering in geschrift en praktijk in religieuze gemeenschappen uit de Lage Landen, 1000–1500: Groningen, 29 september 2006 – Brussel, 5 oktober 2007*, ed. Jeroen Deploige, Brigitte Meijns, and Renée Nip (Brussels: Contactforum Koninklijke Vlaamse Academie van België voor Wetenschappen en Kunsten, 2009), 71–78, at 74–75.

the manuscript's readers are the means by which the book becomes an active instrument of salvation.

In this chapter, I focus on a single codicological unit within MS 4459–70 in order to consider the process through which the manuscript's readers used the song-wound-indulgence complex as a model for embarking on a particular mode of veneration.[9] As I will show, the position of the indulgenced wound within this codicological unit inflects the media that surround it, signaling them as mutually dependent tools for training the inner senses to perceive divinity. The wound is embedded in a series of other media that require visual, haptic, gustatory, and aural engagement in order to take their promised effect on the practitioner. Encasing the wound is Arnulf of Leuven's prayerful song *Carmen de sancta cruce*, which guides the reader from Christ's feet to his face, focusing one by one on the parts of his wounded body as portals to his interior.[10] Even as it inspired spiritual sensations, the disembodied nature of the wound left Christ for the most part physically absent, making it necessary for readers to imaginatively conjure his remaining body parts. Imported into this manuscript and arranged among indulgences, hymns, and illustrations, the prayer became a mechanism by which the manuscript's users entered into dialogue with Christ's body parts; it was not strictly a means of experiencing his physical suffering, but rather a vehicle through which to apprehend his divinity by activating the spiritual senses.

The Cistercian Sensorium

Late medieval Cistercians such as the makers of MS 4459–70 conceptualized the corporeal senses as wholly integrated with the spiritual senses. As Richard Newhauser has shown, the language that Cistercian authors employed to describe their experience of God consistently emphasized not tension but harmony between spiritual and physical

---

9 The unit in question is codicological unit 4, fols. 145–152. The unit consists of seven distinct scripta: an excerpt from Richard of St. Victor's *De discretione naturalium et gratuitorum et diversis motibus anime* (fols. 145r–148v); a report on ten divine visions had by a Cistercian nun (fols. 148v–150r); Arnulf's song (fols. 150r–152r); the first indulgence (fol. 150v); two hymns; and a second indulgence (fol. 152v). In this unit, only the second indulgence is copied in a distinct hand. The manuscript is catalogued in Jan Van den Gheyn, *Catalogue de manuscrits de la Bibliothèque royale de Belgique*, vol. 5 (Brussels: Lamertin, 1906), no. 3161. Additional manuscript analysis of KBR MS 4459–70 can be found in Willem Lourdaux, *Bibliotheca Vallis Sancti Martini in Lovanio* (Leuven: Universitaire Pers, 1978), 480–487; and Albert Ampe, *Jan van Ruusbroec 1293–1381: Tentoonstellingscatalogus*, Catalogi van tentoonstellingen georganiseerd in de Koninklijke Bibliotheek Albert I (Brussels: Koninklijke Bibliotheek, 1981), 22–24.
10 Arnulf (d. 1250) was the fifteenth abbot of Villers.

senses, a continuum between exterior sensation and interior apprehension.[11] This construction of the sensorium is reflected throughout the folios of MS 4459–70, which offer the physical apparatus of the manuscript as a technology to assist the votary in experiencing divinity. For example, toward the end of the manuscript, John of St. Trond included two letters written to the nuns of Vrouwenpark by a monk of Villers named Thomas.[12] Thomas lived at Villers with his brothers Godfrey and Renier and their father, also named Renier, all of whom had entered the monastery in the first quarter of the thirteenth century. He wrote the letters for his sister, Alice, who had taken vows at Vrouwenpark. His letters urged Alice to train her external senses to perceive her environment correctly – that is, spiritually. He offered the chanting of the Psalms as a means of routing her external senses so that they would deliver spiritual significations. Through the chanted, meditative, extended prayer of the psalmody, Alice and her sisters at Vrouwenpark would manage to "vanquish all sins," "make peace between body and soul," and "open" their senses.[13] Engaging the Psalms, the women could defeat the effects of sin and transform the senses from external receptors for transgression into a spiritual means of experiencing Christ.

Like the psalmody, the song-wound-indulgence complex in MS 4459–70 was a mechanism for training the spiritual senses to apprehend divinity. Cistercian references to wound imagery, while often including graphic physical descriptions, instructed votaries to exercise their spiritual senses to engage with the verbal or visual picture. This change in register can be seen, for example, in Cistercian descriptions of the act of sucking from Christ's wound. Although the descriptions involve the somatic experience of putting one's mouth to the wound, what they typically reported as *tasting* was not actually blood but the honeyed substance of their God.[14] For example,

---

[11] Richard Newhauser, "The Senses, the Medieval Sensorium, and Sensing (in) the Middle Ages," in *Handbook of Medieval Culture: Fundamental Aspects and Conditions of the Middle Ages*, ed. Albrecht Classen (Berlin: de Gruyter, 2015), 3:1559–1575, esp. at 1567; see also Caroline Walker Bynum, *Holy Feast and Holy Fast: The Religious Significance of Food to Medieval Women* (Los Angeles: University of California Press, 1987), 153–161. Newhauser points to Bernard of Clairvaux's explication of corporeal parallels: "Sight is related to the holy love (*amor sanctus*) of God; hearing to *dilectio* at a remove from the flesh; smell to the general love (*amor generalis*) of all human beings; taste to a pleasant or social love (*amor iucundus, amor socialis*) of one's companions; and touch to the pious love (*amor pius*) of parents for their young." Newhauser, "The Senses," 1567. On transferring between registers in the physical and spiritual senses, see also Beth Williamson, "Sensory Experience and Medieval Devotion: Sound and Vision, Invisibility and Silence," *Speculum* 88 (2013): 1–43.

[12] These letters are copied onto fols. 255–260. On the letters, see Anthony Ray, "Brothers and Sisters in Christ, Brothers and Sisters Indeed: Two Thirteenth-Century Letters of Thomas, Cantor of Villers, to his Sister Alice, Nun of Parc-les-Dames," in *Partners in Spirit: Women, Men, and Religious Life in Germany, 1100–1500*, ed. Fiona Griffiths and Julie Hotchin (Turnhout: Brepols, 2014), 213–236.

[13] Fol. 259v: "omne peccatum expellit"; "pacem inter corpus et animam facit"; "sensus aperit."

[14] See Caroline Walker Bynum, *Wonderful Blood: Theology and Practice in Late Medieval Northern Germany and Beyond* (Philadelphia: University of Pennsylvania Press, 2007), 14.

Gertrude of Helfta (d. 1302) counseled another member of her order to enter the wound of Christ and from there to suck "the sweetness of the aspirations of the divine heart of Jesus."[15] Elsewhere, Gertrude described imbibing the sanguine beverage of Christ's wound from a golden tube inserted into his heart. Ingesting this matchless brew, she claimed to experience a most gentle sweetness as she learned to sense his ineffable divinity and "felt, saw, heard, tasted, touched" the exquisite sublimity of her union with God.[16] Another example of the transformation in register from the physical to the spiritual senses can be glimpsed in Aelred of Rievaulx's letter to his sister, in which he provides instructions for apprehending divinity. He directs his sister to enter Christ's side wound, the "cavernous gate of his body," in meditation, where she might suck Christ's blood deeply until her lips, "stained with his blood, will become like a scarlet ribbon and your word sweet."[17] Aelred's insistence that his sister enter Christ's wound comes in the context of his discussion of the apostle John, who leaned on Christ's breast to imbibe divine wisdom. Although the wound bleeds and stains her lips, Aelred's focus when offering it to his sister is not on the physicality or suffering experienced by Christ's human body. Rather, the wound in Christ's side is a portal providing access to the experience of God.

In the Cistercian tradition, therefore, the wound could serve as a threshold between the physical and the spiritual senses, an entryway or point of access from the material to the divine. William of St. Thierry (d. 1148), for example, described the senses as a channel linking the physical and spiritual capacities of the human body: "For a sense is one of the five invisible bridges between the invisible incorporeal and the visible corporeal, all in the same body."[18] William's understanding of the senses as a means of linking the incorporeal and corporeal is evident in his devotional writings, in which he identifies the sword of Longinus as the key that opened the door to divine glories. "Those unsearchable riches of your glory," he exhorts, "were hidden

---

[15] "Dulcedinem intentionis de Corde Jesu deificato." Gertrude d'Helfta, Œuvres spirituelles, vol. 3, Le Héraut (Legatus divinae pietatis), ed. Pierre Doyère (Paris: Editions du Cerf, 1968), 302 (lib. 3, cap. 73). English translation from Gertrude of Helfta, The Herald of Divine Love, trans. and ed. Margaret Winkworth (New York: Paulist Press, 1993), 239.
[16] "Ubi quid senserit, quid viderit, quid audierit, quid gustaverit, quidve contrectaverit." Gertrude d'Helfta, Œuvres spirituelles, 126 (lib. 3, cap. 26); The Herald of Divine Love, 191.
[17] "Corporis eius caverna ... sanguine eius fiant sicut vitta coccinea labia tua, et eloquium tuum dulce." Aelred Rievallensis, Opera Omnia, ed. A. Hoste and C. H. Talbot (Turnhout: Brepols, 1971), 671. English translation from Aelred of Rievaulx, "A Rule of Life for a Recluse," trans. Mary Paul Macpherson, in The Works of Aelred of Rievaulx (Dublin: Cistercian Publications, 1972), 1:41–102, at 91.
[18] William of St. Thierry, "The Nature of the Body and Soul," trans. Benjamin Clark, O.C.S.O., in Three Treatises on Man: A Cistercian Anthropology, ed. Bernard McGinn (Kalamazoo, MI: Cistercian Publications, 1977), 101–152, at 140. Original Latin in PL 180:719B: "Est enim sensus unus quilibet de quinque inter invisibile incorporeum, et corpus visibile, invisibile corporeum; quia in eodem corpore."

in your secret place in heaven until the soldier's spear opened the side of your Son."[19] William instructs his readers that by entering the wound they will discover the heart of Christ, "the manna of your Godhead" contained in a "golden vessel."[20] And thus William's meditations include a plea for Christ to "open to us Thy Body's side, that those who long to see the secrets of the Son may enter in and may receive the sacraments that flow therefrom, even the price of their redemption."[21] Like a sacrament, the wound enclosed divine grace, permitting contact beyond Christ's body with his divine substance.

The Prayer to the Wound: Arnulf of Leuven's Carmen

Readers of MS 4459–70 encountered the wound on folio 150v as part of a polyfocal set of devotional practices, embedded within a multiple-verse song, hymns, additional illustrations, reader directions, enumerations, and indulgences.[22] The wound served to animate and illustrate Arnulf's song, forming a subtext to it, drawing readers deeper into the devotional process and coaching them on the proper means of veneration. Arnulf's prayer is the only text in this codicological unit to receive an entry in the manuscript's table of contents, suggesting its primacy. It is a paean to the body of Christ during his Passion, unfolding in seven verses dedicated to his feet, knees, hands, side wound, breast, heart, and face. Chanted or performed, the song produces a "rhetorical action," guiding users in an engagement with the verbal images it offers.[23] The song is dynamic, necessitating both physical action and spiritual engagement with the images it casts. Those who chanted this song properly stepped into a role in which they sustained a dialogue with an image of Christ in their imaginations, narrating their interactions with him: "Behold, I approach you" (*Ecce tibi appropinquo*); "Holy hands, I embrace you" (*Manus sanctae, vos*

---

19 "Investigabiles istae divitiae gloriae tuae, Domine, penes te latebant in coelo secreti tui, donec lancea militis aperto latere Filii tui." William of St. Thierry, *Meditativae orationes*, in PL 180:225D. English translation from *The Works of William of St. Thierry*, trans. Sister Penelope, C.S.M.V. (Spencer, MA: Cistercian Fathers Series, 1971), 1:131.
20 This passage resonates in light of the activation of spiritual senses; William is surely alluding to Rev. 2:17, in which it is said that those who have ears that can properly perceive the spirit will receive "some of the hidden manna."
21 "Aperi nobis latus corporis tui ut ingrediantur qui desiderant videre occulta Filii, et suscipiant profluentia ex eo sacramenta, et pretium redemptionis suae." William of St. Thierry, *Meditativae orationes*, in PL 180:226A; *The Works of William of St. Thierry*, 1:141.
22 The entry is rubricated on fol. 150r as *Oratio quam fecit dominus arnulfus de lovanio quintus decimus abbas villariensis Carmen de sancta cruce ad pedes*. The song is edited in PL 184:1319–1324.
23 Mary Carruthers, *The Experience of Beauty in the Middle Ages* (Oxford: Oxford University Press, 2013), 38.

complector); "How should I respond to you" (*Quid sum tibi responsurus*).²⁴ In this way, the song not only conjured Christ's presence, it also portrayed the supplicants' encounter with him. By performing the song, the singers became intertwined with its subject, Christ's wounded limbs at the moment of his Passion. The song's gestural imagery provided staging that directed practitioners to "embrace" the feet and knees of Christ, "interlock" hands, "taste" the sweetness of his wound, and "gaze" lovingly at his blood-covered face. By performing the song's script, users activated the whole of the song-wound-indulgence complex. For example, singers requested that Christ open his wound so that they could vibrantly taste him ("Oh what a sweet smell/taste this is") and smell him ("Your scent, greater than wine").²⁵ In this way, the song commanded the sensual experience of the wound for the purpose, as will become clear, of stimulating the *spiritual* senses.

The ultimate goal of this sensory apprehension of Christ's wounded body was to request total healing, a restoration of well-being created by reversing the deleterious effects of sin. For example, at Christ's feet, the practitioner utters, "Hail, my salvation, hail, hail dear Jesus," before appealing, "Sweet Jesus, heal everything, restore, and make full like pious medicine. You will heal me here, just as I hope.... Cure me and I will be saved, washing myself in your blood."²⁶ The song unfolds in stages, with the feet, hands, broken knees, side wound, breast, heart, and face of Christ building into a narrative of healing and salvation. Each limb is thus a verbal relic, a point of contact with the medicine of a holy body. Each verse uses the exclamation *salve*, which serves simultaneously as a greeting to one of Christ's limbs and an exhortation for salvation. Arnulf's song thus structures a dialogue between the reader and Christ's body, pausing at each body part to urge Christ's salutary intervention.

In this dialogic process, the song unfolds as part of a series of experiential paradoxes through which Christ's suffering and death are foregrounded as the opportunity for human life, health, and salvation.²⁷ For example, practitioners demanded that a resurrected, absent Christ be made present through their intonation of the song (*emigrare/appare*); as they chanted each verse, a body became visible. Similarly, as they imagined the bitter cruelty of Christ's death, the grit-saturated lesions on his feet, hands, head, and side provided a salubrious cleansing (*lavat sordida*) that erased sin and prepared the way for salvation and eternal life. By conjuring in their imaginations

---

24 Note that the nouns are gendered masculine. Arnulf may well have written the song for his community of monks at Villers, and John of St. Trond may have thought it appropriate to include, unadjusted, in his manuscript.

25 Fol. 151v: "O quam dulcis sapor iste"; "Odor tuus super vinum."

26 Fol. 150r: "Salve meum salutare salve salve Ihesu care ... dulcis Ihesu totum sana tu restaura tu complana tam pio medicamine ... me sanabis hic ut spero. sana me et salvus ero in tuo lavans sanguine."

27 On the paradoxes inherent in wound imagery, see Caroline Walker Bynum, *Christian Materiality: An Essay on Religion in Late Medieval Europe* (Brooklyn: Zone Books, 2011), 94.

the experience of Christ's broken body, readers rendered Christ's death effective and beneficial, transforming their own state from one of sin to one of salvation. They were healed through the experience of his wounding.

This dynamic of healing through wounding, life through death, and presence through absence is perhaps best encapsulated by the stanza on the side wound. This stanza is positioned in the very middle of the song, on folio 151v. The verses praise Christ's side (*salve latus salvatoris*) as a source of salvation that the reader must sense: "I touch you with my mouth" (*ore meo te contingo*). The practitioner is guided to request entry into the wound: "Hide me in this crevice, bring my heart into the depths" (*In hac fossa me reconde infer meum cor profunde*). Within the wound, devotees experienced the taste or smell and the touch of Christ, which was pure sweetness (*O quam dulcis sapor iste qui te gustat ihesu christe tuo tactus a dulcore*).[28] They also sensed his divine odor, which was greater than wine (*Odor tuus super vinum*). The sensory experience of Christ within this wound provided readers with a saving cure (*medela salutifera*).

Although the poem instructed its performers and auditors in this way to taste, smell, feel, and see the body of Christ, there are no signs of users having physically handled the wound image as part of the performance of the song.[29] The wound was activated not through physical touch, taste, and olfaction, but by imaginatively engaging with the song and its accompanying illustrations. Without a graphic of Christ's limbs on the page, the users of MS 4459-70 had to struggle to conjure him, to sense his presence interiorly in their imagination. The song depicts Christ's body parts – feet, knees, hands, breast, heart, and face – in a strictly verbal manner, according to their reception of violent blows during the Passion. Christ's knees, for example, are portrayed as failing to support him as they bent on the wood of the cross.[30] His hands are "stretched out" (*expansis*), dripping blood where they were pierced by nails, and the image of his face is described as fading.[31] When the performers come to the final stanza, on the face of Christ, the prayer offered in the song is a plea for vision, asking that they be allowed to see the face of Christ, departed in heaven though he may be. Arnulf's song structures the stages of a quest to gain sight and other sensory modalities through which performers might apprehend Christ's divine nature with their spiritual senses.

---

28 Here the manuscript reads "tactus" (fol. 151v), which is an aberration from the standardized wording (*victus*).
29 While the wound itself is uniform in color, suggesting that it was not rubbed, the manuscript as a whole shows signs of considerable use.
30 Fol. 150r: "in hoc ligno tamquam reus pendens verus homo deus caducis nutans genibus."
31 Fol. 152r: "viror hinc abcessit." This phrasing marks another scribal aberration from the standard edition. The PL version reads "viror hinc recessit" (PL 184:1323).

The Divine Wound as Aperture

The process of interacting with the wound in MS 4459–70 called for "activation" in the form of flipping back and forth through multiple images, texts, and pages to absorb the entirety of the song-wound-indulgence complex. Although at first glance one might see nothing more than a drawing of a wound framed by hymns and crude illustrations of weapons (Plate X), to sustain an engagement with the varied media on the page required movement, deliberation, and the shifting of registers between song, visual discernment, and interior meditation. The result was potentially cacophonous if not performed with trained awareness.

Although the parts of Christ's body are not depicted graphically, the manuscript does include illustrations to assist the practitioner – images not of Christ's limbs, but of the weapons that caused their injury. They appear as a striking disruption of the text of Arnulf's song on folio 150v, the verso of the page on which the first two verses are inscribed. The disruption is registered codicologically by a break in the mise-en-page, which turns from a single column of text to two. The sole bodily depiction of Christ is of the wound in his side. Around the wound appear words proclaiming that "this is the measure of the side wound of our Lord Christ. Let no one doubt that he himself appeared to a certain person and showed his wound to him/her."[32] The message foregrounds the maker's desire to assert the wound's authenticity, guaranteed by the exactitude of its measurement. On the one hand, it draws attention to the made quality of the wound image: it is an object measured against the real, a replica. But the message also insists that the life-size image is equivalent to the real wound of Christ. "Metric relics" such as this wound were thought to materialize and thus re-present the thing measured, so that the wound-image was transformed into the wound's template, *the* side wound of Christ.[33] Medieval Christians believed that measurement in some sense replicated the template, contained its power. This act of making real through measurement

---

[32] "Hec est mensura vulneris lateris domini mei Jhesu Christi. Nemo dubitet quia ipse apparuit cuidam et ostendit ei vulnera sua." On the illustration, see Berliner, "Arma Christi," 48–51; for the transcription of the inscription, see 125n212. Berliner has argued that MS 4459–70 was the oldest literary indulgence for viewing the *arma Christi*.

[33] On "metric relics," see Rudy, *Postcards on Parchment*, 209–214; and Kathryn M. Rudy, *Virtual Pilgrimages in the Convent: Imagining Jerusalem in the Late Middle Ages* (Turnhout: Brepols, 2011), 97–107. See also Bynum, *Christian Materiality*, 94–99. Bynum's discussion of "the measure of Christ" (94) centers on the medieval presumption that the measure of a person is in some sense his or her replicated self; such an approach to measurement is seen in the practice of donating a unit of wax equal to the measure of the votary's body in exchange for a favor granted by a saint. According to Bynum, "to measure is to absorb the power of the measured self by contact with it" (98). See also David S. Areford, "The Passion Measured: A Late-Medieval Diagram of the Body of Christ," in *The Broken Body: Passion and Devotion in Late-Medieval Culture*, ed. A. A. MacDonald, H. N. B. Ridderbos, and R. M. Schlusemann (Groningen: Egbert Forsten, 1998), 211–238.

was displayed in other devotional practices such as counting the exact number of drops of blood spilled by Christ's crucifixion, quantifying the length of Christ's body or his cross, and undertaking virtual pilgrimages by measuring the distance to a site in string.[34] It was the very act of measurement that transformed the wound from mere representation to real relic, that moved it from the plane of representation to that of real presence and source of power. As a metric relic, the wound in MS 4459–70 defined itself as more than a mere image. The words of measurement announced to the viewer that the wound was not intended solely for observation. Rather, as a relic, it unleashed power over its user; it was meant to be experienced, to take effect. As a bodily relic of Christ resurrected, the wound acted as an earthly point of access to his divine figure. The wound thus signaled an ontological change, guiding the reader toward the veneration of Christ's divinity.

On either side of the wound, words of prayer are inscribed in the form of two hymns dedicated to the wound itself, *Salva plaga lateris* and *O fons aque paradisi*. Like Arnulf's song, the hymns beseech Christ's side wound to provide *salus*, salvation. The wound is portrayed as "true medicine" (*vera medicina*) that effects the purgation necessary for salvation. The rose-colored flux of blood that gushed from Christ's wound secured human liberation from death, activated the purging of sin from the world; it is hailed as a sweet nectar and a potent salve, a *medicina populi* that is the antidote to the lethal poison of sin. It is associated with salvation and sweetness, just as in Arnulf's stanza on the side wound, which describes the wound as containing honey.[35] As Mary Carruthers has noted, medieval natural philosophers and theologians etymologically linked blood with salvific sweetness.[36] Isidore of Seville, for example, derived *sanguinis* from *suavis* because people of sanguine complexion tended toward moderation, generous temperament, and health.[37] Both of the hymns that bookend the wound illustration thus convey its association with Christ's divinity through the dulcet blood within.

The wound's valence as a portal to the divine nature of Christ is further projected in the shape of the wound itself. The wound is fashioned in the shape of a mandorla, positioned directly in the center of the page. This form was common to theophanic

---

34 See Bynum, *Wonderful Blood*, 3; Zur Shalev, "Christian Pilgrimage and Ritual Measurement in Jerusalem," *Micrologus* 19 (2011): 131–150; Sarah Blick, "Votives, Images, Interaction, and Pilgrimage to the Tomb and Shrine of St. Thomas Becket, Canterbury Cathedral," in *Push Me, Pull You: Art and Devotional Interaction in Late Medieval and Renaissance Art*, vol. 2, *Physical and Spatial Interaction in Late Medieval and Renaissance Art*, ed. Sarah Blick and Laura D. Gelfand (Leiden: Brill, 2011), 21–58. See also the essays in Ittai Weinryb, ed., *Ex Voto: Votive Giving Across Cultures* (Chicago: University of Chicago Press, 2015).
35 Fol. 151v: "Salve latus salvatoris, in quo latet mel dulcoris."
36 Carruthers, *The Experience of Beauty*, 81.
37 Carruthers points to Isidore's *Etymologia*, bk. 4, chap. 5: "Sanguis Latine vocatus quod suavis sit, unde et homines, quibus dominatur sanguis, dulces et blandi sunt."

images such as the Transfiguration. As David Areford has shown, the mandorla-shaped wound signaled the presence of Christ's divinity; used as a framing method, it marked the point at which Christ's human body touched his divine nature.[38] The process of entering this wound to experience Christ not strictly in his humanity, but in his divinity, demanded that the practitioner call on his or her interior sensorium. Apprehending the divine, as Bonaventure insisted, required a conversion of external sensory perception of Christ into spiritual understanding. Images of Christ's physical, earthly life, as Michelle Karnes has shown, were for Bonaventure a means of leading the individual to God.[39] The wound in MS 4459–70 guided the reader in this same process of transferring physical sensations into apprehension of Christ's divine presence.

The wound and its accoutrements – measurement, weapons, instructions, indulgence – provide a disruptive force to Arnulf's song so that each sensory modality occasioned by the versified limbs of Christ might be savored. The song's process, and the multisensory perspectives it offered, could not be taken in all at once. Each sensory modality had to be slowly experienced in contemplative fashion, integrated into the sensorium of the practitioner. By means of such an integrative process through which physical modes of perception were converted into spiritual senses, the song-wound-indulgence complex transformed one's very sensory apparatus, enabling the user to experience the wholeness of Christ in his divine nature. This was the meaning of the *salus* repeated throughout the song – practitioners were physiologically altered as a result of its practice, transformed into saved beings.[40]

Activating the Wound: The Indulgences

Having discussed the song and image, I turn now to the indulgences that animate them to take effect. These indulgences are inscribed as promises that, by activating the complex, the practitioner could expect real, efficacious change. The indulgences

---

38 See Areford, "The Passion Measured," 223.
39 Michelle Karnes, *Imagination, Meditation, and Cognition in the Middle Ages* (Chicago: University of Chicago Press, 2011), 99–110. Arguing from Bonaventure's identification of Christ as the exemplar of species (cognitive image), Karnes shows that "species lead the individual to know the object that generated it, and so the impression of divine species, or Christ, on the soul leads the individual back to God" (102). By fusing matter with divinity, Christ, according to Bonaventure's *Itinerarium mentis ad Deum*, made it possible for spiritual concepts to be known through material objects.
40 See also Richard Rolle's discussion in *Melos Amoris* of the "wound of love" that transports the lover by means of the aural reception of heavenly song. This process, as Nicholas Watson has observed, unites the spiritual and physical senses so that the individual is wholly transformed. Nicholas Watson, *Richard Rolle and the Invention of Authority* (Cambridge: Cambridge University Press, 2007).

are not autonomous: they work together with the images and the song, with its instructions for proper sensory engagement with the images, to generate a real transformation of self.

The first indulgence is found at the top of folio 150v, above the wound and *arma Christi*. It serves as a guide to the images below, declaring that "whoever daily looks here in memory of the Passion and the arms of Jesus Christ will receive 40 days of indulgence granted by Pope Leo."[41] Below the indulgence, in two horizontal rows above and below the wound, are tiny depictions of the *arma Christi*. They relay first-person utterances by Christ, addressed to the user from within the image assemblage, explaining that his suffering under these instruments erased the wretched crimes of humanity.[42] Instructional notes also indicate that, two folios over, readers will discover additional depictions of the punishments Christ suffered.[43] Following the instructions, a reader would thumb over the two remaining folios in the unit, where they would discover additional images of the instruments of the Passion and two *more* indulgences for activating them in contemplation.[44] Establishing a list of popes who authorized the indulgence and specifying the number of days of reprieve it granted – three years from St. Peter, one hundred days from thirty popes, forty days from twenty-eight bishops, and forty days from Pope Leo – the first indulgence on folio 152v assured practitioners of the efficacy and authority of the practice. It goes on to calculate the sum of years of indulgence won by this practice: "each week of veneration produces 119 and a half years."[45] By calculating and lumping together the number of days of purgatorial release – that is, multiplying the indulgences offered by various ecclesiastical dignitaries – this indulgence magnified the significance of the devotional practice. In transforming practitioners spiritually by purging them of their sin, the contemplative process also promised to protect them from the terror of sudden death without confession, assuring them that "whoever daily considers these with a devout mind will find no evil death."[46] The indulgences embedded on either side of Arnulf's song thus demarcate the entire set of practices they frame as extraordinarily efficacious.[47]

---

[41] "Quicumque hoc cotidie inspexerit in commemoratione passionis et armorum Ihesu Christi habebit XL dies indulgenciarum datas a leone papa." On the quantifiable aspect of the indulgence, see Flora May Lewis, "Rewarding Devotion: Indulgences and the Promotion of Images," *Studies in Church History* 28 (1992): 19–194; and Kathryn M. Rudy, *Rubrics, Images and Indulgences in Late Medieval Netherlandish Manuscripts* (Leiden: Brill, 2017).
[42] Fol. 150v: "lancea crux clavi spine mors quam toleravi ostendunt qua vi miserorum crimina lavi."
[43] Fol. 150v: "Cetera penalia quaere post duo folia."
[44] Fol. 152v: "Quicumque intuebitur haec arma domini nostri Ihesu Christi quibus nos redemit. De peccatis suis contritis habebit tres annos a beato petro apostolo."
[45] On the calculations on this folio, see Rudy, *Rubrics, Images and Indulgences*, 58.
[46] Fol. 152v: "Item qui cotidie devota mente inspexerit nonquam mala morte peribit."
[47] The second indulgence in this series, on fol. 152v, is a birthing indulgence used for safe delivery in labor, which resonates with the vulval wound image on fol. 150v and hymns to Christ's flowing blood.

Images of the *arma Christi* also accompany the second set of indulgences, drawn neatly in the remaining vertical space on the page (Plate XI). As on the previous page of *arma* illustrations (on fol. 150v), each weapon is labeled. The labels serve to compartmentalize the images, so that users might generate a single meditation on each individual weapon, imagining its role in the process of the Passion.[48] Like the image of the wound, the condensation of the Passion narrative into a single weapon served to elevate the image of that weapon from the level of representation to that of relic.[49] Although these weapons did not purport to be life-size (the way the wound was), they were measured in another sense. Each instrument was drawn and labeled in numerical order of its appearance during the Passion: thirty pieces of silver; one slapping hand; three vestments (white veil, purple robe, black shroud); two swords; two clubs; two whips. Although the wound is not depicted here, an inscription declares that "six thousand six hundred sixty and five wounds" ruptured Christ's body.[50] The computation was part of the devotional exercise, often associated with the recitation of paternosters and aves, one for each wound.[51] With the depiction of tiny, bloodstained footprints, the rubrics indicate that Christ took one thousand steps while carrying the cross, and that with each step he shed blood.[52] The ten footprints pictured, enclosed in little boxes, would be multiplied by one hundred in the imagination of the practitioner. The depictions of the *arma Christi* thus were realized as metric relics in the imagination. Just as the contemplation of the wound steered a transition from external, physical sensation to internal, spiritual experience, so too these weapons activated the spiritual senses of the practitioner. In the process of meditation, their ontological status transformed from representation to real presence. As part of the same process, the indulgence altered the status of practitioners, who moved from

---

On birthing indulgences and Christ's wound, see Mary Morse and Joseph J. Gwara, "A Birth Girdle Printed by Wynkyn de Worde," *The Library* 13 (2012): 33–62; Don C. Skemer, *Binding Words: Textual Amulets in the Middle Ages* (University Park, PA: Pennsylvania State University Press, 2006); Martha Easton, "The Wound of Christ, the Mouth of Hell: Appropriations and Inversions of Female Anatomy in the Later Middle Ages," in *Tributes to Jonathan J. G. Alexander: The Making and Meaning of Illuminated Medieval and Renaissance Manuscripts, Art, and Architecture*, ed. Susan L'Engle and Gerald B. Guest (London: Harvey Miller Publishers, 2006), 395–409.
48 Areford, "The Passion Measured," 215.
49 Areford, "The Passion Measured," 233.
50 Fol. 152v: "Sex sexaginta sexcentaque milia quinque vulnera." These comments are related to the indulgence gained by a year of meditating on the wound. On the calculation of 6665 wounds in relation to the years of indulgence, see Sabine Griese, "Exklusion und Inklusion: Formen der Überlieferung und des Gebrauchs von Literatur im 15. Jahrhundert," in *Codex und Geltung*, ed. Felix Heinzer and Hans-Peter Schmit (Wiesbaden: Harrassowitz, 2015), 175–190, at 180.
51 See Rosemary Woolf, *The English Religious Lyric in the Middle Ages* (Oxford: Clarendon Press, 1968), 240.
52 Fol. 152v: "scitote christus fertur fecisse mille passus ferendo crucem et in quolibet vestigio effudit sanguinem."

illness to health and sin to salvation as they transitioned from considering the suffering of the human Christ with physical senses to apprehending Christ's divinity in the spiritual senses. The entire devotional complex, then, is premised upon a desire for transformation, for passage across registers from the human to the divine, replica to reality, sin to salvation, illness to health.

Wound Readings

The wound in MS 4459–70 was situated at the ontological brink of Christ's human and divine natures, between relic and replica, parchment and flesh. As an aperture, it was the site of transformation, the entryway into spiritual experience, activating the spiritual senses of users so that they might experience Christ's divinity. It registered upon a number of the senses, carrying users from "outward seeing to inner vision," as well as to the imaginative conjuring of Christ's body parts through internal sensations including taste, audition, touch, and olfaction.[53] Even as they experienced divinity in their inner, spiritual senses, the process of apprehending the wound in this manner promised external, physical effects in the form of tears, gesture, and the physiological alterations generated by the modulation of affective intensity. By contemplatively intoning the songs and hymns that surrounded it, practitioners were released of sin, changing in physical composition and achieving a salutary state.[54]

My reading of the wound in MS 4459–70 encourages scholars to consider such imagery as accentuating the continuum of the physical and spiritual senses and their mutually affirming modes of experiencing divinity. Recent scholarship on wound imagery has often associated the physical apprehension of the wound through sight, touch, and taste with a desire to imaginatively experience the physical suffering of Christ. Jessica Barr, for example, examining the wound image in MS 4459–70, has concluded that it underscores a concern with bodily experiences of Christ's suffering. She associates the image with the numerous *Lives* of Liégeois saints, arguing that the manuscript aligns the bodies of its saintly female subjects with that of Christ, so that "word and image work together through the figure of the wounded text to establish a model of embodied religious practice and devotion."[55] Similarly, Nancy Thebaut,

---

[53] Williamson, "Sensory Experience and Medieval Devotion," 21.
[54] Jessica Barr has offered a similar reading, though with different conclusions. Barr notes that the image is surrounded by a hymn (*Salva plaga lateris*) that identifies the wound as "medicina populi" and interprets it as a source of "consolation and healing." She also seeks to interpret the wound within the context of the manuscript, using it to shed light on other texts therein, particularly the five *Lives* of female saints. See Jessica Barr, "Reading Wounds: Embodied Mysticism in a Fourteenth Century Codex," *Magistra* 19 (2013): 27–39, quoted phrases at 37.
[55] Barr, "Reading Wounds," 39.

examining a later manuscript, the fifteenth-century British Library MS Egerton 1821, has argued that wound images in manuscripts enabled the devout to ingest the blood of Christ "visibly and tangibly" in order to "re-feel Christ's suffering."[56] But the wound in MS 4459-70, when read in conjunction with the indulgences and songs, suggests experiences *beyond* the physical, depending on access to Christ's dual nature, at once human and divine.

Queer readings of the vulval wound are especially promising, as they determinedly transgress experiential boundaries, integrating the spiritual and the physical, the erotic and the devotional. Karma Lochrie, for example, understands wound imagery as a site for disrupting neat categories, blending experiences "of mystical devotion, the body of Christ, female desire, and the medical construction of maternity."[57] In such a reading, as Amy Hollywood reiterates, the wound was a synesthetic tool by means of which the reader was invited to "taste, touch, suck, kiss, and enter," thereby making God experiential.[58] Some wound images were said to take spiritual effect only when activated by physical touch – for example, by a kiss. Along these lines, a 1490 woodcut in the Rosenwald Collection of the National Gallery of Art reads, "This is the length and width of the wound of Christ, which was stabbed into his holy side, and whoever kisses it with remorse and sorrow, and also with devotion, will have seven years indulgence from Pope Innocent each time he does this."[59] Apprehended correctly, through spiritual *and* physical sensory perception, wound images promised a specific effect on the individual devotee, either remitting sin, offering visual or gustatory experience, or providing healing. Although no physical signs of rubbing or kissing appear on the wound in MS 4459-70, two tiny droplets of discoloration in its otherwise uniform redness suggest that perhaps the image provoked tears.

Such readings ground the multiplicity of descriptive experiences of wound veneration. What late-medieval authors often described in their experience of Christ's wound was not only suffering, but also delight; not only flesh, but also the godhead. Their sensory experience was not construed in an *either/or* fashion, but rather was simultaneously physical *and* spiritual. Take the example of Lutgard of Aywières, a

---

[56] Nancy Thebaut, "Bleeding Pages, Bleeding Bodies: A Gendered Reading of British Library MS Egerton 1821," *Medieval Feminist Forum* 45 (2009): 175–200, at 178. MS Egerton 1821 is admittedly a much later manuscript and may point to a different set of practices and approaches to Christ's side wound.

[57] Karma Lochrie, "Mystical Acts / Queer Tendencies" in *Constructing Medieval Sexuality*, ed. Karma Lochrie, Peggy McCracken, and James A. Schultz (Minneapolis: University of Minnesota Press, 1997), 180–200, at 188.

[58] Amy Hollywood, *Acute Melancholia: Mysticism, History, and the Study of Religion* (New York: Columbia University Press, 2016), 181–182.

[59] "Das ist die leng vnd weite der wūnden Cristi die Im in sein h. Seitten gestochen wart an dem Creitz wer die mit reū vnd laid aūch mit andacht kūsset als oft er das thūet hat er 7 jar ablas von dem pabst INNOCENTIO." In Areford, "The Passion Measured," 223.

Benedictine-turned-Cistercian nun whose *Life* was written by the Dominican Thomas of Cantimpré (d. 1272). This *Life* was part of the same textual community as MS 4459–70, as it is copied in another manuscript that features many of the same *Lives*, produced at Villers for a nearby women's community.⁶⁰ Thomas describes Lutgard as having regularly gazed at an image of Christ that served to transport her to a spiritual dimension. He states that she would first observe the crucifix with her physical eyes, and that, after a certain time, she was able to perceive Christ with her spiritual senses:

> Whenever she was burdened by any disquiet of heart or body, she would stand before an image of the Crucified One. After she had looked at the image with a steady gaze for a long time, her eyes would close, her limbs would sink to the ground, and she would faint like Daniel "the man of desires," no longer able to stand on her feet. Then, completely rapt in spirit, she would see Christ with the bloody wound in his side and, pressing the mouth of her heart against it, she would suck such sweetness that nothing at all could distress her.⁶¹

In this passage, Thomas provides an estimation of the perceptual stages through which votaries might proceed in order to "activate" the devotional images placed before them. He structures a continuum in which Lutgard first perceives Christ in an image using her physical senses, then transitions into an experience of his real self in her spiritual senses. Thomas's report reveals that he was aware of the distinction between physical images and those conceived in the imagination, and he is careful to demonstrate Lutgard's use of both, her ability to shift from one to the other. First, he states, she stared intently, she "looked" and "gazed"; then, he explains, she closed her eyes, no longer relying on her external visual senses. It is when she terminates her use of external apprehension that, Thomas claims, Lutgard "sees" Christ. She then begins to suck from his wound not with her physical gustatory orifice but with her internal one, the "mouth of her heart." There, what she receives is not a physically or somatically sensible substance, but sweetness, the taste of immaterial divinity. For Thomas, the physical, material image of the wounded Christ was not to be denigrated and not any less valuable than Lutgard's interior apprehension of his divinity. Rather, the image was an opportunity for Lutgard to convert her physical sense of sight to a spiritual register.

---

60 KBR MS 8609–20. Like MS 4459–70, the manuscript also includes the *Lives* of Christina of St. Trond, Alice of Schaerbeek, and Elizabeth of Hungary.

61 Thomas of Cantimpré, "The Life of Lutgard of Aywières," in *The Collected Saints' Lives: Abbot John of Cantimpré, Christina the Astonishing, Margaret of Ypres, and Lutgard of Aywières*, ed. Barbara Newman, trans. Margot H. King and Barbara Newman (Turnhout: Brepols 2008), 211–296, at 229. Original Latin in AA SS 16 June III, 231–263, at 240: "Cum aliquo incommodo cordis aut corporis gravaretur, stabat ante imaginem Crucifixi: et cum diu fixis oculis imaginem inspexisset, clausis oculis et resolutis in terram membris, instar Danielis viri desideriorum, super pedes suos stare non poterat; sed elanguens prorsus rapiebatur in spiritu, et videbat Christum cum vulnere lateris cruentato; et exinde tantam dulcedinem apposito cordis ore sugebat, ut in nullo posset penitus tribulari."

Lutgard was said to have encountered Christ's side wound on several other occasions throughout her *Life*. Each of these episodes takes on new significance when the wound is understood as providing access to a spiritual encounter with Christ's divinity, rather than as part of a strictly somatic form of devotion. For example, Thomas portrays Lutgard as experiencing a vision in which she "pressed her mouth against the wound in his right side. There she drank in so much sweetness.... Thus did her heart inwardly ruminate on the honey of Christ's divinity."[62] Again, the wound here does not generate an experience of Christ's suffering body. Any form of "somatic devotion" that Lutgard might be experiencing during her visionary act of sucking from Christ's wound was entirely internalized within her body.

In fact, when Christ's wound appears to Lutgard, dramatic corporeal experiences seem to happen to *other* people, not to the saint herself. That is, Lutgard's experience of the wound, according to Thomas, had bodily effects on others, a factor contributing to her perceived sanctity. When she contemplated Christ's wound, Thomas reports, Lutgard understood that she was healing others, remedying others of the sin that disturbed their bodies. At one point, Thomas records that Christ's wounds actually spoke to Lutgard, urging her to make use of them, insisting that she "contemplate" them, "lest in vain I shed my blood, lest in vain I endured death." Thomas reports that, "seeing and hearing this," Lutgard understood that she would "mitigate the enkindled wrath of the Father, so that he may not destroy sinners in death but rather, through the mercy of God, 'they may be converted and live.'"[63] In Thomas's reconstruction of Lutgard's encounters with the side wound of Christ, her prayers and interior experiences serve to assist others, purging them of sin and thus prolonging their lives. Similar to the indulgences in MS 4459–70, here Lutgard's contemplation of the wound promised efficacious, salubrious results.

While late medieval wound imagery is certainly fungible and multivalent in meaning, the appearance of Christ's side wound in MS 4459–70 in the context of Arnulf's song and the series of indulgences offers a very specific perspective. Wound imagery, it suggests, was part of a devotional process that positioned users at the border of time and eternity, humanity and divinity, and sin and salvation. "Activating" the wound in MS 4459–70 promised physiological and cosmic effects – the salvation of souls and the healing of bodies. The wound image, importantly, did not denigrate the external senses, nor did it participate in the notion of image-making and visual sensation associated with Gregory the Great's famous dictum

---

62 Thomas of Cantimpré, "The Life of Lutgard of Aywières," 228–229; AA SS 16 June III, 239: "os ejus vulneri dextri lateris applicavit. Ubi tantum dulcedinis hausit.... cor interius ruminabat."
63 Thomas of Cantimpré, "The Life of Lutgard of Aywières," 244; AA SS 16 June III, 244–245: "ne in vanum effuderim sanguinem; ne in vanum sustinuerim mortem.... Labore tuo et fletibus iram patris mitigabis accensam, ut non perdat peccatores in mortem, sed per misericordiam Dei convertantur et vivant." The last words of the passage quote from Ezekiel 18:23 and 33:11.

that pictures served the illiterate, those incapable of true contemplation.[64] Quite the opposite: the wound in MS 4459–70 promised the perfection of the external senses, making them healthier, sharper, and more perceptive of divinity within the world and on the page.

---

64 Gregory's second letter to the iconoclastic Serenus, bishop of Marseilles, is edited in Gregory the Great, *Registrum Epistularum Libri VIII–XIV*, CCSL 140A, ed. Dag Norberg (Turnhout: Brepols, 1982), no. 11. See Celia M. Chazelle, "Pictures, Books, and the Illiterate: Pope Gregory I's Letters to Serenus of Marseilles," *Word and Image* 6 (1990): 138–153.

Alexa Sand
8 Birds in Hand: Micro-books and the Devotional Experience

The connection between books and bodies lies at the root of Christian devotion in the Middle Ages. Word becomes flesh and flesh becomes book, in both the figurative sense of the Gospels and the literal sense of parchment's animal origin. To make or to handle a book was to engage in an intensely somatic experience, rich in both sensory and metaphorical significance. Never was this more the case than when the book itself, by virtue of exaggeratedly small size and formal similarity to other minute objects of devotional performance, such as amulets, miniature reliquaries, or prayer beads, forced its user into an unusually close-up, intimate visual and bodily interaction. Very few small books – those designed to fit easily within the palm of a hand when open – survive from the Middle Ages; their popularity increased markedly in the fifteenth century and gathered momentum in the sixteenth, when miniaturization in printing technology facilitated their production.[1] In the era of manuscript culture, the barriers to producing miniature books were high; without recourse to magnifying lenses, scribes and illuminators working on a small scale needed to have the flawless eyesight of youth but the developed hand skills of maturity. Furthermore, under a certain size, books become difficult to read and even to handle, so the motivations for making tiny codices must lie outside the ordinary functions we associate with medieval manuscripts – to guide a user in prayer or liturgy, to convey learned authority, to entertain or instruct. Thus the limited examples of medieval miniature books bear examination in terms of their somatic and affective power, their agency *as miniatures* rather than as books per se. In this chapter, I examine a series of very small books from the Middle Ages, reflecting on the shifting role of miniaturization in the sensory, emotional, and physical landscape of medieval religiosity.

Miniatures – whether literary or material – have been the subject of much theorization, a natural outcome of the fascination they exercise through distortion of scale. Gaston Bachelard tells us that the miniature requires us to "cross a threshold of absurdity," which activates the imagination as a tool for understanding the vastness of the world.[2] Meanwhile, Susan Stewart observes that the microcosmic ambitions of late medieval and early modern books of hours, calendars, and almanacs

---

[1] Type can be cast and set at almost any scale, eliminating some of the physical limitations on size that exist for scribes. On the history of early modern miniature printing, see Louis Bondy, *Miniature Books: Their History from the Beginnings to the Present Day* (London: Sheppard Press, 1981), 5–7.
[2] Gaston Bachelard, *The Poetics of Space*, trans. Maria Jolas (1969; repr., Boston: Beacon Press, 1994), 149.

corresponded to the "multum-in-parvo" format of miniature codices.³ Both authors point toward one of the miniature's most striking characteristics – namely, its smallness relative to the human body, and its disproportionate ability to affect emotional states of being. Geographer Daniel Montello classifies all spaces "projectively smaller than the body" as "figural spaces"; these, he notes, are spaces that can be investigated haptically – that is, through the perceptual channel of touch – but do not require significant gross-motor movements to be visually or somatically experienced.⁴ The relative physical passivity required for engagement with a very small book means, in a sense, that the object itself scripts a performance of interiority; as I will argue here, the enactment of self-belittlement, of making the self small in order to embody a species of Christomimesis, lies on the boundaries of the spiritual and the physical. Speaking of the late Victorian craze for miniature editions of Romantic literature, Deidre Lynch summarizes, "Miniature books are always *about* the book's peculiar location at the interface of the spiritualized realm of the text and corporealized realm of the text's material supports," offering "a promise of a rich, secret life ('undercover')."⁵

An early, if not the earliest, extant miniature manuscript is the Psalter of Saint Ruprecht – at 37 by 31 mm, it is also one of the smallest books to survive from the entire Middle Ages (Plate XIIa).⁶ Dating to the third quarter of the ninth century, this tiny psalter opens with a prefatory miniature of David composing the Psalms (Plate XIIb), a feature one might expect in a larger-scale prayer book such as the nearly contemporaneous Psalter of Charles the Bald (BnF ms. lat. 1152, 240 x 195 mm).⁷ The first, fiftieth, and hundredth Psalms are written entirely in gold on a crimson-painted ground (Figure 1), just as one might find in luxury psalters of the same period; the text, while tiny, is written out in full, and includes two of the standard prefatory texts: the letter of Jerome and the *Origo prophetiae*, on the sources of the Psalms. Not only do the contents exactly mimic those of a much larger book, but the mise-en-page does so as well: the margins of each page are generous, constraining the text block even further. According to Florentine Mütherich, signs of wear and reader's marks strongly suggest that the book was actively used for prayer and study.⁸ Thus we are looking at

---

3 Susan Stewart, *On Longing: Narratives of the Miniature, the Gigantic, the Souvenir, the Collection* (Baltimore: Johns Hopkins University Press, 1984), 39.
4 Daniel R. Montello, "Scale and Multiple Psychologies of Space," in *Spatial Information Theory: A Theoretical Basis for GIS*, ed. A. U. Frank and I. Campari (Berlin: Springer Verlag, 1993), 312–321, at 315.
5 Deidre Lynch, "Matters of Memory: A Response," *Victorian Studies* 49 (2007): 228–240, at 236. Emphasis in original.
6 Stiftsbibliothek St. Peter, Salzburg, Codex a I 0.
7 Digital facsimile available: http://gallica.bnf.fr/ark:/12148/btv1b55001423q/f8.item.
8 Florentine Mütherich, "Der Psalter von St. Peter in Salzburg," in *Scire Litteras: Forschungen zum mittelalterlichen Geistesleben*, ed. Sigrid Krämer and Michael Bernhard (Munich: Bayerische Akademie der Wissenschaften, 1988), 291–297.

Figure 1: Incipit of Psalter, Psalter of Saint Ruprecht, Stiftsbibliothek St. Peter, Salzburg, Codex a I 0, fols. 1v and 2r. Photograph by Alexa Sand of facsimile edition, *Das Psalterium Sancti Ruperti* (Graz: Akademische Druck- u. Verlagsanstalt [ADEVA], 2007).

a book that functioned both as a legible text of an absolutely standard type *and* as a miniature, talismanic object easily wearable and portable on the body.[9]

In the Carolingian period, personal prayer and devotional piety focused intensely on the Psalter, particularly on its penitential language. Alcuin's *De laude psalmorum*, written in the late eighth century, outlined eight standard uses for the Psalms and identified particular Psalms appropriate to these intentions; Jonathan Black describes the development of Alcuin's brief text into "an extensive program of private devotion, with prayers and other material" becoming intermingled with the Psalm texts over the course of the ninth century.[10] Numerous surviving examples of luxury prayer books reflect the penitential emphasis of Alcuin's "first use": not least of these is the sumptuous prayer book made for Charles the Bald, now in Munich (Residenzmuseum

---

9 For a major study of talismans (textual, wearable ritual objects) in medieval Christianity, see Don C. Skemer, *Binding Words: Textual Amulets in the Middle Ages* (University Park, PA: Penn State University Press, 2006). I discuss this further below. Skemer specifically identifies small, wearable books (libelli) among the category of talismanic objects (125n1).

10 Jonathan Black, "Psalm Uses in Carolingian Prayerbooks: Alcuin's *Confessio Pecatorum Pura* and the Seven Penitential Psalms (Use 1)," *Medieval Studies* 65 (2003): 1–56, at 1.

Schatzkammer, 4 WL).[11] Often described as the first extant personal prayer book for a lay prince, this gemlike manuscript is notably quite small compared to other princely illuminated manuscripts of the period, measuring only 142 by 111 mm. Its famous double-page illumination – the only figural painting in the book – depicts the king in proskynesis before the crucified Christ, with the words of his prayer, spoken in the first person, above his head (Figure 2). Robert Deshman observes that the peculiar wording of this petition – "Oh Christ, you who on the cross have absolved the sins of this world, absolve, I pray, all my wounds for me" – while dependent on monastic formulae, articulates a new ideology of Christomimetic kingship, in which the ruler shares not only in Christ's authority, but also in the suffering of his self-sacrifice.[12]

Figure 2: Dedication miniature, Prayer Book of Charles the Bald, Schatzkammer, Munich, ResMü Schk 4WL, fols. 38v-39r. Photograph: Bayerische Staatsbibliothek München.

The small size and somatic imagery of the Prayer Book of Charles the Bald shed some light on the Psalter of Saint Ruprecht. Designed to amplify and augment the primarily

---

11 Digital facsimile: http://bildsuche.digitale-sammlungen.de/index.html?c=band_segmente&bandnummer=bsb00079994&pimage=00080&l=en.
12 "In cruce qui mundi solvisti crimina, Christe, / Orando mihimet tu uulnera cuncta resolue." Robert Deshman, "The Exalted Servant: The Ruler Theology of the Prayerbook of Charles the Bald," *Viator* 11 (1980): 385–417 (Latin transcription and English translation at 390–391).

penitential mode of private devotion in the period, the prayer book narrows its user's focus to a single pair of pictorial images that provide a bodily template for the physical action of prayer and for an imaginatively constructed corporeal experience of suffering embodied by Christ on the Cross. The Psalter of Saint Ruprecht similarly demands of its user a laser-like focus. A photograph documenting the preparation of the digital images for the facsimile edition gives a sense of the degree to which simply handling such a tiny book, without even engaging with its texts as part of a devotional performance, commands an intensely attentive physical posture: head bowed, hands raised before the heart (Figure 3). The effort of reading such a minuscule, though entirely legible, hand – individual letters are no more than 1.5 mm high, with lines of text spaced approximately 1.2 mm apart – would allow the book's user to identify with the labor of composing the Psalms, depicted in the opening miniature. The incredible degree of refinement in the large incipit capitals, despite their small size, sparks wonderment, an affective state highly appropriate to the language of the Psalms themselves.

Figure 3: Preparing the Psalter of Saint Ruprecht for the facsimile edition. Photograph: Helge Kirchberger Photography.

Furthermore, when one examines this minuscule book, its exaggeratedly small dimensions demand attention to the painstaking labor of its making. We know from scribes' own testimony that scribal work, as a form of prayer or as a commercial endeavor, placed physical and mental demands on its practitioners. Indeed, the complaints of medieval scribes about the arduous nature of their work form a minor literary genre unto itself. Catherine Brown has written of "a veritable somatics of *scriptura*" in early medieval Iberian colophons, including the scribe Florentius's oft-cited and thrice-repeated "I will explain to you in detail how heavy is the burden of writing. It makes the eyes misty. It twists the back. It breaks the ribs and belly. It makes the kidneys ache and fills the whole body with every kind of annoyance."[13] Brown's conclusion that medieval readers were reading "*manuscription* as well as reading a manuscript" is suggestive here.[14] The insistent calling of attention to the body instantiated by a book as small as the Psalter of Saint Ruprecht connects the body of its reader/user – and perhaps wearer – to the hand and body of the scribe, and to the prayerful corporeal activities of copying and illumination in which that scribe engaged. Behind the scribe, too, is the body of the Psalmist, pictured at the beginning of the book in his role as maker (for what is a musician if not a maker of harmonious sounds?). Carl Nordenfalk's exploration of the chain of representation linking the patron and artist/scribe of the Ottonian Archbishop Egbert of Trier's *Registrum Gregorii* to Gregory the Great and his amanuensis Peter, and further back to the Evangelists themselves, suggests that for medieval book owners, scribal labor had a creative and constitutive function beyond that of simply putting words (or pictures) on a page.[15] The Psalter of Saint Ruprecht, in its miniaturization and insignificant heft, hyperbolizes through antithesis the issue of "the heavy burden of writing."

This miniature book's connection to the body can also be understood more literally and immediately, for it is quite likely that it was intended to be worn on a body. Though the late medieval binding is made of plain, unadorned wood boards, in all likelihood the manuscript's original enclosure would have been more luxurious, in keeping with its gemlike quality and its kinship to other high-status prayer books produced in northeastern France in the same period. The Prayer Book of Charles the Bald, for example, was originally bound with ivory plaques set into boards no doubt encased in gold or silver-gilt foil and perhaps studded with gems or enamel. Perhaps the Psalter of Saint Ruprecht traveled in an ornamented pendant case of fine materials, worn as jewelry close to the body when not in active use. Paleographer Bernard Bischoff was the first to suggest that the Saint Ruprecht Psalter might have been worn as an amulet, and to link it to a Carolingian prince, likely Charles the Bald.[16] Mütherich asserts that the little psalter was probably worn "over the heart or on the belt."[17] Could a book

---

[13] Catherine Brown, "Scratching the Surface," *Exemplaria* 26 (2014): 199–214, at 206.
[14] Brown, "Scratching the Surface," 211.
[15] Carl Nordenfalk, "Archbishop Egbert's *Registrum Gregorii*," in *Studien zur mittelalterlichen Kunst 800–1250: Festschrift für Florentine Mütherich zum 70. Geburtstag*, ed. Katharina Bierbrauer, Peter Klein, and Willibald Sauerländer (Munich: Prestel, 1985), 87–100.
[16] Bernard Bischoff, *Paläographie des römischen Altertums und des abendländischen Mittelalters* (Berlin: E. Schmidt, 1979), 42.
[17] Florentine Mütherich, "Der Psalter von St. Peter in Salzburg," 295.

such as this, actually worn over the heart, serve as a point of reference for the scribe Liuthar's famous dedication to Otto III in the Liuthar Gospels (Aachen, Cathedral Treasury), "May God clothe your heart with this book," and the attendant image of the book-as-scroll unfurling across the young Otto's breast?[18]

The notion that a book might be fashioned to double as codex and bodily accessory intended for healing and health (physical or spiritual) is manifest as well in the medical almanacs discussed by Jennifer Borland in this volume; not only are such wearable books formally adapted to their purpose, but they also corporeally engage the user in various series of manipulations and ultimately address the body with their textual and pictorial content. The continuum between the hand of the scribe, the written word on its parchment support, and the body of the reader/user manifests itself as well in the long medieval tradition of what Don Skemer calls "textual amulets." In work particularly relevant to the Psalter of Saint Ruprecht, Skemer identifies a number of small codices of the Gospel of John, including the early eighth-century Stonyhurst/St. Cuthbert Gospel (BL, Add. MS 89000, 137 by 95 mm) and an Italian example that dates even earlier, to the sixth century (BnF ms. lat. 10439, 75 by 60 mm), which he contextualizes as wearable and amuletic.[19] Perhaps it is no coincidence that both of these volumes survive in part because early in their respective histories they were enshrined with bodily relics, the Stonyhurst Gospel with the remains of Saint Cuthbert, and the Italian codex at Chartres, where it was found "in the *chasse* of the chemise of the Virgin" in 1793.[20] The medieval belief in the apotropaic power of John's Gospel, implicit in the histories of these manuscripts and others like them, most of which predate the Psalter of Saint Ruprecht, lends itself particularly well to a small, wearable format.[21] Similarly, the Psalter, and certain Psalms in particular, were understood by medieval commentators to ward off demons or other evils.[22]

---

18 "Hoc auguste libro tibi cor D[eu]s induat Otto": Liuthar Gospels, Aachen Cathedral Treasury, fol. 15v. On the inscription, see Florentine Mütherich, "Zur Datierung des Aachener ottonischen Evangeliars," *Aachener Kunstblätter* 32 (1966): 66–69; also see Eliza Garrison's discussion of the notion of "clothing with a book" in the Liuthar Gospels in *Ottonian Imperial Art and Portraiture: The Artistic Patronage of Otto III and Henry II* (Farnham, Surrey: Ashgate, 2012), 47–50, 59.
19 Don C. Skemer, *Binding Words*, 50–52, 81. On the amuletic function of miniature books and texts in the Islamic context, see Heather Coffey, "Between Amulet and Devotion: Islamic Miniature Books in the Lilly Library," in *The Islamic Manuscript Tradition: Ten Centuries of Book Arts in Indiana University Collections*, ed. Christiane Gruber (Bloomington, IN: Indiana University Press, 2009), 78–115.
20 My translation of the bibliographic note on the fifth unpaginated paper flyleaf inserted into the 1825 binding of the manuscript. The library's notice on Gallica states that the manuscript was seized by D. Poirier at Chartres in 1793. See http://gallica.bnf.fr/ark:/12148/btv1b52503882m/f9.image.r=latin%2010439.
21 On the apotropaic function of John, see Lawrence Nees, "Reading Aldred's Colophon for the Lindisfarne Gospels," *Speculum* 78 (2003): 333–377, at 347–351, n. 48.
22 On the apotropaic function of the Psalms, see Kathleen M. Openshaw, "Weapons in the Daily Battle: Images of the Conquest of Evil in the Early Medieval Psalter," *The Art Bulletin* 75 (1993): 17–38; and

According to most monastic rules, psalmody, alongside the copying of sacred texts (a particularly exalted form of manual labor), fell under the rubric of prayer, the primary "work" of the religious. The miniature Psalter of Saint Ruprecht, then, would seem to have some connection to this monastic setting.

Little, in fact, is known of the origin of this book. Although conventionally named for the founding saint of the Salzburg abbey where it has resided since at least the fifteenth century, it bears no explicit indication of its patronage. Its stylistic affinity with products of Charles the Bald's court school and its miniaturized rendition of courtly conventions of book illumination strongly suggest that it was originally commissioned by and for those closely connected to the Carolingian court in the west. One interesting suggestion made by Mütherich as to how the manuscript made its way from northern France to Salzburg hinges on Irmengard, second daughter of Louis the German and abbess (r. ca. 850–866) of the Imperial Benedictine nunnery of Frauenchiemsee; this house was under the authority of the archbishop of Salzburg, who was also abbot of St. Peter's.[23] Charles the Bald might have given the miniature psalter to his half-niece, perhaps during one of his rare periods of relative cooperation with her father in the late 850s and early 860s, and from her it may have passed to the archdiocese at some point later in the Middle Ages.[24] If indeed the psalter were a gift from one branch of the Carolingians to the other, and one destined for female ownership, this introduces the possibility that somehow female ownership and use may have been linked with miniaturization early on. However, the suggestion of Irmengard as the *destinataire*, attractive as it may be, is tenuous at best.

Books as small as the Psalter of Saint Ruprecht are extremely rare before the advent of printing and its capacity to push miniaturization; as noted, the very fact of the psalter's multum-in-parvo format must have constituted a powerful element in its sensory and imaginative address to its user, as well as its primary challenge to its maker. It is, in short, an object to invoke a kind of gaping and gawking, perhaps mimetic of the stupefaction of the soul in its encounter with the divine. The sensations of awe and humility, both affective and physical in their manifestation, are brought about by the perception of the book as miraculous in its scale and demanding of both user and maker (the delicate and frequent turning of fragile pages, the squinting at minuscule text, the trembling of the hand that had to form such letters). Caroline Walker Bynum, in her oft-cited presidential address to the American Historical Association in 1997, made the point that for medieval theorists, the concept of *admiratio*, which she

---

"The Battle between Christ and Satan in the Tiberius Psalter," *Journal of the Warburg and Courtauld Institutes* 52 (1989): 14–33, at 30.

23 For a biographical note on Irmengard and the Carolingian refoundation of Frauenchiemsee, see Miriam Schmitt, "St. Irmengard: No Poor on the Isle of Chiemsee," in *Medieval Women Monastics: Wisdom's Wellspring*, ed. Miriam Schmitt and Linda Kulzer (Collegeville, MN: The Liturgical Press, Order of Saint Benedict, 1996), 117–134.

24 Mütherich, "Der Psalter von St. Peter," 296.

translates as "wonder," was "a complex set of ideas and reactions" stemming from processes and habits of perception that were "cognitive, non-appropriative, perspectival, and particular," including both physiological response and mental operations of recognition.[25] The notion of wonder as perspectival in character brings us back around to the issue of scale; the very quality of miniaturization, which in the Saint Ruprecht Psalter is its sole singularity (it is otherwise a "normal" kind of psalter), instigates the kind of perspectival shock described by Gaston Bachelard. The point of this shock, this scalar disconnect, is to induce a productive and receptive spiritual state, an open way toward God. Cynthia Hahn has written about the "complex instruction of the body and the senses, the teaching of *reverentia*," or wonder, as a function of medieval reliquaries, and it seems fair to extend this function to a wondrously small book such as the Saint Ruprecht Psalter.[26]

The singularity of the Saint Ruprecht Psalter is integral to its efficacy. It is so much smaller than contemporaneous books of its kind (personal, devotional), that it can only be understood in terms of this singularity. But a book need not go so far down the scale of size to function, in some respects, as a miniature. While almost no evidence suggests that books less than one hundred millimeters on their long edge were produced in any significant number in the period between about 900 and 1200, portable, pocket-sized manuscripts were not unusual, and the connection between these relatively small-format books and the bodies of the saints was strong. In July of 972, Abbot Maiolus (Maieul) of Cluny was taken captive by Muslim brigands from La Garde-Freinet as he crossed the Saint Bernard Pass.[27] Although textual evidence from the time of this event is limited to a short note pleading for ransom that he sent to his monks, later accounts of his life fill in details of the story, employing oral tradition, hagiographic topoi, and perhaps also imaginative reconstruction. Among the details supplied by these later eleventh- and twelfth-century accounts is the fact that Maiolus was traveling with a selection of books. By the middle of the twelfth century, an updated version of Maiolus's life by the monk Nalgod featured an episode in which, after his captivity and the pillaging of his belongings, Maiolus discovers hidden in the folds of his cloak a small book dedicated to the Assumption of the Virgin, which plays an important role in his miraculous release.[28] That this wondrous codex

---

25 Caroline Walker Bynum, "Wonder," *The American Historical Review* 102 (1997): 1–26, at 3.
26 Cynthia Hahn, *Strange Beauty: Issues in the Making and Meaning of Reliquaries, 400–circa 1204* (University Park, PA: Penn State University Press, 2012), 17. See also Hahn's chapter in this volume.
27 For an account of the incident and an analysis of its framing in monastic hagiography, see Scott Bruce, "An Abbot between Two Cultures: Maiolus of Cluny Considers the Muslims of La Garde-Freinet," *Early Medieval Europe* 15 (2007): 426–440; and, at greater length, in Scott Bruce, *Cluny and the Muslims of La Garde-Freinet: Hagiography and the Problem of Islam in Medieval Europe* (Ithaca, NY: Cornell University Press, 2015).
28 Scott Bruce, "Clandestine Codices in the Captivity Narratives of Abbot Maiolus of Cluny," in *Teaching and Learning in Medieval Europe: Essays in Honour of Gernot R. Wieland on his 67th Birthday*, ed. Greti

goes unnoticed even by its wearer/bearer suggests that it is very small indeed, and moreover points to a connection between book and body so intimate as to erase the boundaries between them (Maiolus's saintly body and the little codex both effectuate miracles). It may or may not be the case that the historical Maiolus carried with him a very small codex – what is important here is that, by the middle of the twelfth century, Nalgod could imagine such a codex, and would do so in the context of hagiography.

This situation contrasts with the development, in the middle of the thirteenth century, of a much more distinct and regular practice of fashioning very tiny prayer books for a very specific audience. As the book of hours emerged from its supplementary role in monastic liturgical manuscripts to attain the status of the premier text of lay devotion in the later Middle Ages, the practice of making small books gained momentum. In particular, books of hours and related lay prayer books fashioned for female users (as indicated by the use of feminine word forms in gendered prayers) seem to have been considered particularly well suited to small formats. In her *Gothic Manuscript Illumination in the Diocese of Liege (c. 1250–c. 1330)*, Judith Oliver surveyed the large number of illuminated prayer books, mostly psalters and books of hours, produced in Liège and its environs for the burgeoning religious community of lay women who came to be known as Beguines, as well as for patrons sympathetic to this movement if not themselves committed to its rigorous lifestyle.[29] Many of these books, she notes, were smaller than was usual for psalters or psalter-hours of the thirteenth century, and while some were made for male owners, a great number of them indicate female use.[30] Although the sizes of the Liège manuscripts vary considerably, an example such as the one now in the British Library as MS Royal 2 A.iii, measuring 120 by 85 mm, is roughly typical – compact, but still significantly larger than the Psalter of Saint Ruprecht.

If there was a "standard" size for books of hours and combined psalter-hours in the early period of their popularity, between about 1280 and 1320, it fell somewhere between the dimensions of modern mass-market and B-format paperbacks – that is, between about 170 by 110 mm and 200 by 130 mm.[31] Thus, the smaller average dimensions of the Liège group studied by Oliver stand out, especially because these books come from the very early period of the development of the book of hours as a standalone text for lay devotion. A particularly striking example of this miniaturizing

---

Dinkova-Bruun and Tristan Major, Publications of the Journal of Medieval Latin 11 (Brepols: Turnhout, 2017), 149–162. My sincere thanks to Scott for sharing this essay with me in draft form.

29 Judith Oliver, *Gothic Manuscript Illumination in the Diocese of Liege (c. 1250–c. 1330)*, 2 vols. (Leuven: Peeters, 1988). Also, Judith Oliver, "Devotional Psalters and the Study of Beguine Spirituality," *Vox Benedictina: A Journal of Translations from Monastic Sources* 9 (1992): 199–225.

30 Judith *Oliver, Gothic Manuscript Illumination in the Diocese of Liege*, 115–118.

31 This estimate is based on measurements recorded in my notes, taken over a period of about fifteen years, which include primarily French, Franco-Flemish, and English books of hours and psalter-hours.

approach to the book of hours is also among the earliest extant examples of a freestanding book of hours from the Continent: dated by Oliver and Adelaide Bennett Hagens to around 1270, this is a palm-sized book acquired by the Special Collections and Archives of the Merrill-Cazier Library at Utah State University in 2011, which I will call the Logan Hours (Logan, Utah, being the location of the library).[32] The Logan Hours measures 103 by 74 mm, and is thus among the smallest of the Liège group. Its sixteenth-century binding has been conserved, although it is clear from the disorder of certain quires, missing text, and other disruptions that a less-than-meticulous agent at some point unbound the book and reassembled it after pinching the best of its illuminated pages. The subsequent rebinding was very tight, rendering the book almost impossible to photograph well because it is difficult to open sufficiently (Plate XIIIa).

Oliver and Bennett Hagens were able to ascertain that the Logan Hours contains a partial calendar typical of the Diocese of Liège, though it is missing some specific feasts that would tie it to the cathedral; the same pattern is evident in the suffrages. In particular, both the calendar and the suffrages make mention of Saint Ghislain, a Frankish hermit revered as the founder of an eponymous monastery near Mons, the capital of the Hainault region just to the west of Liège, in the neighboring diocese of Cambrai. Thus it seems possible that the book may have been intended for an individual with ties to both regions and with a particular attachment to Saint Ghislain in particular.[33] In addition to the calendar, the volume contains the hours of the Virgin in the use of Liège, the Penitential and Gradual Psalms, a litany with typical Liégeois saints, the Office of the Dead, and a series of Marian prayers. Although the aforementioned cutting and rebinding obscures the full outline of the program of illumination, the book was also equipped with a set of historiated initials and marginalia; four of the initials survive, along with the labors of the months and signs of the zodiac in what remains of the calendar. The most endearing of the book's paintings are the minuscule golden birds that perch in the margins throughout the text (Plate XIIIb), which may allude to the eagle of Saint John, the dove of the Holy Spirit, or the goldfinch, symbol of the human soul. Or perhaps they are rather the multitude of birds that, according to the prophecy of Ezekiel, will gather and make their nests under the shadow of the great cedar planted on the high mountains of Israel, understood by Christian exegetes of the Middle Ages to be Christ, drawn from the stock of David (Ezekiel 17:23).

---

32 Judith Oliver and Adelaide Bennett Hagens, typescript notes, 1994, based on an examination of the manuscript when it was part of a private collection being prepared for sale to a dealer. These were kindly shared with me by Judy, with Adelaide's permission.

33 This analysis relies heavily on the typescript notes and on Judith Oliver's talk "Gate of Paradise: The New Mercantile Economy and the Book of Hours," presented at Utah State University on 20 November 2015.

Anyone familiar with books of hours will recognize this general ensemble of texts and illuminations, but it bears keeping in mind that the independent book of hours, as opposed to the combined psalter-hours, was still a rare bird in the last few decades of the thirteenth century. What was to become "standard" by 1350 was still taking shape in the laboratory of such books as this. Along with the inclusion of Saint Ghislain, the particular selection of Marian prayers, the unusually abundant avian marginalia, and the now mostly destroyed program of historiated initials, the small size of the Logan Hours is one of many variables that make the book distinctive. Such customization was one of the salient features of books of hours, and no doubt contributed to their growing popularity amongst devout lay folk whose religiosity was shaped by the confessional emphasis of contemporary Mendicant teaching and the intense self-scrutiny and inwardness it fostered.

Why make the Logan Hours so small? Practical explanations, such as to make the book easier to carry in one's purse or in one's hand, arise. However, this would account just as well for those books between 100 and 200 mm in height, and is probably the reason for the much more common dimensions I mentioned earlier. Under 100 mm in height, either the legibility or completeness of the text suffers, or else the book must become awkwardly thick in order to contain the requisite text – this is certainly the case with the Psalter of Saint Ruprecht, which is nearly as thick as it is tall. Even if legibility were not the prime concern of medieval book makers and users – and sometimes the evidence suggests it was not – a totally mechanistic and functional explanation for the smallest books of hours will not suffice. A book such as the Logan Hours is simply smaller than need be from this perspective. The rarity of such items, too, argues for their exceptional dimensions as part of a very particular way of thinking about their relationship to those who would use them as elements of a devotional performance.

What if the small size of the Logan Hours refers to the nature of its content? The primary text in this book was, after all, known in the Middle Ages by its Latin designation, *Officium Parvum Beatae Mariae Virginis*, commonly translated as "The Little Office of the Blessed Virgin Mary." What is "parvum," or "little," about it is its length relative to the full canonical Mass of the Virgin. Furthermore, from its monastic origins in the Carolingian period, this office was most frequently enacted in privacy or quasi-privacy, thus on a smaller scale than the Eucharistic Mass, the benchmark of medieval religious performance. One might also argue that because by the middle of the thirteenth century it could be enacted by anyone of any status, regardless of gender, it was intrinsically lower in prestige than the sacerdotally administered Mass.

The littleness of the Hours of the Virgin did not necessarily make them lesser in terms of religious experience or devotional impact. Theologically, smallness or becoming small was a form of Christomimesis. Thomas Aquinas (d. 1274) put it: "To restore man, who had been laid low by sin, to the heights of divine glory, the Word of the eternal Father, though containing all things within His immensity, willed to become small. This He did, not by putting aside His greatness, but by taking to Himself our littleness."³⁴ Aquinas by no means drew this notion of inversion from thin air. Paul's statement that he is "the least of the apostles" (I Corinthians 15:9) lies at the heart of the rhetoric of self-diminution that saturates the devotional language of Christianity. Mary, at the Annunciation (Luke 1:38), names herself "ancilla," often translated into English as "handmaiden," but more literally a little servant or slave girl. Self-belittlement as a strategy of propitiation in prayer increases steadily from the late eleventh century into the thirteenth.³⁵ Anselm calls himself a "little man" time and again, and littleness is one of the distinctive features of the entire Franciscan project – the Italian "fraticelli" or "little brothers" became the Order of Friars Minor, the humility of mendicancy facilitating their identity with the non-noble classes, or the "little people," in Francis's own words. While the Logan Hours does not show any markedly Franciscan traits, it does belong to a milieu in which Mendicant approaches to spirituality were all-pervasive, and in which many, if not most, lay folk sought spiritual guidance from and gave their confessions to Mendicant clergy.³⁶

The remarkably small size of the Logan Hours suits the devotional program of making the self small in order to become Christlike; its material dimensions reify the spiritual concept of laudable diminution. Also, such small books are cute. "Cute," of course, is not a medieval concept, but it may just be one of the few aesthetic affective triggers that has a real basis in the evolution of the human brain. Philosopher John Morreall identifies the aesthetics of the cute as based in the feelings of tenderness and protectiveness stirred in human adults by human infants, and by extension felt toward adults with infantile characteristics that make them adorable, similarly configured animals, and inanimate objects that, like infants, are "small relative to things of (their) kind" and visually present "a certain innocence and non-threateningness like that of a baby."³⁷ Late medieval and early modern

---

34 "Aeterni patris verbum sua immensitate universa comprehendens, ut hominem per peccata minoratum in celsitudinem divinae gloriae revocaret, breve fieri voluit nostra brevitate assumpta, non sua deposita maiestate." Thomas Aquinas, *Compendium Theologiae: Compendium of Theology*, trans. Cyril Vollert (St. Louis: B. Herder Book Company, 1947), bk. 1, chap. 1 ("Scope of the Present Work"), accessed 18 April 2016, http://dhspriory.org/thomas/Compendium.htm#1.
35 For the link between gendered language and the embrace of the small in the rhetoric of devotion, see Caroline Walker Bynum's important essay on the non-alignment of biological sex and spiritual gender identity, "'... And Woman His Humanity': Female Imagery in the Religious Writing of the Later Middle Ages," in *Gender and Religion: On the Complexity of Symbols*, ed. Caroline Walker Bynum, Stevan Harrell, and Paula Richman (Boston: Beacon Press, 1986), 257–288, reprinted in Caroline Walker Bynum, *Fragmentation and Redemption: Essays on Gender and the Human Body in Medieval Religion* (New York: Zone Books, 1991), 151–179.
36 On the Mendicants and the Beguines in the Low Countries, see Walter Simons, *Cities of Ladies: Beguine Communities of the Low Countries, 1200–1565* (Philadelphia, PA: University of Pennsylvania Press, 2001), 116–120.
37 John Morreall, "Cuteness," *British Journal of Aesthetics* 31 (1991): 39–47, at 45.

artists certainly tapped into the cute as a strategy for heightening the affective tenor of devotional experience. For example, cuteness seems to be a factor in the proliferation from 1250 to 1350 of small ivory statuettes of the Virgin and Child that emphasize the ludic, tender exchange between mother and infant, exaggerate the childlike features of Mary's face (large eyes, small nose and chin, rounded cheeks), and attend to such adorable traits of the infant as the rings of chubby flesh around his wrists and ankles and the soft curve of his belly and buttocks (Figure 4). Sianne Ngai, theorizing cuteness in relation to contemporary art, defines it as "an aesthetic disclosing the surprisingly wide spectrum of feelings, ranging from tenderness to aggression, that we harbor toward ostensively subordinate and unthreatening

Figure 4: Virgin and Child ("Rattier Virgin"), elephant ivory, Paris, 1280–1300. Collection: The Victoria and Albert Museum, London, V&A 200–1867. Photograph courtesy of the Board of Trustees of the Victoria and Albert Museum.

commodities."[38] Her identification of the response to "cute" as rooted in such visceral feelings as "tenderness" and "aggression" is telling; the small book, and the (perhaps) small body and/or soul it indexes, arouse strong feelings precisely because there is something not quite certain about their subordination.

Cuteness and miniaturization may be attractive for psychosexual reasons, as Ngai suggests and as Susan Stewart famously argued in her ubiquitously quoted *On Longing*, or for more evolutionary ones such as those Morreall posits. Perry Nodelman's account of why miniature heroes and heroines are so pervasive in modern children's literature also has something to do with it; he writes, "So when these small beings prevail over insurmountable odds, as they always do, they represent a potent version of the wish-fulfillment fantasy: the very small can triumph over the dangerously large, the very powerless over the exceedingly powerful."[39] Although Nodelman is thinking of *The Indian in the Cupboard* and *Thumbellina*, the idea of the small and meek conquering the great and proud brings us back around to Christ making himself small in order to conquer Satan by redeeming Adam's sin. It also describes the situation of many of the owners of these early books of hours – namely, devout laywomen.

The Logan Hours was certainly intended for female use, with many feminine word forms in the prayer section. A conceptual link emerges that connects small books to individuals who were socially constructed as small in importance and in power, and who also built their identities around making themselves small through prayer just as Christ made himself small through incarnation. At a moment in the history of the development of lay piety when laywomen's spiritual ambition sometimes threatened the patriarchal order of the Church, making feminine piety small and self-effacing was a survival strategy, as well as a cordon of containment. In those instances when a female book owner initiated the commission of a very small book, the choice may have reflected, to some degree, an interest in the devotional power of the small. On the other hand, as Madeline Caviness has suggested regarding the diminutive Hours of Jeanne d'Évreux (discussed below), sometimes the choices made about the content and format of prayer books for female users were made "against" the envisioned owner, embedding constraining messages about her sexuality, spirituality, and social

---

38 Sianne Ngai, "Our Aesthetic Categories," *PMLA* 125 (2010): 948–958, at 949. Ngai explores this idea further in her book *Our Aesthetic Categories: Zany, Cute, Interesting* (Cambridge, MA: Harvard University Press, 2012), 53–109, where she is primarily concerned with the way cuteness "constrict[s] the gap between consumer and commodity" in a capitalist context (71). Relevant to premodern miniature books, however, she situates "cute" in relation to the hyperpassivity of the object: "there is a sense in which the cute thing is the most reified or thinglike of things, the most objectified of objects or even an 'object' par excellence" (93). This she connects to a kind of reflective mimesis, as described by Benjamin and Adorno, as an "assimilation of the subject to the object" (101). It is precisely the slippage between small book and "small person" that concerns me here.
39 Perry Nodelman, *The Pleasures of Children's Literature* (White Plains, NY: Longman, 1992), 199.

role.⁴⁰ But as Caviness notes, the longer Jeanne owned the book that at its outset (intentionally, in her account) enforced a sternly repressive spiritual regimen on the impressionable bride of fourteen, the less efficacious it may have become in its ideological browbeating.⁴¹ The equation of smallness and female subjectivity thus cuts both ways. On the one hand, it may help the marginalized female devotee to articulate and perform her spiritual agency under the radar, while on the other hand it may reinforce a male-centered ideology in which the diminution of the feminine functions as a strategy to neutralize the perceived threat of a powerful and unregulated form of religiosity.

The Logan Hours comes from the region of northwestern Europe most closely associated with the power – and the problems – of female lay piety in the thirteenth century. The Beguine movement had its roots in the Diocese of Liège with Mary of Oignies, and by the 1270s, the presence of these irregular but extremely self-disciplined religious women in the towns and cities of the Low Countries was an established fact. One of the few Beguine women to leave a substantial body of written evidence in her own voice, the Dutch mystic Hadewijch, explicitly invokes the commonplace of the smallness of humanity compared to the greatness of God's love just before describing herself as "too far from having obtained full growth."⁴² While consistent with a long tradition of monastic self-denigration, Hadewijch's belittling of herself also functions as an evasion of the possible (indeed probable) accusation that, as a laywoman daring to write on theological matters, she exceeded her authority and possibly transgressed into heresy. The threat of such allegations was real. As Paul Mommaerts notes, numerous papal and comital acts in the 1230s and 1240s attest to the near-constant persecution of *mulieres religiosae*.⁴³ Hadewijch herself mentions a "beguine who was killed by Master Robbaert for her perfect Love," referring to the

---

40 Madeline Caviness, "Patron or Matron? A Capetian Bride and a *Vade Mecum* for Her Marriage Bed," *Speculum* 68 (1993): 333–362.
41 Caviness, "Patron or Matron?," 343: "The reading response that I am establishing for the Cloisters Hours is that of the very young bride; in later life she would have been less susceptible." She characterizes the book's intended effect upon Jeanne as a "psychological clitoridectomy" (365), a claim that has raised objections among some scholars, who view it as too damning and limited a view of the marginal misconduct: see, for example, Lucy Freeman Sandler, "The Study of Marginal Imagery: Past, Present, and Future," *Studies in Iconography* 18 (1997): 1–49, at 30–32.
42 Hadewijch, "Letter 30: Answering the Demand of God's Trinity and Unity," in *Hadewijch: The Complete Works*, trans. Columba Hart (Mahwah, NJ: Paulist Press, 1980), 119. For the Middle Dutch text (based on the 1947 edition of J. van Mierlo), see the website Digitale bibliotheek voor den Nederlandse letteren, http://www.dbnl.org/tekst/hade002brie01_01/hade002brie01_01_0031.php). A new edition of the Middle Dutch text is forthcoming: Paul Mommaers and Anikó Daróczi, *Hadewijch: Brieven – Middelnederlandse Tekst* (Leuven: Peeters, 2017).
43 Paul Mommaerts with Elisabeth Dutton, *Hadewijch: Writer, Beguine, Love Mystic* (Leuven: Peeters, 2004), 32.

Dominican inquisitor Robert le Bougre, who burned at the stake his share of accused heretics between 1235 and 1238.[44]

A century or so after the creation of the Logan Hours, Julian of Norwich would write evocatively of the hazelnut, describing it as "a littil thing... in the palme of my hand," which Christ shows to her, telling her, "It is all that is made."[45] This image once again evinces the notion of the universe contained within the small and insignificant. However, as Liz Herbert McAvoy notices, the nut also alludes to the Song of Songs, in which, she writes, "the tiny nut of little value takes on an inordinate significance in its association with the *hortus inclusus* which is also the location of sexual desire and its fulfillment."[46] Thus a small and replete object could function as a metaphor for the female body, at once smaller than the average male body (both physically and in terms of intellect and spiritual potential, according to medieval gender theory) and containing the immense potential to generate something much larger than itself (that is, a lineage or a great number of progeny). A tiny book such as the Logan Hours could likewise encompass almost the entire universe: the calendar of the year; images of earthly labor and heavenly constellations; the salvific life of Christ, as told through the devotions to Mary contained in the hours as well as through pictures; the commemoration of the dead; and of course numerous songs of praise to the Virgin Mother in whose immaculate womb – another almost impossibly small container – was borne the living incarnation of God.

Although extraordinarily small books of hours remained unusual, if the survival rate of such volumes is any measure, their production does seem to have continued as the book of hours grew in importance as the central text of lay devotion. The gendered element of the miniature, its appropriateness to a female book-user, also remained relevant. In a landscape populated primarily by "paperback"-sized books for all manner of users and at all levels of production from the most basic to the most luxurious, the miniature examples stand out as belonging almost exclusively to the category of the ultra-deluxe. Just as elaborate programs of illumination were a hallmark of high-prestige books for the wealthiest and most refined of clientele, so too were very small books the province of an elite audience. The most famous example of an extremely small and extremely sumptuous book of hours is the one created for Queen Jeanne d'Évreux, illuminated by Jean Pucelle between 1324 and 1328. At 92 by 62 mm, it is even smaller than the Logan Hours, and famously fits in the palm of a hand when fully open. In a virtuoso turn of miniaturization, the three-line initial *D* of the Matins

---

44 Mommaerts with Dutton, *Hadewijch*, 8.
45 Julian of Norwich, *The Shewings of Julian of Norwich*, ed. Georgia Ronan Crampton (Kalamazoo, MI: Medieval Institute Publications, 1994), 1.5.148-149, http://d.lib.rochester.edu/teams/text/the-shewings-of-julian-of-norwich-part-1.
46 Liz Herbert McAvoy, *Authority and the Female Body in the Writings of Julian of Norwich and Margery Kempe* (Cambridge: D. S. Brewer, 2004), 84.

Figure 5: Jean Pucelle, The Betrayal of Christ/The Annunciation, opening to the Matins of the Virgin, Hours of Jeanne d'Évreux, Paris, 1324–1328. Collection: Metropolitan Museum of Art, New York, The Cloisters Collection, 54.1.2, fol. 15v-16r. Photograph made available by the museum under a Creative Commons Zero license.

of the Virgin contains an image of the young queen herself, kneeling with her book in her hands (Figure 5). The queen is less than ten millimeters high, her book-within-the-book perhaps two millimeters. Yet, as many have noted, much rides on this very little woman (or girl, given her extreme youth at the time of her marriage to Charles IV), for it was on her ability to produce a legitimate male heir that the Capetians staked their hopes for dynastic continuity (she failed in this regard, giving birth only to three daughters). Both Joan Holladay and Madeline Caviness have observed that the book constantly worries at issues of sexual purity, reproductive fertility, and lineage, either browbeating or gently directing Jeanne toward her role as a vessel for dynastic continuity.[47] Like Julian's little hazelnut, the Hours of Jeanne d'Évreux – and, moreover,

---

[47] Madeline Caviness, "Patron or Matron?"; Joan Holladay, "The Education of Jeanne d'Évreux: Personal Piety and Dynastic Salvation in Her Book of Hours at the Cloisters," *Art History* 17 (1994): 585–611.

the initial *D* with the tiny queen and her even-tinier book inside it – encloses something enormous and almost beyond containment: namely, the relationship between the Capetian dynasty, in all its ideological, historical, physical, and legendary manifestations, and the Incarnation and Passion of Christ. There is pathos in this.

The fourteenth century saw the development of very large-format books of hours (and other devotional texts) for princely patrons, to such an extent that Jean de Berry's "Petites Heures" (BnF ms. lat. 18014), at 212 by 145 mm, is actually on the large end of the standard dimensions developed in the earlier period. Very small books are few and far between. In general, books produced for the French and Burgundian courts in this period grew ever more impressive in scale, giving the lie to their function as "private" devotional aids. But this would begin to change in the mid-fifteenth century, and I close with a few examples of the ways in which the vogue for miniaturization that swept through northern Europe in this period returns to the connection between book, body, and affect already present in the Psalter of Saint Ruprecht.

The *Codex Rotundus* (Hildesheim, Dombibliothek Hildesheim, Hs 728), a book of hours from Bruges, dated to around 1490–1492, is notable both for its form and its size. Its circular folios measure only 90 mm in diameter (Figure 6). It contains three full-page tondo miniatures and thirty historiated initials all painted by a Flemish

Figure 6: Codex Rotundus, Bruges, 1490–1492. Collection: Dombibliothek, Hildesheim, HS 728. Photograph: Dombibliothek Hildesheim.

artist, probably for Adolf of Cleves, Lord of Ravenstein, who had recently married his cousin, Anne of Burgundy, one of the Philip the Good's illegitimate daughters. The book's unusual circular format aligns it with the sort of multifunctional jewelry that was fashionable in Burgundian court culture; enclosed in a jeweled binding and hung as a pendant on a belt or necklace, it would have approximated the large, curvilinear forms of pendants of the time, such as that worn by Margaret of Austria in Jean Hey's 1490 portrait (New York, Metropolitan Museum of Art). Combining piety and display, such a bauble would have allowed Adolf, or perhaps more likely Anne, to wear the hours as talismanic protection and as adornment.

This conception of the book-as-jewelry developed further in the sixteenth century. About two decades later than the *Codex Rotundus*, a minuscule prayer book created for Queen Claude of France as a companion to an equally small and precious book of hours features fully illuminated margins depicting the life of Christ on every folio, along with historiated initials and full-page miniatures that represent a variety of related subjects (New York, Morgan Library, MS M.1166; Figure 7); its pages measure 69 by 49 mm. Each opening has the jeweled quality of a reliquary, the entire surface

Figure 7: Prayer Book of Claude of France, Tours, France, ca. 1517. Collection: Pierpont Morgan Library, New York, MS M.1166. Photograph: Pierpont Morgan Library.

Figure 8: Portrait of Henry VIII, English psalter in the translation of John Croke, London, ca. 1540. Collection: British Library, London, MS Stowe 956. Photograph: Margaret Jean Langstaff.

glittering with high-chroma colors and gold. These formal features, so similar to those that Hahn identifies with reliquaries' inducement of wonderment, correspond to the wondrous scale of the object. Although it is not clear from the library's records whether the red silk-velvet binding and golden clasps are original, they certainly complement the book's interior, just as a velvet case highlights the beauty of a spectacular necklace or ring. The book is of a size that would have allowed it to be slipped into a small, embroidered, perhaps bejeweled case and easily carried on a belt, which was a widespread practice by this time. Perhaps the most famous example of such a "girdle-book" is the miniature psalter that Anne Boleyn reportedly handed to one of her ladies-in-waiting just before she climbed the scaffold.[48] At 40 by 30 mm, it approaches the Psalter of Saint Ruprecht's extreme dimensions. Equipped with a gilt binding complete with loops for attachment to a chain, it contains a single miniature depicting Henry VIII (Figure 8).

---

[48] British Library, MS Stowe 956. Psalter in the English translation of John Croke, ca. 1540. For the legend that this was the book handed off by Anne Boleyn at her execution, see Robert Marsham, "On a Manuscript Book of Prayers in a Binding of Gold Enamelled, said to have been given by Queen Anne Boleyn to a lady of the Wyatt Family: together with a Transcript of its Contents," *Archaeologia* 44 (1873): 259–272.

As the (unsubstantiated) legend of "Anne Boleyn's" miniature psalter suggests, tiny books made to be worn or carried close to the body are in some sense always already constituted as talismans or reliquaries, imbued with pathetic affect – tokens of loss and longing (as Stewart suggests). However, there is more to these books than nostalgia. Tapping into a Christian rhetoric of smallness and enclosure centered around the God-bearing body of the Virgin Mary, "ancilla Dei," the miniature book format was well suited to the text of the hours, or to the Psalms that made up the primary material of the office. In reducing the book to very small dimensions, the makers of these objects demanded of their potential users an intensely bodily, internalized attention. The multiple levels at which the body registers the miniature scale of the book – visual, tactile, relational, and intellectual – must have enriched the devotional experience and facilitated an acting-out of the very doctrine of incarnation in imaginative terms.

Jennifer Borland
9 Moved by Medicine: The Multisensory Experience of Handling Folding Almanacs

Objects cannot be perceived, much less used, without our senses, and that sensory experience is often directed by the form the objects take. In the case of the small medieval manuscripts commonly described as "folding almanacs," the specialized way in which they engage their users activates the senses differently than books in a traditional codex form do. These almanacs – compact manuscripts that contain a variety of information relevant to health, including calendars, solar and lunar eclipses, astrological material, and other tables and diagrams – are usually made of six to ten parchment sheets folded up and bound together, averaging 6 cm wide and 12 cm long (Plates XIVab). Through their particular format, these pocket-sized books choreograph their handling practices: specific sensory experiences are generated by the multiple and habitual unfoldings and refoldings of their folios. While sight is naturally a primary sense used in the act of reading, the folding almanacs instigate a physical experience for their users that is different from that of most books, one that heightens haptic and auditory engagement. In this chapter, I consider how the senses are engaged by these almanacs, arguing that the specific form of these unusual books grants them agency, activating their materiality and manipulating the experiences of users.

As small, portable books that were likely used in the context of medical consultation and treatment, the folding almanacs inherently draw specific attention to the bodily, sensory experiences of both illness and healing. Their content relates directly to the body of the patient, offering information used by the practitioner to assess and treat that body. Some examples take this correspondence even further, including depictions of bodies that inevitably refer to the actual ones being healed with the help of the books. While the images of the zodiac man or the bloodletting man have functions more diagrammatic than instructive within these books, they nevertheless serve as reminders of the embodied nature of medieval health care. Treating and being treated were already heightened sensory experiences, further amplified by the multisensory engagement these complicated books required from their handlers.

Note: I want to express my gratitude to Fiona Griffiths and Kathryn Starkey for inviting me to contribute to this volume, and for their generosity throughout the process. Thanks as well to Karen Overbey, my co-conspirator in the research of these fascinating books.

https://doi.org/10.1515/9783110563443-010

The Sensory Experience of Books

This chapter focuses on how the senses were involved in experiencing objects, and in particular how they were involved in the physical manipulation and comprehension of books. Books, of course, are not static objects; they contain images and information that are fundamental to a comprehensive understanding of them. As Richard Newhauser has argued, the senses were fundamental to medieval knowledge acquisition; they were the "foundation of cognition," in the words of Michael Camille.[1] The complex mechanics of medieval manuscripts, and especially the folding almanacs with their necessity for elaborate manipulations, required sustained engagement with multiple senses in ways not required by other types of objects. In discussions by Camille, Mark Cruse, Maura Nolan, Jonathan Wilcox, and others, the intimacies of book use demonstrate that the senses were essential for the richest experience of reading.[2]

The multisensory nature of the act of reading folding almanacs creates an experience that one might describe as phenomenological. Not coincidentally, in his introduction to *Sensory Perception in the Medieval West*, Simon C. Thomson notes the resonances between considerations of sensory experience and the embodied perception articulated by phenomenology.[3] Phenomenology offers a philosophy for describing bodily experience – or, in the words of one of its key theorists, Maurice Merleau-Ponty, one's "being-in-the-world."[4] Thinking phenomenologically about medieval objects and spaces allows one to acknowledge the interconnected nature

---

1 Richard G. Newhauser, "Introduction: The Sensual Middle Ages," in *A Cultural History of the Senses in the Middle Ages*, ed. Richard G. Newhauser (London: Bloomsbury Press, 2014), 1–22; Michael Camille, "Sensations of the Page: Imaging Technologies and Medieval Illuminated Manuscripts," in *The Iconic Page in Manuscript, Print, and Digital Culture*, ed. George Bornstein and Theresa Tinkle (Ann Arbor: University of Michigan Press, 1998), 33–54, at 33. See also Richard G. Newhauser, "The Senses, the Medieval Sensorium, and Sensing (in) the Middle Ages," in *Handbook of Medieval Culture: Fundamental Aspects and Conditions of Medieval Culture*, 3 vols., ed. Albrecht Classen (Berlin: Walter de Gruyter, 2015), 3:1559–1575; Richard G. Newhauser and Corine Schlief, eds., "Pleasure and Danger in Perception: The Five Senses in the Middle Ages and the Renaissance," special issue, *The Senses and Society* 5, no. 1 (2010).
2 Camille, "Sensations of the Page"; Mark Cruse, "Matter and Meaning in Medieval Books," *The Senses and Society* 5 (2010): 45–56; Maura Nolan, "Medieval Habit, Modern Sensation: Reading Manuscripts in the Digital Age," *The Chaucer Review* 47 (2013): 465–476; Jonathan Wilcox, "The Sensory Cost of Remediation: or, Sniffing the Gutter of Anglo-Saxon Manuscripts," in *Sensory Perception in the Medieval West*, ed. Simon C. Thomson and Michael D. J. Bintley (Turnhout: Brepols, 2016), 27–51. More recently, Helga Lutz has begun to consider the specifically spatial experience of the codex as compacted space – a phenomenon that is even more extreme in the folded almanacs. See Helga Lutz, "Folding Bodies into Books," in *Presence and Agency: Rhetoric, Aesthetics and the Experience of Art*, ed. Caroline van Eck and Antje Wessels (Leiden: Leiden University Press, forthcoming).
3 Simon C. Thomson, "Sensory Perception in the Medieval West: Introduction," in *Sensory Perception in the Medieval West*, ed. Simon C. Thomson and Michael D. J. Bintley (Turnhout: Brepols, 2016), 1–5.
4 Maurice Merleau-Ponty, *Phenomenology of Perception*, trans. Colin Smith (1945; repr., London: Routledge, 2005).

of the senses in most experiences, rather than focusing on the action of individual senses. Such an approach provides a critical apparatus for investigating user reception through the concept of a "lived body" that experiences the world and also impacts that world, a notion that resonates with medieval materiality. My own work has frequently considered medieval spaces and objects, including manuscripts, through the lens of phenomenology, which informs my approach to sensory engagement as well.[5]

Reading a book involves, in the words of Maura Nolan, "a repertoire of bodily motions and gestures" that are activated by the handling of the book, creating a phenomenological experience that engages all of the senses.[6] Both Nolan and Jonathan Wilcox consider the multisensory nature of medieval book reading in part by contrasting that experience with the inevitable limitations of digitized manuscripts, which really only engage one sense: that of sight. According to Wilcox, "the tactile is everywhere in the operation of a real book, but absent from the digital simulacrum."[7] He goes on to describe how the materiality of the book is asserted through that tactility, stating, "Parchment alerts an attentive hand to the difference between flesh side and hair side, while the book asserts values of weight and heft, portability and haptic involvement of those who hold it."[8] That haptic involvement on the part of the user is especially pronounced with the folding almanacs and the many manipulations they encourage.

Books have a sensory impact on their viewers: the senses play a role in facilitating use or comprehension of an object, but an object may direct or control the sensory experience as well. Medieval perception was affected by both animate and inanimate entities and things – or, as Chris Woolgar asserts, "the sensorium extended to and was affected by qualities of objects and beings round about them."[9] A number of scholars of the senses have pointed to the notion of object agency in the formation of sensory

---

[5] Jennifer Borland, "Unruly Reading: The Consuming Role of Touch in the Experience of a Medieval Manuscript," in *Scraped, Stroked, and Bound: Materially Engaged Readings of Medieval Manuscripts*, ed. Jonathan Wilcox (Turnhout: Brepols, 2013), 97–114, plates 225–230; Jennifer Borland, "Audience and Spatial Experience in the Nuns' Church at Clonmacnoise," *Different Visions: A Journal of New Perspectives in Medieval Art* 3 (2011): 1–45; Jennifer Borland, "Encountering the Inauthentic," in *Transparent Things: A Cabinet*, ed. Karen Eileen Overbey and Maggie M. Williams (New York: punctum books, 2013), 17–38.
[6] Nolan, "Medieval Habit, Modern Sensation," 465. See also Elaine Treharne, "Fleshing Out the Text: The Transcendent Manuscript in the Digital Age," *postmedieval* 4 (2013): 465–478; and Kerr Houston, "Surface and Substance," The Material Collective Blog, accessed 4 April 2018, http://thematerialcollective.org/surface-substance/.
[7] Wilcox, "The Sensory Cost of Remediation," 39. For another perspective on accessibility and digitization in relation to the folding almanac BL Harley MS 937, see Chelsea Silva, "Opening the Medieval Folding Almanac," *Exemplaria* 30 (2018): 49–65.
[8] Wilcox, "The Sensory Cost of Remediation," 39. Wilcox organized the hands-on manuscript workshop at University of Iowa in 2008 in which I participated, and he also edited the resulting publication, *Scraped, Stroked, and Bound: Materially Engaged Readings of Medieval Manuscripts* (see n. 5 above).
[9] Chris Woolgar, "The Social Life of the Senses: Experiencing Self, Others, and Environments," in *A Cultural History of the Senses in the Middle Ages*, ed. Richard G. Newhauser (London: Bloomsbury Press, 2014), 23–43, at 43.

experience; for instance, Thomson has suggested that an "audience's sensory perception could be exploited or piqued by objects and experiences in the medieval world."[10] In thinking about the power these books have to manipulate their users, I draw on Jane Bennett's ideas about active objects and their potential for animation.[11] In the case of the folding almanacs, movement and resistance to movement are the most pronounced actions they make, engaging the user primarily through tactility and sound.

The particular format of the folding almanacs requires a different sort of engagement than does the traditional codex form seen in most medieval manuscripts. The user's senses are not just engaged by the act of reading; the unusual manipulation necessitated by the almanacs' form – the repeated opening and closing of folios, the folding and unfolding of the parchment – itself directs the user's experience and stimulates the senses. My argument here, that the folding almanacs direct the sensory experience of their users, builds on previous work that explores another facet of their format. Elsewhere, Karen Overbey and I have contemplated the portability and potential performativity of these manuscripts. We consider the way in which their manipulation could have facilitated medical efficacy through an almost ritualistic performance of folding and unfolding, enacted by the handler for the benefit of the patient or audience, animating the space of the consultation.[12] Building on that previous work but moving in a different direction, in this chapter I think more about the effect of such manipulations on the handlers themselves. As Newhauser has pointed out, "sensory organs were not just passive receptors of information, but actively participated in the formation of knowledge."[13] The folding almanacs actively engage the senses of their handlers – through sight, but also through touch and sound – to facilitate cognition and understanding of their medical content within the embodied exchange of health consultation. By consenting to actively engage the folios of these manuscripts, the handlers themselves are moved.

The Format and Organization of Folding Almanacs

The folding almanacs have been described as essentially calendar books, meant to provide guidance for determining the best time for the treatment of a particular ailment. The notion of propitious times was pertinent in a variety of cultural contexts and, according to Hilary M. Carey, can "be seen as part of popular rather than learned

---

10 Thomson, "Sensory Perception in the Medieval West: Introduction," 1.
11 Jane Bennett, *Vibrant Matter* (Durham: Duke University Press, 2010).
12 Karen Eileen Overbey and Jennifer Borland, "Diagnostic Performance and Diagrammatic Manipulation in the Physician's Folding Almanacs," in *The Agency of Things in Medieval and Early Modern Art: Materials, Power and Manipulation*, ed. Grażyna Jurkowlaniec, Ika Matyjaszkiewicz, and Zuzanna Sarnecka (New York: Routledge, 2018), 144–156.
13 Newhauser, "Introduction: The Sensual Middle Ages," 21.

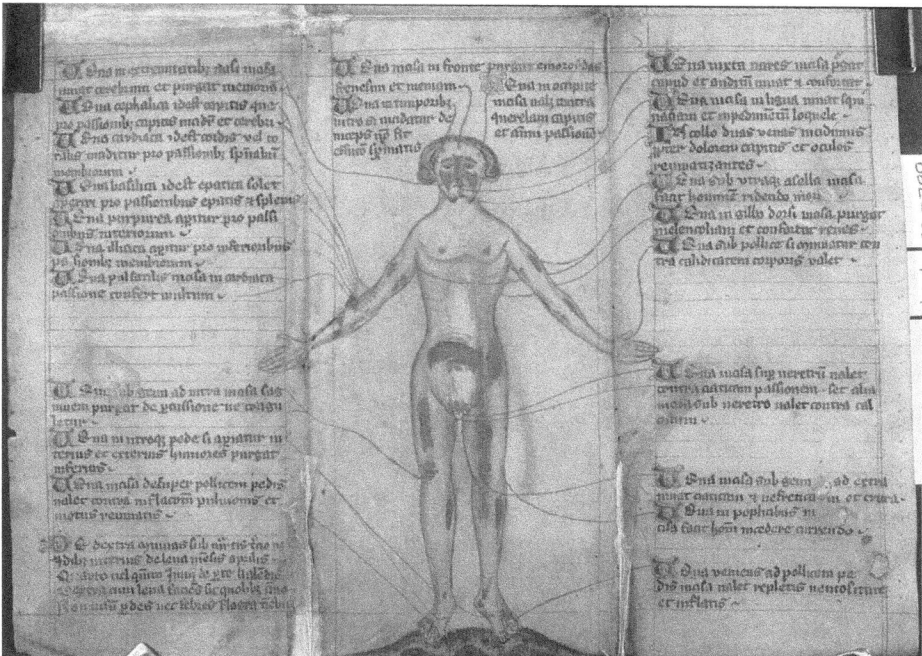

Figure 1: Bloodletting man, ca. 1406, Collection: British Library, London, Harley MS 5311, fol. 10v, detail. Copyright The British Library Board.

culture."[14] The folding almanacs supplied what was needed to determine the phases and movements of the moon before undertaking a procedure.

Most of these manuscripts are made up of just a few folios, all folded individually to create a pocket-sized object. In some cases, the leaves are folded into thirds; in others, fourths. The extant manuscripts do not always have the same content or number of folios. Carey describes the organization of one of the tri-fold variations this way: "Each folio is divided into two horizontally and three vertically, making six recto and six verso sections, with an upper half 'a' and a lower half 'b' on each side."[15] A hypothetical representative example might contain ten leaves, of which folio 1 could display the table of movable feasts, the calendar canon, and a vein man as in Figure 1.[16] Folios 2 through 5

---

14 Hilary M. Carey, "Astrological Medicine and the Medieval English Folded Almanac," *Social History of Medicine* 17 (2004): 345–363, at 361–362. That said, these books were more advanced than the basic, "more popular regimen of noting good and evil days of the month."
15 Hilary M. Carey, "What is a Folded Almanac? The Form and Function of a Key Manuscript Source for Astro-medical Practice in Later Medieval England," *Social History of Medicine* 16 (2003): 481–509, at 497. J. P. Gumbert includes useful diagrams of various types: Gumbert, *Bat Books: A Catalogue of Folded Manuscripts Containing Almanacs or Other Texts* (Turnhout: Brepols, 2016), 19–23.
16 Good examples of this format are BL MS Harley 5311 and Wellcome MS. 8932.

might contain the calendar, which looks similar to the calendars in late medieval books of hours. Each month occupies half of one side of a folio, with three months depicted on each of the four folios, the text filling the spaces in columns that are usually demarcated by the folds. The fourth space of each folio is what remains visible when it is completely folded up, and it is left blank except for the title of the folio's contents (for example, "April, May, June" in Figure 2). Lunar tables and a corresponding canon, and

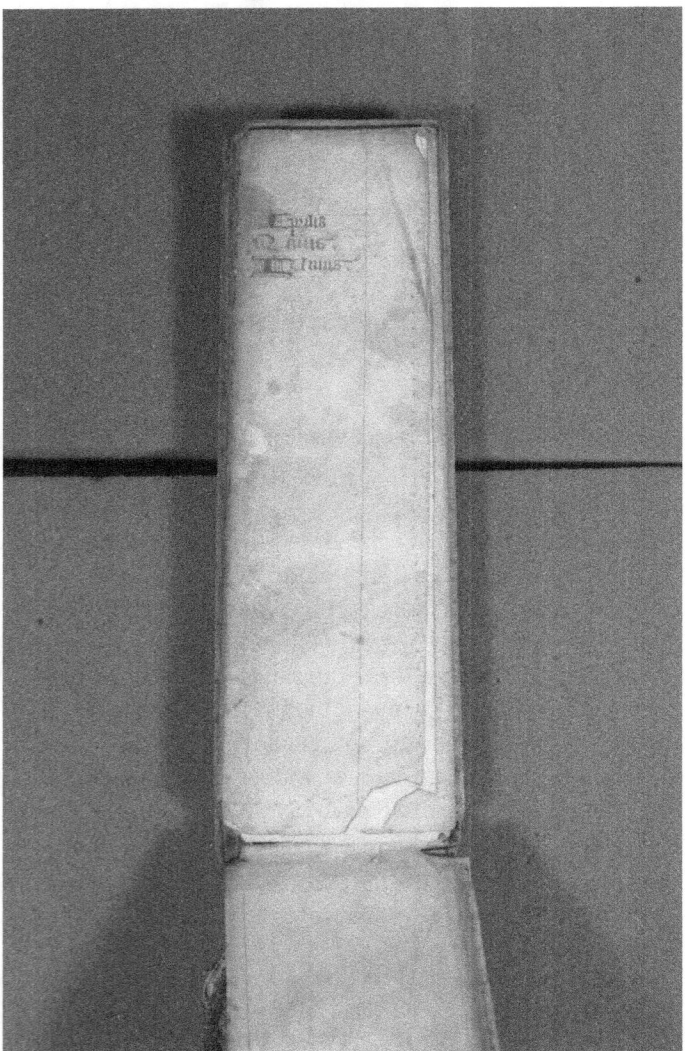

Figure 2: Titles for April, May, June calendars, *Almanach, tabula festorum, mobilium ab anno 1364 usque annum domini 1462*, York, England, between 1406 and 1424. Collection: The Rosenbach, Philadelphia, MS 1004/29, fol. 3. Photograph: J. Borland.

often the zodiac man, might appear on folio 6 (Plate XIVb). Folios 7 through 9 could display eclipses, often spectacularly illuminated with gold: folio 7 might display solar eclipses with a canon, and folios 8 and 9 could show lunar eclipses (Plate XV). We might also find a diagram of the Sphere of Apuleius, a prognostication device, as well as vessels containing urine samples along with a canon, on folio 9 (Plate XVI). Finally, folio 10 could contains a tract on astrological prediction.

The sophisticated organization of the folding almanac's information highlights its remarkable symbiosis of form and content, with both elements working together to create an unusual and singular type of book. More than forty folding almanacs with this type of astro-medical content have survived, most made in England during the fifteenth century.[17] The specific folded format of this group of manuscripts, along with their limited geographic and temporal scope, is remarkable. Since these innovative pocket-sized books contain information that was also available in traditional codex form, their makers were using an unconventional and sophisticated format for existing content.[18] The organization of this information within the folding almanac is ingenious: it is tightly laid out on each folio and positioned so that it can be easily read by the holder of the manuscript regardless of how fully a folio has been unfolded (in fact, viewed from any other position, the material will be upside down). It is only possible to open one folio at a time; thus, each time a folio is viewed, the page must be folded back up before another one can be opened.

The folding almanacs produced in fifteenth-century England are not the only books created in this manner, but they represent the largest group: thirty-one out of the sixty or so folded manuscripts catalogued by J. P. Gumbert.[19] Gumbert states that books made in this format have three distinct features: (1) they have folded leaves which cannot be read unless unfolded; (2) the leaves are not grouped into quires, but instead have tabs on one edge, which are gathered and sewn together "into a stub"; and (3) the book is held by the stub, and the text on the unfolded leaf is read "from outer (=upper) edge toward the stub."[20] These characteristics demonstrate the primary differences between these manuscripts and other small medieval codices, such as tiny books of hours or girdle books. The folding book served a specific function, and seems to have appeared in the thirteenth century as a solution to the problem of "how to make something that is small outside but large inside."[21] It accommodates a sizeable amount of text while being small enough to be carried on one's person. Such folded books do eventually disappear, except in the case of one type of text that particularly benefited from the "large inside" made possible by

---

17 Thirty-one English folding almanacs are currently known. Carey lists twenty-nine in "What is a Folded Almanac?" J. P. Gumbert catalogues sixty-three books total using this format, of which forty-four are almanacs (thirty English and fourteen Continental). Gumbert, *Bat Books*.
18 Carey, "Astrological Medicine," 362.
19 Gumbert, *Bat Books*.
20 Gumbert, *Bat Books*, 17–19.
21 Gumbert, *Bat Books*, 23.

this format: calendars, and especially almanacs.[22] These texts might only be a few leaves thick if created in codex form, which would be awkward; their wide tables do best with larger leaves, which would be far too big to carry on a girdle or belt.[23] In the case of the folding almanac, form and content work together to create an ingenious solution, making objects that are functional, accessible, and informative.

For most of the surviving almanacs, a user would have begun by holding the entire closed manuscript in their palm, much as one might hold a smartphone today. Usually the tab or binding would be held facing the user, while the opposite, open edge of the manuscript would be oriented away from them.[24] The handler would then select a folio based on the titles written on the folded, closed folios – in fact, the orientation of these titles can be used to determine the proper orientation of the manuscript as a whole (Figure 2). These titles appear on the verso and face outward when the tri- or quarter-fold is closed, but are hidden from the viewer once the opening of the folio commences. The user would then bend the other closed folios away from the selected one, in order to open up sufficient space around it for unfolding. The selected folio would next be opened, first by unfolding it horizontally, which would result in gaining access to the first of the three half sheets that contain content – this first half sheet, the reader will note, is facing the right direction to be read by the handler. If the user then required access to the other two half sheets, they would fully open the folio away from them, in order to view the entirety of the recto side, which usually contained two half sheets of content oriented correctly for the reader. To access another folio, the open folio would first have to be closed, reversing the order of unfolding that already took place. Although each instance of use would be somewhat unique, depending on the idiosyncrasies of user, illness, time of year, and other factors, the process of opening and closing sequential folios might eventually become somewhat mechanical or habitual, as the handler became familiar with the nuances of the specific book, its folded pages, its binding, and the feel and sound of manipulating these different elements.[25]

This complicated process not only reflects the unique experience of using one of these almanacs, but also demonstrates the careful attention that went into their planning, organization, and production. Several copies have survived unbound, giving us a particularly good sense of the mechanics of their construction. For example, MS

---

[22] Gumbert, *Bat Books*, 24. Carey suggests that by the sixteenth century, a folded almanac was "an old-fashioned object": Carey, "Astrological Medicine," 355. Perhaps a move away from health care by itinerant physicians led to the decreased usefulness of such books – if such practitioners were no longer common, there was no longer a need for mobility (or for such a marker of authority).

[23] Gumbert, *Bat Books*, 24.

[24] But this is not always the case; sometimes a book employs both orientations, depending on the folio.

[25] For a video of a conservator handling MS. 8932 at the Wellcome Library, see https://wellcomelibrary.org/item/b20605055#?c=0&m=0&s=0&cv=0 (accessed 27 November 2017).

Lansdowne 331 at the British Library was unbound and later rebound as a codex; the binding tabs have been lost or removed, and the sheets were sliced in two before being bound (Figure 3). Taken from an example of the quarter-fold type, the two columns on either side of what is now the spine of the book do not match, and much of the manuscript appears upside down. Such examples keenly demonstrate how this information has been shaped to fit the format of the folding book, and how this format works differently than the bound codex.

Figure 3: Almanac folios rebound in codex (two columns of September on left, two columns of August upside down on right), British Library, London, Lansdowne MS 331, 11v-12r, ca. 1463. Copyright The British Library Board.

While the reader might have used the almanac as a tool to impact engagement with a patient, the manner in which this was done would have been largely controlled by the format of the book itself. To begin with, the size of the book, the size of its text, and the way in which it must be opened to be made sense of are all deliberately designed for a single user. One cannot easily set the book on a table to read it; instead it must be held, making it difficult to fully share the reading experience the way one might with a larger codex, which two or more people could have used together. Although it was possible for two people to view one of these manuscripts, with one person handling it while an observer stood next to the handler and

Figure 4: Codex lying flat, medieval bookbinding model, University of Iowa Libraries, Preservation/Conservation Department.

was shown specific folios, the tangible experience of manipulating the book could not have been shared.

There is also no easy way to hold more than one folio open at a time; in fact, simply unfolding a single folio is rather cumbersome, requiring deft maneuvering with both hands. The design of the manuscript dictates this particular method of unfolding; the specific manner in which a handler manipulates the book has been predetermined. The experience of touching is much more pronounced in a book like this, compared to folios in a codex. Of course, manipulating a codex also requires touching, but the 180-degree flexibility of many medieval bindings would have allowed some books to rest open (Figure 4). Thus readers often would have had to use both hands only when opening the codex; from then on, they could turn the pages with just one hand, allowing for largely hands-free reading. In contrast, folding almanacs demand constant, two-handed touching. The experience of viewing these books in libraries today underscores this difference, as the reader of a folding almanac is often allowed a greater amount of handling than is usually granted with the average codex.[26] This necessity is also one reason why some libraries will not allow handling of folding almanacs at all, not even by their conservators. The heightened haptic engagement necessary to fully understand them is driven by the format of the object itself, which incorporates the necessity for touching and movement.

---

[26] This was a pronounced experience for me when viewing folding almanacs in the reading rooms of various libraries.

Using the Folding Almanacs in Health Care

Astrological medicine like that found in the folding almanacs was a key aspect of late medieval health care, one that engaged the senses in both diagnosis and treatment. Practitioners relied on their senses to detect signs of specific illnesses, especially given the lack of additional tools of scientific testing. Faith Wallis points out that trained physicians were able to combine sensory data with scientific doctrine, setting them apart from other practitioners through their "knowledge of this hidden world" inside the patient's body.[27] Not unlike in the act of reading, sight and touch were the dominant senses in diagnosis, especially in the common practices of taking a patient's pulse and of uroscopy, the "specialized art of seeing" used to analyze urine samples.[28] Urine may have also been occasionally smelled and even tasted, although sight was the predominant sense used in uroscopy. In the case of other conditions and circumstances, the smell of armpits or the sound of a patient's voice might have been used to establish a prognosis and treatment regimen.[29] The insertion of a diagnostic tool like the folding almanac into the space of consultation, in which the doctor relied on both his own senses and the sensory experiences described by the patient, would have integrated the book and its handling into an already heavily sensorial exchange.

Generally speaking, most medieval medicine was based on the theory of *complexio* – complexion or temperament – which was essentially derived from classical traditions of Hippocratic medicine and, later, Galen.[30] The theory proposed that health was related to the balance of the qualities of hot, wet, cold, and dry within a human body. It was thought that this balance was impacted by the four humors – blood, phlegm, yellow bile, and black bile.[31] The balance of these humors was tied to characteristics both physical and psychological; an individual's character was described as sanguine, phlegmatic, choleric, or melancholy.[32] Each person's

---

[27] Faith Wallis, "Medicine and the Senses: Feeling the Pulse, Smelling the Plague, and Listening for the Cure," in *A Cultural History of the Senses in the Middle Ages*, ed. Richard G. Newhauser (London: Bloomsbury Press, 2014), 133–152, at 134.
[28] Wallis, "Medicine and the Senses," 141.
[29] Wallis, "Medicine and the Senses," 152.
[30] Nancy Siraisi, *Medieval and Early Renaissance Medicine: An Introduction to Knowledges and Practice* (Chicago: University of Chicago Press, 2009).
[31] Siraisi, *Medieval and Early Renaissance Medicine*, 105. See also the many useful introductory essays on medieval medicine in David C. Lindberg and Michael H. Shank, eds., *Cambridge History of Science*, vol. 2, *Medieval Science* (Cambridge: Cambridge University Press, 2011), especially Emilie Savage-Smith, "Medicine in Medieval Islam," 139–167; Vivian Nutton, "Early-Medieval Medicine and Natural Science," 323–340; Danielle Jacquart, "Anatomy, Physiology, and Medical Theory," 590–610; and Katharine Park, "Medical Practice," 611–629. For more on the Islamic tradition, see Peter E. Pormann and Emilie Savage-Smith, *Medieval Islamic Medicine* (Washington, D.C.: Georgetown University Press, 2007).
[32] Siraisi, *Medieval and Early Renaissance Medicine*, 106.

healthy balance was different, and maintaining the balance of these humors was the essence of medieval medical care. Phenomena that impacted the body's health were categorized as naturals, nonnaturals, and contranaturals: naturals were the fundamental elements within the body, such as the temperaments, humors, and body parts, while contranaturals were pathological conditions or diseases.[33] The nonnaturals, however, were especially pertinent to the understanding of the causes and treatment of disease: they usually comprised the factors of air, food and drink, sleep and wakefulness, motion and rest, evacuation and repletion, along with the passions of the mind, and sometimes included bathing, sexual practices, and physical activity as well.[34]

Calendars are common in a variety of genres; they are relevant to devotion when they are incorporated into books of hours, and to astrological medicine when included in the almanacs. Treatment and prognosis of patients was not limited to prescribing a change in diet, an herbal remedy, or bloodletting; to ensure successful healing, practitioners also took into consideration facets of astrological medicine, specifically following the theory of "critical days," a branch of medical astrology that dealt with calendar dates and thus the phases of the moon.[35] The type of material found in fifteenth-century English folding almanacs can also be found in codex form. English almanacs were based on the larger works of two astronomers from Oxford: John Somer and Nicholas Lynn.[36] The folding almanacs were among the simplest types of medical almanacs, in contrast with more robust almanacs that supplied more thorough information on the planetary positions throughout the year and would have existed in larger codex form.[37] Most of the folding almanacs do not diverge from the calculations of Somer and his successor Lynn and are somewhat generic; even though

---

[33] Chester R. Burns, "The Nonnaturals: A Paradox in the Western Concept of Health," *The Journal of Medicine and Philosophy* 1 (1976): 202–211, at 203. See also Siraisi, *Medieval and Early Renaissance Medicine*, 101.

[34] Jacquart, "Anatomy, Physiology, and Medical Theory," 602; Luis García-Ballester, "On the Origin of Six Non-natural Things in Galen," in *Galen und das hellenistische Erbe: Verhandlungen des IV. Internationalen Galen-Symposiums*, ed. Jutta Kollesch, Diethard Nickel, and Claudius Galenus (Stuttgart: Franz Steiner Verlag, 1993), 105–115; Pedro Gil Sotres, "Regimens of Health," in *Western Medical Thought from Antiquity to the Middle Ages*, ed. Mirko D. Grmek (Cambridge: Harvard University Press, 1998), 291–318, 395–399; Marilyn Nicoud, *Les Régimes de Santé au Moyen Âge* (Rome: École française de Rome, 2007).

[35] Siraisi, *Medieval and Early Renaissance Medicine*, 135.

[36] See Carey, "Astrological Medicine"; Gumbert, *Bat Books*; and Linne R. Mooney, *The Kalendarium of John Somer* (Athens: University of Georgia Press, 1998). Gumbert considers an almanac's reliance on either Somer or Lynn as a way to organize his catalogue, and finds that Somer is used in the earlier fifteenth century but that eventually Lynn's text takes precedence.

[37] "In the end, various kinds of medical almanacs were produced which supplied information at a variety of levels of astrological expertise to meet the needs of physicians." Carey, "Astrological Medicine," 350.

these compact almanacs were designed as "personal objects," they rarely display markers of ownership or individualization.³⁸

Physicians were not especially common in fifteenth-century England, and even in places where access to such physicians might be available, they were not the only healers or even the primary ones. Much healing probably still took place in the home, while university-trained physicians primarily served wealthier lords and prelates.³⁹ Almanacs were most likely taken into the field by trained practitioners whose practices were not in court or urban settings, but rather in the vicinity of busy provincial towns like Norwich or York.⁴⁰ Such practitioners may have had some professional training, but they likely based their practice on primarily empirical knowledge of remedies and prognosis. Especially in England in this period, practitioners of all types – barber-surgeons, university-trained physicians, or skilled laywomen – gained training through a wide variety of avenues.⁴¹ Regardless of the specific training of the practitioner, the excessive dirt and other signs of wear displayed by many of the surviving folding almanacs suggest abundant use by their owners.

The small size, portable format, and abbreviated texts of the folding almanacs provided the basic reference material for diagnosis of common complaints, but the usefulness of these small books for healthcare practitioners may have also resided in the way they conveyed the appearance of learned expertise. The almanacs, carried visibly on the belt and activated during the course of a patient's consultation with the doctor, undoubtedly suggested prestige and authority.⁴² In fact, the folding almanacs appear at a time when medical hierarchies were becoming increasingly specialized and there was notable public concern about issues such as the licensing of practitioners and other means of assessing competence.⁴³

---

38 Carey, "Astrological Medicine," 355–356.
39 Rawcliffe, *Medicine and Society in Later Medieval England*, 105–124.
40 Carey, "Astrological Medicine," 355–360. See also Peter Murray Jones, "Information and Science," in *Fifteenth-Century Attitudes: Perceptions of Society in Late Medieval England*, ed. Rosemary Horrox (Cambridge: Cambridge University Press, 1994), 97–111, at 109; and C. H. Talbot, "A Medieval Physician's vade mecum," *Journal of the History of Medicine and Allied Sciences* 16 (1961): 213–233, at 218–219. Thomas Fayreford (fl. 1400–1450) and John Crophill (d. 1485) were two such provincial practitioners, known through their surviving commonplace books, which include medical treatises and records of patients treated, BL MS Harley 2558 (Fayreford, in Latin) and BL MS Harley 1735 (Crophill, in English). See Peter Murray Jones, "Thomas Fayreford: An English Fifteenth Century Medical Practitioner," in *Medicine from the Black Death to the French Disease*, ed. Roger French (Aldershot, UK: Ashgate, 1998), 156–183; E. W. Talbert, "The Notebook of a Fifteenth-Century Practicing Physician," *Studies in English* 22 (1942): 5–30; and James K. Mustain, "A Rural Medical Practitioner in Fifteenth-Century England," *Bulletin of the History of Medicine* 46 (1972): 469–476.
41 Carey, "Astrological Medicine," 352. See also Rawcliffe, *Medicine and Society in Later Medieval England*.
42 Overbey and Borland, "Diagnostic Performance and Diagrammatic Manipulation."
43 Katherine Park, "Medical Practice," 624; Carole Rawcliffe, *Medicine and Society in Later Medieval England* (Stroud, Gloustershire: Sutton, 1995), 105–126.

Although their content is similar to that found in other calendar or astrological codices, it was the design of the folding almanacs that probably appealed to a wide range of users from diverse social backgrounds.[44] The innovative, almost exclusively English design of these almanacs establishes them as specialized tools that nonetheless became increasingly familiar to both patients and practitioners in the period. The novelty of their format may also have appealed to elite bibliophiles or others interested in medicine. Carey, for instance, argues for a range of users, including physicians but also people generally interested in astrology: "a social range similar to that reflected in the appearance of their books," which vary from luxurious to roughly executed.[45] The proliferation of folded almanac production in the fifteenth century mirrors the increased practice of collecting many genres of books, including encyclopedic texts, practical health-care and household guides, and newly vernacularized texts. Gumbert also suggests that these books would have been of interest to a variety of educated laypeople with appropriate resources.[46] While the specific content of the folding almanacs suggests use by itinerant health practitioners interested in having this information in portable form, these books likely also had a wider book-collecting audience. Precise users of the folding almanacs are unknown, yet it is helpful to consider the likely audiences in order to think through why they were formatted in this way and how that format was implicated in their use.

Audiotactility and Agency

The power and authority associated with these objects may not only be due to their specialized charts and diagrams or their sartorial display, but also the way they were manipulated within a context that included other talismanic practices.[47] Health management would have made an attempt to use all possible methods for curing illnesses and healing injuries, and these would have included amuletic charms on small parchment scraps, either read aloud or placed on the body; jewelry, gems, and other talismans worn on the body for protection or cure; pilgrim badges; and visits to local (or sometimes distant) saints' shrines or other holy places.[48] Medical texts often recommend

---

44 Carey, "Astrological Medicine," 361.
45 Carey, "Astrological Medicine," 357–358.
46 Gumbert, *Bat Books*, 24.
47 Overbey and Borland, "Diagnostic Performance and Diagrammatic Manipulation."
48 The charms were even sometimes written directly on the body or ingested. Peter Murray Jones describes a charm that is to be written on the cheek: Jones, "Amulets: Prescriptions and Surviving Objects from Late Medieval England," in *Beyond Pilgrimage Souvenirs and Secular Badges*, ed. Sarah Blick (Oxford: Oxbow, 2007), 92–107. Lea T. Olsan discusses charms written on consumable items that

charms and the creation of amulets as part of treatment.⁴⁹ The folding almanacs were also worn on the body, potentially making them talismanic or amuletic too.

The folding almanacs may have sometimes hung directly on the belt, or they may have been carried in a small hanging purse or pouch. Other portable objects were probably also kept in those pouches or hung alongside the almanacs: rosaries, jewelry or gems, pilgrim badges, coin purses, *materia medica*, and textual amulets could all have been carried alongside a small, encased manuscript.⁵⁰ Talismanic connotations were attached to folding almanacs in part because of how they were worn, creating an association with other types of things that hung from the belt or girdle. Many of the extant folding almanacs have two limp covers, sometimes made of leather, sometimes covered in textiles. Some have the remnants of cords attached, and several leather slipcases also survive, in which the book would have been kept when not in use.⁵¹ Amulets, talismans, and pilgrim badges, of course, are all examples of objects that gained efficacy by appealing to the senses – that is, through their proximity to the body. The affinities between these kinds of objects and the folding almanacs indicates that they were similarly associated with the benefits of immediate sensory access. The talismanic quality of an almanac was amplified by the content accessed by its handler.

This sensory experience of reading is further augmented by the recalcitrance of the materials, more pronounced in the folding almanacs because they ask parchment to behave differently than it does in conventional codices. Unlike paper, parchment has a collagen-based fibrous structure that resists reshaping.⁵² It is always inclined to unfurl, as though channeling a memory of its earlier physical state as the skin curving over an animal's back: in the words of Christopher Clarkson, "[it] is not natural for parchment to lie flat."⁵³ Many covers of medieval codices were clasped or locked shut when not in use to prevent such curling and buckling. Meanwhile, changes in

---

were then ingested: Olsan, "Charms and Prayers in Medieval Medical Theory and Practice," *Social History of Medicine* 16 (2003): 343–366. See also Don C. Skemer, *Binding Words: Textual Amulets in the Middle Ages* (University Park: Penn State University Press, 2006).
49 Jones, "Amulets"; Olsan, "Charms and Prayers."
50 Skemer, in his discussion of how textual amulets were worn or carried, points out that "once folded or rolled, individual amulets could be carried in linen, velvet, or silk sacks, slung over the person's shoulder or suspended from the belt like girdle books and *vade mecum* folding books." *Binding Words*, 160.
51 Gumbert, *Bat Books*, 22–23.
52 For recent examples of studies that explore the material properties of parchment, see Alenka Možir, Irena Kralj Cigić, Marjan Marinšek, and Matija Strlič, "Material Properties of Historic Parchment: A Reference Collection Survey," *Studies in Conservation* 59 (2014): 136–149; Sarah Fiddyment et al., "Animal Origin of 13th-Century Uterine Vellum Revealed Using Noninvasive Peptide Fingerprinting," in *Proceedings of the National Academy of Science* 112 (2015), 15066–15071.
53 Christopher Clarkson, "Rediscovering Parchment: The Nature of the Beast," *The Paper Conservator* 16 (1992): 5–26, at 6.

temperature and humidity over time can lead to a loss of moisture that results in hardening and brittleness: once folds have been pressed into place, this hardening can cause them to hold their shape. Thus the act of *unfolding* is also resisted by the manuscript's pages. In a medieval codex, each piece of parchment, or bifolio, has only a single fold at the center; it is joined at this fold with other bifolios in a quire or gathering, which is then sewn into the binding of the book. If we think about how the codex is constructed, this center fold is sometimes – probably most of the time – fully folded when the book is closed; even when the book is open, that fold is rarely flattened completely. Thus its crease stays within a comfortable range. In a folding almanac, there are many additional folds; greater manipulation has been performed upon the piece of parchment. In a tri-fold almanac, for example, three folds are made, the last two of those to already doubled-up parchment. Once these folds have been made and the folios have stayed folded over many centuries, the books are audibly reluctant to unfold (Figures 5–6). When we handle them today, the folded pages can be quite

Figure 5: British Library, London, Stowe MS 1065, ca. 1482, manuscript in folded state, tied. Copyright The British Library Board.

Figure 6: British Library, London, Stowe MS 1065, fol. 6, unfolded state of rest once handler releases parchment. Copyright The British Library Board.

resistant, crunching and crackling as they are opened. These small books and their noisy pages shape their users' sensory experiences, forcing the handler to grapple, literally, with the physical reality of the object.

Every medieval manuscript made of parchment is going to creak and crackle some of the time.[54] But the parchment sheets of folding almanacs are exponentially noisier than those of the average codex; the folding and unfolding required of the reader consistently makes remarkably satisfying sounds.[55] This may be amplified by the type of parchment used in folding almanacs. These are usually not elite books in the traditional sense, even though they are often illuminated with colorful images and gold leaf. The parchment tends to be of the thicker and more robust type, perhaps chosen for these books – given that they might sustain a high level of handling when used in the field – because it was sturdier. The number of surviving and *intact* almanacs that also show a great deal of wear seem to suggest that this was the case.

---

54 While the original parchment may have been suppler when it was made than it is today, modern parchment samples suggest that even new parchment can still be quite audibly resistant to manipulation such as folding.
55 These satisfying crunches seem to generate a pleasure similar to that of cracking a joint or popping bubble wrap, which often seems to have a calming, stress-reducing effect.

Thicker parchment would have held up longer, but it would have also been harder to bend.

But it is not just that the parchment has been forced to accept more folds, and then to keep them (since the resting state of an almanac is folded); it is also expected to completely unfold on demand. These conflicting states are in tension with each other, and are further complicated by the parchment's original curvature. The parchment itself pushes to open up and stretch, but the deep folds also cause it to snap back from its flattened state. And this stress is manifest in movement and in noise, demonstrating the different physical forces at play in these folios. Given this constant tension between open and closed, folded and unfolded, their preferred state would probably be somewhere in between. These are objects that not only move on their own, but also may resist the actions of their handlers. They are dynamic, creating a rush of air and a snapping sound. Such factors, essential to the parchment sheets folded within an almanac, dictate how the user engages with the book, and what that user has to do to make the book work in the desired manner.

These parchment pages enact or respond to the laws of physics: crunching and crackling when you unfold them and springing back into folded form as soon as you loosen your grip, their thick parchment pushing back against the user and making noises in protest. Is this an example of Jane Bennett's notion of "thingly power" – that is, "the curious ability of inanimate things to animate, to act, to produce effects dramatic and subtle"?[56] Her argument for understanding matter not as dead but as having material agency is folded into a call for us as humans to be more attentive, through our senses, to the "channels of communication" created by objects and matter: "an actant never really acts alone," but is dependent on collaboration.[57] It may not really be much of a challenge for us to accept that our experiences, even our movements or actions, can be influenced by the matter and objects around us; perhaps the more tricky aspect of Bennett's assertions has to do with *how* we describe or imagine thingly power.

The assertiveness of the folding almanacs, their apparent self-determinacy, lends itself to anthropomorphism. Although scholars generally avoid anthropomorphizing their subjects, Bennett makes the case that anthropomorphism can be valuable and legitimate. As she observes, "a careful course of anthropomorphism can help to reveal [the] vitality" of objects, while our "encounters with matter ... expose a wider distribution of agency."[58] It is especially challenging to resist such language with a folding almanac; Gumbert's observation that such manuscripts "hang upside-down and all folded up" when in rest but "lift up their heads and spread their wings wide" when in

---

56 Bennett, *Vibrant Matter*, 6.
57 Bennett, *Vibrant Matter*, 21.
58 Bennett, *Vibrant Matter*, 122.

action demonstrates the animated status of these books.[59] The recognition that things have agency reveals, according to Bennett, a world of "lively matter" through "the inflection of matter as vibrant, vital, energetic, lively, quivering, vibratory, evanescent, and effluescent."[60] Those adjectives assert the capacities of objects to engage our senses, to move us.

A book's weight, the size of its text, page markings like chapter headings, rubrics, and page numbers, the presence of images – all of these factors contribute to the experience of using it, activating specific habits of reading.[61] According to Nolan, "habit is deeply connected to sensation," with the various sensory cues generated by objects like books activating "habitual behaviors" in the user.[62] In the case of the folding almanacs, the characteristics of these compact manuscripts are notably unique compared to the much more common codex form found in modern printed books as well as most medieval manuscripts. The manuscript's weight as it hangs in a pouch on one's belt, the book's heft in the hand, the series of foldings and unfoldings of the individual folios that might occur over the course of a diagnostic session – the folding almanac would have created very different habitual reading behaviors than a codex, generating a specific set of embodied motions and gestures that engaged specific senses in distinctive combinations.

Nolan and others bring attention to the "multimodal" or "cross-modal effects" of reading, arguing that the simultaneous engagement of multiple senses encourages information processing and even readerly well-being.[63] Michelle M. Sauer, specifically writing about the role of sound in the production of parchment and the reading of books made of parchment, cites recent research that indicates that "auditory-tactile stimulation" can be "a means to increase health and well-being."[64] She goes on to propose that the combination of touch and sound "might have produced a mental state in the (medieval) reader that made them particularly receptive to spiritual experience."[65] Beatrice Kitzinger has also argued that a spiritual benefit is inherent in the "activation" of a manuscript, the instrumentality of which facilitates "apprehension" through the senses but also beyond them, toward an understanding of the scope

---

[59] This also leads to his idiosyncratic description of them as "bat books." Gumbert, *Bat Books*, 19.
[60] Bennett, Vibrant Matter, 112.
[61] Nolan, "Medieval Habit, Modern Sensation," 466.
[62] Nolan, "Medieval Habit, Modern Sensation," 466.
[63] Michelle M. Sauer, "Audiotactility & the Medieval Soundscape of Parchment," in "Medieval Sound" forum, ed. Dorothy Kim and Christopher Roman, *Sounding Out*, 17 October 2016, https://soundstudiesblog.com/2016/10/17/audiotactility-the-medieval-soundscape-of-parchment/.
[64] In "Audiotactility & the Medieval Soundscape of Parchment," Sauer cites Esko O. Dijk et al., "Audio-Tactile Stimulation: A Tool to Improve Health and Well-Being?," *International Journal of Autonomous and Adaptive Communications Systems* 6 (2013): 305–323.
[65] Sauer, "Audiotactility & the Medieval Soundscape of Parchment."

of Christian time.⁶⁶ There were certainly health benefits associated with the content of the folding almanacs, and the performative manipulation of these almanacs may have generated further confidence in both the practitioner's authority and the manuscript's efficacy.⁶⁷ While the direct health benefits of this multisensory engagement were likely minimal, such engagement may well have enhanced the book's amuletic properties in the minds of both patient and practitioner.

Books also reflect the limits of what is reasonable in terms of discernment or understanding, exhibiting a kind of logic of comprehensibility that is linked to physical engagement. Sensation has a role in forming a handler's reading habits, but those habits are also directed by the manuscript layout, which "opens a window onto medieval habits of representation and reading."⁶⁸ Bodily limitations determine the limitations of a book, in terms of how much information can be processed by the eye at once, or what can be held by the hand.⁶⁹ Such considerations are especially pertinent to the almanacs because of their specific form. Did they seem as controlling, as recalcitrant, to original users as they might to us today? During a period of regular, active use, the parchment leaves of a folded almanac may have been suppler and more yielding than they are now. Without regular use, however, they would likely lose some flexibility and settle into their folds, making them resistant as well as noisy.⁷⁰ Even if these folding almanacs demonstrated greater flexibility when newly made and regularly used, the noise of unfolding would have always been fundamental to the experience of them – especially with the thicker parchment of which they were often made.

Conclusion

To access the full efficacy or impact of folding almanacs requires sensory engagement specific to these books and their particular format-content combination. The physics of this format insist on a particular way of being used, one that might have even altered how the content was absorbed. The format facilitated an especially performative use within the spaces of medical treatment, but such manipulation was not

---

66 Beatrice Kitzinger, "The Instrumental Cross and the Use of the Gospel Book Troyes, BM MS 960," *Different Visions* 4 (2014): 1–33, http://differentvisions.org/articles-pdf/four/kitzinger-instrumental-cross.pdf. The introduction to this issue of *Different Visions* is also useful: Karen Eileen Overbey and Benjamin C. Tilghman, "Active Objects: An Introduction," *Different Visions* 4 (2014): 1–9, http://differentvisions.org/articles-pdf/four/introduction.pdf.
67 Overbey and Borland, "Diagnostic Performance and Diagrammatic Manipulation."
68 Nolan, "Medieval Habit, Modern Sensation," 467.
69 Nolan, "Medieval Habit, Modern Sensation," 469.
70 I appreciate parchment maker Jesse Meyer's expertise in helping me think through the characteristics and behaviors of parchment; email message to author, 21 December 2016.

generated solely by the handlers; the handlers were also manipulated *by* the almanacs. Through their construction they generated, and continue to generate, forces, movement, and sounds that encourage a particular type of use; this use potentially increased their efficacy along with the well-being of those who used them or were in their presence.

In other words, the significance, power, and efficacy of the folding almanacs are tied up in their handling as much as in their content. While folding almanacs contained specific information with a practical function and were probably used to gain access to that content at least some of the time, there was also an important performative aspect to their use, activating the potential space between practitioner and patient. This performance – whether witnessed by a patient or simply experienced by the handler – would have eventually become habitual, ritualized, even talismanic. It would have contributed to the aura of the knowledge contained inside the book, knowledge that was activated by and through handling. Although the closed almanac is potentially a symbol of knowledge when displayed on a belt, the book's power is wrapped up in the "mechanics of physical contact" that are required for its usefulness to be fully realized.[71] The movement, the engagement of touch and hearing and other senses, the ritualized combinations of unfoldings and refoldings – these are necessary for that full power to be engaged. Bennett describes the impact of objects as "enchantment" in an effort to get at "the agency of things that *produce* (helpful, harmful) effects in human and other bodies."[72]

In an important discussion of textual amulets, Don C. Skemer suggests that proximity and tangibility are key to these objects' efficacy. Just as textual amulets were made more powerful by being worn, the manipulation of the almanacs, and the sensory engagement inherent in that use, were made more powerful through "physical agency."[73] In a sense the almanacs are like textual amulets, but it is not just touching or sensing them that makes them powerful. It is their form and the complicated series of actions that they produce: the promise of privileged knowledge is only fully realized through a kind of ritualized or habitual movement that is directly linked to their form. A folding almanac maintains these various levels of use, layering amuletic visibility and proximity onto an even more direct physical engagement through the handling of the book and the medical treatment of patients' bodies. The deep connection between habit and sensation is based in the physical book that "orchestrates" that habit; as articulated by Nolan, the material book's "conventions act as triggers for habitual behaviors, which in turn function as a means of ordering both the physical sensations of reading and the immaterial content of the work."[74] This

---

[71] Skemer, *Binding Words*, 127.
[72] Bennett, *Vibrant Matter*, xii.
[73] Skemer, *Binding Words*, 134.
[74] Nolan, "Medieval Habit, Modern Sensation," 467.

connection between the handling of a book – more specifically, a folding almanac – and the habitual behaviors or conjured ideas that result from that handling, brings to mind Sauer's discussion of the power of auditory-tactile stimulation. Beyond mental or intellectual well-being, the use of books like these suggests that the habitual can move into the spiritual, even the magical, to create well-being. The folding almanac directs the physical movement of the handler, maybe even provoking mental, emotional, and spiritual benefits at the same time. Sensory engagement with a folding almanac involves being *moved* on multiple levels.

Richard Newhauser
10 "putten to ploughe": Touching the Peasant Sensory Community

The Good Plowman and Peasant Agency

To the rest of the historiographical evidence that illustrates peasant agency in medieval England we can add the positively valued activity of the plowman in the art and literature of the later Middle Ages. The good plowman depicted in these contexts supplements the data that has been gathered in recent investigations into the range of choices available to peasants, the forces that shaped those options, and the milieux of peasant societies and their effects on peasant decision-making.[1] In particular, historians who have examined peasant societies have demonstrated in various ways the cohesiveness of village life, pointing, for example, to the way in which communal control of agriculture in village communities affected economic growth, or to the fact that strong peasant communities could restrain increases in money rents demanded of them and even hold rents lower than what landlords might otherwise have been able to charge.[2] Furthermore, as R. B. Goheen argued some time ago, peasant agency extended to politics as well, since "medieval English peasants participated in the crown's provincial politics partly at least on their own terms and for their own ends, and in the process they influenced both the form and content of these politics."[3] But such social and political histories largely

---

Note: I would like to express my gratitude to Arthur Russell and Katie Walter for reading and commenting on an earlier version of this chapter. Thanks also to those who commented helpfully at the Third International Workshop of the research project "The Senses: Past and Present," University of Bern, Switzerland, 10–13 October 2017; and the Sensory Experience Workshop convened at Stanford University, 14 October 2016. An abbreviated form of this chapter was published in Spanish translation as "Tacto y arado: creando la comunidad sensorial campesina," trans. María Ocando Finol, in *Abordajes sensoriales del mundo medieval*, ed. Gerardo Fabián Rodríguez and Gisela Coronado Schwindt (Mar del Plata, Argentina: Universidad Nacional de Mar del Plata, 2017), 105–128, accessed 13 November 2017, http://giemmardelplata.org/en/archivos/librosyactas/.

---

1 Anne DeWindt, "Historians and Peasant Agency: Studies of Late Medieval English Peasants," in *Crisis in the Later Middle Ages: Beyond the Postan-Duby Paradigm*, ed. John Drendel, The Medieval Countryside 13 (Turnhout: Brepols, 2015), 95–125.
2 Rosemary L. Hopcroft, "The Social Origins of Agrarian Change in Late Medieval England," *American Journal of Sociology* 99 (1994): 1559–1595; Junichi Kanzaka, "Villein Rents in Thirteenth-Century England: An Analysis of the Hundred Rolls of 1279–1280," *Economic History Review* 55 (2002): 593–618; Bruce Campbell, "The Agrarian Problem of the Early Fourteenth Century," *Past and Present* 188 (2005): 3–70. See also DeWindt, "Historians and Peasant Agency," 105.
3 R. B. Goheen, "Peasant Politics? Village Community and the Crown in Fifteenth-Century England," *The American Historical Review* 96 (1991): 42–62, at 42.

overlook the sensory elements that contributed to the self-identity and unity of peasant communities. Kellie Robertson has very clearly delineated the ways in which fourteenth-century England produced a view of two bodies in those who labored: a theological and idealized one, and a juridically regulated one created in the wake of the labor laws promulgated in the second half of the century.[4] I hope to supplement this perspective here by focusing on one of the senses – namely, touch, studied from within the sensory life of peasant society, and its actualization at the moment of grasping an iconic peasant object, that is to say, the plow – as a key element in the expression of peasant agency. As such, this chapter strives to serve as one step in examining a particular aspect of the historical sensorium of the late fourteenth century, especially in England.[5]

The emergence of the figure of the good plowman as a central and decisive character in Middle English poetry is one of the remarkable features of English literature in the fourteenth century. This figure, to be sure, is identified with the image of the fruitful, industrious peasant and not the sinful tiller of the soil who is the kin of Cain,[6] or the recalcitrant agricultural laborer pictured in English and Continental manuscripts as unwilling to work – for example, the peasant portrayed at the foot of the tree of vices in the psalter that Robert de Lisle commissioned for his daughters and gave to them in 1339 (Figure 1 and Plate XVIIa).[7] The good peasant is also to be differentiated from the figure of the indolent plowman, as seen in an allegory of Sloth sitting near his idle plow (and opposed to the virtuous figure of Labor sowing seeds) in a late thirteenth-century copy of the *Somme le roi* (Plate XVIII).[8]

As Paul Freedman has observed, "If medieval understanding of the dependence of society on the toil of the lowly was ambivalent, it did at least include the possibility of endowing symbols such as plowing with favorable moral connotations."[9] These implications could reach as far as the spiritualization of the plowman as a Christlike savior of society and the Church, which he becomes in the course of William Langland's fourteenth-century poem *Piers Plowman*, to which I will

---

4 Kellie Robertson, *The Laborer's Two Bodies: Literary and Legal Productions in Britain, 1350–1500* (Houndmills, UK: Palgrave Macmillan, 2005), especially 13–50.
5 For the phrase "historical sensorium," see Lauren Berlant, *Cruel Optimism* (Durham: Duke University Press, 2011), 3.
6 On the distinction between the industrious and the sinful peasant, see, for example, Jonathan Alexander, "Labeur and Paresse: Ideological Representations of Medieval Peasant Labor," *The Art Bulletin* 72 (1990): 436–452.
7 Lucy Freeman Sandler, *The Psalter of Robert de Lisle in the British Library* (1983; repr., London: Harvey Miller, 1999). Images of British Library MS Arundel 83 (II) are available online at http://www.bl.uk/manuscripts/FullDisplay.aspx?ref=Arundel_MS_83 (accessed 10 January 2017).
8 Frère Laurent, *La Somme le roi*, ed. Édith Brayer and Anne-Françoise Leurquin-Labie (Paris: Société des Anciens Textes Français, 2008).
9 Paul Freedman, *Images of the Medieval Peasant* (Stanford: Stanford University Press, 1999), 35.

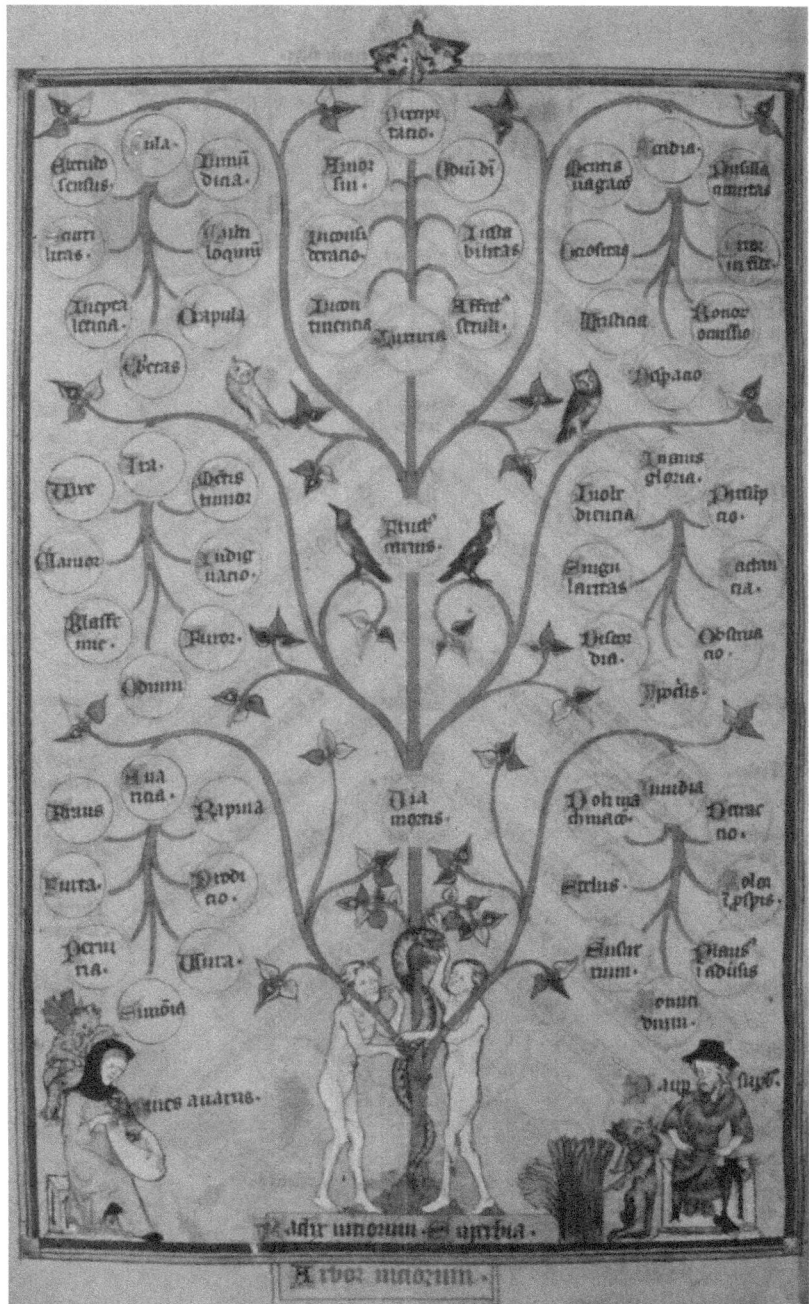

Figure 1: The De Lisle Psalter, given by Robert de Lisle to his daughters on November 25, 1339; the tree of vices. British Library, London, MS Arundel 83 (II), fol. 128v. Copyright The British Library Board.

return later in this chapter.¹⁰ Or the favorable connotations could remain secular but nonetheless thoroughly idealized as an expression of the expectations placed upon the peasant estate; this is what we find in Geoffrey Chaucer's portrait of the Plowman, who is, together with the Parson, part of a diptych of virtuous, rural poverty contained in "The General Prologue" of *The Canterbury Tales*:

> With hym ther was a Plowman, was his brother,
> That hadde ylad of dong ful many a fother;
> A trewe swynkere and a good was he,
> Lyvynge in pees and parfit charitee.
> God loved he best with al his hoole herte
> At alle tymes, thogh him gamed or smerte,
> And thanne his neighebor right as hymselve.
> He wolde thresshe, and therto dyke and delve,
> For Cristes sake, for every povre wight,
> Withouten hire, if it lay in his myght.
> His tithes payde he ful faire and wel,
> Bothe of his propre swynk and his catel.
> In a tabard he rood upon a mere.¹¹

(With him [the Parson] there was a Plowman, who was his brother,/Who had hauled many cartloads of dung;/He was an honest and good worker,/Living in peace and true *caritas* [love]./He loved God most of all with his entire heart/At all times, whether it was advantageous to him or caused him discomfort,/And after that [he loved] his fellow human being exactly as himself./He used to thresh and moreover make ditches and dig,/For Christ's sake, for every poor person,/Without pay, if it was within his power to do so./He paid his tithes very properly and completely,/On both his own labor and his possessions./He rode in a workman's loose garment on a mare.)

---

10 For the spiritual context of the plowman and his labor, see Stephen A. Barney, "The Plowshare of the Tongue: The Progress of a Symbol from the Bible to *Piers Plowman*," *Mediaeval Studies* 35 (1973): 261–293. The image of the plowman as the idealized guide for the Church should be compared to the view of plowmen in Roman antiquity as men creating the agricultural foundation for those who heroically direct the affairs of state and ensure Rome's greatness. See, for example, the view of the plow and plowing in Virgil's *Georgics* explicated in Robert McKay Wilhelm, "The Plough-Chariot: Symbol of Order in the *Georgics*," *The Classical Journal* 77 (1982): 213–230.

11 Geoffrey Chaucer, "The General Prologue," *The Canterbury Tales*, I.529–541, in *The Riverside Chaucer*, ed. Larry D. Benson, 3rd ed. (Boston: Houghton Mifflin, 1987), 32. All translations from Middle English are my own. On the idealization of the Plowman in Chaucer's work and the way he exemplifies an ideal of communal responsibility, see Mark Bailey, "The Ploughman," in *Historians on Chaucer. The 'General Prologue' to the Canterbury Tales*, ed. Stephen H. Rigby, with the assistance of Alastair J. Minnis (Oxford: Oxford University Press, 2014), 352–367, at 365–367. On Chaucer's Plowman, see also Daniel F. Pigg, "With Hym Ther Was a Plowman, Was His Brother," in *Chaucer's Pilgrims: An Historical Guide to the Pilgrims in the Canterbury Tales*, ed. Laura C. Lambdin and Robert T. Lambdin (Westport: Greenwood Press, 1996), 263–270.

The Good Plow as Peasant Object

Not only plowmen but also the plow itself was able to attract wholly positive associations, as we can witness, for instance, in the concept of "plow sanctuary," the notion that the plow afforded legal protection to a criminal in the same way that a church did or, with regard to the "king's peace," in the way that seeking protection on a royal highway did. As Ranulf Higden's *Polychronicon* puts it, in a late fourteenth-century translation by John Trevisa:

> Molinicius, kyng of Britouns, was þe þridde and twenty of hem, and þe firste þat ȝaf hem lawe. He ordeyned þat plowȝmen solowes, goddes temples, and hiȝe weies, þat ledeþ to citees and townes, schulde haue þe fredom of sucour; so þat eueriche man þat fley to eny of þe þre for socour for trespas þat he hadde i-doo schulde be safe for pursuyt of alle his enemyes.[12]

> (Molinicius was the twenty-third king of the Britons and the first lawgiver among them. He commanded that plowmen's plows, temples of the gods, and highways leading to cities and towns should have the right of providing refuge from prosecution, so that everyone who flees to any of these three for protection because of a criminal act he has committed should be safe from charges brought by all his enemies.)

As stated here, it is plowmen's plows that offered legal protection against criminal prosecution. The specification of the plows as those employed by peasants (and not those owned by the lords of manors, etc.) is surely an acknowledgment of the critical role played by the men who till the land for food production and their special need for defense when exposed in remote fields.[13] The special status of these people becomes associated with their most iconic object. Plowmen and plows are interdependent in the associative understanding of peasant society; together they form part of an object-based medieval history yet to be written.

The plow is an object that is integral to peasant society beginning perhaps four thousand years ago, and typically it was depicted in the medieval period as engaging the physical touch of only the peasantry.[14] As seen in many illustrations of tilling,

---

[12] "Statuit Molmutius rex Britonum vicesimus tertius et primus eorum legifer, ut aratra colonum, templa deorum, viaeque ad civitates ducentes, immunitate confugii gauderent, ita ut nullus reus ad aliquod istorum trium confugiens pro tuitione ab aliquo invaderetur." Ranulf Higden, *Polychronicon*, 1.45, in *Polychronicon Ranulfi Higden monachi Cestrensis; together with the English Translations of John Trevisa and of an Unknown Writer of the Fifteenth Century*, ed. Joseph Rawson Lumby and Churchill Babington, 9 vols., Rerum Britannicarum medii aevi scriptores 41 (London: Longmans, Green, and Co., 1865–1886), 2:42–45. In the Middle English, "solowes" are plows. For the Latin *colo, colonis* (peasant), see the *Dictionary of Medieval Latin from British Sources*.

[13] See the very helpful analysis by James H. Morey, "Plows, Laws, and Sanctuary in Medieval England in the Wakefield *Mactacio Abel*," *Studies in Philology* 95 (1998): 41–55, at 45.

[14] Frederic L. Pryor, "The Invention of the Plow," *Comparative Studies in Society and History* 27 (1985): 727–743. See also Michael Partridge, *Farm Tools Through the Ages* (Reading: Osprey, 1973), 36–57.

the plow frequently in use in England in the High and later Middle Ages represented a further development of the scratch plow, or ard; this was the heavy plow (Latin *aratrum*, *carruca*). It consisted of a beam (Latin *temo*) from which first a coulter (Latin *culter*) descended,[15] which opened a thin strip in the ground, followed by the plowshare (Latin *vomer*) that cut a deep furrow into the soil; the soil then rode up along the moldboard and was turned over.[16] In the case of the swing plow, the beam could be stabilized by the use of a foot (Latin *pes*) (Figure 2). A wheel or wheels could also be employed for stabilization (Plates XVIII and XVIIb), a development documented as early as the first century by Pliny the Elder.[17]

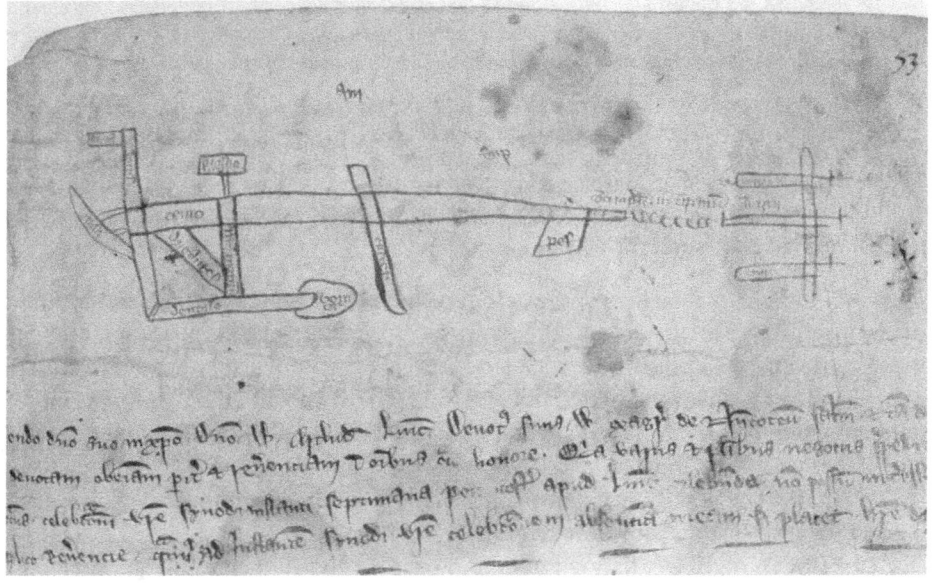

Figure 2: Cartulary of the Cistercian nunnery of Nun Coton (now Coltham), English, late thirteenth century; a swing plow with coulter. Bodleian Library, Oxford, MS Top. Linc. d. 1, fol. 53r. Reproduced with permission of the Bodleian Libraries, the University of Oxford.

Plows were pulled by farm animals, with the standard size of the plow team being eight animals for a lord's demesne (at times mixing oxen and horses). On the other

---

15 For archaeological evidence of an early (ca. 1050–1230 CE) plow beam and coulter discovered in Ireland, see Caroline Earwood and Keith Beattie, "A Medieval Plough from Drumlee, County Antrim," *Ulster Journal of Archaeology* 67 (2008): 118–125.
16 I have adopted the Latin terms from the diagram of the plow in Figure 2.
17 Pliny the Elder, *Natural History*, 18.48.172, in Pliny, *Natural History*, trans. Harris Rackham, William H. S. Jones, and D. E. Eichholz, 10 vols., Loeb Classical Library 371 (Cambridge, MA: Harvard University Press, 1938–1963), 5:296–297.

10 "putten to ploughe": Touching the Peasant Sensory Community — 231

Figure 3: Jean Miélot, *Miracles de Nostre Dame*, ca. 1456, Flemish, miniatures by Jean Tavernier, completed for Philip the Good of Burgundy, from the library of Charles the Bold, Duke of Burgundy 1467–1477; plowing scene with image of the soul of a covetous but devout plowman received by the Virgin. Bodleian Library, Oxford, MS Douce 374, fol. 89r. Reproduced with permission of the Bodleian Libraries, the University of Oxford.

hand, as is suggested by many manuscript illuminations, peasants were apparently able to make do in plowing their rented land as tenant farmers, or on common fields,[18] or when performing required service on a lord's fields, with much smaller plow teams consisting of two pairs (or even a single pair) of oxen (Plates XIXa and XIXb). Smaller plow teams could also be composed of a pair of horses (Figure 3 and Plate XVIIb).[19] Along with being depicted in manuscript illuminations, smaller plow teams are also documented by the archival evidence.[20]

---

[18] Eric Kerridge, *The Common Fields of England* (Manchester: Manchester University Press, 1992). Cf. Warren O. Ault, *Open-Field Farming in Medieval England: A Study of Village By-laws* (London: Routledge, 1972).
[19] See also Patricia Basing, *Trades and Crafts in Medieval Manuscripts* (London: British Library, 1990), fig. 13 (plates I and II).
[20] John Langdon, *Horses, Oxen and Technological Innovation: The Use of Draught Animals in English Farming from 1066–1500* (Cambridge, UK: Cambridge University Press, 1986), 62–74, 229–244.

The reality of these smaller plow teams not only makes it apparent why manuscript illuminations often show fewer than eight animals, but it has also proven important in assessing some references to tilling in literary texts: plowing could hardly be presented in medieval drama with a full team of eight animals, but it was very possible to do so using just a pair of horses, for example in the Wakefield play *The Killing of Abel*.[21] In all events, the heavy plow greatly extended the amount of land that could be tilled by the peasant, and this factor was prized in the plow well into the early modern period. As an anonymous author of the early seventeenth century put it, "The Plough, which now is generally in vse, can compasse with the aide of two or one, as the Country requires, an Acre or two in a day. Threescore ordinarie Countrie labourers, can hardly digge an Acre at two Spades, whereof I haue made triall."[22]

Touching the Peasant Sensory Community: Interobjectivity

As George Homans observed years ago in a now classic study of English villagers in the thirteenth century, "The plowshare was the villein's badge of office.... The plow was his life."[23] As an extension of Homans's observation, I am suggesting here that the touch of the plow can be seen as one of the sensory experiences that defined a stereotypical peasant activity, and that laying hands on the plow demarcated one essential characteristic of the "sensory community" of the rural peasantry. Up to now, scholarly attention has mainly been attracted by other senses used to define the peasant community that are contained in medieval textual sources external to this community – in particular the olfactory sense. Chaucer notes the many cartloads of dung associated with his Plowman, and in this way he draws on earlier traditions that associated the rural peasantry with distinctive, scatological odors. The early thirteenth-century preacher Jacques de Vitry, for example, inscribed this connection between the peasantry and dung in an exemplum: A peasant who had been brought up around the smells of animals passed by the spicers' section of a city and was overcome by the

---

21 *The Killing of Abel*, in *The Towneley Plays*, re-ed. George England, with notes by Alfred Pollard, EETS es 71 (London: Oxford University Press, 1966), 9–22. See, for example, Margaret Rogerson, "The Medieval Plough Team on Stage: Wordplay and Reality in the *Mactacio Abel*," *Comparative Drama* 28 (1994): 182–200.
22 *God Speede the Plovgh* (London: John Harison, 1601), A2v–A3r. Practical advice on when to plow is found earlier in fifteenth-century Middle English texts on husbandry, such as the translation of Walter of Henley's book (see below, n. 45) from the late fifteenth century, or the translation of Palladius, *De re rustica*, completed for Humphrey, Duke of Gloucester, ca. 1442–1443: *Palladius on Husbondrie*, ed. Barton Lodge, 2 vols., EETS os 52, 72 (London: N. Trübner & Co., 1873–1879).
23 George Caspar Homans, *English Villagers of the Thirteenth Century* (New York: Norton, 1941), 243.

odors of herbs and spices being ground up. He fainted, unable to regain consciousness, as if he were half dead. But as soon as he was returned to the stench of fumes and dung at his home, he was successfully revived.[24] In the same way, an unrefined taste in food – coarse, dark bread or pottage and beer made from oats, for example – and the feel of unrefined clothing – e.g., loose-fitting garments of rough material in ill repair, etc. – were taken as sensory markers for the peasantry.[25] Yet these sensorial stereotypes must be set against the tendency, especially pronounced in England in the latter half of the fourteenth century, for the lower orders to imitate the habits of those above them in the social hierarchy. This tendency was encouraged by economic and social changes during the period. Following the initial spread of the Black Plague in the mid-fourteenth century, the supply of labor decreased dramatically, wages went up, and seignorial obligations on the peasantry decreased. As a result of these and other developments, laborers' spending power increased appreciably. The peasantry was able to afford a more varied diet and to aspire to imitate aristocratic fashions, such as the tight-fitting clothes favored at court.[26] There was much outrage among moralists of the time at these articulations of peasant agency, by which peasants expressed their desire to escape the sensory standards of their station and in this way to redefine by themselves the limitations of their identity. As a good example of the outrage voiced by those outside the peasantry, we can point to the work of John Gower. His *Vox Clamantis* (composed mostly between 1378 and the earlier part of 1381) complains about the gustatory demands of hired laborers. In the *Visio Anglie*, which Gower added later to the beginning of the *Vox*, the peasants of the Rising of 1381 are depicted as domestic and wild animals unwilling to consume the common food of beasts. Instead, they demand the refined repast of the upper orders: pigs refuse to drink water but want wine, dogs refuse table scraps and demand instead well-fattened meat, etc.[27]

---

24 Jacques de Vitry, *The Exempla or Illustrative Stories from the Sermones Vulgares of Jacques de Vitry*, ed. Thomas Frederick Crane, Publications of the Folk-Lore Society 26 (London: David Nutt, 1890), 80 (no. 191). See Kathryn Reyerson, "Urban Sensations: The Medieval City Imagined," in *A Cultural History of the Senses in the Middle Ages*, ed. Richard G. Newhauser, A Cultural History of the Senses 2 (London: Bloomsbury, 2014), 45–65, at 45. The exemplum was used widely in different variations; see Frederic C. Tubach, *Index exemplorum: A Handbook of Medieval Religious Tales*, 2nd ed., FF Communications 204 (1969; repr., Helsinki: Academia Scientiarum Fennica, 1981), no. 3645.
25 It is clear, of course, that taste and touch intersect in sensorial terms: some of the earliest meanings of "taste" refer to touching or exploring by means of the sense of touch. See the recent essay by Ben Highmore, "Taste as Feeling," *New Literary History* 47 (2016): 547–566.
26 Harry Kitsikopoulos, "England," in *Agrarian Change and Crisis in Europe, 1200–1500*, ed. Harry Kitsikopoulos (New York: Routledge, 2012), 23–56, at 36–39; Christopher Dyer, *An Age of Transition? Economy and Society in England in the Later Middle Ages* (Oxford: Oxford University Press, 2005), 126–172.
27 John Gower, *Visio Anglie* (*Vox clamantis* 1), 4.361–364 (pigs), 5.383–384 (dogs), in John Gower, *Poems on Contemporary Events: The Visio Anglie (1381) and Cronica tripertita (1400)*, ed. David R. Carlson, trans. A. G. Rigg, Texts and Studies 174 (Toronto: Pontifical Institute of Mediaeval Studies

In contrast to these widely documented olfactory, gustatory, and haptic experiences and associations, the implicit connection between the peasant and the plow persisted through the late Middle Ages as a central characteristic of the peasantry – and it persisted regardless of changes in the rural economy. This connection was activated through the haptic sense when the hand touched the plow, for as Bartholomew the Englishman observed, the sense of touch refers to all parts of the body but it is centered in the palms of the hands and the soles of the feet.[28] This important role played by the touch of the plow in defining the sensory community of the peasantry has barely been evaluated up to now. It is a sensory experience left unarticulated in texts written about the peasantry in the later Middle Ages, one whose significance must be teased out from its largely self-understood, naturalized place in the conception of what work amounts to in peasant communities and what defines the sensory life of the peasantry.

Through the pioneering work of Constance Classen, David Howes, and others, the senses have become an object of scholarly investigation for many disciplines, reaching beyond the earlier dominance of psychology to include now the widest range of academic fields in the humanities and social sciences.[29] Speaking of the senses as socially and culturally constructed, rather than as essential or zoetic elements,[30] implicates the way in which social identity is defined within sensory communities – that is to say, social groups in which the members "share common ways of using their senses and making sense of sensations."[31] In some ways analogous to what Barbara Rosenwein has written of emotional communities, we can also observe that sensory communities are groups in which people are linked cohesively through norms of interpretation of sensory experience and subscribe to the same valuation (or devaluation) of those sensory experiences.[32] The interpretive norms embodied in sensory communities make up part of the somatic factors involved in describing what Pierre Bourdieu termed "habitus": dispositions of social structures and history that

---

Press, 2011), 52 (pigs), 54 (dogs). On Gower and taste, see Richard Newhauser, "John Gower's Sweet Tooth," *The Review of English Studies* N.S. 64 (2013): 752–769.

28 Bartholomeus Anglicus, *Liber de proprietatibus rerum*, 3.21 (Strasburg, 1485): "Hic autem sensus licet sit in omnibus partibus principaliter tamen viget in volis manuum et in plantis...."

29 See, for example, David Howes and Constance Classen, *Ways of Sensing: Understanding the Senses in Society* (London: Routledge, 2014).

30 I employ *zoe* as opposed to *bios*, treating this pair of terms in the sense used by Giorgio Agamben. See Agamben, *Homo Sacer: Sovereign Power and Bare Life*, trans. Daniel Heller-Roazen (Stanford: Stanford University Press, 1998).

31 Phillip Vannini, Dennis Waskul, and Simon Gottschalk, *The Senses in Self, Society, and Culture: A Sociology of the Senses* (London: Routledge, 2012), 7–8.

32 Defining emotional communities, Barbara H. Rosenwein has written that they are "groups in which people adhere to the same norms of emotional expression and value – or devalue – the same or related emotions." Rosenwein, *Emotional Communities in the Early Middle Ages* (Ithaca, NY: Cornell University Press, 2006), 2.

condition perception.³³ The social groupings involved here establish sensory regimes and enforce standards that are reflected in concepts of the hierarchy of the senses and other aspects of the sensorium, but since social identity also has a political character, sensory communities are subject to resistance by conflicting or insurgent or "reinterpretive" understandings of the senses.³⁴ Sensory communities may be as small as temporary gatherings of people at a banquet, all participating in a series of tastes, smells, sights, and so on. On the other hand, a sensory community can also encompass the breadth of one of the medieval estates – in the present case, the peasantry – and its shaping of somatic awareness through sight, hearing, taste, smell, and touch that defines the cohesiveness of the group.³⁵ The haptic sense is bidirectional: when someone leans against a wall, her back both touches the wall and is touched by the wall. The social order of touch, then, also regulates what a sensory community considers fitting to be touched by, expressed in particular through the clothing that it finds appropriate for itself or that is imposed on it, either by direct domination in the form of sumptuary laws and the like, or by the less coercive form of cultural hegemony that Antonio Gramsci termed "consent."³⁶ In the Middle Ages (as also now), "class distinctions were impressed on the skin through the use of symbolically potent textiles."³⁷ But the social and communal context of the haptic sense can also be observed in implicit regulations concerning who can touch whom and who can touch what.

The haptic contact between plow and plowman was activated at the plow handle(s), or stilt(s) (Latin *stiva* and *ansa*), when the peasant reached out to "putten (himself) to ploughe" to guide it while plowing – and, we must now add, given the fact that objects have agency, when the handle(s) of the plow also offered a site for the touch of the plowman's hand. In terms of what has come to be known as the "new materiality,"³⁸ the capacities of an object (here, a plow) are activated, or become actual,

---

33 Pierre Bourdieu, *Distinction: A Social Critique of the Judgement of Taste*, trans. Richard Nice (London: Routledge, 1984), 170.
34 Richard Newhauser, "The Senses, the Medieval Sensorium, and Sensing (in) the Middle Ages," in *Handbook of Medieval Culture: Fundamental Aspects and Conditions of the European Middle Ages*, ed. A. Classen, 3 vols. (Berlin: De Gruyter, 2015), 3:1559–1575, at 1573. On the politics of the senses, see Davide Panagia, *The Political Life of Sensation* (Durham: Duke University Press, 2009).
35 Cf. Vannini, Waskul, and Gottschalk, *The Senses in Self, Society, and Culture*, 59.
36 Antonio Gramsci, *Selections from the Prison Notebooks of Antonio Gramsci*, ed. and trans. Quentin Hoare and Geoffrey Nowell Smith (London: ElecBook, 1999), 145, accessed 10 January 2017, http://abahlali.org/files/gramsci.pdf.
37 Constance Classen, *The Deepest Sense: A Cultural History of Touch* (Urbana, IL: University of Illinois Press, 2012), 9. On the importance of the skin and flesh in defining what is human, see Katie Walter, "The Form of the Formless: Medieval Taxonomies of Skin, Flesh and the Human," in *Reading Skin in Medieval Literature and Culture*, ed. Katie L. Walter (New York: Palgrave Macmillan, 2013), 119–139.
38 Manuel DeLanda, "The New Materiality," *Architectural Design* 85 (2015): 16–21. See also Jane Bennett, *Vibrant Matter: A Political Ecology of Things* (Durham, NC: Duke University Press, 2010);

only when it interacts with other things (soil, the plowman's hand). By "activation" or "actualization," I refer to the functional contact between a sensory organ (here, the hand) and an object of sensation (the plow) as they participate in bringing about a specific activity (plowing). Because this actualization of objects in connection with humans is necessarily mediated through the human senses, we can say that both thinking sensually, in terms of sensory anthropology, and taking account of objects as actants will lead us to the interface between things and the sensory experiences connected with those things that together form part of the life of the sensory community that is defined by them. As Bruno Latour has observed, it is the interaction of objects and humanity that goes to make up "the weaving of social life," and, using the same metaphor, he has asserted that when we take account of this interaction we "can weave the properties of objects with those of the social."[39] For Latour's sociology, inanimate beings exert social force because they have an effect on the environment in which they exist, but if the interaction of objects and subjects has gone largely unexpressed and undescribed, Gordon Sammut, Paul Daanen, and Mohammad Sartawi have depicted the way in which this situation of object-subject cooperation is in fact an aspect of ideology, understood as the tacitly accepted, unexamined naturalization of cultural phenomena. Interobjectivity makes it clear that for "human beings who have been fully enculturated into a given environment, the meaning of objects with which we interact in the course of our day-to-day life is immediately and nonconsciously intelligible to us."[40] Interobjectivity thus designates a study that stands at the crossroads of both material culture, which is so important to contemporary medieval studies, and sensory experience, with its expanding significance for the study of the Middle Ages. Interobjectivity also accepts, as Diana Coole and Samantha Frost have written of critical materialism, that "society is simultaneously materially real and socially constructed."[41] By focusing on the intercorporeality of the sensorial, this approach emphasizes the continuity of object and subject.[42] Taking interobjectivity into account, then, we can say that it is insufficient to describe the plowman-plow interaction merely as the manipulation of a farm implement.[43] The human occupation

---

Stacy Alaimo, *Bodily Natures: Science, Environment, and the Material Self* (Bloomington: Indiana University Press, 2010).
39 Bruno Latour, "On Interobjectivity," *Mind, Culture, and Activity: An International Journal* 3 (1994): 228–245, at 235–236.
40 Gordon Sammut, Paul Daanen, and Mohammad Sartawi, "Interobjectivity: Representations and Artefacts in Cultural Psychology," *Culture & Psychology* 16 (2010): 451–463, at 452.
41 Diana Coole and Samantha Frost, "Introducing the New Materialisms," in *New Materialisms: Ontology, Agency, and Politics*, ed. Diana Coole and Samantha Frost (Durham: Duke University Press, 2010), 1–43, at 27.
42 Yannis Hamilakis, *Archaeology and the Senses: Human Experience, Memory, and Affect* (Cambridge, UK: Cambridge University Press, 2014), 116.
43 See Latour, "On Interobjectivity," 235.

and the occupational object function together (and of course they do so in a context composed of other things as well: the soil, the animals that make up the plow team, etc.); neither the human hand nor the plow as object is complete without the other. Moreover, the social element enacted here to complete this interaction is somatic, part of the body – and that is to say the sensory life – of the society in which it occurs.

The Peasant Community and the Aristocracy

The interaction of plow and peasant mediated through the sense of touch when one is said in Middle English to "putten (himself) to ploughe" implicates numerous social forces, including the idealization of estate functionality and the potential for peasant agency. The flawless nature of Chaucer's Plowman is predicated on his carrying out the twin commandments of *caritas* (love of God and love of one's fellow human beings), but also on his willingness to help other poor people and, furthermore, to pay his tithes. He is not only an impeccable example of virtuous rural labor within the context of a Christian measurement of the good, but his agency is also contained within the context of the hierarchical, class-bound expectations of the peasantry. As Michael Camille noted in an important examination of illuminations of tillage, depictions of medieval plowmen implicated "an association between ploughing and the proper organization of society."[44] The idealization of tilling the soil seen in Chaucer's Plowman stands out in contrast to less sanguine views of plowmen held by landowners and estate managers who wrote on husbandry,[45] and also to more aggressive, less contained actions by the peasantry in England in 1381 when peasants rose up against a series of oppressive taxes and indentured labor.[46] The Peasants' Revolt came as a shock to authors like Chaucer as well as to artists who painted scenes of plowing that reached back to earlier traditions of an idealized social order expressed by the harmony of the estates as a way to replace realistic images of the contemporary peasantry with a more aristocrat-centric ideal. Indeed, Chaucer's Knight attempts to reclaim this ideal by appropriating the metaphor of plowing for his own virtuous narration. Describing the enormity of his task in telling his tale and his humble

---

[44] Michael Camille, "Labouring for the Lord: The Ploughman and the Social Order in the Luttrell Psalter," *Art History* 10 (1987): 423–454, at 431.
[45] Walter of Henley, a Dominican prior writing ca. 1286, recommended using a mixed plow team of horses and oxen "pur ceo ke la malyce des charuers ne suffrent mye la charue aler hors del pas" (because the malice of ploughmen will not allow the plough [of horses] to go beyond their pace). *Walter of Henley's Husbandry* [...], ed. and trans. Elizabeth Lamond (London: Longmans, Green, and Co., 1890), 10–11.
[46] On the 1381 rising, see Steven Justice, *Writing and Rebellion: England in 1381*, The New Historicism 27 (Berkeley: University of California Press, 1994).

abilities to complete the job, he says: "I have, God woot, a large feeld to ere,/And wayke been the oxen in my plough"[47] (I have, God knows, a large field to till,/And the oxen in my plow team are weak). But the Miller, the very figure of an aggressive English peasantry,[48] reappropriates the metaphor for himself,[49] thereby denying the Knight even a verbal ability to lay hold of the plow – and in much less polite terms than Piers Plowman uses in Langland's poem to assert his own exclusive interaction with the implement, as will be seen later.

The text known as the *Early South English Legendary Life of Mary Magdalen* (though it is not actually part of the early *South English Legendary*, it is included in a copy of that collection from ca. 1300) presents the ideal of tillage as poor relief in describing Martha's actions when she takes over the family's property from Lazarus and Mary Magdalen:

Martha nam hire brothur lond and hire sustres also,
And dude heom teolien wel inough, ase wys man scholde do;
Tharewith heo fedde alle heore men and clothede heom also,
Povere men and wummen, that weren neodfole and in wo.[50]

(Martha took her brother's land and her sister's also,/And ordered them to be plowed carefully, as a wise man should do;/Therewith she fed all her people and clothed them also,/Poor men and women, who were in a state of want and need.)

The same inculcation of neighborliness inscribed in Chaucer's Plowman is seen here as well, when Martha assumes the authority of the role of male landowner (but not the labor of the plowman himself). The plowman's hand that is laid on the plow, as ordered by Martha, is taught in this way the sociability of touch,[51] an aspect of what I have elsewhere termed the "edification of the senses."[52] In the *Life of Mary Magdalen*'s

---

47 Chaucer, "The Knight's Tale," *The Canterbury Tales*, I.886–887, in *The Riverside Chaucer*, 37.
48 See Lee Patterson, "'No Man His Reson Herde': Peasant Consciousness, Chaucer's Miller, and the Structure of the *Canterbury Tales*," in *Literary Practice and Social Change in Britain, 1380–1530*, ed. Lee Patterson, The New Historicism 8 (Berkeley: University of California Press, 1990), 113–155.
49 Chaucer, "The Miller's Prologue," *The Canterbury Tales*, I.3159–3160, in *The Riverside Chaucer*, 67. See Brent Addison Moberly, "'Wayke Been the Oxen': Plowing, Presumption, and the Third-Estate Ideal in Late Medieval England" (PhD dissertation, Indiana University, 2007), 12–18.
50 *Early South English Legendary Life of Mary Magdalen*, vv. 59–62, in *Middle English Legends of Women Saints*, ed. Sherry L. Reames, TEAMS (Kalamazoo: Medieval Institute Publications, 2003), 61.
51 Touch as a factor in interpersonal relations was the focus of study by two psychologists in the 1960s who understood sociability demonstrated in touching as the opposite of social alienation. See Sidney M. Jourard and Jane E. Rubin, "Self-disclosure and Touching: A Study of Two Modes of Interpersonal Encounter and Their Inter-relation," *Journal of Humanistic Psychology* 8 (1968): 39–48.
52 Richard G. Newhauser, "Introduction: The Sensual Middle Ages," in *A Cultural History of the Senses in the Middle Ages*, ed. Richard G. Newhauser, A Cultural History of the Senses 2 (London: Bloomsbury, 2014), 1–22, at 12–17.

idealization of poor relief, the plowman's haptic sense is instructed to play its role in serving the common good: coming to the aid of the impoverished is contextualized in ethically positive terms. The gap between the view of the senses as the portals of potential sinfulness, on the one hand, and the senses as the foundation of epistemology, on the other hand, may seem to present an impasse that cannot be overcome, for in this perspective, the means of perception would also be the agents undermining cognition and, as others have argued, this would result in an incoherent connection of perception and the will.[53] But if the senses might be thought to potentially destabilize cognition, we can observe that the connection of perception and the will still achieves coherence in the Middle Ages in a process of training the interpretation of sensory data – that is to say, through educating the senses. Insofar as this process amounts to the socialization of perception that can go so far as to encompass an ascetic *custodia sensuum*,[54] it overlaps with what Michel Foucault termed "discipline,"[55] but edification involves much more than this. It includes such important elements of the social as the modification of the interpretation of sensory data through scientific knowledge (as seen in the influential clarification of optical illusions by texts of Perspectivist optics beginning in the thirteenth century),[56] the shaping of the user experience of devotional objects and books,[57] or something as ubiquitous as the sensory training of apprentices in a trade. But even beyond these historical elements of edification, the method of modal anthropology, or the anthropology of the senses, that I have attempted to pursue here,[58] which establishes the multiplicity of the modalities of perception as a continuum between the life of the mind and the life of the body, provides the foundation on which to see perception, will, and cognition as steps in the same process.

---

53 Joachim Küpper, "Perception, Cognition, and Volition in the *Arcipreste de Talavera*," in *Rethinking the Medieval Senses: Heritage, Fascinations, Frames*, ed. Stephen G. Nichols, Andreas Kablitz, and Alison Calhoun (Baltimore: Johns Hopkins University Press, 2008), 119–153.

54 See Pierre Adnès, "Garde des sens," *Dictionnaire de spiritualité*, 17 vols. (Paris: G. Beauchesne et ses fils, 1932–1995), 6:117–122.

55 Michel Foucault, *Discipline and Punish: The Birth of the Prison*, trans. Alan Sheridan (1977; repr., New York: Random House, 1995).

56 See Richard G. Newhauser, "Morals, Science, and the Edification of the Senses," in *Optics, Ethics, and Art in the Thirteenth and Fourteenth Centuries: Looking into Peter of Limoges's Moral Treatise on the Eye*, ed. Herbert L. Kessler and Richard G. Newhauser, with the assistance of Arthur J. Russell, Text – Image – Context: Studies in Medieval Manuscript Illumination 5, Studies and Texts 209 (Toronto: Pontifical Institute of Mediaeval Studies, 2018), 7–16; Richard Newhauser, "Peter of Limoges, Optics, and the Science of the Senses," in "Pleasure and Danger in Perception: The Five Senses in the Middle Ages and the Renaissance," special issue, *The Senses & Society* 5 (2010): 28–44.

57 See the recent work by Arthur J. Russell, "The Moral Sense of Touch: Teaching Tactile Values in Late Medieval England" (PhD dissertation, Arizona State University, 2016).

58 See most recently François Laplantine, *The Life of the Senses: Introduction to a Modal Anthropology*, trans. Jamie Furniss (London: Bloomsbury, 2015); David Howes, "Senses, Anthropology of the," in *International Encyclopedia of the Social & Behavioral Sciences*, ed. James D. Wright, 2nd ed., 26 vols. (Oxford: Elsevier, 2015), 21:615–620.

Manuscript illuminations focusing on peasants plowing often present images of peasant tillage designed for the eyes of the upper levels of society who owned the valuable books in whose margins the plowmen were depicted laboring. The animals at work pulling the plow as well as the plowmen's feet in the furrows of the fields are generally not mud-covered or dirty. Likewise, the peasant clothing portrayed in some scenes of farm work is not what laborers might be expected to have worn, but has been cosmeticized for aristocratic taste, as is the case in the Luttrell Psalter (Plate XIXb). There, the plowman's clothing is brightly colored and lined with green material, his coat is orange, and his hood is a deep purple, all of which indicate a much higher level of fashion than typical peasant wear.[59] Something similar can be said, taking an example from a later period, about the plowman in the foreground of Pieter Bruegel's *Landscape with the Fall of Icarus*, extant in two versions of the painting attributed to Bruegel (Plate XX).[60]

Among the number of dissonant and curious details in the painting,[61] those connected with the plowman stand out. He uses only one horse to pull a heavy plow, which would have placed a great strain on the animal that farm laborers would have known to avoid. He is also depicted in a posture that seems to show him stepping away from the plow, in effect leaving his work unfinished in the middle of the field. And he is dressed in expensive and formal clothing that aligns him with the aristocracy more than the peasantry. Recently, the accumulation of these details has yielded an interpretation of this figure as a veiled reference to King Philip II of Spain, hated in the Netherlands for his interest only in the objects seen lying on the ground in the painting to the left of the horse's hind foot: the dagger (representing war with France) and the purse (signifying taxation of his Flemish subjects to finance war).[62] Regardless of whether this kind of allegorical hermeneutic is consistent with the rest of the details in the painting, it has already been made clear that artistically enhancing the clothing of peasants while they plow is not without precedent. From the perspective of aristocratic viewers (or later, the wealthy bourgeoisie), this enrichment of peasant clothing added to the appreciation of tilling the soil as a noble activity and to a disarming of the potential aggression of contemporary peasants. In Bruegel's painting, it is precisely this ideal of plowing that the plowman seems to turn away from, an attitude that might be seen to parallel Icarus's lack of care, or perhaps his hubris, in completing his escape from Crete.

---

[59] Camille, "Labouring for the Lord," 427–428. For a pathos-filled description of the clothing worn by peasants while plowing, see below, 241–242.

[60] Christina Currie and Dominique Allart, *The Brueg(H)el Phenomenon: Paintings by Pieter Bruegel the Elder and Pieter Brueghel the Younger with a Special Focus on Technique and Copying Practice*, 3 vols., Scientia Artis 8 (Brussels: Royal Institute for Cultural Heritage, 2012), 844–848.

[61] See Philip McCouat, "Bruegel's *Icarus* and the Perils of Flight," *Journal of Art in Society*, 2015, accessed 10 January 2017, http://www.artinsociety.com/bruegels-icarus-and-the-perils-of-flight.html.

[62] Yoni Ascher, "Bruegel's Plowman and the Fall of Art Historians," *IKON* 7 (2014): 225–234.

Touching the Peasant Sensory Community: Gender

The view of working with the plow presented by manuscript illuminations in highly decorated books hardly comes from the perspective of peasants themselves, and nevertheless some details in the illuminations highlight a few important factors related to the plow's role in the sensory community of the peasantry. First of all, while only one figure guides the plow, he is often depicted as working with others. That is to say, tilling is frequently a communal activity, or even a familial one, since one of the essential characteristics of peasant farms was that they centered on the family unit.[63] While one person lays a hand on the plow, another works alongside him breaking up clods or digging up large obstacles (Figure 3), or more often urging on the plow team with a large goad (Figure 4 and Plate XIXb). The family works together in this way, as can be found in the description of plowing in *Piers the Plowman's Crede*, composed between 1393 and 1401 in alliterative verse. The text also articulates many Lollard themes in its harsh criticism of the fraternal orders in England, and it testifies to the influence of William Langland's *Piers Plowman* by focusing on the plainspoken wisdom of a good peasant whom the narrator introduces in the act of plowing. The description of the plowman brings together many of the details mentioned already:

> And as I wente be the waie, wepynge for sorowe,
> And seigh a sely man me by, opon the plow hongen.
> His cote was of a cloute that cary was ycalled,
> His hod was full of holes, and his heer oute,
> With his knopped schon clouted full thykke.
> His ton toteden out as he the londe treddede,
> His hosen overhongen his hokschynes on everiche a side,
> Al beslombred in fen as he the plow folwede.
> Twey myteynes, as mete, maad all of cloutes;
> The fyngers weren forwerd and ful of fen honged.
> This whit waselede in the fen almost to the ancle,
> Foure rotheren hym byforn that feble were worthen.
> Men myghte reken ich a ryb, so reufull they weren.
> His wijf walked him with, with a longe gode,
> In a cutted cote, cutted full heyghe,
> Wrapped in a wynwe schete to weren hire fro weders,
> Barfote on the bare ijs, that the blode folwede.[64]

---

63 R. H. Hilton, *The English Peasantry in the Later Middle Ages: The Ford Lectures for 1973 and Other Studies* (Oxford: Clarendon, 1975), 13.
64 *Piers the Plowman's Crede*, in *Six Ecclesiastical Satires*, ed. James Dean (Kalamazoo, MI: Medieval Institute Publications, 1991), 420–436, accessed 10 January 2017, http://d.lib.rochester.edu/teams/text/dean-six-ecclesiastical-satires-piers-the-plowmans-crede.

(As I walked along the road, weeping with sorrow,/I saw a simple man near me who was clinging to the plow./His tunic was made of rags called "checked cloth,"/His hood was full of holes and his hair stuck through,/With his lumpy shoes stuffed tightly with rags./His toes stuck out as he trod over the land,/His leggings hung over his ankles on both sides,/All soiled with dirt as he followed the plow./Two mittens, matching [the shoes], made of rags;/His fingers were harmed and fully covered with dirt./This person was befouled with filth almost to his ankles,/Four oxen before him that had grown feeble./People could count each rib, so pitiful they were./His wife walked with him with a long goad,/In a shortened tunic, cut quite high,/Wrapped in a winnowing sheet to protect her from the weather,/Barefoot on the ice, so that blood flowed after her.)

Figure 4: William Langland, *Piers Plowman*, fourteenth century, Trinity College, Cambridge, MS R.3.14, fol. 1v. Copyright The Master and Fellows of Trinity College, Cambridge. International License: http://trin-sites-pub.trin.cam.ac.uk/james/viewpage.php?index=1365.

The pathos of this scene supports the role of the plowman and his wife working together. Their physical misery and – unlike in the depictions of plowmen in manuscript illuminations – their dirt-covered limbs heighten the transgressive spiritual authority with which the plowman comes to speak with the narrator. No representative of the four orders of friars (Franciscans, Dominicans, Augustinians, Carmelites) encountered by the narrator can explain the Apostles' Creed to him, but the humble plowman Piers can do so, and in the plain language of the peasantry.

A second important factor that emerges from both literary and visual depictions of the plowman is indicated by this figure's title itself: he is a plow-*man*.[65] No matter

---

65 For the importance of literary sources in the construction of masculinity, see Stefan Horlacher, "Configuring Masculinity," in *Configuring Masculinity in Theory and Literary Practice*, ed. Stefan Horlacher, DQR Studies in Literature 58 (Leiden: Brill, 2015), 1–10.

how much the work of tilling the soil is depicted as communal, the hand that touches the plow is that of a man. In other words, to "putten (oneself) to ploughe," in the literal sense of the phrase, is to enact an important feature of specifically peasant masculinity, an element of the construction of the male gender in the Middle Ages that has been insufficiently studied up to now. The hand on the plow is part of the plowman's sensory engagement in an action that has been taken as constitutive of a basic and traditional construction of manhood – namely, being a provider for one's family – and perhaps all the more pointedly so because of the importance of family labor on peasant farms.[66] As a masculine-gendered form of work, it also reaches beyond some of the elements that have been taken to define manhood through kinship ties, rituals, or marriage.[67] And it further adds to the view of an adult masculinity seen in those means of becoming a man in late medieval England,[68] especially in the social life of men in villages, such as the customs of pledging (in which pairs of men became responsible for each other's behavior) and tithing (in which larger groups kept the peace by providing financial surety if one of their number committed a crime against the peace), customs that were important means for youths to enter the homosocial group of men.[69] The masculine hand on the plow further particularizes the gender role ascribed to the first man, making it part of a naturalized iconography of peasant masculinity defined in contrast to the traditional and more universalized (because it is not class-specific) role attributed to the first woman, as seen in the well-known proverb: "When Adam delved and Eve span, who was then a gentleman?"[70] As has been seen already, this view of the plowman as a representative of essentially male labor characteristic of the peasantry could be variously treated: it might affirm his place in an idealized view of class structure (Chaucer, the Luttrell Psalter), sound a

---

[66] Vern L. Bullough, "On Being a Male in the Middle Ages," in *Medieval Masculinities: Regarding Men in the Middle Ages*, ed. Clare A. Lees with Thelma Fenster and Jo Ann McNamara, Medieval Cultures 7 (Minneapolis: University of Minnesota Press, 1994), 31–45, at 34.
[67] Jade M. Nobbs, "History, Western," in *International Encyclopedia of Men and Masculinities*, ed. Michael Flood et al. (London: Routledge, 2007), 301–305, at 302.
[68] For a thorough examination of youths becoming men in the later Middle Ages in the context of knighthood, university training, and urban craft workers, see Ruth Mazo Karras, *From Boys to Men: Formations of Masculinity in Late Medieval Europe* (Philadelphia: University of Pennsylvania Press, 2003).
[69] Derek G. Neal, *The Masculine Self in Late Medieval England* (Chicago: University of Chicago Press, 2008), 14–20.
[70] Catherine Batt, "The Idioms of Women's Work and Thomas Hoccleve's Travails," in *The Middle Ages at Work: Practicing Labor in Late Medieval England*, ed. Kellie Robertson and Michael Uebel (New York: Palgrave Macmillan, 2004), 19–40; Albert B. Friedman, "'When Adam Delved…': Contexts of an Historic Proverb," in *The Learned and the Lewed: Studies in Chaucer and Medieval Literature*, ed. Larry D. Benson, Harvard English Studies 5 (Cambridge, MA: Harvard University Press, 1974), 213–230.

dissonant note about his place in that order (Bruegel), or emphasize his critical distance from parts of the Church (*Piers the Plowman's Crede*), etc.

The expected masculinity of the plowman's work is one of the factors underlying the view of the gendered sexuality of plowing itself, making it possible to read a lyric such as "The Plowman's Song" with a strong, even salacious, reference to male sexual activity. The poem was copied by John Shirley as the work of Geoffrey Chaucer in the course of the 1420s and is preserved today in London, British Library MS Additional 16165.[71] This "Balade" has never been accepted as an authentic part of the Chaucerian canon, though what has been understood as its striking sexual imagery might well be accommodated among Chaucer's genuine works. It begins:

> Of alle crafftes oute blessed be þe ploughe,
> So mury it is to holde to by hinde:
> For whanne þe share is shoven inn depe ynoghe,
> And þe onlere kerveþe in his kuynde
> Þe tydee soyle þat doþe þe lande vnbynde,
> Ageyns þe hil "Tpruk in, tpruk out" I calle,
> For of my ploughe þe best stott is balle.[72]

(Among all professional implements the plow should be blessed,/It is so enjoyable to hold on behind it:/For when the plowshare is shoved in very deep,/And the coulter [?], as is his nature, cuts into/The bountiful soil, which makes the land open up,/Facing the mound I call, "Pft in, pft out,"/For pounding is the best steer in my plow team.)[73]

Though at least one early scholar thought it was too coarse to attribute such a meaning to the poem,[74] a reading of its emphasis on the vigorous action of penetrating the land as synonymous with male activity during coitus is partially endorsed by the male-gendered representation of working with the plow to begin with.[75]

---

[71] On the date of Shirley's work on the manuscript, see Ralph Hanna III, "John Shirley and British Library, MS. Additional 16165," *Studies in Bibliography* 49 (1996): 95–105, at 98–100.
[72] "The Plowman's Song," ed. Julia Boffey and A. S. G. Edwards, in "'Chaucer's Chronicle,' John Shirley, and the Canon of Chaucer's Shorter Poems," *Studies in the Age of Chaucer* 20 (1998): 201–218, at 217–218.
[73] In a personal communication, Tony Edwards has confirmed that "onlere" is the reading of the manuscript. It may be a scribal mistake for "cutere" (i.e., coulter). Note that "stott" ("steer") can also be used to designate a "slut": see *The Middle English Dictionary*, s.v. "*stot* (n)" [def. 2a.], accessed 10 January 2017, http://quod.lib.umich.edu/m/med/.
[74] Eleanor P. Hammond, "Omissions from the Editions of Chaucer," *Modern Language Notes* 19 (1904): 35–38.
[75] The sexual imagery is emphasized by Ordelle G. Hill, *The Manor, the Plowman, and the Shepherd: Agrarian Themes and Imagery in Late Medieval and Early Renaissance English Literature* (Selingrove: Susquehanna University Press; London and Toronto: Associated University Presses, 1993), 80.

The Peasant Hand Touching the Plow: Piers Plowman

To "putten [or *senden*] honde to ploughe" was proverbial in its extended sense in Middle English to mean to "undertake a task," as it had also been in biblical usage (and as it continues to be used idiomatically in English today). The translation of Luke 9:62 in the Wycliffite Bible, for example, follows the Latin closely:

> Nemo mittens manum suam in aratrum et aspiciens retro aptus est regno Dei.
> [No man sendynge his hond to the plouʒ, and biholdinge aʒen, is able to the rewme of God.][76]
> (No man putting his hand to the plow, and looking back, is fit for the kingdom of God.)

But "to put oneself to the plow" never fully shed its literal semantic field.[77] And the implications of the plow and the plowman's touch, which functioned in important ways to define the sensory community of the peasantry, continued to attract the attention of writers and artists as a site for the examination of a broad palette of social issues, as they do importantly in *Piers Plowman*. Langland's allegorical poem was written and rewritten over the course of the fourteenth century in what are called the A-, B-, and C-versions during the periods 1368–1374 and 1379/81–circa 1385.[78] The "plow" as a unit of arable land (a further meaning of Old English *ploʒ*, Middle English *plouʒ*) has been studied recently as a locus for questions about orality, English law, and the rational justification for taxation in Langland's text, and a defining issue in the "*Piers Plowman* tradition." As Stephen Yeager has demonstrated, Piers's appellation of "plowman" encompasses a paradox in the English legal system, implicating both an idealized alternative to the corrupt administrators of ecclesiastical and royal institutions, who were seen as abandoning traditions, and at the same time a wistful construct created by those same administrators that deployed all the ameliorative features of the plowman examined already in this chapter.[79] Though Piers is only infrequently seen to be in contact with a plow,[80] he is clearly identified as a

---

[76] Cited in *The Middle English Dictionary*, s.v. "*hond(e)* (n)" [def. 1c.(b)].
[77] *The Middle English Dictionary*, s.v. "*plough* (n)" [def. 1b.(a)].
[78] See John Bowers, "Dating *Piers Plowman*: Testing the Testimony of Usk's *Testament*," *Yearbook of Langland Studies* 13 (1999): 65–100; George Kane, "The Text," in *A Companion to Piers Plowman*, ed. John A. Alford (Berkeley: University of California Press, 1988), 175–200; J. A. W. Bennett, "The Date of the A-Text of *Piers Plowman*," *PMLA* 58 (1943): 566–572; J. A. W. Bennett, "The Date of the B-Text of *Piers Plowman*," *Medium Ævum* 12 (1943): 55–64. On the possibility of a fourth, early working version of the poem, see William Langland, *Piers Plowman: The Z Version*, ed. A. G. Rigg and Charlotte Brewer, Studies and Texts 59 (Toronto: Pontifical Institute of Mediaeval Studies Press, 1983).
[79] Stephen M. Yeager, *From Lawmen to Plowmen: Anglo-Saxon Legal Tradition and the School of Langland* (Toronto: University of Toronto Press, 2014), chap. 5; Stephen M. Yeager, "The New Plow and the Old: Law, Orality, and the Figure of the Plowman in Passus B 19," in *Truth and Tales: Cultural Mobility and Medieval Media*, ed. Fiona Somerset and Nicholas Watson (Columbus: Ohio State University Press, 2015), 60–78.
[80] As has been noted by others, Piers enters the poem only infrequently. See, for example, T. P. Dolan, "The Plowman as Hero," in *Heroes and Heroines in Medieval English Literature: A Festschrift Presented*

plowman in the poem, and the activity of plowing is foregrounded in an illumination in one important manuscript witness of the text (Figure 4).

The question that takes up most of Passus VI is the plowing of the half acre, an allegorical action that makes visible the question of what constitutes work and who is to engage in manual labor for the benefit of society – that is to say, how the good society would look when everyone worked for a unified goal. This Passus also dramatizes the new economic relationships in rural England in that Piers himself, as a plowman and a representative of peasant agency, is the one who tells both knights and peasants what to do in the field, and he pays the laborers in money, not in the use of the land. The poet notes:

> At heigh prime Piers leet the plough stonde,
> To oversen hem hymself; whoso best wroghte,
> He sholde be hired therafter, whan hervest tyme come.[81]

> (At high prime Piers let the plow stand,/To oversee them [i.e., the workers] himself; whoever worked best/That person should be hired later on, when harvest-time came.)

Here he is reflecting and reframing the principles of the Ordinance of Laborers (1349) and Statutes of Laborers (1351, 1388), which ordered pay only for honest work and required laborers to remain an entire year on the job.[82] Piers assigns the tasks involved in plowing and sowing the half acre in an orderly division of labor along traditional lines: he himself engages in plowing, other laborers are set to dig ditches and turn over the ridges of the furrows, and women are given the task of sewing up grain sacks. Piers's view of gendered labor distinctions is part of the expression of a masculine ethics in the poem.[83] In the project of restoring the social order following the corruption of society allegorized earlier in the poem in the Lady Meed episode, Piers's decision to give himself the task of working with the plow is in line with the gendered view of male peasant labor. But then a knight suggests that he might take over the task of plowing:

---

to André Crépin on the Occasion of his Sixty-Fifth Birthday, ed. Leo Carruthers (Cambridge, UK: D. S. Brewer, 1994), 97–103.

81 William Langland, *Piers Plowman*, B.6.112–114, in *The Vision of Piers Plowman: A Critical Edition of the B-Text Based on Trinity College Cambridge MS B.15.17*, ed. A. V. C. Schmidt, 2nd ed. (1995; repr., London: Dent; Rutland, VT: Charles E. Tuttle, 1997), 100.

82 On *Piers Plowman* and fourteenth-century statutes on labor, see Anne Middleton, "Acts of Vagrancy: The C Version 'Autobiography' and the Statute of 1388," in *Written Work: Langland, Labor, and Authorship*, ed. Steven Justice and Kathryn Kerby-Fulton (Philadelphia: University of Pennsylvania Press, 1997), 208–318; David Aers, *Community, Gender, and Individual Identity: English Writing, 1360–1430* (London: Routledge, 1988), 26–30.

83 See the perceptive analysis of labor and marriage in Langland's poem in Isabel Davis, *Writing Masculinity in the Later Middle Ages*, Cambridge Studies in Medieval Literature 62 (Cambridge, UK: Cambridge University Press, 2007), 12–37.

> "By Crist!" quod a knyght thoo, "he kenneth us the beste;
> Ac on the teme, trewely, taught was I nevere.
> Ac kenne me," quod the knyght, "and by Crist I wole assaye!"[84]

("By Christ!," said a knight then, "he [i.e., Piers] is instructing us in the best way;/But concerning the plow team, to tell the truth, I was never given instruction./But teach me," said the knight, "and by Christ I will try to do it!")

Echoing the knight's rhetorical structure, Piers politely rejects this offer, reserving the plow and the results of its interaction with the plowman for the peasantry, namely to provide food for all of society. It is not just Piers's personal righteousness that justifies him in declining the knight's proposal,[85] but also the plowman's understanding of his position as representative of the sensory community of the peasantry. As he explains, with specific reference to the somatic context of his labor:

> "By Seint Poul!," quod Perkyn, "ye profre yow so faire
> That I shal swynke and swete and sowe for us bothe"[86]

("By Saint Paul," said Piers, "you offer yourself so graciously/But I'll work and sweat and sow for both of us")

Of course, Piers's words assert the ideal of a harmonious social order based on the functional model of estates theory, in which every estate in society fulfills its traditional duty, but these words also have the effect of claiming the plow, from the perspective of the peasantry, as the purview of a plowman alone. Moreover, they articulate the position of peasant masculinity in a confrontation with the manhood of knights. On the one hand, Piers asserts his role as a manual laborer whose task is to provide food for his family and, in more general terms, for the community that he is attempting to create and strengthen.[87] On the other hand, the knightly model of masculinity depends on the exercise of violence to exert dominance over other men – those of a knight's own class as well as social inferiors – and on the practice of modes of courtly conduct.[88] Here, in Piers's terms (and, literally, on his turf), peasant agency

---

84 *Piers Plowman*, B.6.21–23, ed. Schmidt, 96.
85 Alan J. Fletcher, "The Social Trinity of Piers Plowman," *The Review of English Studies* 44 (1993): 343–361, at 349.
86 *Piers Plowman*, B.6.24–25, ed. Schmidt, 96.
87 On the importance of the family in *Piers Plowman*, see M. Teresa Tavormina, *Kindly Similitude: Marriage and Family in Piers Plowman*, Piers Plowman Studies XI (Cambridge, UK: D. S. Brewer, 1995). On Langland's plowman and the cohesiveness of peasant communities, see Chris Dyer, "Piers Plowman and Plowmen: A Historical Perspective," *The Yearbook of Langland Studies* 8 (1994): 155–176, at 167–169.
88 Karras, *From Boys to Men*, 20–66.

exercises its rights in the object-subject cooperation that defines its characteristic sensory experience.

To be sure, the attempt to create a utopian community under the direction of the peasantry falls apart when too many people refuse to work. At that point, Piers calls on the knight to threaten the malingerers with violence, Hunger has to be invoked to coerce labor out of fear of famine, and eventually some of the laborers refuse to work unless they get better food and higher wages – which recalls the image of the obstinate peasant in the shadow of the tree of vices with which this chapter began. And here, Langland turns to examine a key ethical issue central to a community defined by labor: namely, the dissonance between the theological ideal of a shared humanity to be loved (and fed) by peasant labor, because all humans have been saved through Jesus's sacrifice,[89] and, in contrast, the legal-political construction of labor that leads to a need to distinguish between those who work and those who refuse to do so and instead simply beg.[90] Through all of this, the connection between Piers and the iconic object of the peasantry remains a constant, to the point that when Wastour (personifying those who want only to eat up what others have produced) declares his unwillingness to work, he curses both Piers and his plow in scatological terms.[91] The weave of plowman, plow, and agricultural service persists, mediated through the haptic sense when the plowman's hand grasps the plow, as the province of the peasantry. Through Piers's claim, the peasant prerogative of touching the plow is foreclosed to the aristocracy, and it is contextualized by Langland in the specific legal, social, and economic conditions of late fourteenth-century England in which peasant agency has been shown to operate.

---

89 *Piers Plowman*, B.6.207, ed. Schmidt, 104.
90 Emily Steiner, *Reading Piers Plowman* (Cambridge, UK: Cambridge University Press, 2013), 83–92.
91 *Piers Plowman*, B.6.155, ed. Schmidt, 102.

Beth Williamson
Reflections on Sensory Reflections: An Afterword

As John Arnold observed in 2014:

> In recent years, there has been ever more nuanced and insightful work into the nature of medieval piety, the feel and experience of medieval faith. This has been notably interdisciplinary in nature, coming from literary scholarship, archaeological study, art history, and most recently musicology, bringing a focus on the senses, the emotions, sacred spaces, handling holy objects, reflecting inwardly on the divine.[1]

This observation occurs in an essay by Arnold on histories and historiographies of medieval Christianity, in a final section entitled "Where Now?". The placement of this comment at the endpoint of the essay, which looks forward rather than backward, indicates that the kinds of work that Arnold mentions – including approaches focusing on the senses and on interactions between people and material objects – were to some extent still part of the future that had yet to come. In that future, Arnold suggests, such new types of histories might benefit from developments such as further engagement with the relations between culture, materiality, and power. He also suggests that the recent focus on the experience of belief had often led scholars back to normative sources and to a concentration on social or spiritual elites, and that it was not yet well determined whether these new areas of history focusing on experience "worked" as well for ordinary laypeople as for the elites.[2]

In my 2011 epilogue to a volume of essays concerning the art and architecture of Bristol Cathedral I traced some similar developments.[3] There I too noted the emergence of work over the past twenty years that had paid serious attention to the body and the senses, and to embodied, or physical, experience. Toward the end of that epilogue, as I began to look ahead, I suggested that music and aural culture as they relate to the human experience of religious buildings would be a desirable area for future research in architectural history and the history of religious practice. This present volume lies, as its editors point out, at the intersection of two fields that are already vibrant: medieval material culture and medieval sensory experience. In placing its center of gravity at that particular point, it addresses several issues necessary to the

---

1 John H. Arnold, "Histories and Historiographies of Medieval Christianity," in *The Oxford Handbook of Medieval Christianity*, ed. John H. Arnold (Oxford: Oxford University Press, 2014), 2–41, at 38.
2 Arnold, "Histories and Historiographies," 39.
3 Beth Williamson, "Epilogue," in *The Medieval Art, Architecture and History of Bristol Cathedral: An Enigma Explored*, ed. Jon Cannon and Beth Williamson (Woodbridge: The Boydell Press, 2011), 300–309.

next steps of research in histories of art and material culture: it responds to the call made by John Arnold, and it also furthers the kind of research I was hoping to see more of when I wrote my own epilogue in 2011.

First, then, this volume answers John Arnold's call to look more closely at whether we can make new cultural histories concerning the feel and experience of medieval faith "work" for our inquiries into the experiences of people outside the social and spiritual elites. As Fiona Griffiths and Kathryn Starkey observe in their introduction: "Not only do objects often tell a different story than texts (even, in some cases, directly disproving the claims of the written record), but they often shed light on communities and aspects of medieval life and culture that texts – produced in literate, generally elite, and often male clerical environments – do not address."[4] The chapters herein offer up a set of proposals for reconstructing or reproducing sensory experiences in connection with a variety of objects. At the same time, the editors and contributors keep in mind that, while it may be possible to reproduce the essentials of a sensory experience by looking at, or touching, an artifact from the past (or by using any other of the human senses), it is not possible to unproblematically reproduce medieval consumption or interpretation.[5] Nonetheless, they take up the methodological opportunities and challenges of object-based histories – of histories that genuinely treat objects as primary sources – in the ways that medievalists who have embraced the "material turn" have proposed that we should all be doing for some time now.[6] Such approaches not only give objects their proper due, and admit that artifacts can be part of the scholarly armory in the writing of medieval histories, but also acknowledge that objects elicit "traces of ephemeral and physical experiences that were rarely fully described or articulated in texts."[7] In other words, objects not only can be given a status *alongside* texts as evidence of medieval experience, but in some cases they can perform as evidence in ways that go *beyond* what texts offer. Most importantly, the essays in this volume show that these objects can indeed answer John Arnold's call to discover whether histories that focus on experience can provide us with insights into the lives of some of those historical subjects who operated outside the realm of the social and spiritual elites. This is because of "the importance of objects and sensory reception *together* as constitutive of the very identity of medieval communities," as the editors put it.[8] That being the case, we can clearly see that when historical work on the experience of medieval faith (or medieval secular life) and on the interactions

---

[4] See Fiona Griffiths and Kathryn Starkey, "Sensing Through Objects," above, at 13.
[5] Griffiths and Starkey point, in their Sensing Through Objects (11–12), to Mark M. Smith's caution on this point. See Mark M. Smith, "Producing Sense, Consuming Sense, Making Sense: Perils and Prospects for Sensory History," *Journal of Social History* 40 (2007): 841–858.
[6] See the works cited in Griffiths and Starkey, "Sensing Through Objects," at [13n32].
[7] Griffiths and Starkey, "Sensing Through Objects," 20.
[8] Griffiths and Starkey, "Sensing Through Objects," 20.

between people and material culture takes that same material culture itself more seriously as a form of primary evidence, different questions can be asked about the past and different answers proposed.

Secondly, several essays in the volume concentrate on sound, thus furthering the agenda I had hoped for in 2011 of expanding the study of past listening and hearing within the investigation of historical objects and environments. Here there are investigations into actual sounds produced by physical objects (such as bells adorning jewelry, in chapter 3) and into the visual record of sound (such as music notated in an illuminated songbook, in chapter 1). It is important to pause at this point, and to make clear the intellectual and methodological differences between attempting to reconstruct the medieval experience of sound (or to produce an "authentic" medieval sound in performance) and taking seriously the fact that sound played a part in people's own experiences and their understandings of the world. It is more or less impossible to "hear as others heard," just as it is more or less impossible to see as others saw. But this does not mean that the effort to work in that direction is necessarily wasted. To ask questions about past experience is valuable, and to try to construct methodologies for broadening the questions that we can ask is an endeavor to be supported.

If we seek to understand what it felt like to walk in an urban piazza in medieval Florence, for example, or pray in a Lady Chapel in a medieval English cathedral, most of us, as scholars, would feel that it is better to visit those locations than not to. We would of course seek to understand the ways in which the built environment of those spaces had been altered by new buildings, or larger windows, or the removal of statues, or the destruction of stained-glass windows. It might never be possible for us to mentally (let alone physically) reconstruct the medieval built environment of such places. We would know that the people inhabiting the spaces had changed, the practices enacted in the spaces had changed, the religion, the politics, the whole world had changed. And yet many of us who operate within those fields of cultural history that are inflected by anthropological methods and concerns, given the ability to visit a space that we were researching, would think it more valuable to see, inhabit, and experience that place than not to do so, even if it were clear that there were scant overlaps between our actual experience of the space in the present day and a medieval person's experience of it. This is at least partly because we understand that a space is activated by presence, action, movement, sounds and smells, light and shadow. Therefore, to activate that space ourselves, with our own presence, our own actions, our own perceptions of sound and smell, light and shadow, goes some way toward thinking about how that space worked in the past.

The ways in which the past is a foreign country where they do things differently are multiple.[9] The people who inhabited the Florentine piazza or the English Lady Chapel were different from us, of course, with their different levels of education, dif-

---

9 The allusions in this sentence refer, of course, to the opening line of L. P. Hartley's 1953 novel *The Go-Between*.

ferent beliefs, different life expectancies, different concerns. The sounds and smells were different too, and the light and shadow. Nonetheless, to experience those spaces ourselves and to remind ourselves through our bodily senses that there *were* sounds and smells, and light and shadow, as well as death and fear, or carnival and celebration, in those or any other past spaces, is a step toward understanding something more about medieval experience. Even if our own experience of moving through such a space cannot reproduce, or reconstruct, an individual historical subject's experience, it can remind us to ask more about the things that would have acted upon another person's experience and consciousness. Knowing, as I do, that the thirteenth-century chapel of Merton College, Oxford, was often rather cold on a dark winter's Sunday afternoon, even in the late twentieth century, and that my own experience of singing an Advent responsory there was often accompanied by the awareness that my hands were cold and my nose colder still, is useful. It reminds me to think harder than I otherwise might about the embodied experience of medieval people's devotional or liturgical activity – about how worship felt, for instance, on winter evenings as opposed to summer mornings. Some might think of this simply as paying attention to context – the temporal context of a particular liturgy in a particular geographical location, as well as the spatial context of a particular chapel. But I think there is more here: without paying attention to the sensory dimension of a historically, geographically, and spatially contextualized experience, one may know *that* something might have taken place and that an individual might have experienced it, but one knows less about *how* it might have taken place.

Equally, when it comes to understanding how a medieval individual might have experienced reading from, or looking at, a medieval manuscript, almost all scholars who seek to take seriously not just what is written or painted on that manuscript's pages, but also the ways in which texts and images relate to one another within the book and how long it takes to flip from one major illuminated page to the next (or, more diligently, to read all the text in between those major illuminations), would prefer to handle the manuscript. The British Library's wonderful "Turning the Pages" virtual book software allows one to flip the pages of the books that are featured and see in great detail many of the texts and images within them.[10] However, it cannot allow a reader to feel how heavy a large manuscript missal can be, which might make one experience the book as especially "weighty" in the sense of its importance as well as its simple heft. Nor can it allow a reader to feel the skin of the parchment pages, which might lend an extra dimension to one's understanding of the phrase "Word made flesh." Such sensory experiences lend added suggestions – added reflections – to an attempt to understand what it was like to use a book or walk through a space.

In advocating the use of practices that attempt to draw out aspects of past experience through attention to current sensory experience, scholars sometimes come

---

[10] http://www.bl.uk/onlinegallery/virtualbooks/viewall/index.html.

up against accusations of "speculation." Speculation, and interpretation, are central to many scholarly attempts to understand the past through many different kinds of evidence, be it material evidence, visual evidence, or textual evidence. Nonetheless, speculation about the experience of medieval individuals based upon the embodied or sensory experience of twenty-first-century individuals comes under criticism from some quarters, as the editors point out above. They note that "medievalists have not typically embraced reenactment or re-creative experience as credible sources of knowledge about the past," but that within fields such as theater and performance studies, reenactment has gained a stronger foothold.[11] Other fields, too, have begun to embrace such practices, with well-respected results. Since 2009, Professor John Harper of the University of Bangor, Wales, has led a research project entitled "The Experience of Worship in Late Medieval Cathedral and Parish Church."[12] In this project, a key aim is to explore ways in which the understanding of late medieval English liturgy might be increased through practice-led research and enactment.[13] Medieval Sarum liturgies were enacted in Salisbury Cathedral, the building for which they were written, and also in the small medieval parish church of St. Teilo, originally at Llandeilo Tal-y-bont, Wales, and now reconstructed at St. Fagans National Museum of History in Cardiff. This allowed exploration of the kinds of adaptation of the liturgy that could have been required for its use in a smaller building with much less space and fewer clergy. Service books and other liturgical artifacts were created, including a gradual, a choirbook, a painted reredos, a double-sided lectern, and an organ, along with other furnishings and vestments. These were based upon surviving medieval examples, or fragments of examples (three fragmentary medieval organs survive which, combined, provided the model for the organ for this project). Similarly, the lectern was based upon the one at Ranworth parish church in Norfolk.[14] All artifacts were created using techniques and materials that were as close as possible to those available in the Middle Ages.

The results of the Experience of Worship project are serious and stimulating, and could not possibly be dismissed – as other types of re-creative, creative, or imaginative activity have been – as a pastime for "the mad, the vain and the foolish."[15] The performances of various late medieval liturgies in different spaces and with different kinds of arrangements allowed the project team, and other participants, to observe

---

11 Griffiths and Starkey, "Sensing Through Objects," 14.
12 http://www.experienceofworship.org.uk/.
13 The project team consistently prefer the term "enactment" to "reenactment," in recognition of the fact that the performances of medieval liturgies that were a central feature of the project were not "reenacting" an exact experience that had been lived before, but "enacting" one in the present day. This enactment can shed light upon past experience but does not pretend to "reenact" – to enact again and enact accurately – some notional "model" of late medieval liturgical performance.
14 See http://www.experienceofworship.org.uk/artefacts/.
15 See Griffiths and Starkey, "Sensing Through Objects," 15, above, for the editors' discussion of the short shrift given to reenactment-type activities by certain scholars and in certain scholarly areas.

and record different types of sensory experiences, as well as reflections about these experiences, as a way of reaching toward some answers to largely unanswered questions about the late medieval liturgy and people's responses to it.[16] These enactments also stimulated the posing of further questions, and it is in this regard that paying proper attention to sensory experience is, perhaps, at its most effective. In a similar way, handling medieval artifacts and posing questions about the experiences activated by such sensory engagement can deepen and enrich our understanding of the objects thus handled, even if the particular questions posed are not answered, or cannot be fully answered. The work of eliciting the questions is equally important, as it develops methods and methodologies related to the study of late medieval artifacts, their physical settings, and the swirl of sensory information and impressions that would have accompanied a subject's engagement with the object. So, to take one example from this volume – the folding almanacs considered by Jennifer Borland – it is clear that attention to the particularity of the almanacs' folded and unfolded forms, and to the physical process of opening and closing the almanacs when using them, allows several kinds of information and questions to emerge. To hold and manipulate these almanacs oneself augments one's understanding of them in very particular ways. To touch and use these almanacs, to activate them, not only provides object-based information, and information about the objects themselves, but also feeds into the asking of better, more methodologically and theoretically informed questions about them.

The same can be said of touching, using, and activating other medieval objects and using the tools of one's own sensory perception to further appreciate their materiality. There has been much scholarly concentration of late on medieval materiality within art history, visual culture, and histories of religion.[17] Within that work on materiality there have been various strands of research that use contemporary sensory experience to respond to medieval objects and to ask further questions about medieval experiences and responses. A particularly fruitful example of this

---

[16] The main publications from this project are, to date: *Late Medieval Liturgies Enacted: The Experience of Worship in Late Medieval Cathedral and Parish Church*, ed. Sally Harper, P. S. Barnwell, and Magnus Williamson (Aldershot: Ashgate, 2016); *Lady Mass according to the Use of Salisbury: The Votive Cycles of the Daily Mass as celebrated in the Lady Chapel in honour of the Blessed Virgin Mary*, ed. Sally Harper, John Harper, and Matthew Cheung Salisbury (London: British Academy / Early English Church Music, 2017); John Harper, *Old Sarum and its Customary: Liturgical practice in the first cathedral at Salisbury* (Woodbridge: Boydell, forthcoming 2018). Video recordings of the enactments are available at http://www.experienceofworship.org.uk/enactments/introduction/.

[17] See, among others: Lisa Reilly with Libby Parker, Aden Kumler, and Christopher R. Lakey, eds., "*Res et significatio*: The Material Sense of Things in the Middle Ages," special issue, *Gesta* 51 (2012); Karen Eileen Overbey and Benjamin C. Tilghman, eds., "Active Objects," special issue, *Different Visions: A Journal of New Perspectives on Medieval Art* 4 (2014), http://differentvisions.org/issue-four/; Beth Williamson, "Material Culture and Medieval Christianity," in *The Oxford Handbook of Medieval Christianity*, ed. John H. Arnold (Oxford: Oxford University Press, 2014), 60–75.

sensory work is the collection of essays edited by Maggie M. Williams and Karen Eileen Overbey entitled *Transparent Things: A Cabinet*.[18] Nancy M. Thompson's essay in this collection, "Close Encounters with Luminous Objects: Reflections on Studying Stained Glass," meditates upon her own sensory encounters with the objects of her study and allows those sensory encounters to generate imaginative responses to them, considering the business of their making as well as later human encounters with the glass. Thompson writes: "When I am in the presence of a window and can, as much as a historian can, experience it in the present, I can more sensitively construct the window's historical meaning."[19] Her own close sensory contact – and emotional connection – with the historical object allows her to "imagine what viewing a stained-glass window might have been like for a medieval person."[20] Note that Thompson does not claim that her own sensory response to the window, or her emotional connection with it, allows her to fully *answer* the question of what it might have been like for a medieval person to view this window. The attempt is not to replicate the historical experience of past people. But to acknowledge and use one's own human sensory and emotional responses encourages a scholar to add empathetic and imaginative engagement with the object to all the other evidence and material that she brings to bear in her attempts to analyze and understand it.

Alexa Sand, writing about ivory statues of the Virgin Mary, shows in a different way how sensitivity to sensory experience can help to elicit deeper interpretations of the objects under investigation.[21] She investigates how sensory experience could be invoked conceptually in these objects by virtue of a number of strategies. Even if, as Sand suggests, the statues were not necessarily routinely handled and stroked by their medieval owners, because of the high cost and value of elephant ivory in the Middle Ages, the statues are nonetheless haptic, "oriented towards a sense of touch in their materiality and their conception as representational objects."[22] In the case of certain of these ivory statues, their makers have banked on two types of sensory awareness. They capitalize upon the owner's knowledge of the sensuous feel of ivory, its smoothness and warmth under the fingertips, and they provoke the owner's imagination of touch by evoking it over and over again in their form and iconography. The intimacy of the embraces between Virgin and Child, the holding of the child's foot by his mother, the child's grip on his mother's veil or other clothing, all help to

---

18 Maggie M. Williams and Karen Eileen Overbey, eds., *Transparent Things: A Cabinet* (Brooklyn, NY: punctum books, 2013), open access at http://punctumbooks.com.
19 Nancy M. Thompson, "Close Encounters with Luminous Objects: Reflections on Studying Stained Glass," in *Transparent Things: A Cabinet*, ed. Maggie M. Williams and Karen Eileen Overbey (Brooklyn, NY: punctum books, 2013), 57–67, at 66.
20 Thompson, "Close Encounters with Luminous Objects," 67.
21 Alexa Sand, "Materia Meditandi: Haptic Perception and Some Parisian Ivories of the Virgin and Child, ca. 1300," *Different Visions* 4 (2014): 1–28.
22 Sand, "Materia Meditandi," 5.

keep the viewer's mind on the sense of touch, evoked as an inner sense rather than as a physical action.[23] As Sand puts it, these sculptures "beguile the sense of touch and instate it at the center of the practice of devotional seeing."[24] Here, then, Sand is not as explicit as Thompson about her own sensory response to the objects of her study as a route to the consideration of medieval sensory experience and response. But her own sensory responses – her own looking, and her haptic imaginings – work together with her awareness both of the materiality of the objects she studies and of the ways in which sensory processes were understood in the Middle Ages. Together, all these aspects of sensory engagement and analysis produce another rich response to a collection of medieval objects, which can then be usefully applied to other objects in an attempt to forge more sensory histories of the object and of devotional practice.

Others, too, in other fields beyond art history and material culture, are using their own sensory responses to offer them additional ways of thinking about the experiences of medieval people in relation to objects of material cultural production. Emma Dillon begins the prologue to her 2012 book *The Sense of Sound* with an evocation of the modern sounds of Exeter High Street. She describes her own encounters with the sounds she heard in that place during her childhood, and in particular her own attentiveness to the absence of a long-heard, oft-repeated sound once it had disappeared. A particular street musician, who used to stand outside the city's Marks and Spencer store and whom Dillon regularly heard in her own forays up the High Street, was suddenly, a few years before the writing of her book, no longer there. She writes: "When he vanished a few years ago (I hope to a new pitch, in a new town), to be replaced by the fiasco of barking and crooning, his memory provoked something more complicated than nostalgia: a kind of heightened aural awareness, attentive listening made acute by absence."[25] This awareness allowed her to, as she puts it, "call upon the living to help explain the sounding past," as well as to think about the affect of song, to remember the capacity of music to participate in a landscape of human experience, and to perform the experiment of "listening to a medieval repertory whose wider sonic environment is now almost completely silent."[26]

Thus, each study of an object, or artifact, or building, or song, that attempts to analyze these things at least partly through the active orchestration and observation of sensory experience provides more information about the object in question than we could otherwise obtain. Additionally, though, and crucially, each instance of sensory engagement with such artifacts can also provide further information

---

23 For another approach to sensory experience and the inner senses, see Beth Williamson, "Sensory Experience in Medieval Devotion: Sound and Vision, Invisibility and Silence," *Speculum* 88 (2013): 1–43.
24 Sand, "Materia Meditandi," 23.
25 Emma Dillon, *The Sense of Sound: Musical Meaning in France, 1260–1330* (Oxford: Oxford University Press, 2012), 4.
26 Dillon, *The Sense of Sound*, 4, 6.

about those sensory creatures, the medieval human beings who might have handled them. Direct sensory engagement with medieval objects, or with medieval (or once-medieval) urban or ecclesiastical spaces, can also shed further light on objects and spaces that *cannot* be accessed with direct and personal experience – whether for reasons of restricted access or because they are lost or fragmentary – and on the questions that can legitimately be asked of them. The questions (as well as the answers) that can be generated by such direct sensory engagement allow for the application of similar answers and questions to other objects and artifacts that cannot currently be engaged with by sensory means.

Thus I wholeheartedly endorse the suggestion of the editors of this volume that "examining objects from the perspective of the sensory pushes the boundaries of what we can know about medieval experience in a sometimes speculative but always productive way."[27] Sensory reflections upon objects, and sensory reflections derived from engagement with those objects, not only increase our knowledge about the objects themselves but also enrich the methodological field. They expand the boundaries of what we can know about medieval objects and artifacts and broaden the horizons of what we can ask about objects, artifacts, beliefs, and experience.

---

27 Griffiths and Starkey, "Sensing Through Objects," 15.

Index

'Abbasid 80, 81, 86, 132
Abencerrajes, Hall of the 116, 117, 134, 139, 140
Activation 13, 15, 18, 20, 118, 146, 163, 168, 171, 221, 236
Adab 80
Adalhard, abbot of Corbie 55
Admiratio 188–189
Admonitio generalis 51, 57
Adoration of the Cross 160
Aelred of Rievaulx 167
Aesthetics 29, 34, 118, 133, 135, 137, 140–141, 193
Agency 19, 181, 196, 203, 205, 216–222, 233, 235, 237, 246
– peasant agency 225–228, 247, 248
'Ajab 132, 135, 141
Alan of Lille 6
al-Andalus 120, 122, 133, 134
Albertus Magnus 1
Alcuin: *De laude psalmorum* 183
Alhambra Vases 17, 116–141
Alhambra 17, 116–141
al-Jāḥiẓ 86
Almanac 203–224, 254
al-Washshā' 80, 81, 90
Amphora 128
Amulet 19 181, 186, 187, 216–217, 223
Amuletic 187, 216–217, 222, 223
Ancilla Dei 202
Animals
– peasants as 230, 232–233, 237, 240
– plowing with 225–232, 237, 240
Anne Boleyn 201, 202
Anthropology
– modal 239
– sensory 236, 239
Apostles' Creed 242
Ard 230
Aristotle 1, 3, 4, 9, 21
– *De sensu et sensato* 3, 4
Arma Christi 18, 163, 174, 175
Arnulf of Leuven
– *Carmen de sancta cruce* 165, 168–170
Artifice 117, 119, 121, 122, 132, 134, 135, 137
Astrology 214, 216
Audiotactility 216–222
Autoethnography 13
Avicenna 1

Baillet-en-France 56, 71, 73
Bartholomew the Englishman 234
Bayeux Tapestry 108
Beguines 190, 196
Behrens-Abouseif, Doris 95, 140, 141
Bible: Luke 9:62
– Wycliffite Bible 245
Black Plague, the 233
Blood 13, 166, 167, 169, 170, 172, 175, 177, 213
– bloodletting 80–81, 203, 214–215
Bloodletting man 203, 207
Bonaventure 173
Boniface of Mainz 64
Book of hours 190–192, 197, 199, 200
Bourdieu, Pierre 234–235
Bruegel, Pieter 244
– *Landscape with the Fall of Icarus* 240, 286
Büraburg bei Fritzlar 60, 63, 64, 65, 67, 70, 71, 72, 73, 75
Busnoys, Antoine 16, 22, 23, 27, 28, 36, 37, 39, 41, 42, 43, 48
Byzantine 17, 77, 81, 82, 90, 91, 145, 158, 159

Caesarea 82, 84, 88
Cairo Geniza 79, 85
Cambrai 143, 144, 191
Camille, Michael 3, 30, 204, 237
Caritas 228, 237
Carolingian Empire 51, 54, 60, 63, 76
Castrum 64
Champlevé 144, 155, 159
Chansonnier 30, 36, 37, 41
Chasse 18, 144, 146–159, 162, 187
Chaucer, Geoffrey
– *The Canterbury Tales* 19, 228, 238
– knight in 237–238
– Miller in 238
Chiasm 137
Choirbook 253
Christomimesis 19, 182, 192
Ciborium 146, 152, 153, 154, 159
Cistercian 18, 164, 165–168, 230
Classen, Constance 10, 13, 234, 235
Clement of Alexandria
– *Paedagogus* 93–94

Cloisonné 102, 108, 109, 113, 159
Codex Rotundus (Hildesheim, Dombibliothek Hildesheim Hs. 728) 199
Comares Hall 119, 128, 138, 139
Complexio 213
Consent 206, 235
Contratenor 23–27, 37–46
Coole, Diana 236
Corpus Christi 164
Council of Meaux-Paris 51
Crete 240
Custodia sensuum 239
Cute 193–195

Daanen, Paul 236
Digitization 111, 205
Dijon Chansonnier 16, 22, 28, 33, 36, 38, 41
Dinar 84
Discantus 23–26, 37, 38–46
Dospĕl Williams, Elizabeth 16–17, 20, 78, 87, 89, 121
Dowry lists 78

England 3, 19, 104, 209, 215, 225–226, 230, 237, 241, 243, 246, 248
Evangelists 186
Eyesight 73, 181

Fatimid 84, 88
Ferrandis Torres, José 126, 127
Flax 52, 56, 61–63, 67–71, 74–76
Fleury Monastery 142
Fortuny Marsal, Mariano 124–125, 130
Foucault, Michel 239
Fountain 17, 117, 121, 130, 131, 137, 140
Frauenchiemsee 188
Freedman, Paul 226
Freer Vase 121, 122, 125, 128, 130–133, 135, 136, 137
Friars 193, 242
Frost, Samantha 236
Fuller Brooch 14, 104

Galen 1, 213
Gaugerik, Saint 143
Gerard of Harderwyck 1
Gertrude of Helfta 167
Ghislain, Saint 191, 192

Girdle book 18, 201, 209
Goheen, R.B. 225
Gondulphus, Saint 149, 156
Gospel of John, 5th or 6th century (Paris, BnF MS Latin 10439) 187
Gospel 181, 187
Gower, John
– *Visio Anglie* 233
– *Vox Clamantis* 233
Gramsci, Antonio 235
Granada 127, 130, 133, 136, 138, 139
Grotesques 22, 29, 30
Guennol triptych 160
Gynaecea (textile workshops) 51

Habitus 234
Hadewijch 196
Hands 68–69, 185, 212, 232, 234
– as sensory organs 206, 236–237
Haptic 15, 19, 117–119, 121, 165, 182, 203, 205, 212, 234, 235, 239, 248, 255, 256
Hedwig of Silesia 9
Henry of Ghent 6
Higden, Ranulf
– *Polychronicon* 229–230
Historiography
– object-based 250–251
Holy Week 51
Homans, George 232
Howes, David 10, 12, 13, 234
Hrabanus Maurus
– *De universo* 57, 58
Humors 27, 30, 213–214
Hyperopia 73

Ibn al-Haytham 140
Ibn al-Khatib 119, 133–134
Ibn Zamrak 116, 133–134
Icarus 240
Incarnation 19, 152, 195, 197, 199, 202
Indulgence 4, 18, 163–165, 166, 168, 169, 171, 173–175, 177, 179
Injury 59, 69, 171, 216
Interobjectivity 232–237
Irmengard, Abbess of Frauenchiemsee 188

Jacques de Vitry 232, 233
Jaén 120, 126

Jeanne d'Évreux 195, 197
– Hours of Jeanne d'Evreux (New York, The Cloisters, 54.1.2) 198–199
Jane Bennett 220, 235
Je m'esbaïs de vous mon cuer 16, 22, 24, 48
Jerez de la Frontera 120, 123
Jerez Vase 120, 123, 126–127
Jerome 5–6, 8, 182
Jewelry 11, 15–17, 19, 77, 78–85, 86–89, 92–96, 98, 99, 103, 109, 112, 113, 114, 121, 186, 200, 216, 217, 251
John Gower
– *Vox Clamantis* 233
John of St. Trond, Brother 164, 166, 169
Julian of Norwich 197

Khirbat al-Mafjar 86, 87–88
Killing of Abel, The (Wakefield) 232
Kitāb al-Muwashshā (*The Brocaded Book*) 80, 81–82
Kurban Bayram 13

Lady Chapel 251–252
Lambert, Saint 149, 151, 155, 162
Langland
– Piers Plowman 19, 245–246
Langland, William
– *Piers Plowman* 226–227, 238, 241, 242
– Hunger in 248
– knight in 238, 248
– Piers in 241–242, 245, 248
– plowing half acre 246
– Wastour in 248
Latour, Bruno 236
Laurent, Friar
– *Somme le roi* 226
Lazarus 238
Libellus 152
Liège 148, 150, 151, 154, 155, 160, 161, 162, 176, 190, 191, 196
Linen production 56, 59, 62–63, 67, 68
Liuthar Gospels 187
Llandeilo Tal-y-bont 253
Logan Hours (Logan, Utah, Merrill-Cazier Library Special Collections and Archives COLL V BOOK 422) 191
Lollard 241
London, British Library MS Stowe 956 (Psalter in English translation of John Croke) 201

Longthorpe Tower, England 3
Loom weight 16, 52, 57, 63, 65, 66, 71, 75
Looms 51, 52, 53, 57, 73, 74, 75
Lotharingia 18, 144, 154, 162
Louvegne 149
Luster ceramics 117, 127
Lutgard of Aywières 177–178
Luttrell Psalter 240, 243–244

Magdalen, Mary 238–239
Maieul. *See* Maiolus, Abbot of Cluny
Maiolus, Abbot of Cluny 189–190
Málaga 126, 127
Malmédy 148, 149, 151
Mandorla 172–173
Manipulation 19, 102–104, 108, 187, 204, 205–206, 218, 222–223, 236
Manuscript illuminations 19, 231–232, 240, 241–242
Manuscripts
– Cambridge, Trinity College MS R.3.14 242, 246
– Hildesheim, Dombibliothek Hildesheim Hs. 728 199
– Logan, Utah, Merrill-Cazier Library Special Collections and Archives COLL V BOOK 422 279
– London, British Library MS Additional 16165 244
– London, British Library MS Additional 35313 283
– London, British Library MS Additional 42130 285
– London, British Library MS Additional 54180 284
– London, British Library Additional MS 89000 187
– London, British Library MS Arundel 83 (II) 226, 227, 283
– London, British Library MS Royal 12 F xiii 285
– London, British Library MS Stowe 956 (Psalter in English translation of John Croke) 201
– Munich, Residenz Museum Schatzkammer 4 WL 183–184
– New York, Morgan Library MS M.1166 200
– New York, The Cloisters, 54.1.2 198
– Oxford, Bodleian Library MS Douce 374 231
– Oxford, Bodleian Library MS Top. Linc. d. 1 230
– Paris, BnF MS Latin 10439 187

– Salzburg, Stiftsbibliothek St. Peter, Codex a I 0 182, 183, 278
– Wellcome Library, London, Ms. 49 6, 7
Martha 238–239
Mary Magdalen, Early South English Legendary Life of 238–239
Mary of Oignies 196
Masculinity
– knightly model of 247–248
– peasant model of 19, 243–244, 247
– in village society 243
Mass 159, 192
Materia medica 217
Materiality
– critical 236–237
– new 235–237
Matins 197–198
Medical almanac 16, 187, 214
Mendicant 192, 193
Metric relics 171, 175
Meuse River valley 18, 144, 162
Micro-book 181–202
Middle English 19, 226, 228, 229, 232, 237, 245
Millefiori 103, 108
Minuscule 18, 185, 188, 191, 200
Mirror neurons 13
Mise-en-page 26, 27, 29, 171, 182
Molinicius (King of the Britons) 229
Molmutius. *See* Molinicius (King of the Britons)
Monulphus, Saint 149, 156
Mosan. *See* Meuse River valley
Muhammad 133, 134
Mulieres religiosae 164, 196
Multum-in-parvo 182, 188
Muqarnas 117, 140
Musée national du Moyen Âge 8
Musical notation (fifteenth century) 24, 31

Nasrid 17, 116–141
Nationalmuseum, Stockholm 120, 126, 130
Nedunyot 79
Niche 117, 119, 128, 135

Ockeghem, Johannes 23, 28, 37
Officium Parvum Beatae Mariae Virginis 192
Old English 99, 105, 112, 245
Olfactory sensation 59, 68, 79, 88, 121, 232, 234
Opus anglicanum 54–55

Ordinance of Laborers 246
Origo prophetiae 182

Parchment 19, 60, 176, 181, 187, 203, 205, 206, 217–220
Passion, the 142, 162, 163, 170, 174, 175, 214
Peasant agency. *See Agency*
Peasant communities. *See also* Sensory community
– imitation of aristocracy by 237–240
– masculinity in 241–244, 247
Peasants' Revolt (in England) 237
Pelagia 79–80, 81, 92, 93
Performance practice 25, 26, 32, 34–35
Period ear 32
Perspectivist optics 239
Phenomenology 204–206
Philip II (King of Spain) 240
Physician 73, 213–216
Piers the Plowman's Crede 241, 244
Pilgrim badge 216–217
Pin Beater 16, 52, 57, 61, 72, 75
Pit house 64
Pliny the Elder 230
Plow
– as unit of arable land 245–246
– connection with peasantry 19, 225–228, 229–237
– heavy plow 230, 232, 240
– parts of 234
– positive associations of 229–232
– sanctuary 229
– scratch plow (ard) 230
– swing plow 230
– team (oxen and horses) 230–231
Plowing
– as communal activity 225, 241
– on family farms 243
– as masculine activity 19, 243–244, 247
– as peasant characteristic 241–242
– as sexual activity 244
Plowman
– Chaucer's portrait of 228
– cosmetization of in art 240
– negative image of 30, 226, 237–238, 240
– positive image of 225, 229–230
– spiritualization of 226–227
Plowman's Song, The 244
Polyphonic songbook 23, 24, 25

Polyptych 54, 55
Portability 127–128, 143, 205, 206
Posthole 57, 61
Poverty
– poor relief 238–239
– rural 228, 234
Prayer book 182–186, 189–190, 195, 200
Prayer-book of Charles the Bald (Munich, Residenz Museum Schatzkammer 4 WL) 183–184
Prayer-book of Claude of France (New York, Morgan Library MS M.1166) 200
Prudence 6–8
Psalms, the 166, 182, 183, 185, 202
– Seven Penitential Psalms 149
Psalter 18, 56, 72, 74, 182–190, 192, 199, 201–202, 226, 278, 283, 285
Psalter of Saint Ruprecht (Salzburg, Stiftsbibliothek St. Peter, Codex a I 0) 183, 184–188, 190, 192, 199, 201, 278

Qur'an 77, 85, 95, 139–140

Rattier Virgin 14–15, 194
Reenactment 13–14, 117, 253
Relics 18, 19, 53, 69, 142–162, 172, 175, 176, 187
Reliquary 18, 142–162
Remaclus, Saint 18, 144
Repoussé 106–107, 114
Responsory 252
Riccio, Andrea
– *Shepherd Daphnis Playing a Pipe, The* 10–12
Richard of Fournival
– *Bestiaire d'amour* 6, 14
Risālat al-qiyān (Epistle on Singing-Girls) 86
Robert de Lisle 226, 227, 283
Robertson, Kellie 226
Rondeau cinquain 23
Rondeau 23–24, 27, 37, 43–46
Rosenwein, Barbara 20, 234
Ruprecht, Saint 18, 182–190, 183, 192, 199, 201, 278

Saint-Amand 152
Sainte-Croix, Liège 160
Sammut, Gordon 236
San Giorgio al Velabro 274

Sartawi, Mohammad 236
Sarum 253
Sceatta, sceattas 104
Scop 112, 113
Scriptorium 164
Senses
– edification of 149–150, 238–239
– guarding of 6
– hearing 1–3, 9, 31, 96, 104–105
– inner 7–8, 165, 176, 256
– moral ambiguity of 92
– outer 7–8
– sensory actualization 226, 235–236
– sight, and optical illusions 239
– smell 1, 3, 8–9, 12, 13, 14
– taste 1, 3, 8–9, 12, 71, 97, 235
– touch, bidirectional, of plow, sociability of 234–235, 237–238
Sensorium
– hierarchy of senses in 104–105, 108–109, 234–235
– historical 13, 112, 226
Sensory analysis 36–38, 67–76, 78–81, 92–95, 133–140, 204–206, 217–218, 225–248
Sensory community
– definition of 232, 234, 236, 245
– peasant 225–248
Servatius, Saint 149, 153, 155–158, 162
Shears 16, 51–52, 55, 57, 66, 67, 72
Sheep 51, 55, 59, 60
Shepherd Daphnis Playing a Pipe, The 10–12
Shirley, John 244
Sins
– Sloth 226
Sint-Servaaskerk 153, 156, 157, 275
Sinzendorff, Ambassador Joachim von 126
Smoothers 56, 61, 68, 69
Social organization
– idealized in art 237–238
Somme le roi. See Laurent, Friar
Sphere of Apuleius 209, 282
Spindle whorl 16, 52, 57, 61, 63, 65, 66, 70, 71, 75
Spindle 16, 51, 52, 57, 61, 65, 66, 70–72, 75
Spinning 59, 61–62, 69–71, 74–76
Spolia 146, 147, 159
Statutes of Laborers 246
Stavelot 18, 144–154, 155, 158–159, 160, 275
Stonyhurst (Cuthbert) Gospels (London, British Library Additional MS 89000) 187

Sumptuary laws 235
Sūrat al-Aḥzāb 94
Sūrat al-Nūr 95
Sutton Hoo 108, 271
Synesthetic 106, 108, 110, 115, 177

Tabarrūj 94
Talisman 183, 200, 202, 216–217, 223
Tertullian
– *De cultu feminarum* 93–94
Textile 50–76, 80, 92, 98, 117, 118, 119, 124, 132, 135, 136, 137, 141, 217, 235
Thirty Years' War 126
Thomas Aquinas 1, 192–193
Thomas of Cantimpré 3, 178
Tongeren-Maastricht 148, 149, 156
Trevisa, John 229
Triptych 18, 144, 158–162
Triumphus sancti Remacli, the 148–149, 151, 155
True Cross, the 144, 158–160, 162

Umayyad 77, 86, 132
Unicorn tapestries, Musée national du Moyen Âge in Paris 8

Veni Creator Spiritus 149, 150, 154
Victoria and Albert Museum 15, 116, 136, 194
Villers 18, 164, 165, 166, 169, 178
Villiers-le-Sec 56, 71–73
Vitry, Jacques de 232, 233

Vrouwenpark 164, 166

Walafrid Strabo
– *Hortulus* 51–52, 75
Walters Art Museum 10, 11, 14, 143, 152
Weaving 52, 57, 61, 66, 69, 71, 73–76, 108, 236
Wellcome Apocalypse (Wellcome Library, London, Ms. 49) 6, 7
Westphalia 63
Wibald, Abbot 18, 144, 146–147, 148, 152, 158–160
Wijnaldum-Tjitsma 52, 57, 60–61, 62, 63, 66–73, 75
William of St. Thierry 167, 168
Wonder. *See Admiratio*
Wool production 51, 60, 75, 90
Work
– estates theory of 247–248
– for benefit of society 246–247
– gendered 244–246
– of peasants 30, 225
– theological ideal of 20–21

Yeager, Stephen 245

Zīnah Tabarrūj 94–95
Zīnah 94–95
Zodiac 191, 203, 209
Zodiac man 203, 209
Zoomorphs 101, 102, 108

Plates

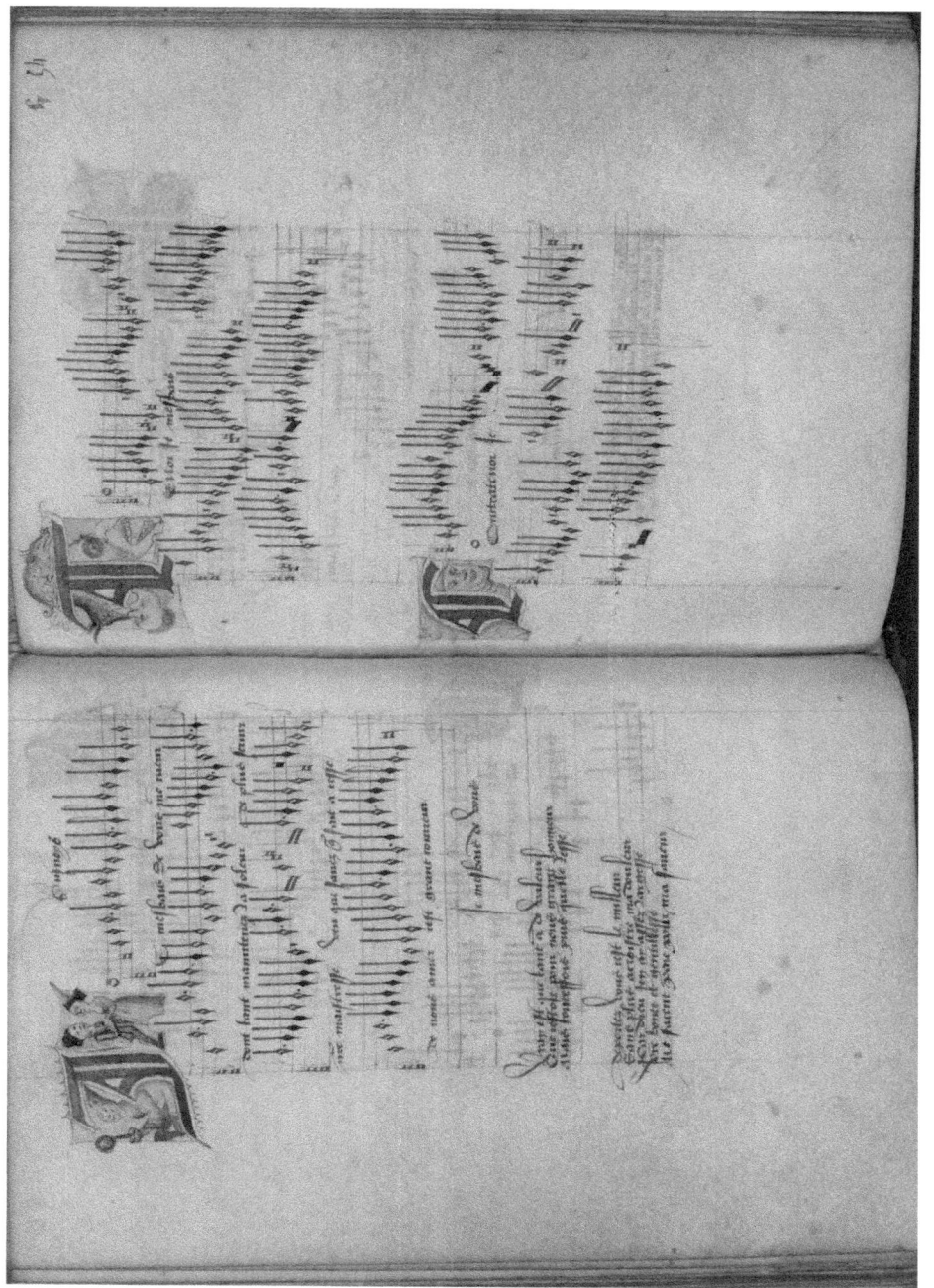

Plate I (Rodin): Antoine Busnoys, *Je m'esbaïs de vous mon cuer*, in the "Dijon Chansonnier," Bibliothèque Municipale, Dijon, MS 517 (formerly 295), fols. 53v–54r.

Plate II (Dospěl Williams): Courtesan, ink and watercolor on paper, ca. eleventh century, The Israel Museum, Jerusalem, B65.04.0165. Photograph courtesy of Harvard Fine Arts Library, Digital Images & Slides Collection, d2011.06753.

Plate III (Dospĕl Williams): Sculpture of a woman, Khirbat al-Mafjar, Jordan, eighth century. Collection: Rockefeller Museum, Jerusalem. Photograph: Elizabeth Dospĕl Williams.

Plate IV (Herman): Disc brooch, gilt copper-alloy composite with gold filigree, garnet cloisonné, and white shell inlay, early seventh century, Sarre, Kent. Collection: British Museum, London, 1860,1024.1. Photograph copyright the Trustees of the British Museum.

Plate Va (Herman): Shoulder clasps, gold with garnet and glass cloisonné, late sixth or early seventh century, Sutton Hoo, Suffolk. Collection: British Museum, London, 1939,1010.4 and 1939,1010.4a. Photograph copyright the Trustees of the British Museum.

Plate Vb (Herman): Disc pendant, gold with filigree, glass, and garnet cloisonné, mid- to late seventh century. Portable Antiquities Scheme, SUR-883362. Photograph copyright Surrey County Council.

Plate VI (Blessing): Gazelle Vase, late fourteenth to early fifteenth century, Museo Nacional de Arte Hispanomusulman, Granada, inv. no. 290. Image: Album/Art Resource, NY.

Plate VII (Blessing): Freer Vase, late fifteenth century, Freer Gallery of Art and Arthur M. Sackler Gallery, Smithsonian Institution, Washington, D.C., F1903.206a-b, gift of Charles Lang Freer.

Plate VIIIa (Hahn): Shrine of Saint Amandus, early thirteenth century, with later additions, Walters Art Museum, Baltimore, accession number 53.9. Courtesy of The Walters Art Museum.

Plate VIIIb (Hahn): View of ciborium, San Giorgio al Velabro, Rome, seventh century with many restorations. Photograph copyright Cynthia Hahn.

Plate IXa (Hahn): Reliquary of Saint Gondulphus, twelfth century, originally held in the treasury of Sint-Servaaskerk, Maastricht. Collection: Royal Museums of Art and History (Cinquantenaire Museum), Brussels. Image courtesy of Kleon3 CC 3.0.

Plate IXb (Hahn): Stavelot Triptych, ca. 1156–1158, Pierpont Morgan Library and Museum, New York. Copyright Art Resource.

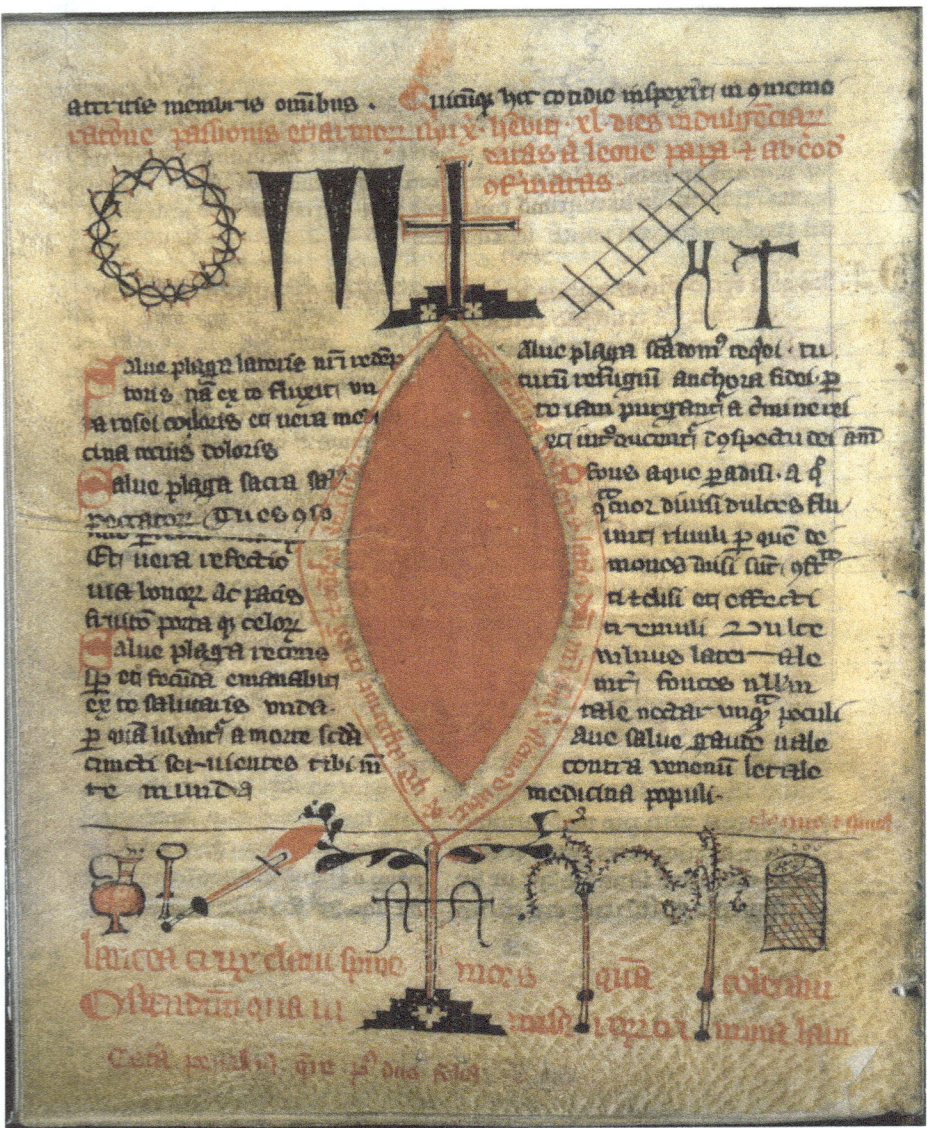

Plate X (Ritchey): Measured side wound of Christ surrounded by arms of Christ, hymns, and indulgence. Miscellany compiled by John of St. Trond in 1320. Royal Library of Belgium, Brussels MS 4459–70. Fol. 150v. Copyright Royal Library of Belgium.

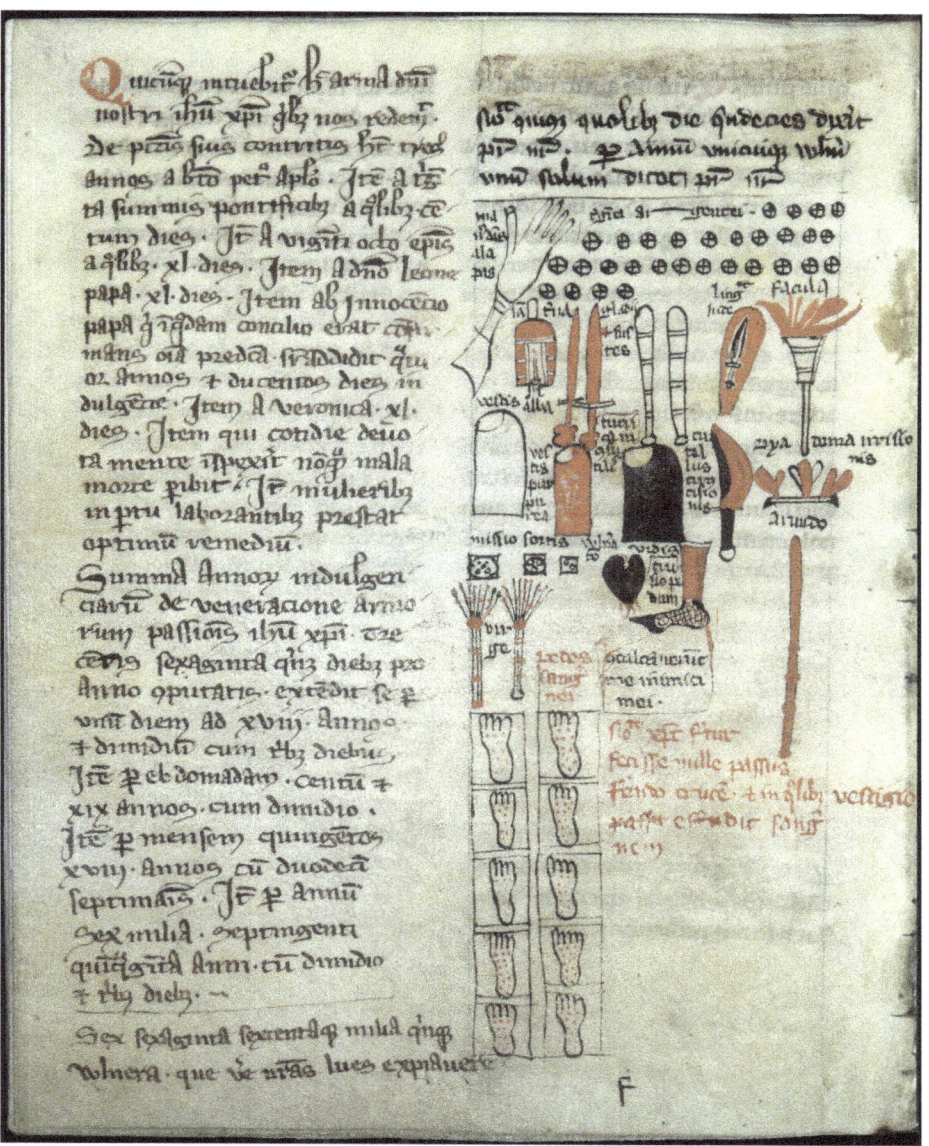

Plate XI (Ritchey): Arms of Christ and indulgences. Miscellany compiled by John of St. Trond in 1320. Royal Library of Belgium, Brussels MS 4459–70. Fol. 152v. Copyright Royal Library of Belgium.

Plate XIIa (Sand): Psalter of Saint Ruprecht, Stiftsbibliothek St. Peter, Salzburg, Codex a I 0. Photograph: Helge Kirchberger Photography.

Plate XIIb (Sand): David as composer, Psalter of Saint Ruprecht, Stiftsbibliothek St. Peter, Salzburg, Codex a I 0, fol. 1r. Photograph: Helge Kirchberger Photography.

Plate XIIIa (Sand): Opening initial to Psalm 6, Penitential Psalms, Logan Hours, Utah State University Special Collections and Archives, COLL V Book 422, unfoliated. Photograph: Andrew McAllister.

Plate XIIIb (Sand): Detail of a marginal bird, Logan Hours, Utah State University Special Collections and Archives, COLL V Book 422, unfoliated. Photograph: Andrew McAllister.

Plate XIVa (Borland): Wellcome Library, London, MS. 8932, 1415–1420? Photograph: Wellcome Collection.

Plate XIVb (Borland): Wellcome Library, London, MS. 8932, fol. 5. Photograph: Wellcome Collection.

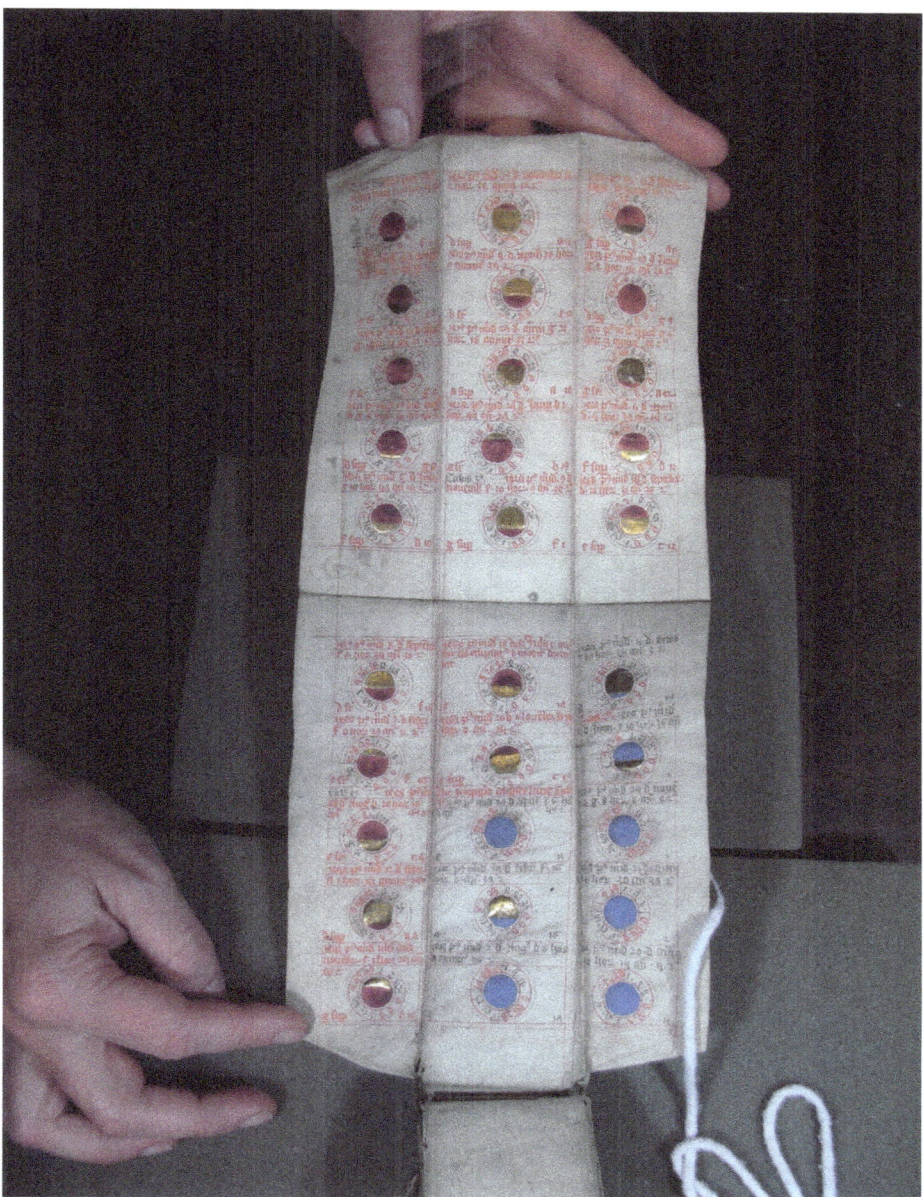

Plate XV (Borland): Solar and lunar eclipses, *Almanach, tabula festorum, mobilium ab anno 1364 usque annum domini 1462*, York, England, between 1406 and 1424. Collection: The Rosenbach, Philadelphia, MS 1004/29, fol. 7. Photograph: J. Borland.

Plate XVI (Borland): Sphere of Apuleius and urine chart, ca. 1406, Collection: British Library, London, Harley MS 5311, fol. 2r. Copyright The British Library Board.

Plate XVIIa (Newhauser): The De Lisle Psalter, given by Robert de Lisle to his daughters on November 25, 1339; the tree of vices (detail). British Library, London, MS Arundel 83 (II), fol. 128v. Copyright The British Library Board.

Plate XVIIb (Newhauser): London Rothschild Hours (Hours of Joanna I of Castile), southern Netherlands, compiled ca. 1500 for a female member of the Spanish court or royal family, perhaps Joanna I, Queen of Castile and Aragon. September Labor: men plowing and sowing. British Library, London, MS Additional 35313, fol. 5v. Copyright The British Library Board.

Plate XVIII (Newhauser): The *Somme le roi*, a manuscript produced in Paris, probably for King Philip IV, completed ca. 1295. Top: "Prouesce" (fortitude) contrasted with "Peresce" (sloth). Bottom: David vs. Goliath, and Labor. British Library, London, MS Additional 54180, fol. 121v. Image in public domain.

Plate XIXa (Newhauser): Breviary, English, early thirteenth century; plowing with oxen (detail). British Library, London, MS Royal 12 F xiii, fol. 37v. Copyright The British Library Board.

Plate XIXb (Newhauser): Luttrell Psalter, commissioned by Sir Geoffrey Luttrell, lord of the manor of Irnham in Lincolnshire, written and illustrated ca. 1335–1340 in England; men plowing. British Library, London, MS Additional 42130, fol. 170r. Copyright The British Library Board.

Plate XX (Newhauser): Pieter Bruegel the Elder (attrib.), *Landscape with the Fall of Icarus*, ca. 1560s(?), Royal Museums of Fine Arts, Brussels. Wikimedia Commons: public domain.

www.ingramcontent.com/pod-product-compliance
Lightning Source LLC
Chambersburg PA
CBHW080407230426
43662CB00016B/2348